THE BUSINESS ENVIRONMENT

CHALLENGES AND CHANGES

SECOND EDITION

Ian Brooks
and Jamie Weatherston

Faculty of Management and Business
Nene College of Higher Education

FINANCIAL TIMES

Prentice Hall

An imprint of **Pearson Education**

Harlow, England · London · New York · Reading, Massachusetts · San Francisco
Toronto · Don Mills, Ontario · Sydney · Tokyo · Singapore · Hong Kong · Seoul
Taipei · Cape Town · Madrid · Mexico City · Amsterdam · Munich · Paris · Milan

Pearson Education Limited
Edinburgh Gate
Harlow
Essex CM20 2JE
England

and Associated Companies throughout the world

Visit us on the World Wide Web at:
http:/www.pearsoneduc.com

First edition published 1997
Second edition 2000

ISBN 0 273 64690 7

British Library Cataloguing-in-Publication Data
A catalogue record for this book can be obtained from the British Library

Library of Congress Cataloging-in-Publication Data
A catalog record for this book is available from the Library of Congress

10 9 8 7 6 5 4
06 05 04 03 02

Typeset by 43 in 9.5/12 Centennial light
Printed in Great Britain by Henry Ling Limited, at the Dorset Press, Dorchester, DT1 1HD

HD31 BRO

THE BUSINESS ENVIRONMENT

CHALLENGES AND CHANGES

We work with leading authors to develop the strongest educational materials in business and management, bringing cutting-edge thinking and best learning practice to a global market.

Under a range of well-known imprints, including Financial Times Prentice Hall, we craft high quality print and electronic publications which help readers to understand and apply their content, whether studying or at work.

To find out more about the complete range of our publishing please visit us on the World Wide Web at: http://www.pearsoneduc.com

To
Connor, Lucy, Cara, Hannah and Bernie
and to
Alice, Jack and Dawn

ACKNOWLEDGEMENTS

We are grateful to the following for permission to reproduce copyright material:

Fig. 7.2 reproduced with permission from *Regional Studies, 27/8*, Carfax Publishing Company (R. Martin, 1993); Exhibit 3.1 from 'Competing in the Global Economy: "Knowledge is Power" emerges as big idea for the economy: reversing the decline', Financial Times (K. Brown, 17 December 1998); Exhibit 3.2 from 'Chain Reaction: It is not just globalisation which is forcing companies into cross border mergers. Deflation is also playing a big part', Financial Times (P. Martin, 17 November 1998); Exhibit 3.3 from 'The risks from world trade', Financial Times (23 November 1998); Exhibit 3.4 from 'Industry counts cost of losing duty-free sales Economic consultancy suggests that 19 000 jobs could be lost', Financial Times (J. Willman, 27 February 1998); Exhibit 4.3 from 'ICI & Glaxo join forces to replace CFCs', The Times (16 January 1995); Exhibit 4.4 from 'Persil Power tears £57 million hole in Unilever profit', The Times (22 February 1995).

Whilst every effort has been made to trace the owners of copyright material, in a few cases this has proved impossible and we take this opportunity to offer our apologies to any copyright holders whose rights we may have unwittingly infringed.

A Companion Web Site accompanies *The Business Environment* by Brooks and Weatherston

Visit ***The Business Environment*** Companion Web Site at www.booksites.nct/brooks to find valuable teaching and learning material including:

For Students:
- links to further internet resources, related to each chapter of the book

For Lecturers:
- A secure, password protected site with teaching material
- A syllabus manager that will build and host a course web page
- A full, downloadable instructor's manual, including:
  - teaching guidance for each chapter
  - guidance and answers to questions within the book
  - further notes on case studies and guidance on integrating them into teaching
  - overhead transparency masters to assist in learning

CONTENTS

PART II
CASE STUDIES

PREFACE

The need for a second edition of *The Business Environment: Challenges and Changes* reflects the importance of the subject in undergraduate and professional educational programmes. A clear understanding of the theories and models outlined in the text provides a fundamental building block for the study of corporate strategy, a subject which is included at more advanced levels of the business curriculum.

The overall structure of the second edition remains the same. In it we try to blend theory with practical examples to allow students to apply those theories. However some changes have been made in response to requests and observations by readers, for example key concepts have been added at the beginning of each chapter. Useful web sites are also included at the end of each chapter (these were live when the book went to press). Attention has been given to the development of material to do with information technology, social dynamics, Europe and globalisation. New case studies are included, others have been reviewed. The cases have been carefully selected to illustrate an array of organisational types and operating environments. Practical examples, throughout the text, have been replaced or updated. The structure of the book is explained in Chapter 1. We provide a brief outline here.

Chapter 1 sets the scene on the business environment and delineates the scope of the book. It recognises that a number of interrelated environmental forces act upon a variety of types of organisation which can be differentiated by, for example, their prime objectives or their legal status; the environment influences different types of organisation in different ways. These forces are grouped under LE PEST C, but form an interrelated and complex whole acting at a number of geo-political scales. Additionally, the impact of individual perception and organisational filters and the influence they have on the business environment and forecasting is explored.

Chapter 2 seeks to identify the nature and complexity of the competitive environment and to determine how its dynamic nature and structure affects both the level of competition that an organisation faces and the future profitability of organisations. The international character of competition and the importance of the EU are identified as a key issues. We introduce some of the tools and models that organisations can use to understand their own position and that of their competitors.

Markets left to their own devices may become anti-competitive, intervention may be necessary. Governments can also provide support for new, fledgling industry to allow them to grow and become competitive in the international arena. We look at this role at national level and in the European Union.

In Chapter 3 the four main macroeconomic goals, employment, growth, low inflation and trade are explored in some detail and we consider the changes in government priorities within the macroeconomic environment in recent decades. We discuss the international macroeconomic environment, with particular reference to the European Union and the internationalisation of markets and how organisations are required to respond to macroeconomic factors, such as interest rate changes and the removal of trade barriers, which are outside of their direct control.

Chapter 4 takes a broad view of the technological environment. It begins by defining technology and draws distinctions between knowledge and innovation. Considerable attention is given to the funding of research and development (R&D) in major industrial economies and the relevance of R&D to different sectors is considered. Some general technologies affecting organisations are considered including advanced manufacturing technology and information based technologies. The effects of technology on organisations and people are discussed. The chapter concludes by considering the management of technology and of technical professionals.

Chapter 5 looks at three broad aspects of the dynamic and multi-faceted social environment, that is, national culture, demographic restructuring and various social changes, and examines the complex interactive relationship between organisations and a social community or society. This relationship takes place within a local, national and regional cultural context.

The chapter opens with a discussion of national culture which, it is argued, influences all organisational and environmental activity. It investigates demographic issues at a local, national and international scale and assesses their influence upon organisations. Finally, it takes a closer look at a number of critical social phenomena and identifies some of the key consequences of social dynamism for commercial and other organisations. Issues such as crime, health, the family and the changing face of organised labour will be considered.

Chapter 6 is set in the context of actions taken at a global, national and local scale. Environmental campaigners and business people are increasingly recognising the importance of agreeing trade-offs between economic development and performance. As it is often difficult to confine ecological problems to issues that can be dealt with by individual countries, it is becoming increasingly apparent that 'world solutions' need to be sought.

The more serious ecological concerns are looked at and the extent of their impact is investigated. The basic economic arguments which help us understand how firms are able to pollute the environment are explored and the range of actions which can be taken by governments to monitor and regulate the output of pollutants from economic activity identified. We end the chapter by examining the different approaches adopted by businesses towards environmental issues, discussing the impact of these upon consumers and noting the extent of consumer power in respect of ecological issues.

Chapter 7 focuses on key political issues and offers an insight into the potential impact of the law on organisations. Political decisions, made at all geo-political levels, are examined and an assessment of their impact on organisations is made. The European Union, which will continue to have a significant impact on organisations, is given special attention. The chapter also looks at support for industry and regions, and discusses a number of issues connected with democratic institutions.

A number of key areas of legal terminology important to the context of the book as a whole are outlined and the ways in which law may be classified are identified. Sources of law and the nature of the court system are also summarised.

Chapter 8 focuses on public organisations and their 'unique' business environment. The role of Political (with a big 'P') forces in creating a dynamic and complex public sector business environment are explored and major structural shifts that have changed the face of the public sector are identified. The privatisation process is ongoing in many countries. This and other measures, such as market testing and competitive tendering, has reduced the role of government in the economy and increased commercialisation, competition and value for money. As a result of these processes, many government services in the United Kingdom and elsewhere have been exposed to competitive forces. Additionally, benchmarking and other mechanisms aimed at increasing competition and consumer involvement have been developed since the early 1980s.

An examination is also made of shifting political ideologies, economic and social circumstances and global environmental changes as they influence public organisations and how the government of the day often filters and interprets these external forces.

Chapter 9 has focuses upon the nature of change in the business environment and organisational, individual, group and government responses to environmental dynamism. The chapter notes that the business environment is increasingly complex, dynamic, and uncertain for many organisations, individuals, groups and governments. Major economic, political, technological and social changes have transformed the business environment in the last two decades necessitating organisational change and increased flexibility. There may be a trend towards high profile 'shock events' and non-linear chaotic patterns in many areas of the natural world (to some extent such patterns are also observable in the business world) which suggests that organisations might do well to make contingency plans. The nature of the business environment calls into question the validity of organisational approaches to long-term planning and suggests the need for processes which build in flexibility and adaptability. Turbulent environments demand government attention. The future role of government is likely to remain a fiercely debated issue for some time.

Thanks to all those who have helped to put the book together by providing chapters, case studies and information.

THE BUSINESS ENVIRONMENT

1

THE BUSINESS ENVIRONMENT

Ian Brooks

LEARNING OBJECTIVES

On completion of this chapter you should be able to:

- define the term business environment and understand a number of models of the contextual environment of organisations;

- know the prime variables which comprise the external environment;

- recognise that environmental forces acting at a variety of geographical scales and political tiers influence organisations;

- understand that the business environment is unique to each organisation;

- recognise that human processes influence our understanding of the business environment;

- understand the prime sources of complexity and dynamism in the business environment;

- critically assess the nature and value of environmental forecasting techniques and styles;

- recognise the complex relationship between organisation and environment and the influence of the environment on structure and strategy;

- understand the nature of the strategy formulation process;

- map environmental stakeholders' power/interest;

- conduct a sector impact analysis;

- identify environmental variables, sources of information and forecasting techniques.

KEY CONCEPTS

- business environment
- PEST analysis
- environmental stakeholders
- geo-political scales
- dynamism and complexity
- environmental determinism/two-way relationship
- enactment

- perceptual and organisational knowledge filters
- subjective and objective forecasting
- impact analysis, brainstorming, Delphi, scenario planning
- strategy, structure and strategic planning
- SWOT analysis

ENVIRONMENTAL FORCES

Whether it is a financial institution, a university or a multinational chemical manufacturer, no organisation exists within a vacuum. It is very likely, for example, to have a number of competitors, to be subject to local government planning restrictions, obliged to comply with national or European pollution regulations and subject to fluctuations in the fortunes of the local, national or global economy. The business environment comprises an array of 'forces' acting upon organisations, often with far-reaching implications. In order to fully appreciate the nature of the business environment it is first necessary to analyse the various forces at play. Only then can we attempt to develop a more integrated and holistic understanding of environmental activity. Thus following this introductory chapter this text unravels these powerful forces and illustrates how each may affect organisations.

This introductory chapter explains the rationale and scope of the book and demonstrates the fundamental characteristics of the business environment, its relationship with organisations and the implications for organisational structure and strategy. We start by defining the business environment and by classifying the forces at play. The chapter then develops a model of the business environment which forms the basis of our approach. We briefly explain the diverse nature of organisations and take a closer look at various approaches to environmental forecasting before discussing the relationship between the business environment and organisational activity. The role of the business environment in influencing the strategic direction of organisations is addressed and some of the complex issues are debated. Naturally, many of the issues raised are further developed in later chapters and the prime theme of dynamism and complexity is explored in depth in Chapter 9.

The focus of this book is on the organisation in its environment rather than on the individual, group or government and their external environments. Figure 1.1

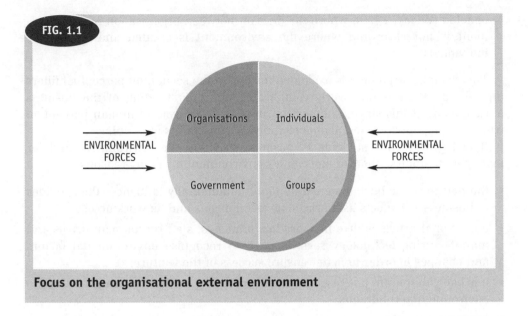

FIG. 1.1

Focus on the organisational external environment

demonstrates that focus. Public sector organisations are singled out for special attention in Chapter 8, partly because of the unique and dynamic environmental influences acting upon this sector and partly because more frequent reference is made to commercial organisations elsewhere in the book.

The business environment: a definition

The word 'environment' does not merely refer to the natural or ecological environment, although that may be an important consideration for many organisations. It is a general concept which embraces the totality of external environmental forces which may influence any aspect of organisational activity. Similarly, the word 'business' is used to imply any type of organisation, whether it be a commercial profit-making enterprise, a government agency or a non-profit-making charitable trust. Consequently, we will use the terms 'business' and 'organisation' interchangeably. Hence 'the business environment' is a broad and all-embracing term which encompasses any and all influences which are external to the organisation in question. We will elaborate upon this definition below.

Defining the environment poses an intellectual problem although a number of eminent researchers have categorised the different approaches (see Smircich and Stubbart, 1985; Mansfield, 1990). Wilson (1992) has suggested three broad conceptions of the business environment, each of which is covered in some detail in this book. He argues that the business environment may be viewed as:

- an objective fact, a clear measurable and definable reality;
- a subjective fact, its particular characteristics being dependent on individuals' interpretation and perceptions;

- enacted (Weick, 1979), where the division between organisation and environment is not clear and where the environment is created and defined by individuals.

This complex argument is explained further in the section on perceptual filters (pp. 16–18). It need not overly complicate our understanding of the business environment at this stage, although awareness of the role of human perception when defining environmental opportunities or constraints is useful.

It is important for students of business to study the environment and for managers to analyse their organisation's environment for many reasons:

- the nature of the business environment fundamentally influences the activities of business – it affects its markets, its technologies and its workforce;
- operational activities, like new product launches, staff recruitment drives and manufacturing technology reviews need to recognise environmental factors and changes in order to better ensure success of the venture;
- it is likely that profit and organisational well-being are fundamentally related to environmental conditions;
- strategic planning needs to take into consideration likely changes in the business environment.

A classification of environmental forces

The simple acronym 'PEST' (standing for Political, Economic, Social, Technological) serves well as an *aide-mémoire* when considering the array of environmental forces influencing business activity. In fact if the acronym is enlarged to 'LE PEST C' (to include Legal, Ecological and Competitive) it encompasses most areas of concern in this field. Figure 1.2 illustrates this categorisation

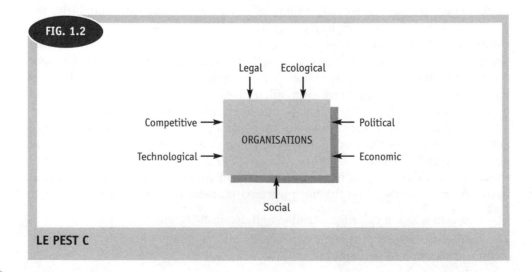

FIG. 1.2

Legal   Ecological

Competitive →   ← Political

ORGANISATIONS

Technological →   ← Economic

Social

LE PEST C

of the business environment. This text concentrates on each of these forces and the interaction between them.

PEST analysis enables students or managers to assemble a logical and comprehensive picture of their environment. However, it is the interrelationship between the apparently different factors which adds not only complexity and uncertainty but also richness and greater accuracy to the analysis. Figure 1.3 illustrates a simple PEST analysis of Scania, a multinational, Swedish-owned truck manufacturer.

There are a number of important aspects of Scania's environment which will influence the company's strategic and operational decision making. Some of these factors lie within Scania's control, such as aspects of truck design to meet Euro standards and fuel efficiency targets, while many others, such as fluctuations in the value of the Swedish krona, are beyond its influence.

There are numerous other, sometimes graphic, representations of the business environment. Daft (1992) demonstrates pictorially his typology of environmental forces (Figure 1.4). This 'dartboard' configuration gives the organisation pride of place in the centre while radiating from it are eight categories of environmental concerns. This typology is similar to the LE PEST C acronym suggesting, as it does, that all environmental forces fall within one or more of these specified categories.

For analytical purposes Peace and Robinson (1994) separate a firm's external environment into three categories although it is not the intention of this book to focus, in any detail, on the internal or operating environment of the organisation. They refer to

- the 'remote environment', such as global and domestic political, social and technological concerns – this is akin to the contextual environment outlined above;
- the 'industry environment' or its competitive forces; and
- the 'operating environment' which comprises a rather mixed group of actors including suppliers and customers.

The day-to-day activity of organisations includes interaction with the 'task environment' (Dill, 1958) including an organisation's relationship with its customers, suppliers, trade unions and shareholders. However, this book focuses on the broader contextual environment which permeates and extends beyond the immediate task environment.

Robbins (1992) suggests that the prime forces for change within organisations derive from forces acting within their environment. Specifically, he suggests the following typology of forces: the nature of a workforce, technology, economic shocks, social trends, world politics and competition. These and other dynamic environmental forces will be explored within this book.

Classifications of the type outlined above attempt to model the environment and although they tend to simplify reality, they help us in identifying and understanding what are complex environmental processes and forces. They serve as useful tools to aid our analysis of the environment. The 'real' environment is a complex

FIG. 1.3

Legal

- Block Exemption: impending removal of EU regulation 123/85 leading to cancellation of motor franchise arrangements enabling dealers to seek multi-franchises; Block Exemption renewed 1995, removed 200
- EU transport regulations/harmonisation; working hours directive (drivers); emissions standards (Euro 1, Euro 2, Euro 3); maximum truck sizes
- maximum legal truck sizes likely to increase – may reduce truck demand due to scale efficiencies

Ecological

- Euro 1, 2 and 3 regulations impose increasingly stringent emissions and noise limits requiring redesign of engines and other parts
- environmentalist transport lobby aims to increase rail freight and reduce the numbers of large trucks on the road
- stringent standards require more frequent engine service and emission checks
- increasingly aware and active public concern over health issues; quality of life and road congestion

Political

- national and European government transport policies
- investment in rail freight terminals and other infrastructure following privatisation
- pressure to regulate road haulage companies further, e.g. driver hours, registration requirements
- reductions in centrally funded road building; toll roads
- excise duty on diesel; levels of road tax on trucks

Economic

- effects of economic cycles, which are pronounced in this industry, dramatically affecting new truck sales
- currency fluctuations; especially of Swedish krona/Euro against sterling and non-European currencies
- Single European Currency - UK entry?
- intrest rates: many trucks purchased on financing arrangement often organised through Scania Finance Ltd – the lower the rates, other things equal, the higher the sales

SCANIA IN THE UK

Social and demographic

- societal lobby of governments to reduce or control road traffic and congestion
- changing shopping habits influencing rates of growth and geographical distribution of retailers

Technological

- complexity in truck design and on-board aids, e.g. on-board computers, engine management systems, trans European navigation, communications
- Channel Tunnel; increases in rail freight?
- Continual improvements in fuel consumption and emissions control as manufacturers seek competitive advantage while complying with Euro standards
- alternative fuels
- alternative transportation systems
- improved technologies and quality increasing service intervals

Competitive

- changing customer base; from small haulage operators to large fleet management organisations – increased buyer power
- Growth of rental market; non-manufacturing suppliers, e.g. Ryder, BBS
- convergence in design and 'quality' characteristics among main players leading to increasing competition
- marque loyalties of declining importance; lifetime cost considerations; after-sales market of increasing importance
- whole package concept (e.g. trucks, financing and after-sales services
- possible future Japanese or Far Eastern incursion into European truck market
- new entrants' excursion into large and lucrative after-sales market (as in car industry e.g. Kwik-Fit)

PEST analysis: Scania in the UK

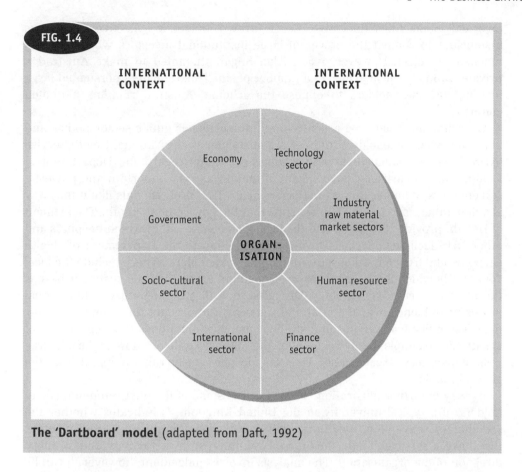

FIG. 1.4

The 'Dartboard' model (adapted from Daft, 1992)

array of interrelated forces; we merely compartmentalise them for simplicity and to gain insight. Often a number of forces within the environment combine to influence an organisation. It is when reading case studies or analysing real organisations that the complexity of the business environment becomes apparent, yet understanding of the individual elements of that environment will enable you to better appreciate the nature and dynamism encountered.

Environmental stakeholders

All organisations, whatever their size, have a number of stakeholders. A stakeholder is a person, organisation, interest group or other body which holds a 'stake' in the business. In addition to having an interest in the activities of the organisation, some stakeholders have power to influence those activities. Institutional shareholders such as large insurance companies, for example, are powerful stakeholders in many commercial companies and consequently have considerable influence, if they wish to use it, upon the nature of company objectives. In 1995 many small shareholders in British Gas plc objected to pay and bonus increases awarded to the Chief Executive, Cedric Brown, but their collective action was insufficient to combat the power of large institutional investors who were less inclined to object. However, when Alan Sugar attempted to make Amstrad a private company the activities of a number of small shareholders persuaded large institutional shareholders to oppose the scheme. Amstrad remains a quoted company.

Governments often hold a controlling influence over public sector bodies and hence are vital stakeholders in those organisations. In the National Health Service (NHS) hospital management and medical personnel regard the Department of Health and the particular government of the day as very important and powerful stakeholders. Whether they as managers or medical professionals like it that way is a debatable issue but the fact remains that the government, via the Department of Health, provides the funds and the legal framework within which hospitals and other NHS facilities operate. However, in addition to the Department of Health each hospital trust has other 'environmental stakeholders'. These include the local community which the hospital serves. One might argue that this customer base is the most important stakeholder. Of course not all stakeholders will hold equal power or influence over the affairs of the organisation, and the community may have less influence over hospital strategic activities than does the Department of Health. For example, many regional health authorities do not now undertake free cosmetic surgery, except in severe cases, despite considerable demand from the general public.

By way of further illustration, Table 1.1 lists some of the environmental stakeholders of a typical university in the United Kingdom. It indicates whether the stakeholders have high, medium or low power over the university and whether they have a relatively high, medium or low interest in the activity and strategic direction of the organisation. The analysis involves judgement; however, it can be carried out for any organisation with which you are familiar. It should also be noted that, due to volatility in the business environment, stakeholder power and interest is itself dynamic. Figure 1.5 shows how one might 'map' stakeholder power and

TABLE 1.1   Environmental stakeholders: higher education

Environmental stakeholders	Power to influence strategy	Level of interest in activities
Government: Department of Education	HIGH	LOW
Students	MEDIUM	HIGH
Quality assessment bodies	HIGH	MEDIUM
Local government	LOW	LOW
Local residents	LOW	MEDIUM
Funding body	HIGH	MEDIUM
Other regional HE institutions	MEDIUM	MEDIUM
Taxpayers	LOW	LOW

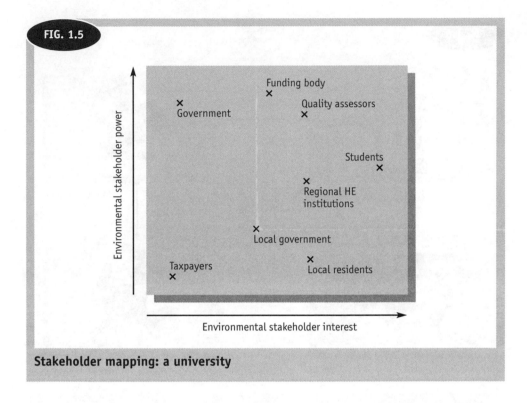

FIG. 1.5

Stakeholder mapping: a university

interest in an organisation using the data from Table 1.1. This graphically illustrates which stakeholders wield most power and influence. Such an analysis provides a useful analytical tool for managers to assess the relative power and influence of each of their environmental stakeholders. It may prove invaluable in the strategic management process.

Geo-political scales

This book studies the business environment at a range of geo-political scales. The 'geo' in this case refers to 'geographical' scale while the political implies levels or tiers of government. Hence at the local level in most countries there is a tier of government which is responsible for certain activities within a relatively small area. Similarly there is a tier of government, often very important and influential, at a national scale. In Europe the European Union (EU), and in South-East Asia ASEAN, form a further level of government. The EU, for example, has created enormous change, not least in trading relations, patterns of trade and alterations in product specifications. It is a dynamic force in organisations across Europe and indeed elsewhere.

Most organisations are influenced by environmental forces operating at different geo-political levels, as illustrated in Figure 1.6. For example, Scania interact with their environment at a variety of scales. At the local level in the United

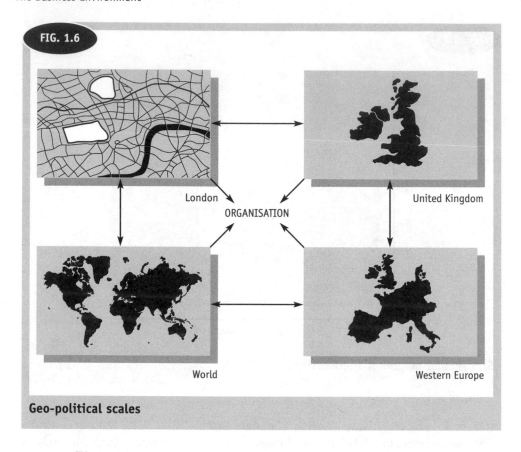

FIG. 1.6

London

United Kingdom

ORGANISATION

World

Western Europe

Geo-political scales

Kingdom their head office is located in Milton Keynes, England, and a move to an alternative location within the town is planned. The decision where to locate will be subject to local government planning restrictions which will in turn be influenced by national laws and EU directives. Also, Scania employs a large number of skilled, experienced and professional staff who currently live in or near Milton Keynes. Hence factors within the local environment (i.e. local government and local labour supply) are important to the activities of Scania (GB) in Milton Keynes. However, Scania is also subject to environmental dynamism at the national, European and global scales. Table 1.2 illustrates two influences upon Scania (GB) at four geo-political scales. It also categorises these forces into legal, ecological, political, economic, social, technological and competitive (LE PEST C). Many environmental issues, such as EU engine emission regulations, are themselves the outcome of a diverse range of influences acting in cohort. Hence, as illustrated in Table 1.2, the nature of the laws governing truck engine emissions within the EU is influenced by a complex consortium of ecological, social, technological, political and legal forces. Conflicting pressures are brought to bear on the European government from ecological pressure groups, social and political philosophies and organisational lobbyists. The outcome is, in this case, a compromise 'solution' enshrined in law.

TABLE 1.2 Factors operating within Scania's business environment at four geo-political scales

Geo-political scale	Environmental issues For example:	Environmental forces
Local	A: Milton Keynes town planning regulations (Scania GB headquarters)	A: Political, legal, social, ecological
	B: Local skilled labour supply conditions	B: Social, economic, competitive
National	A: Value of sterling against the Swedish krona/Euro	A: Economic, political
	B: Government freight transport policy	B: Political, social, competitive
European Union	A: Emissions control and truck size regulations	A: Ecological, technological, political, social, legal
	B: Trading relations and concessions to non-EU countries	B: Political, competitive
Global	A: GATT negotiations to pursue free trade agreements	A: Political, legal, competitive
	B: Kyoto Conference (1998) CO_2 emission targets	B: Ecological, social, political

Unfortunately, it is not always simple or practical to distinguish between the business environment at various geo-political scales as these influences are often so interrelated and complex that they can only be fully appreciated collectively. Some forces will operate at a number of different levels and manifest themselves in a variety of ways. Hence it may fall upon local government to enforce pollution controls that originated at global inter-governmental conferences. Even many small, local companies are increasingly aware that forces operating at the European level, such as product specification directives emanating from Brussels, have a direct and often profound influence on their business. For example, many local butchers' shops are finding it increasingly difficult to comply with European Union health and safety regulations. For some it is proving to be the proverbial last straw.

Not all organisations are influenced equally by the business environment. In fact what may prove to be a real threat for one organisation could be a wondrous opportunity for growth and profitability for another. For example, the technological advances made in the design, production and marketing of personal computers and the consequent reduction in their cost and improvement in quality have led to enormous increases in their demand for household and business use. These technological forces have, however, virtually proved a death blow to the manufacture of mechanical and even electronic typewriters and have reduced the demand for mainframe computers for certain applications. In reality every organisation has a complex array of environmental influences with which it interacts and which are, in their entirety, quite unique.

Hence the business environment is a complex array of forces acting with often unpredictable and unequal force upon organisations at a variety of geographical and political scales.

The organisation–environment relationship

The relationship and direction of influence between the environment and an organisation is not one-way, simple or static. The belief that the activities of organisations are entirely determined by the environment in which they operate is described as environmental determinism. Although we know that the environment influences business activity it is by no means certain that absolute determinism is apparent even for the smallest of organisations. Organisations have tentacles of influence which help form and give shape to the business environment. In other words there is not a one-way causal relationship between environment and organisation. We have argued above that it would be rather naive to assume that organisations themselves do not play a major part in influencing their environment. The reality is that many profoundly shape their environment and that facing numerous other organisations. The simplest example is that of a number of competing companies in an industrial sector. The activity of one, say the introduction of a new product range, will influence the activity and success of another. Figure 1.7 indicates this two-way influence between organisation and environment.

Each organisation forms part of the business environment of other organisations, as competitors, allies, suppliers, buyers and so forth. No organisation is isolated and without any influence on its own environment and that of others. Many organisations, especially sizeable and/or influential ones, exert considerable pressures for change in their business environment. Hamel and Prahalad (1994) argue that companies can only control their future if they know how to influence the destiny of their industry. For example, the Direct Line company in the United Kingdom has revolutionised the insurance and financial services industries. They have effectively marketed and delivered a quick and efficient 'telephone line' service. This has reduced their overheads, when compared to normal broker services, rapidly increased their market share and enabled them to maintain highly competitive rates which have 'squeezed' more traditional competitors. They, and the numerous companies now mimicking them, have changed the

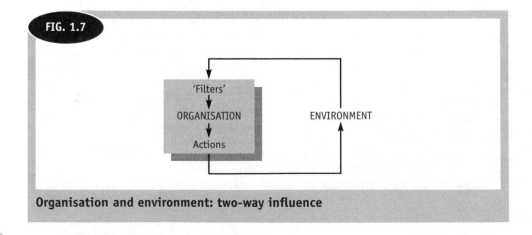

FIG. 1.7

Organisation and environment: two-way influence

business environment for insurance and financial services companies. A similar process is likely to occur as the World Wide Web (WWW) is used for marketing and purchasing consumer goods; for example, the 'virtual' supermarket may rapidly lead to fundamental changes in shopping habits in the next decade with enormous potential knock-on effects on current businesses and their operations.

Sometimes organisations within a business sector collaborate with each other in order to maintain a stable environment within known competitive conditions. For example, many European motor manufacturers had for some time succeeded in persuading the European Union to extend the 'block exemption' scheme for motor distributor dealerships. That is, manufacturers can still demand that their dealerships distribute, service and repair solely their vehicles. Hence motor manufacturers maintain control over their distribution channels which act as a strong barrier to entry for any new makes that might want to enter the market. The investment required to establish a comprehensive distributor network is immense and effectively deters many potential entrants and limits the penetrative capabilities of others. The conditions of competition are thus maintained – business as usual. Now that the removal of block exemption has been agreed, competitive conditions in that industry will change.

A model of the business environment

The model of the business environment illustrated in Figure 1.8 indicates how the various environmental forces, acting at a variety of scales, pass through what we

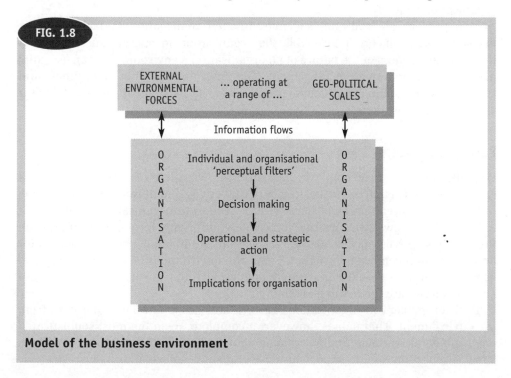

FIG. 1.8

Model of the business environment

refer to as 'perceptual filters'. These filters, which are explained more fully below, comprise all the internal mechanisms within organisations which enable managers to construct their own view of environmental realities. For example, an organisation may not have an active environmental scanning capability and hence may miss numerous potential opportunities, while others may be managed by eternal optimists who are convinced of their organisations' invincibility even when faced with hostile environmental influences. For all intents and purposes, these perceptual filters actually change and shape 'reality' for organisations. They influence the way organisations look at their environment and what they see. Consequently, we must not underestimate their power and influence. The failure of the UK motorcycle industry, which has been virtually wiped out, was in large part due to its inability to accept that the business environment was rapidly changing. Design, product and process changes, largely developed in Japan, were ignored by British manufacturers who failed to perceive and react either to these environmental changes or to evolving customer requirements.

Information about an organisation's environment may take a variety of forms: for example, it may comprise sophisticated data from a strategic management information system or, conversely, an apparently minor snippet of information gleaned by a powerful senior manager. There is little evidence to suggest that organisations are more likely to act on concrete data than on the opinion or impression of its senior personnel. Environmental information is always the result of 'human' analysis. It has passed through the complex perceptual filters which exist within every organisation. However, this information will not influence all organisations equally.

Managers at all levels utilise environmental information to facilitate their decision making in order to enable the organisation to operate successfully. A thorough awareness of the nature of an organisation's environment is an essential prerequisite for strategic management. The environment often determines, and always influences, the future course of action of organisations. It acts as a force for change in organisations.

Perceptual filters

Organisations and their employees assist in the 'creation' of their own business environment such that the actual nature of that environment remains as much one of human interpretation as of hard 'reality'. Different organisations in the same industry often view environmental forces quite differently from one another, even though those forces may in fact be very similar. Additionally, organisations filter and interpret incoming information about the environment and how managerial cognition, organisational culture and politics all influence this process. These statements require further explanation.

Decision-makers in organisations receive and assimilate incoming data from the environment. That data is, however, incomplete. Even the most sophisticated environmental scanning and forecasting activities can only collect and process a small proportion of all important environmental information. Most strategic decision-makers are primarily concerned to learn about those changes which might influence their activity and as such they continuously make decisions regarding the importance or significance of 'new' information. It is quite possible, therefore, that person A will ignore data or dismiss it as unimportant while person B, even in the same organisation, may take this same information on board and 'allow' it to influence their decision-making process. This difference in 'reception' may be attributed to differences in the individuals' backgrounds, their position in the organisation, or how welcome or potentially threatening the information is to the receiver. Just as individuals differ so do organisations and whole industrial sectors.

Our individual and collective perception only enables us to 'see' and interpret in certain ways. It is these perceptions that drive individual and business actions. Weick (1979) suggests that individual and organisational actions might in turn influence change within the environment. A hypothetical example will help illustrate this phenomenon. Let us assume that Forefront, a computer software house, perceive that the competitive environment in which they operate is changing. These perceived changes encourage them to develop a technologically superior Windows^{TM} environment software product. They also perceive that numerous smaller software companies may begin to encroach on their other activities if they do not focus research and development (R&D) activity in these areas. Faced with a decision, Forefront decide to increase their efforts in R&D in the Windows^{TM} market. This entails reducing their R&D spend and management attention elsewhere. After two years Forefront have successfully produced and marketed their Windows^{TM} product and remain the market leaders. However, there has been a cost. The neglect of their other software products has meant that competitors have overtaken them in market share terms in these other product lines. Their original perception of their environment led them to a particular strategic management decision. As a result of that decision Forefront, in this example, have enacted their environment. That is, their actions have assured that their perceptions became a reality. Their actions, to focus on the Windows^{TM} environment at the expense of their other products, have led other 'environmental actors' (that is, their competitors) to adjust their strategic policy to take advantage of the opportunity. Forefront's perceptions and subsequent actions have become a self-fulfilling prophecy.

Miller (1988) argues that managers' perception of their environment has a greater influence on organisational decision making and eventual strategic direction than does more objective information. He is not alone in this belief. Boyd *et al.* (1993) suggest that this raises some major concerns regarding the reliability and validity of managers' perception. They argue, for example, that managers often make broad generalisations based on a small number of cases. Huber (1985) contends that these and other shortcomings are inevitable due to the perceptual and cognitive limitations of managers. Some managers and organisations, in facing an uncertain business environment, perceive their environment as more certain than it actually is. This is particularly true of those managers who have a low tolerance for confusion or ambiguity.

In summary, the main influences upon individual and organisational perception are:

- characteristics of individuals, such as background, education and duration of employment within the organisation;
- organisational culture;
- organisational politics, structures and control mechanisms;
- history and development of an organisation;
- industrial sectors and their norms.

QUESTION

Discuss why two organisations in the same sector might 'see' their environment in quite different ways.

Dynamism and complexity

Throughout this book we stress the dynamic nature of environmental forces; however, we recognise that the degree or extent of dynamism is not equal for all organisations or environments. For example, at present the extent of environmental flux affecting a high street solicitor, although not negligible, is less than that influencing BP or General Motors. It may be the case, of course, that BP have a far greater influence over their environment than does the solicitor's office, so dynamism is not necessarily a handicap, especially if that very dynamism preserves and enhances the competitive strengths of the firm.

Complexity in the environment is a product of a number of interrelated factors and the degree of environmental uncertainty, possibly caused by dynamism, plays a major part. An organisation faced with an uncertain environment is, other things being equal, in a far less advantageous position than one facing stability. However, yet again all is not straightforward, for many organisations become complacent when faced with a set of known environmental parameters. A significant change in one or more of those characteristics often leaves the inflexible organisation unable to cope. Environmental complexity also tends to increase for organisations operating at a variety of geo-political scales. A transnational manufacturing and marketing organisation is likely to encounter dynamic environmental forces at local, national and global scales. Figure 1.9 can be used to 'map' an organisation's position according to the levels of complexity and dynamism in its environment. By way of illustration we have located the approximate position of a number of 'generic' organisations.

When faced with a complex, uncertain and dynamic environment some organisations and many individual managers attempt to simplify that environment; at least in their own minds. Bourgeois (1985), however, recommends that organisations face up to and actively confront that difficult environment.

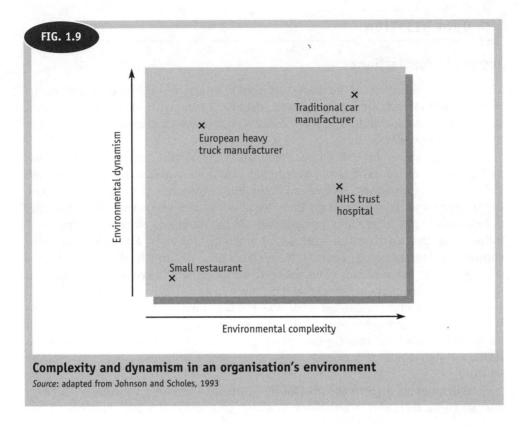

FIG. 1.9

Complexity and dynamism in an organisation's environment
Source: adapted from Johnson and Scholes, 1993

Other researchers have argued that attempts to reduce environmental uncertainty may lead to poor long-term organisational performance. The themes of dynamism and complexity will be developed throughout this book and the consequences for organisations, government, individuals and groups further explored in Chapter 9.

QUESTIONS

1. Using the information in Figure 1.3, identify three variables in Scania's environment (a) which are totally outside of the organisation's control, (b) over which Scania have some, albeit minimal, influence, and (c) which it may attempt to alter and further influence for the benefit of the organisation.

2. For an organisation with which you are familiar (e.g. workplace, university, school, a case study from this book) identify two environmental forces for each of the LE PEST C categories. Establish the geo-political scale(s) at which each force may operate.

3. Carry out an environmental stakeholder analysis of a organisation with which you are familiar. Place this information on a grid as shown in Figure 1.5. What does this tell you about management priorities and their chief concerns?

THE ORGANISATION

Types of organisations

The term 'organisation' or 'business', as used in this book, embraces a wide range of legal entities with diverse objectives. Table 1.3 lists, with examples, the main types of organisation in the UK. Each country will have variations upon these yet in many ways they are similar.

As organisations differ fundamentally from one another in their legal status and primary objectives it is not surprising that the environmental forces which influence them also vary. In fact environmental pressures may encourage some organisations to actually change their legal status and objectives. For example, deregulation and increasing competition in the financial services industry is influencing the activity and success of building societies and life assurance companies. Due to overcapacity, technological changes and further potential for economies of scale some have merged while others have been swallowed up by larger companies. Merger activity may in turn lead to a change in legal status. For example, in August 1995 the Halifax Building Society and the Leeds Building Society formally merged and later became a public limited company with its shares quoted on the London stock exchange. This has now enabled the Halifax to acquire, for example, the Birmingham Midshires Building Society in 1999.

Organisational objectives profoundly influence an organisation's activity and strategic direction. Knowledge of these objectives will help determine the

TABLE 1.3   Types of organisation

Types of organisation	United Kingdom examples	Global examples
Government Civil Service Departments and Agencies	Ministry of Agriculture Food and Fisheries	Ministero Scuola Ed Educatione (Italy)
Local Government Organisations	Gloucestershire County Council	
Incorporated by Royal Charter or by Act of Parliament (Public Corporations)	BBC (by Royal Charter) Post Office (by Act of Parliament)	Air France
Quasi Autonomous Non-Governmental Organisations (Quangos)	Higher Education Funding Council Executive (HEFCE)	UMNO (Malaysia)
Sole Trader	The King of Balti's	Kobayashi Electronics (Japan)
Partnership	Peat Marwick McLintock	
Charity Organisations	Oxfam	International Red Cross
Private Limited Company	Virgin Atlantic	
Cooperative	Cooperative Retail Society	Cooperativa Di Consumatori (Italy)
Public Limited Company (PLC)	BP	Heineken (Holland)
Building Societies and Friendly Societies	Bradford & Bingley Building Society	

TABLE 1.4   Organisational objectives

Type of organisation	Prime objective
Commercial company (e.g. Shell plc)	To maximise shareholder value
Charity (e.g. Oxfam)	To relieve poverty, distress and suffering in any part of the world
General hospital (e.g. Kettering General Hospital NHS Trust)	To provide quality health care for the local community

importance of different environmental forces and changes. Table 1.4 gives a flavour of the range of objectives that exist in just three types of organisation.

In addition to the legal status and prime objectives of organisations there are numerous other factors which may profoundly effect the nature of the organisation–environment relationship. These include

- organisational structure;
- size of the organisation;
- type of technology used;
- cultural and political context of the organisation;
- organisational and individual perceptual filters.

These and other factors will, subtly or otherwise, alter the importance of any particular environmental variable. For example, a large and diversified organisation may cope better with a proposed new EU regulation (because of its ability to influence the outcome by lobbying) than a smaller more specialised firm. Conversely, it is frequently argued that small firms tend to be more flexible and able to cope with environmental uncertainty than large, sluggish organisations.

ENVIRONMENTAL FORECASTING

Forecasting in a dynamic and complex environment

We have argued that managers' perception influences their vision and assessment of the business environment. These processes are based on subjective judgements of the environment. However, many organisations attempt to form and utilise more objective environmental measures. The following section explores some of these objective, and other more perceptual, measures, while the role that organisational culture and outlook plays in influencing views of the environment is discussed in the final section of this chapter.

Managers with strategic responsibilities in organisations are often frustrated by the difficulty of predicting changes in the environment. It is frequently the case, especially in smaller organisations, that little formal long-term forecasting takes place. It is viewed as such an uncertain science that time is not spent attempting to foresee what is often regarded as the unforeseeable. Instead managers prefer to be influenced by a combination of information resulting from their accumulated experience in business and a variety of perceptual measures of their environment. This may, however, prevent organisations from acting proactively, so that they are always in a position of having to react to a change thrust upon them.

There are many examples of companies which have failed due to their reliance upon incorrect forecasts or the inability of management to react appropriately to environmental evidence. A good example is that of the car industry in the USA in the 1970s. Over 20 per cent of its market share had, by 1980, been lost to foreign manufacturers who produced smaller, more fuel-efficient vehicles. The American manufacturers had failed to appreciate that global political and economic conditions would lead to large increases in oil prices, and that social factors, such as greater female economic and geographic mobility, were 'conspiring' to create a preference for smaller cars. In the early 1980s US car companies made losses in excess of $5 billion (£3.1 billion). Japanese car manufacturers, on the other hand, had anticipated the future need for fuel-efficient cars with lower servicing costs or, as many commentators have argued, they planted the idea in consumers' minds. More recently, the closure of a number of plants around the world, including some in Scotland and in the north-east of England, which produced semiconductors was the outcome of a dramatic fall in global prices because of massive over-supply and currency fluctuations in South-East Asia. Closures of relatively new plants in the UK were costly mistakes for both the producing companies and the workforce.

At best, assessing the potential impact of likely changes in the environment offers organisations an advantage over their competitors by enabling decision-makers to narrow the range of options. Measures will always entail some element of subjectivity, if only in the processes involved in collecting the data. The accuracy and, therefore, the value of such forecasts will often depend on the 'richness' of data, itself a product of managers' choice of communication media. Boyd *et al.* (1993) argue that 'richness' is a product of the speed of feedback, variety of communication channels utilised, and the 'personalness' of the information. Nevertheless, it is clear that, in a dynamic and complex business environment, attempting to forecast sometimes discontinuous trends is fraught with difficulty. One need only look at the frequent inaccuracies of the UK Treasury predictions of medium-term inflation and GDP growth despite that agency's 'closeness' to the economy and privileged access to data. However, to do nothing is also a dangerous course of action for an organisation, as is over-reliance on internal sources of information rather than external channels. It is quite possible, under such circumstances, that a state of inertia could set in, which would ill equip organisations to accurately forecast changes in the environment and which may lead to poor quality decision making and organisational underperformance.

Approach to forecasting

Peace and Robinson (1994) suggest that strategic decision makers need to take a step-by-step approach to forecasting (see Figure 1.10). Their model outlines five steps:

- selection of environmental variables that are critical to the organisation;
- selection of sources of information about those variables;
- evaluation of forecasting techniques;
- integration of the results of forecasting into the strategic management process;
- monitoring and evaluation of the critical aspects of these forecasts.

Some variables may be so obviously important to the well-being of the organisation that they become, in a sense, self-selecting. For example, a company which smelts aluminium will be concerned about likely changes in the price of electricity as this forms a major cost in the production process. Other variables will be identified, usually by senior managers with experience in the organisation and within the sector. However, it is critical to select variables that may be important in the future and not just rely on those which have been critical in the past. It is not a difficult task to select the key variables, although a little lateral thinking may prove useful. It is likely that you could select many key variables for each of the case study organisations at the end of this book. In order to keep the list of variables manageable it is recommended that you omit factors that have little chance of occurring.

There are numerous sources of information about the business environment. These include government statistics and forecasts regarding economic variables such as inflation and growth rates, research findings estimating changes in commodity prices, informed opinions on political, social or technological changes,

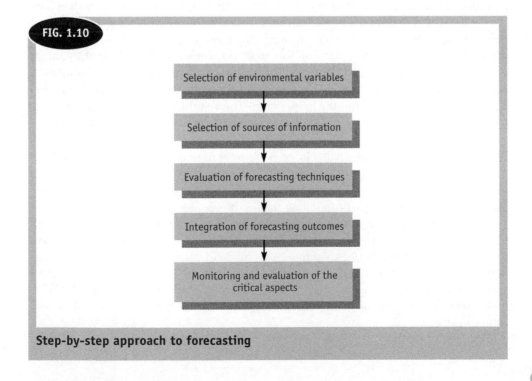

FIG. 1.10

Selection of environmental variables

Selection of sources of information

Evaluation of forecasting techniques

Integration of forecasting outcomes

Monitoring and evaluation of the critical aspects

Step-by-step approach to forecasting

and so forth. A considerable amount of information is merely 'picked up' by managers keeping their eyes and ears open and continually scanning their business environment for opportunities or threats resulting from imminent change. Although quantitative measures of environmental variables carry a certain credibility, more judgemental and subjective approaches are likely to prove more practical and even more accurate. You will note from our discussion of perceptual filters that subjectivity impinges on all human activity – not least upon the manager when sensing changes in the business environment.

Forecasting techniques

Using sophisticated computer techniques and relying primarily on numerical data, some companies and many governments attempt to model changes in the environment. These models often utilise economic data and attempt to estimate future economic variables, such as interest rates and the external value of currencies. There are many private consultancy companies that specialise in developing such models for government and commercial clients. However, as environmental stability is very much a phenomenon of the past, modelling of this type has been subject to considerable 'bad press'. Such models find environmental flux and discontinuity difficult, if not impossible, to predict.

Far less expensive to develop, and often just as accurate, are time series and judgemental models. Time series models attempt to identify trends in variables based on historical data or cyclical factors and extrapolate them into the future. For example, a simple time series model may look at the population of a country at five-year intervals over the past hundred years then use this evidence to predict future demographic changes. This method does not, however, allow for environmental discontinuity where the 'rules' of the past no longer apply. A slightly more sophisticated model may add additional variables, such as likely changes in birth rates and predictions concerning the migration of people which may have a bearing on the population of the country in question. The resulting demographic forecasts may prove useful for strategic planners in government and some organisations.

Judgemental models are those based upon the informed opinion of people in the relevant field. For example, sales force personnel may be asked to estimate likely future trends in sales potential, taking into consideration all likely variables. Their experience 'on the ground' may prove invaluable and lead to more accurate forecasts than sophisticated modelling techniques could achieve.

Brainstorming is another common, rather creative, method of generating ideas and forecasts. Brainstorming can usefully be employed to estimate future trends in technology development, for example. A number of informed people are encouraged to generate ideas and forecasts in a group setting. Many of these ideas may appear fanciful but trends in technological development often lead to 'fanciful' outcomes! Such techniques can generate useful judgemental ideas about potential future events.

The Delphi method of forecasting is a more systematic technique than brainstorming. This method attempts to gain consensus among a group of people, such as a senior strategic management group. For example, a company senior management team may meet and aim to forecast their likely competitive position in five years' time. They will discuss all relevant variables and start to agree on as many points and issues as possible in an attempt to develop the most likely and most widely held view. This can then be used in the strategy process.

Scenario development recognises judgemental and non-quantitative information such as changing fashions. Scenarios are 'pictures' or 'stories' of what might be the case some time in the future. They draw upon both subjective and more objective data. Hence a company may develop two or three likely scenarios for some future date and take these into consideration in their planning process. They may develop contingency plans to cope with each scenario should it arise. The multinational oil giant, Shell, has made extensive use of scenario 'planning'.

Finally, a number of organisations and consultancies have developed 'political risk' ratings for countries around the world. These take into consideration the stability and predictability of nations and their governments, and advise commercial organisations and governments on the risks involved in overseas investment.

Impact analysis

One simple, yet effective, way of forecasting the effect of environmental changes on organisations is to conduct an impact analysis. This involves ascertaining a series of potential environmental changes and assessing the probable effect of these on a range of organisations, usually direct competitors. Table 1.5 illustrates a simple impact analysis of the heavy truck industry. The effect of a change is first assessed

TABLE 1.5   Impact analysis in the truck industry

Environmental scenario	Scania	ERF	Mercedes Trucks
Ecological Strict new European Union environmental protection legislation (i.e. Euro standards 2 and 3)	— Track record in R&D on environment-friendly engines and truck design, nevertheless changes will require extra investment	——— UK company, too smalll to invest sufficiently in environmentally-friendly R&D	—— R&D expenditure on environment-orientated technology but without outstanding quality reputation of Scania
Economic Sweden join EMU and adopt the Euro; UK and sterling remain out of Euro	++ Reduces transaction costs and uncertainty in Euro countries	— Little effect on UK market but uncertainty and transaction costs remain with exports	++ Reduces transaction costs and uncertainty in Euro countries
Political Governments enforce movement of 'heavy' freight to railways and restrict the use of heavy trucks	—— Will adversely affect the sale of trucks, servicing and parts sales as Scania do not produce light trucks and vans	—— Will adversely affect the sale of trucks, servicing and parts sales as ERF do not produce light trucks and vans	— Mercedes is protected to a degree by having sizeable market shares in motor vehicles of all sizes but heavy truck sales would suffer

QUESTIONS

1. Select an organisational case study and identify an array of environmental variables which influence the company.
   (a) Which of these variables may management be able to forecast?
   (b) What are the likely sources of information to facilitate forecasting?
   (c) What approaches and methods of forecasting might be employed?
   (d) What would be some of the difficulties in accurately forecasting changes in these variables?

2. Conduct an impact analysis for a sector of industry with which you are familiar.

3. Using library and other information sources and accessing historical data assess whether previous predictions of environmental parameters were accurate. For example, the United Nations and the OECD predict all manner of economic, technological, social and demographic trends. What are the causes of any inaccuracies?

as either a positive (+) or negative (−) influence. Positive influences are those where there will be a benefit to the company financially or otherwise. Changes which may lead to strongly positive effects are given a ++ or even +++ rating. The impact analysis may then involve a brief explanation of the plus/minus score.

It can be seen from the impact analysis in Table 1.5 that changes in environmental regulations will adversely effect all truck manufacturers; however, some are better prepared due to their scale and a history of concern for such issues. A realignment of exchange rates will not affect all three companies in the same way.

Impact analysis enables managers or analysts to assess the effects of environmental change on an organisation and upon its competitors. Clearly, where such changes are likely to adversely affect an organisation more than its competitors then contingency planning needs to be considered.

ENVIRONMENTAL ANALYSIS AND STRATEGIC PROCESS

Strategy and structure: environmental influence

Most early organisational theory and management research assumed a largely stable business environment. Hence proponents of the Classical School and of Scientific Management argued that organisations should be machine-like and feature centralised authority, clear lines of command, specialisation and the division of labour and numerous rules and regulations. However, such mechanised and bureaucratic organisations, typified by hierarchical structures and a fervent adherence to the power-control role of management, are poorly suited to dynamic and complex environments. By the 1940s in North America and increasingly also in Europe, the deficiencies of the 'classical' organisation became apparent. Technological changes, increasingly complex markets and social, political and cultural changes created new demands on organisations which many were ill-equipped to manage. Although many of the basic principles identified by classical management theorists, such as Fayol and Taylor, remain entrenched within many 'modern' organisations, other environmentally sensitive changes have occurred. The Human Relations School (late 1930s onwards), typified by the work of Chester Barnard and landmark studies by the Tavistock Institute, together with the Hawthorne studies, signalled change. In the search for greater effectiveness and flexibility within organisations, emphasis has shifted towards the consideration of 'people' issues such as motivation and leadership. A better motivated and well led workforce will prove to be more flexible and capable of coping with environmental change and complexity.

A study of electronics companies in the United Kingdom by Burns and Stalker (1961) attempted to establish why some companies were able to cope with changes in their environment, specifically dynamism in their product markets, while others were inept in this regard. They argued that successful innovators had developed an 'organic' structure while those with 'mechanistic' structures were less able to adapt. Lawrence and Lorsch (1967) found a similar relationship between the business environment and the internal structure of the firm in the United States. Where they differed from earlier researchers was that they did not believe that organisations or their environments were uniform or unchanging. They postulated that the more turbulent and complex the environment the greater the degree of difference between sub-parts of the organisation. Hence they argued that successful companies were those that developed appropriate degrees of differentiation between specialist departments while simultaneously promoting integration calling on common goals.

In environments that are certain and stable, organisations will tend to develop a form and structure which is most efficient in relation to that environment, probably one with a high degree of managerial control and mechanistic structures and systems. If an organisation's environment is uncertain and complex, managers design structures with greater in-built flexibility. However, perception may play a part in this process – that is, managers in organisations which have an organic structure may perceive the environment as being dynamic and uncertain while those in more mechanistic structures may perceive their environment as being more certain; the reality may be quite different. Nevertheless, there are many firms in the company graveyard whose managers 'perceived' their environments as being stable and certain when in fact they harboured destructive dynamic forces.

There has been considerable research in more recent years concerning the relationship between groups of organisations and their collective environment. Grinyer and Spender (1979), for example, argued that organisations in a particular industry sector, such as the motor vehicle industry or the higher education sector, have a tendency to develop 'recipe knowledge' about how to operate in that business. This recipe knowledge influences their collective view of the industry environment. They argue, however, that companies who continually develop their recipe knowledge in line with changes in the environment are likely to succeed and prosper at the expense of their more sluggish competitors. These organisations are not imprisoned by the recipe.

As argued in the section above on environmental forecasting, it is often suggested that the success of commercial firms depends on their ability to foresee and subsequently act upon environmental information. Miles and Snow (1978) have identified various types of organisation which possess quite different capabilities and motivations in this respect. Their typology of organisations refers to the 'style' in which they operate strategically. This style influences their relationship with the business environment and is, in turn, influenced by that environment. Hence 'defender' organisations, they argue, attempt to create a stable environment which suits their non-dynamic structure and strategy, while 'prospectors' view their environment as ever-changing and seek continual strategic and structural adjustments to cope with changes. They are continually searching for new opportunities and in the process may create change and uncertainty for others within their competitive environment. They identify two other categories of organisation, 'analysers' and 'reactors'. The former are capable of acting in both stable and unstable environments, a quality of considerable value. 'Reactors' act only when environmental change 'forces' them to do so. They are not 'proactive' organisations. Boyd *et al.* (1993) state that 'given these differences in internal versus external focus, one would expect a greater potential for environmental misperception among defenders or reactors, relative to analysers'.

All four types of organisation, it is argued, 'enact' or create their environment. What they choose to see and how they choose to interpret that environment is quite unique to each organisation. Hence a defender may view ostensibly the same environment as a prospector yet see stability and continuity all around while the prospector sees only change and opportunity. Clearly each organisation filters data to suit its own capabilities and concerns. Executives selectively misinterpret aspects of their environment. These filters include individual managers' cognitive processes, organisational culture and politics, other group or team factors and the strategic orientation of the organisation. Therefore, as stated above, it is quite possible for two organisations to view the same environmental change as either a glorious opportunity for growth and prosperity or, depending on their perception, a catastrophe threatening organisational survival.

More recently the development of Chaos Theory has stressed that, because of the unpredictability and constant flux which characterise the business environment, organisational structure and strategy need to be fundamentally reappraised. This interesting development is further developed in the final chapter of this book.

Strategic planning

The strategic planning process in organisations is the subject of considerable attention in the field of business and management. The academic and, increasingly, the practitioner worlds are engaged in lively debate over issues such as the nature of strategy formulation. To put it rather simplistically there are two broad schools of thought – the rationalist and subjectivist approaches.

The rationalist approach argues that strategic planning is, or certainly should be, undertaken in a logical and largely linear fashion. It is suggested that organisations monitor their business environment and analyse their internal resource position in order to assess what strengths and weaknesses they have which might facilitate the exploitation of environmental opportunities and the avoidance of environmental threats. A stakeholder analysis is also important at this stage.

PEST analysis, or the many variants upon it described above, is usually undertaken within organisations as a prelude to a more strategically orientated technique – a SWOT analysis. This acronym stands for Strengths, Weaknesses, Opportunities and Threats. As part of a strategic process of analysis an organisation may assess its strengths and weaknesses from an internal resource perspective. For example, it may conclude that it is in a sound financial state and that it utilises modern, effective technology. Its weaknesses may, for example, be an under-trained and poorly motivated staff.

It is the latter two elements of this acronym which are of particular relevance here for it is in the business environment where both opportunities and threats can be found. As a vital strategic tool businesses often attempt to identify such opportunities that they may seek to exploit and threats that they attempt to avoid.

Similarly, a popular model suggests that the initial stages of strategy formulation lie in gaining an appreciation of the degree of uncertainty in the organisation's environment. This is proceeded by an audit of environmental influences. The strategic planner then conducts a structural analysis of the immediate competitive environment of the organisation before analysing the organisation's strategic position (Johnson and Scholes, 1993). Johnson and Scholes explain that 'the aim of such analysis is to develop an understanding of opportunities which can be built upon and threats which have to be overcome'. Organisations can then adapt to their environment and by actively managing environmental relationships can in turn shape the changes that are occurring. The task of rational strategic management in this scenario involves reading the environment and then 'creating initiatives that will resonate with the changes that are occurring' (Morgan, 1989).

Senior management generate a series of strategic options from which choices are later made after due analysis and consideration of all parameters. The chosen strategies are then implemented.

Thus it is assumed that actual or predicted changes in the environment lead to planned strategic change in organisations. Strategic planning, therefore, is an attempt to match organisational capabilities with environmental opportunities. Hence the dominant paradigm is that organisations are in a state of 'dynamic equilibrium', continually adapting to their environment. These planning activities, it is argued, are essential for organisations to cope with environmental dynamism.

Strategic planning often tends to adopt a three- to five-year time scale, during which time the business environment of most organisations will alter significantly. However, it should be stressed that proponents of the rational approach do stress the need for 'reality embellishments' such as feedback loops (for example, to enable further environmental scanning to influence decisions at a later stage) and consideration of the role of organisational culture, politics and other contextual, non-rational, issues in the planning process.

This argument brings us to an alternative perspective on strategy formulation, the subjective approach. These alternative views are often based both on empirical research and intuitive judgement and attempt to explain the actual processes that take place in organisations. They tend to be less prescriptive. As argued above, organisations are not entirely rational or logical in their environmental sensing or decision-making processes. Organisation-level filters of an intensely 'human' nature disrupt mechanical linear planning processes. They influence the nature and quality of information available and severely limit the range of strategic choices likely to be entertained. They also add an inescapable richness and reality to organisational activity. It is rather pointless to assume, as some traditional rational models imply, that organisational culture, politics and other human processes can, somehow, be easily managed, ignored or stopped from fundamentally influencing organisational activity.

Hamel and Prahalad (1989), in a study of numerous organisations in Europe, America and Japan, question the almost taken-for-granted assumption that successful organisations adapt or seek to 'fit' their environment. They argue that firms that do seek adaption to their environment are prone to imitation and repetition as competitors do likewise. Many successful organisations use resources more creatively and challenge environmental assumptions. They are able to influence the environment of their competitors and, in part at least, create their own environment. This process, referred to as 'enactment', is discussed above. However, the simple rational model of strategic planning pays little attention to the notion of enactment or the way in which organisations influence their business environment.

We have argued above that organisations and individuals enact their environment and may view similar information in quite different ways. This is a non-rational process. When we make this assumption we suggest that environments are not fixed and measurable in a strict sense. They are ever-changing and open to multiple interpretations. Additionally, internal processes of strategic planning are not as the Rationalist School would suggest. Often crucial business decisions are based on very limited data, moulded by personal considerations or cultural norms and implemented by political expediency. Some organisations will have sophisticated planning departments; others will be strategically 'led' by a dominant stakeholder such as the managing director. There is not a great deal of evidence to suggest that one style is a guarantee of greater success than the other.

Although interesting, this subject is complex. You are very likely to investigate it in further detail if you are engaged on a structured business or management course which leads to considerations of strategic management or corporate policy. It is, however, wise at this stage to appreciate the arguments of both schools of thought and develop a broad understanding of organisational processes and academic debates.

Chapter 9 explores the essential nature of the business environment in more detail, continuing many of the debates above. It argues that rapid and sometimes discontinuous change calls for major alterations in strategic planning processes and demands organisational flexibility.

QUESTIONS

1. What is the relationship between the degree of uncertainty in the business environment and organisational structure? Attempt to explain this relationship.

2. What is an organic structure? How might an organic structure make an organisation more able to cope with environmental change and with product innovation?

CONCLUSION

Having set the scene and defined the parameters within which we will study the business environment, this book now takes a closer look at the individual environmental forces which influence organisations. Chapters 2–7 run through the LE PEST C forces; Chapter 8 focuses on the somewhat unique aspects of the public sector environment which is so often neglected in business environment texts. Each chapter will explore the forces at play and the implications of these for organisations. The final chapter revisits many of the themes discussed above and further develops and explores them, focusing in particular on the influence of the business environment on organisations, individuals, groups and governments. The case studies which form Part II of this book support this material.

SUMMARY OF MAIN POINTS

This chapter has aimed to 'set the scene' on the business environment and to delineate the scope of this book. A number of vital issues and concepts have been covered. The key points are:

- There are a number of interrelated forces acting upon organisations which emanate from the external environment of the organisation.
- For the purpose of analysis, these forces can be placed in distinct categories, but in reality they form an interrelated and complex whole.
- Environmental forces act at a number of geo-political scales.
- The relationship between organisation and environment is not clear-cut, as information flows from the environment to the organisation but also from the organisation to the environment.
- There is a variety of types of organisation which can be differentiated by, for example, their prime objectives or their legal status – the environment influences different types of organisation in different ways.
- Individual perception and organisational filters influence how the business environment is viewed.
- Forecasting the business environment is problematic due to change and complexity, yet many methods exist and are widely used.

- There is a relationship between the business environment and both the structure and strategy of organisations.

- There is considerable debate concerning the nature and process of strategic policy formulation but an understanding of the business environment is essential for successful strategic management.

REFERENCES

Bourgeois, L.J. (1985) 'Strategic goals, perceived uncertainty and economic performance in volatile environments', *Academy of Management Review*, 28, 548–73.

Boyd, B.K., Dess, G. and Rasheed, A.M.A. (1993) 'Divergence between archival and perceptual measures of the environment: causes and consequences', *Academy of Management Review*, 18 (2), 204–26.

Burns, T. and Stalker, G.M. (1961) *The Management of Innovation*, London: Tavistock.

Daft, R.L. (1992) *Organisational Theory and Design*, West Publishing.

Dill, W.R. (1958) 'Environment as an influence on managerial autonomy', *Administrative Science Quarterly*, 2, 409–43.

Grinyer, P. and Spender, J.C. (1979) 'Recipes, crises and adaption in mature businesses', *International Studies of Management & Organisation*, 9, 13.

Hamel, G. and Prahalad, C.K. (1989) 'Strategic intent', *Harvard Business Review*, May–June, 63–76.

Hamel, G. and Prahalad, C.K. (1994) *Competing for the Future*, Harvard Business Press.

Huber, G.P. (1985) 'Temporal stability and response-order biases in participant descriptions of organizational decisions', *Academy of Management Journal*, 28, 943–50.

Johnson, J. and Scholes, K. (1993) *Exploring Corporate Strategy: Text and Cases*, 3rd edn, Hemel Hempstead: Prentice Hall.

Lawrence, P.R. and Lorsch, J.W. (1967) *Organisation and Environment*, Cambridge, MA: Harvard Graduate School of Business Administration.

Mansfield, R. (1990) 'Conceptualizing and managing the organizational environment', in Wilson, D.C. and Rosenfield, R.H. (1990), *Managing Organizations: Texts, Readings and Cases*, London: McGraw-Hill.

Miles, R.E. and Snow, C.C. (1978) *Organizational Strategy, Structure and Process*, New York: McGraw-Hill.

Miller, D. (1988) 'Relating Porter's business strategies to environment and structure', *Academy of Management Journal*, 31, 280–308.

Morgan, G. (1989) *Creative Organisational Theory: A Resourcebook*, Sage.

Peace, J.A. and Robinson, R.B. (1994) *Strategic Management: Formulation, Implementation and Control*, 5th edn, Chicago: Irwin.

Robbins, S.P. (1992) *Essentials of Organisational Behaviour*, 3rd edn, Hemel Hempstead: Prentice Hall International.

Smircich, L. and Stubbart, C. (1985) 'Strategic management in an enacted environment', *Academy of Management Review*, 10 (4), 724–36

Weick, K. (1979) *The Social Psychology of Organizing*, Reading, MA: Addison Wesley.

Wilson, D.C. (1992) *A Strategy of Change*, Routledge.

2

THE COMPETITIVE ENVIRONMENT

Jamie Weatherston

LEARNING OBJECTIVES

On completion of this chapter you should be able to:

- recognise the difficulties that businesses face in a dynamic competitive environment;
- understand the traditional microeconomic view of competition and be able to apply its models to a business situation;
- be aware of the classification of markets and appreciate how competition in markets differs;
- appreciate the factors on which competition is based;
- distinguish between the various tools of competitive analysis and apply them to commercial examples;
- be familiar with the role of government and regulatory authorities in the market at different geo-political scales and be able to assess measures of intervention;
- illustrate how public interest is served in market activities.

KEY CONCEPTS

- market economy
- price mechanism
- market structures
- monopoly
- oligopoly
- monopolistic competition
- nature of products and services
- concentration

> **Key concepts continued**
>
> - market entry
> - barriers to entry
> - economies of scale
> - experience curve
>
> - competition
> - collusion
> - contestable markets
> - Porter's five forces

INTRODUCTION

In this chapter we will seek to identify the competitive environment and determine how its dynamic nature affects both the level of competition that an organisation faces and the future profitability of organisations. It has been suggested by Thompson and Strickland (1995) that when crafting an organisation's strategy one of the major tasks facing decision-makers is an assessment of the company's external environment, in particular the industry and competitive conditions in which the organisation operates. The structural characteristics of an industry play a key role in determining the nature and intensity of competition within it (Grant, 1995). Using the traditional microeconomic approach we will outline the basic economic problem and the approach of economic systems to that problem, and examine how resources are allocated in differing economies. We will identify the conditions that determine the level of complexity in a market and investigate each of the market structures to which these conditions apply. An exploration of market structures and an understanding of the differences between the structures presented by economists provides a useful starting point for this analysis.

Organisations will always attempt to reduce the dynamism and uncertainty of the market in which they trade. Many tactics, both fair and foul, can be employed in this endeavour. A major part of this chapter will be devoted to the identification and analysis of the tactics displayed. The huge sums of money that some organisations invest in research and development and advertising may be necessary to maintain the organisations' position in the market and raise a barrier to prevent others from entering that market. Coca-Cola, for example, spend huge sums of money on advertising. Similarly, the need for research and development spending in the pharmaceutical industry limits entry by other organisations. Other activities, for example, entering into agreements that restrict competition, evidenced by the cement cartel, may have a similar effect. This type of collusive activity may be against the interests of consumers. If that is the case then regulatory authorities need to become involved. We will examine the role and the activities of these bodies at three geo-political levels, local, national and global. The concept of contestable markets will provide the reader with an additional interpretation of the market.

Michael Porter's (1980) structural analysis of competitive forces (the five forces model) establishes the factors which determine industry profitability and competitiveness. This model originates from the traditional approach and provides a useful basis from which strategists can begin to build a picture of their competitive position. Competitor analysis can also be used in conjunction with the five forces model to create a more in-depth analysis of the position. Throughout the chapter we will be identifying the tools and techniques which are needed to carry out an investigation of the competitive environment. The starting point for our analysis is the traditional economic view.

THE TRADITIONAL ECONOMIC VIEW

The basic economic problem is how to allocate scarce resources among the almost limitless wants of consumers in society. Choices have to be made about what and how to produce and for whom goods and services should be produced.

An examination of the theory as it applies to two theoretical types of economy is useful, that is, the command economy and the market economy.

The command economy

In a command economy the questions of allocation are answered by the state. The state decides on the volume of production, the types of goods and services produced, the type of work each citizen will do, the ways in which they will be rewarded, the level of pollution control and many other aspects of life. Individual citizens must accept a large measure of direction in their daily life.

The market economy and the price mechanism

The market economy is at the other end of the spectrum. Within this system the consumer is 'king'. Choices made by consumers directly affect the allocation of resources in the economy. Consumers aim to gain the maximum 'utility', or satisfaction, from the goods that they purchase, and are, therefore, concerned about the price they have to pay for items they consume. They express their choices by the prices they are willing to pay for goods.

In the market economy firms choose the methods by which to produce goods and services. They are concerned, primarily, with the costs of making their products or providing their service and the revenues they receive. In this situation firms aim for the greatest return on their investment.

Ideally, the price mechanism allows people to buy what they want, subject to income constraints. The nature and quantity of what is produced will be influenced by consumer preference, expressed through buying behaviour. The ways in which goods are produced will be decided by competition between producers who will seek to produce at lowest cost. The number of people who are able to buy the goods and services will also be decided by the market. Those whose services are in greatest demand will receive the greatest rewards, in terms of wages, and so have the greatest buying power. This mechanism registers people's preferences and transmits them to the firms who produce the goods for consumers to buy.

The consumer is central to the system via the operation of supply and demand. Demand influences price and price influences supply. (A full analysis of demand and supply is given in Chapter 6.) Ultimately the use of scarce factors of production – that is, land, labour, and capital – is dictated by the demands or wants of individuals. When consumers want more of a good than is being supplied, price increases, resources are attracted to the industry and supply expands. When demand falls the opposite effect occurs. There is obviously a time lag involved in the operation of the price mechanism. The speed of the effect varies depending on the situation. In a manufacturing context it is very difficult to transfer production quickly from one good to another, in response to a change in consumer demand, because of the specific nature of machinery or the need to re-train labour. The new toy bonanza at Christmas clearly falls into this category. When demand for Teletubbies rose in the run up to Christmas 1997 or for Buzz Lightyears in 1996 it was impossible for the manufacturers to increase supply to meet the huge surge in demand.

The traditional microeconomic view of competition emphasises the role of market structures in the market economy.

A market is a set of arrangements by which buyers and sellers are in contact to exchange goods and services.   (Begg *et al.*, 1994)

This view is based on the structure–conduct–performance (s–c–p) paradigm which tells us that demand and supply establish the basic conditions of the market. This, in turn, prescribes the market structure, the conduct of the organisation in the market and its performance, for example, its turnover and profit (see Figure 2.1).

Readers may be unfamiliar with economic theories relating business activity to market structure. As competition is based on these theories it is necessary to have an understanding of some of the concepts raised by microeconomics.

Economists distinguish between various types of market which are classified into four general types: perfectly competitive, monopoly, oligopoly, and monopolistic competition. The classification and correspondingly the level of competition is based largely on

- the nature of the product that is supplied, which in turn is determined by demand and cost conditions facing the market,
- the number and concentration of firms in the market, and
- market entry conditions including the existence of barriers to entry and the level of information available to firms and customers.

We will now look at each of these factors.

The nature of the product or service

It is important to differentiate between products or services offered as their nature will affect competition. It is usual to distinguish between homogeneous and

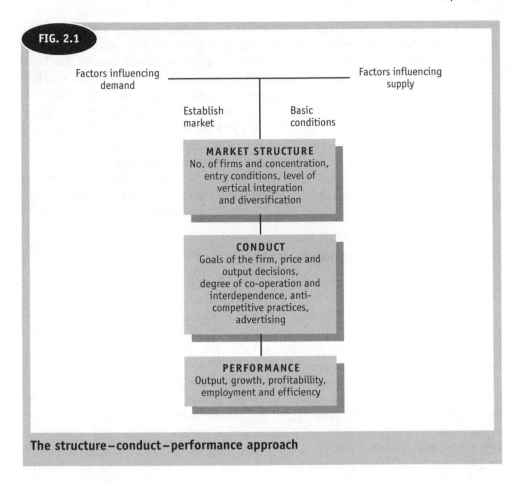

FIG. 2.1

The structure–conduct–performance approach

heterogeneous products, that is, products of the same sort and those of different sorts.

If a number of organisations are selling an identical or homogeneous product then the ability of producers to set the price of that product is reduced. For example, the price that a small clothes retailer can charge for a standard white shirt or blouse may be constrained by other similar retailers in the locality. Competitive behaviour is limited because the individual organisation has no market power. If the product is differentiated in some way – for example, if a shirt or blouse has a designer label – then the seller has an increased ability to decide the price, and other aspects of competition, because the product is differentiated.

This ability to differentiate products is recognised as essential and is used widely by organisations. Marketing is an important differentiating tool that is effective in promoting brand image. Brand recognition and customer loyalty are often important advantages held by incumbents (that is, organisations that already have an established position in the market). The car industry produces heterogeneous products since each model is different, though each still has the fundamental characteristics that distinguish it as a car. Even if different models look very similar it may be possible for manufacturers to create a difference through marketing. The world market for soap powders is dominated by two companies, Procter & Gamble (P&G) and Unilever. They do not sell only one homogeneous product each, but have a range of differentiated products, targeted at particular segments of the market. This process of differentiation has increased recently. From 1937 to 1980 P&G launched only seven detergents onto the market. This compares with the introduction of fourteen new lines from 1989 to 1994. By 1998 P&G had 26 detergents available in the UK market. The effect of this upsurge of launch activity was to further fragment the market. In both of the industries discussed above, because organisations have the power over their market, it is inevitable that they will compete actively with each other in all respects. This aspect will be considered in more detail when looking at the market for goods and services.

Number of firms and concentration

If there is just one organisation in the market then there is no competition. That organisation is a monopolist and, if not restrained by regulation, capable of making substantial profits. Although it is not a pure monopolist, BT's position in the telecommunications market has allowed it to make enormous profits since privatisation despite having to meet substantial redundancy costs. Table 2.1 provides some detail.

The level of profit from its activities in the home market has increased BT's ability to compete in international markets, utilising its size in an extremely competitive environment. However, success in the home market is no guarantee of triumph on a global scale. BT's planned £35 billion merger with Cable and Wireless failed in July 1996. In September 1997 the takeover of MCI, America's second-largest long-distance carrier, to form Concert and become the world's fourth-biggest telecom company, was thwarted when WorldCom bid $30 billion for MCI, valuing the company at $41.5 a share, rather than BT's offer worth just $40 a share (Alexander, 1997).

As the number of organisations in the market rises, competition increases and the ability of organisations to protect their profits declines. Hamburger stalls at any festival or sporting event, or ice-cream sellers on a beach, for example, face intense competition as consumer choice is multiplied.

TABLE 2.1   BT profits 1994–1998

Year	Profits (£m)
1994	2756
1995	2662
1996	3019
1997	3203
1998	3219

Source: BT Company Accounts, year ended 31 March 1998

It is not only the number of organisations that decides the extent of competition in a market. The level of concentration also affects the nature of competition. Concentration measures the share that the largest companies have of the total market output and reveals the extent of the domination by those large companies. Market concentration can be measured by the concentration ratio (CR).

The n-firm concentration ratio is the market share of the n largest firms in an industry.

Let us take an example of an industry with a turnover of £150 million where the five largest organisations have a combined share of £90 million. The concentration ratio of the five largest organisations is the output of the five largest firms divided by the total market, that is

$90/150 \times 100 = 60\%$

The five-firm concentration ratio is 60 per cent, that is CR5 60. The most commonly used measures are the four- and five-firm concentration ratios. Table 2.2 shows

TABLE 2.2   Concentration ratios of supermarkets and building societies

Leading supermarkets and superstores by turnover (£m) 1996–97	Turnover (£m)	Estimated share of mortgage business by leading building societies (£m) 1995	Gross advances (£m)
J. Sainsbury	14312.0	Halifax	10019
Tesco	13887.0	Woolwich	3130
Asda Group	6952.2	Nationwide	3129
Safeway	6589.7	Alliance & Leicester	2946
Somerfield	3200.6	National & Provincial	2367
Wm Morrisons	2176.0	Northern Rock	2263
Waitrose	1460.8	Bradford & Bingley	2245
Savacentre	737.9	Birmingham Midshires	1924
Budgens	320.5	Bristol & West	1113
Netto Foodstores	293.3	Britannia	904
		Other BS	3674
		Other	1975
		Banks	21237
Total	49930.0	Total	56926

Concentration ratios:
Retailers CR4:
    top four retailers' turnover £41740.9m
        $41740.9/49930.0 \times 100 = 83.6$
        CR4 84

Building societies CR5:
    top five lenders £21591m
        $21591/56926 \times 100 = 37.9$
        CR5 38

Source: adapted from *Supermarket and Superstores Market Report 1998*, 15th edn, ed. L. Barfe, Keynote Ltd, Hampton, Table 10, p. 18, and *Building Society Market Report 1996*, 10th edn, ed. P. Smith, Keynote Ltd, Hampton, Table 28, p. 39

the market share of the leading UK supermarket chains and building societies in the mortgage market along with concentration ratio calculations.

In this example the four biggest retailers have 84 per cent of sales (CR4 84). In the building society example the top five firms account for only 38 per cent of the market (CR5 38), although concentration is likely to increase as more societies convert to banks or are taken over by large financial conglomerates.

The concentration ratio should give an indication of the amount of competition within an industry. Industries with low concentration ratios, building societies in this case, may be more competitive because each organisation is competing with similarly sized rivals. No one organisation in this market wields more market power than the others. It is also apparent that the less concentrated an industry, the lower the barriers to entry (and vice versa). If there are few barriers to entry then new organisations can enter the market relatively easily and capture market share. This effectively increases competitive pressures in that industry. (See below for further explanation of barriers to entry.)

Alternatively, a high concentration ratio may indicate a smaller degree of competition, as in the retail sector, where it should be possible for each organisation to protect its share. This is particularly likely to occur if the market is still growing. We will analyse this in more detail when looking at the market for goods and services.

Evidence suggests that market concentration increased sharply until the 1980s, since when there has been little change in most sectors, though there is evidence of a resurgence of small-firm activity in recent years. One sector which has seen substantial change in market concentration is that of building societies, where merger activity and the abandonment of mutual status is ongoing.

The number of organisations and their concentration is not the only important factor to consider when analysing an organisation's competitive position. Table 2.3 shows two markets, each with a CR5 80. In market A the second-largest organisation has a market share of just 44 per cent of that of the largest organisation. In market B the two second-largest organisations are much closer in size to the largest, and the rest of the market is more evenly distributed amongst the top five. The competitive nature of these markets is likely to be very different, even though the CR5 is identical.

The CR3, that is the market share of the top three producers, in the UK cigarette market was estimated, between 1994 and 1996, to be 90 (see Table 2.4). If this

TABLE 2.3 Relative size within a market

Firm	Market A	Market B
1	43	23
2	19	16
3	10	16
4	5	13
5	3	12

TABLE 2.4   Market share in the UK cigarette market

Company	1994 (bn sticks)	1995 (bn sticks)	1996 (bn sticks)
Gallaher	36.5	31.4	31.7
Imperial	33	29.5	31.1
Rothmans/PM	12	10.4	10.5
Other	9.2	8.3	8.1
Total	90.7	79.6	81.4

Source: adapted from *Cigarettes: The Supply Structure*, January 1997, Figure 6;
Cigarette manufacturers: United Kingdom market shares, 1994–96, Mintel

concentration ratio is used as the only measure it could be inferred that the UK cigarette market was not particularly competitive. However, this could not be further from the truth.

The concentration of a market is only one indicator which should be appraised in conjunction with others when assessing the competitiveness of a market. These examples illustrate a basic problem with the concentration ratio measure, that it gives no information about inequality or the relative market share within the group of organisations selected.

Herfindahl–Hirschman Index (HHI)

An alternative indicator which attempts to overcome the problem of the concentration ratio measure is used in the United States where concentration and market dominance is measured by the Herfindahl–Hirschman Index (HHI). This measure is used by regulatory authorities in the USA, particularly when considering merger activity.

The HHI measures not only the number of organisations in the market but also the inequality between them, in terms of market share. A score of over 1800 points on the HHI represents a highly concentrated market. A merger which creates a market with this level of concentration will raise concerns (Fishwick, 1993). On examination of the data in Table 2.2 we can calculate an approximate HHI score for the top ten performers in the retail sector of 2043 and a score of 781 for the building societies (for calculation see Griffiths and Wall, 1997). The lower the index, the more competitive the market.

A merger of Asda and Safeway, proposed in 1998, would clearly have sent the HHI still higher, representing a highly concentrated market, with no room for merger activity. The 1992 US guidelines specify that the score on the post-merger HHI has to be less than 1000 for the merger not to have an adverse effect on competition in the market. Although not subject to this rule it is likely that the Asda/Safeway merger would not have been allowed by the Monopolies and Mergers Commission, so the proposal was dropped by the companies concerned.

Market entry conditions

Many markets present severe barriers to entry to prospective competitors while in others barriers are almost non-existent. It is clearly easier to open a small restaurant than to establish a Formula One racing team! The barriers in each case are very different. Barriers to entry can be categorised into two groups, so-called innocent barriers and those deliberately erected to prevent entrants.

Barriers erected deliberately

In some cases incumbents may take action to restrict entry. This could involve increasing expenditure on R&D, the introduction of new technology, advertising, legal action or rewarding customers through fidelity rebates. Barriers founded on reputation – for example the use of predatory pricing which lowers the price paid by the consumer – can be very effective in making new entrants think twice about the attractiveness of the market. This tactic has been used by newspapers and is said to have been applied by bus operators, such as Highland Scottish Omnibuses, Southdown Motor Services Ltd and Sussex Coastline Buses Ltd. Brand proliferation, as has happened in the detergent market (see above), also acts as a barrier to entry. Multiple brands, produced by the same manufacturer, compete against each other but also present an effective barrier to new products. It is difficult for a new entrant to establish a large market niche with only one product.

One instance where barriers to entry could be described as being relatively high and created by the scale of advertising is the cola market. The advertising budget for Coca-Cola's Classic was $131 million in 1996 (Langton, 1998). The two market leaders spent large amounts on advertising and promotion in 1997, with Coca-Cola doubling its UK advertising and promotion budget to £40 million (Marshall, 1997). This limited the progress rivals could make. Table 2.5 indicates that Virgin's market share actually fell, perhaps as a result of differences in advertising spend.

Virgin also had to overcome strategic barriers created by Coca-Cola who were able to grant discounts to stores that were able to sell high volumes of their product and so limited the space available to Virgin Cola. Virgin did not reach an agreement with Tesco to stock their cola until 1997 (Marshall, 1997). Later in the summer of 1997 Virgin concluded agreements with the Asda, Somerfield, Woolworths and

TABLE 2.5   Market share of colas, 1994 and 1997

Name	1994 % market share	1997 % market share
Coca-Cola	44.2	31.4
Pepsi	20.1	12.7
Virgin	8.7	5.3
Other	27	50.6

Source: The Times, 20 February 1997

Morrisons. Table 2.5 does, however, also show that the own-label brands were able to gain market share even in the face of this advertising onslaught.

Innocent barriers

Innocent barriers arise when an organisation has absolute cost advantages. In this case the incumbent organisation is able to produce at such a cost that it is uneconomical for another organisation to try and enter the market because their unit costs are, in comparison, much higher. The unit cost is the cost of producing one unit of output. In this situation organisations are said to benefit from economies of scale.

Barriers to entry will be investigated in more detail below.

Economies of scale

Figure 2.2 shows a situation where an increase in size of plant from 10 000–30 000 units results in a fall of average total cost (ATC) from £1000 to £500 per unit (average total cost is total cost divided by output, i.e. TC/O). A large plant with a capacity of 50 000 units reduces ATC even further, to £300 per unit.

Figure 2.3 shows that average costs per unit of production fall as output rises. Costs fall not at a uniform rate but at a declining rate, producing the typical

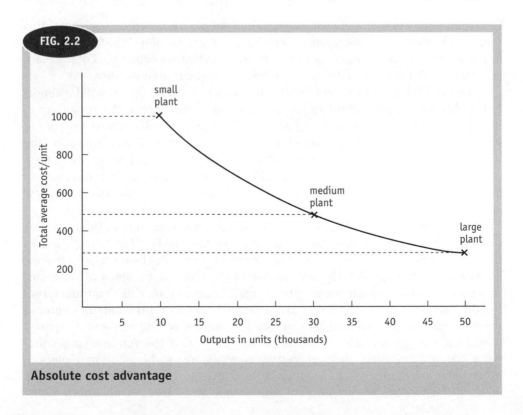

FIG. 2.2

Absolute cost advantage

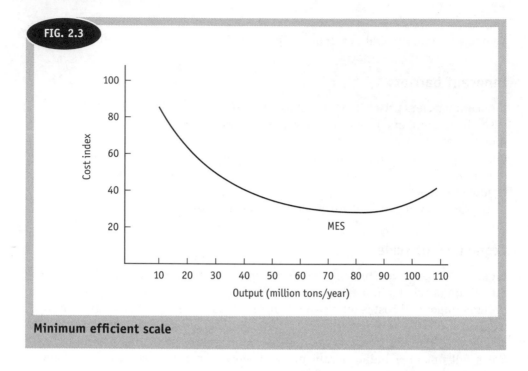

FIG. 2.3

Minimum efficient scale

U-shaped long-run average cost curve. When the curve becomes horizontal this output is known as the minimum efficient scale of production (MES), in this case, approximately 80 million tons per year. In some industries economies of scale are substantial, for example, in telecommunications and car manufacture.

If the MES is large in relation to the total market demand then it will be almost impossible for a new entrant to successfully enter the market. An organisation trying to enter the market at lower levels of output, e.g. 30 million tons per year in the example in Figure 2.3, would be at a severe cost disadvantage to the incumbents. The price that the new entrant would have to charge to break even would be much higher than those charged by the incumbent organisations that are experiencing economies of scale, and so it would be very difficult for the new organisation to attract customers.

The possibility of successful entry into the market is slim, unless the organisation were able to target a particular segment of the market that is regarded as unimportant by the incumbents. The new entrant would still face a tough struggle as it would be a formidable task to establish a brand image and customer recognition over a very narrow product range. Japanese motorbike manufacturers Honda, Yamaha, Suzuki and Kawasaki managed to achieve this when they entered the American and United Kingdom motorbike markets, selling only small-capacity machines. The incumbents in the market did not realise the subtle changes that were occurring. Rather than operating in a secure, stable, national market, protected from competition by the high costs of transportation and communication or by the ignorance of foreign companies, they were now in an international market competing against knowledgeable and efficient overseas rivals. The result of this inability to recognise change resulted in the almost total collapse of motorcycle manufacture in Europe and America (see Exhibit 2.9 on Honda). Daewoo, the Korean conglomerate, has penetrated and attained a credible position in the car market with a distinctive selling and marketing strategy which has enabled them to reduce costs. Global competition can wipe out previously concrete advantages. Organisations need to be able to respond to change quickly if they are to survive in the fiercely competitive global market. Lean production methods and flexible manufacturing have helped Japanese industry. The importance of innovation to support competitiveness by reducing costs and increasing quality should be recognised. The technological revolution of the past few decades has transformed retail services. Computerised information technology has facilitated the reorganisation of distribution systems and increasingly efficient stock-handling methods have enabled retailers to benefit from economies of scale (see also Exhibit 2.1).

It must also be recognised that capital investment in plant and equipment can lead to overcapacity if market growth is slow. The result could be severe for some companies and industries. A number of Japan's large-scale steel plants faced

EXHIBIT 2.1

Financial services direct

Over the past 15 years the financial services industry has seen substantial changes in the way the sector operates. Companies like Direct Line and First Direct, part of the HSBC group, have pioneered a new type of business enterprise.

Direct Line began in 1985 by slashing the cost of insurance. It is now one of the biggest providers of motor insurance and has emerged as a key player in traditional financial services and banking sectors providing mortgages, savings accounts, pensions and personal loans.

First Direct established the United Kingdom's first telephone bank when it identified the need to cut costs in a mature market and to attract customers by offering a different type of product. Virgin Direct, founded in 1995, has undercut providers of pensions, insurance, and investment products, including unit trusts. Other organisations in the sector have responded to the challenge. Halifax announced 24-hour telephone banking in January 1998. One of the biggest advantages of direct selling is the low operating cost that it offers a company, enabling it to do away with highly paid advisers in expensive traditional high street branch networks. Lower costs can be passed on directly to consumers.

These companies utilise the power of telecommunications and computing, selling direct to the public over the telephone. The downside is that the tactic requires heavy investment in IT, call centres and training.

The success of the direct sales companies has forced other financial services providers to re-think their strategy.

closure in 1998 due to the severe recession being experienced in Japan and the Far Eastern 'Tiger' economies.

It is not only economies of scale that confer advantages on organisations. We can use the experience curve phenomenon to further illustrate how advantages of incumbency can accrue to organisations.

Experience curve

The experience curve effect provides additional insight into the problems of entering a market. The experience curve was first described and popularised by the Boston Consulting Group (BCG), an American consultancy company, in 1968.

BCG observed, during studies of company performance, that incumbents in any market segment benefited from the experience that they had accumulated. The study showed a direct and constant relationship between aggregate growth in volume of production and declining cost of production. That is, as production volume increased the company became more efficient at producing the product, and the cost per unit of that production therefore declined. At first cost per unit fell rapidly and then more slowly as learning opportunities were exhausted. This resulted in a progressively declining gradient exhibited in the experience curve (see Figure 2.4). It has been claimed that costs fall by around 15 to 30 per cent with each doubling of output.

Experience curve savings are particularly important if price levels for a product are relatively similar, because what makes a company more profitable than its competitors is the level of its costs. If an organisation can increase output relative to its competitors then it will move down the experience curve more quickly, reducing costs, and thus widening cost differentials.

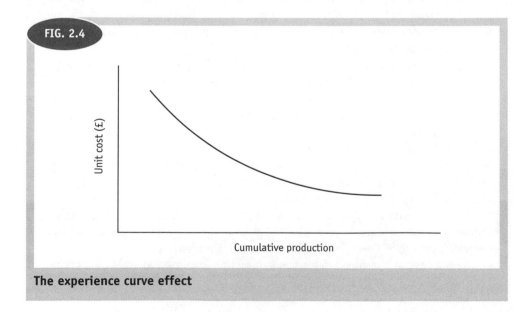

FIG. 2.4

Unit cost (£)

Cumulative production

The experience curve effect

BCG put forward three reasons why this fall in unit costs may occur. These were due to specialisation, learning and economies of scale. We have examined the last of these reasons above and will explore the first two here.

Specialisation

It usually becomes increasingly possible to design narrow and focused jobs as scale of production grows. Ford's car plants were at the forefront of this move in the 1920s and 1930s. Increasing specialisation through the division of labour should bring advantages. These are summarised by Beardshaw (1992):

- increase in skill and dexterity means the task can be carried out more expertly;
- time saving through reducing down time, the time in which a worker is idle, and the time saved on training;
- individual aptitudes can be utilised so individuals can concentrate on what they do best;
- machinery can be further utilised – modern production techniques, starting with the Ford Motor Company's own production line, are able to make full use of machinery because of specialisation of the workforce;
- breaking down the process into separate tasks allows for closer management control.

Learning

It is important to understand that organisations as well as individuals learn. As tasks are undertaken more frequently, individuals can learn and become more proficient at their work. Labour costs should decline. Similarly, an organisation should be able to learn and put in place efficient systems and procedures which should also translate into cost savings. Learning is likely to be the most important component in the experience curve for organisations in high-technology industries. Maintenance of learning and its conversion into organisational knowledge is a key element of competitive advantage for many high-tech companies. Japanese companies have been at the forefront of the global learning process, adapting the American philosophy of total quality management and advancing the ideas. This has led to the development of 'quality circles', 'kaizen' or continuous improvement, 'just-in-time manufacturing', 'right first time, every time' and many more management techniques which some Western companies are still coming to terms with.

Mansfield (1994) illustrated this point by reference to Texas Instruments, a major producer in the highly competitive global markets for semiconductor chips and other electronic products. When the semiconductor industry was relatively young, Texas Instruments priced its product at less than its then current average cost of production in order to increase its output and its total cumulative production. Believing that the experience curve, through the learning component, was relatively steep, it hoped that this would reduce its average costs to such an extent that it would be profitable to produce and sell at this low price. This strategy was extremely successful. As Texas Instruments continued to cut price, its rivals began to withdraw from the market, its output continued to increase, its costs fell further, and its profits increased.

Boeing's domination of the world aircraft market is in part due to learning by experience, gained from early entry into the market, which has been translated into more efficient operations. That Boeing's dominant position in the market seems to be under threat may, in turn, be due to other manufacturers, particularly the relatively young European competitor Airbus Industrie, having closed the gap on Boeing in terms of learning and experience. The combined effects of experience and economies of scale mean that many big companies gain substantial advantage. Not only are costs lower but visibility in the marketplace is also greater.

The ease of entry into a market is probably the major factor influencing competition. If organisations can enter a market at relatively little cost they are likely to seize the opportunity. Various strategies, as we have seen, are available to organisations that enable them to construct barriers that prospective competitors find difficult to overcome. One of the main deterrents to organisations entering a market is the risk of losing valuable funds in the venture. We explore this further by examining the contestable market approach below.

At this stage it is useful to undertake a closer examination of the market for goods and services. As in the business world very few organisations operate within perfectly competitive markets, we can concentrate our analysis on the monopolistic, oligopolistic and monopolistically competitive markets. We will draw on the ideas introduced in this section.

QUESTIONS

1. Comment, using Table 2.4, on why the market for cigarettes seemed to be declining from 1994 to 1996.

2. How were the supermarkets able to increase the market share of their colas in the face of competition from the main rivals in the market?

3. Using Exhibit 2.1 and key concepts introduced in this section, analyse how companies in the financial services sector have changed the competitive structure of the market.

4. Using market research data, calculate the CR5 for a market of your choice. Comment on your findings.

THE MARKET FOR GOODS AND SERVICES

In this section we will investigate the different competitive environment that organisations will face in monopoly, oligopoly and monopolistic competition and probe some of the issues surrounding each configuration. Table 2.6 summarises the characteristics of these markets.

TABLE 2.6 Models of market structure

Characteristics	Perfect competition	Monopolistic competition	Oligopoly	Monopoly
No. and size of sellers	Many, small	Many, small	Few, large	One, no close substitutes
Type of product	Homogeneous	Differentiated	Differentiated or homogeneous	One
Entry barriers	None	None	Low, some	High
CR (%)	0	Low	High	100
Example	Fruit and vegetable markets	High street clothes retailers	Airlines, car manufacturers	Regional Water Boards (UK)

Monopoly

The economist's view

Economists view monopolists as the sole supplier of an industry's output, producing goods and services for which no substitute is available. In this extreme case a monopoly is said to have a concentration ratio of 100, it being the only organisation supplying the market. Those monopolies that enjoy massive economies of scale are called natural monopolies; in this case there is only room for one firm producing at minimum efficient scale – for example, water, gas and electricity suppliers. The market power of these organisations is controlled by regulatory authorities (see below). Monopolies can arise because of barriers to entry that prevent competition. These barriers may be due to actions taken by incumbents or innocent barriers. De Beers' very strong position in the supply of diamonds relies on its central selling organisation controlling 80 per cent of world trade in rough diamonds.

Monopolists, because of their protected position, need not be overly concerned by the threat of new organisations entering the industry in the short or medium term.

It is possible for the monopolist to make monopoly or abnormal profits in the long run, unlike in a competitive industry where profits are eroded by new organisations entering the market. Indeed companies which hold monopoly positions, and are able to maintain large profits, are not uncommon. The utilities, privatised in the United Kingdom during the 1980s and 1990s, on the whole enjoy monopoly positions in their home market. Their annual reports are widely reported in the media, and profit announcements are often accompanied by a furore from consumer groups who are concerned that profits are being made at the expense of the consumer (see BT's profits in Table 2.1).

The view of the authorities

An alternative view of monopoly is employed by the competition authorities. In the UK an organisation is said to be a scale monopoly if it has over 25 per cent of the relevant regional or national market. If two or more organisations are involved by agreement or conduct that prevents, restricts or distorts competition then the monopoly is said to be complex. In 1995 Sega had a 38 per cent share of the UK combined video games console and games software market and is, by this definition, a monopoly. Its main rival, Nintendo, had a share of just under 25 per cent. The entry of Sony into the market, with their play station console, in 1995 added a vital competitive element. Although an organisation does not control the whole of the market, its market position may confer on it enormous power.

Problems associated with monopoly

Lack of competition in the market may mean that there is a danger that a monopolist can take action that may adversely affect the consumer. Results could include

- restriction of output, as the monopolist can create a shortage, depriving consumers while increasing its profits;
- price fixing, as the monopolist can restrict supply to those who can afford to pay higher prices;
- regulation of terms of supply, as the monopolist can impose harsh terms on consumers;
- removal of consumer choice – for example, the situation for consumers buying cars in the former Communist states of Eastern Europe was dire.

Exhibit 2.2 illustrates some of these potential problems.

Because monopolists may try to manipulate the market against the wishes of the consumer, it is necessary for other forms of control to be applied to the market.

EXHIBIT 2.2

Monopoly references

The President of the Board of Trade, Margaret Beckett, referred the Ladbrokes/ Corals merger to the MMC. She stated that the organisations had ceased to be distinct enterprises and had assets of over £70 million. It was later rejected.

Source: DTI Press Notice P/28/256, 31 March 1998

An investigation of the charges made by Vodaphone and Cellnet for calls made from fixed phones to their mobile phones and charges made by BT for calls made to mobile phones was called for by the Director General of Telecommunications, Don Cruikshank. He referred the case to the MMC to see whether charges were against the public interest. This followed a situation when the organisations concerned had failed to reduce their charges when asked by Oftel in December 1997.

Source: OFTEL Press Release 17/98, 5 March 1998

Wall's Ice Cream was referred to the MMC on the grounds that Birds Eye Wall's Ltd (BEW) was pursuing or had pursued anti-competitive practices. The organisation was said to have refused to supply wrapped ice cream to wholesalers who are not dedicated distributors or where ice cream was supplied to non-dedicated distributors it was on less favourable contractual terms. Further BEW were alleged to grant discounts to retailers who purchased BEW wrapped ice cream from dedicated distributors but not to retailers who purchased BEW wrapped ice cream from other suppliers.

Source: OFT Press Office No. 61/97, 22 December 1997

Control of monopoly power

The imposition of strict controls provides a challenge to the monopolist's position and its ability to make profits. Control of monopoly can take a number of forms. In an effort to limit the dangers of monopoly power many monopolies have to be regulated by the government or its agencies. Control of monopolies is not only the province of national government but is increasingly coming under a higher tier of control, that of the European Union. The main regulating body in the UK was until recently the Monopolies and Mergers Commission (MMC). The MMC had to determine whether the referred monopoly or proposed merger operated against the public interest and recommend action to ensure the maintenance of competition. The MMC was replaced by the Competition Commission under the Competition Act 1998 (see Exhibit 2.3 for details).

In the United Kingdom the privatisations of the 1980s and 1990s also spawned the growth of regulatory bodies such as OFTEL, OFGAS and OFFER, to provide a framework to control those newly privatised monopolies. (Further examination of this can be found in Chapter 8.)

EXHIBIT 2.3

The Competition Act 1998: a new regime

The Competition Act 1998, which received royal assent in November 1998 and comes into force on 1 March 2000, introduces a new domestic competition regime in the United Kingdom by outlawing cartels and other anti-competitive agreements and the abuse of a dominant position.

'It provides a strong deterrent against cartels and abuses of market power', suggested Margaret Beckett (ex President of the Board of Trade). However, agreements that provide balanced benefits, shared between consumers and business, will be permitted. The Director General of Fair Trading (DGFT) is responsible for enforcing the new legislation and has strong investigatory powers. The MMC was replaced by the Competition Commission on 1 April 1999.

Exhibit 2.3 continued

Anti-competitive agreements

Prohibition is based on Article 85 (see Chapter 7). Agreements will be prohibited that have the object or effect of preventing, restricting or distorting competition in the United Kingdom. These prohibitions replace the Restrictive Trade Practices Act 1976 (RTPA) and the Resale Prices Act 1976 (RPA).

Process

DGFT decides if prohibitions are infringed and the level of fines and other penalties to be imposed. Beneficial effects are assessed by DGFT for exemption. Appeal is to the Competition Commission.

Abuse of a dominant market position

Prohibition is based on Article 86 (see Chapter 7). Abuse of a dominant market position in the United Kingdom is prohibited. The kind of conduct that may constitute an abuse is:

- imposing unfair purchase or selling prices, or other unfair conditions;
- limiting production, markets or technical development to the prejudice of customers;
- applying dissimilar conditions to equivalent transactions with other trading parties thus placing them at a competitive disadvantage; and
- making contracts subject to the acceptance of other obligations which are irrelevant to the subject matter of the contract.

Most of the Competition Act 1980 is repealed and the Act also provides for the amendment of the Fair Trading Act 1973 (FTA) to strengthen the DGFT's investigative powers in respect of monopoly investigations, including complex monopolies.

Process

DGFT decides if prohibitions are infringed and, if so, the level of penalties to be imposed.

- *Criteria* – Whether either prohibition is infringed is decided upon based on a test on the effect it has on competition.
- *Investigation* – the DGFT has strong investigatory powers, including forcible entry/search powers.
- *Fines* – Penalties of up to 10 per cent of United Kingdom turnover can be levied.

Third party rights to challenge companies and seek damages are included and alleged anti-competitive agreements and behaviour may be halted during investigation.

Source: adapted from DTI Press Release P/97/662, 16 October 1997, Competition Bill to benefit consumers and business and the MMC web site at www.open.gov.uk/.

Regulation of monopolies can also have a detrimental effect. BT is restricted by government legislation from entering the market for cable television. The rapidly changing technology and the ability of other domestic and foreign competitors to enter the market may be to the long-term disadvantage of BT. The ability of the United Kingdom's biggest telecommunications company to compete in the world market might be harmed.

It is evident from this brief analysis that the UK government is intent on strengthening competition law by prohibiting anti-competitive behaviour. Monopolists do not have free rein over their market. It is up to organisations within the market to be particularly aware of how changes in the regulatory regime are going to affect them in the future and design organisational responses to meet those changes. Of increasing importance is the response of consumers to monopolists. For example, the drought in some areas of the United Kingdom in 1995 provoked an outcry from consumers and consumer groups. It is in the interests of the water companies to listen to the problems of their consumers or the government may be forced to take action. Being proactive and implementing self-control, as opposed to being constrained by tight regulation, is often considered beneficial in the long run.

The economist Joseph Schumpeter (1883–1950) also recognised the transient nature of the monopolist's position. He suggests that a monopoly will eventually be circumvented by technology and innovation and that barriers to entry are not a serious problem to a competitive market in the long run. The position of BT, for example, has substantially altered from its position as a monopoly provider of telecommunications in the UK prior to privatisation in August 1984. Not only have regulations resulted in more competition, but the development of mobile phones, and more recently the Internet, will have enormous implications for BT as it strives to maintain its position.

Oligopoly

Oligopoly is defined as a market in which a small number of producers compete with each other. In some cases two organisations dominate – for example in the detergent market where Procter & Gamble and Unilever are dominant, or in the UK mobile phone market where Vodaphone and Cellnet hold sway. This form of oligopoly is known as a *duopoly*.

Because of the small number of competitors each organisation has to consider how its actions will affect the decisions of its competitors. Organisations are interdependent, which means that action by one organisation will solicit a response from its competitor(s). This is particularly important in regard to pricing decisions. It is likely that any change in price will be copied by competitors, with the effect of reducing profits for all organisations. Freedom of manoeuvre for an organisation is very restricted, not because of fear of entry into the market, but because of this interdependence of organisations within the market. The consequence of this is relative price stability in the market, with competition based on quality, branding, advertising and service. For example, Procter & Gamble and

Unilever were the biggest advertisers in 1996 and Langton (1998) reported that the advertising budget of Coca-Cola Classic and McDonalds in 1996 were $131 million and $599 million respectively.

The grocery market provides a good example of an oligopolistic market in operation. Four organisations account for the bulk of sales. Each company must take account of the reaction of the others when it formulates its policy since its optimal strategy will depend, in part, on the response of competitors. The sector is explored briefly in Exhibit 2.4.

EXHIBIT 2.4

The retail environment

Since the 1970s there has been a dramatic change in the retail environment of many Western economies (Bromley and Thomas, 1993). In the 1980s the UK experienced a massive and sustained concentration of capital within grocery retailing (Wrigley and Lowe, 1996). The main supermarket retailers (those owning/operating ten or more retail outlets) have gained market share at the expense of independents and co-operatives. Between 1982 and 1990 the market share of the top five grocery retailers increased from under 25 per cent to 61 per cent of national grocery sales, with a superleague of firms appearing in the industry.

The key players in the market are Tesco, J. Sainsbury, the Asda Group and Safeway who collectively were reported to have a market share of 66 per cent in 1996 (see Table 2.7).

TABLE 2.7   Grocery market shares, 1994–96

Retailer	1994 %	1995 %	1996 %
Tesco	19.3	21.8	22.5
J. Sainsbury	22.0	21.1	20.7
Asda	11.7	11.7	12.8
Safeway	9.2	9.6	10.3
Kwik Save	6.9	6.6	6.5
Co-ops	6.6	6.6	5.5
Somerfield	4.8	4.5	4.5
Wm. Morrison	3.6	4.0	4.2
Iceland	3.4	3.2	2.9
Waitrose	1.4	1.6	1.6
Aldi	0.3	0.8	0.9
Netto	0.6	0.7	0.8
Others	11.0	8.0	7.0

Source: AGB Sharetrack/Mintel

In February 1998 Somerfield announced plans to merge with Kwik Save Group giving the company 7 per cent market share and making it the fifth largest operator (Hamilton, 1998). This took the CR5 to nearly 70.

The merger was partly in response to the growing competition Kwik Save faced from other discounters, including Aldi and Netto, and the discount lines of the major retailers which effectively left Kwik Save stuck in the middle. The market share of second division supermarkets is being squeezed still further. It fell from 16 per cent to 13.5 per cent in 1997. This trend is set against the background of wide-ranging socio-economic change (see Chapter 5).

Price competition appears to be less significant than the battle for customer loyalty (Barfe, 1998). Loyalty is sought by advertising and value added services. Advertising puts in place barriers to entry and creates brand awareness. The advertising spend of the top four retailers in 1997 was £109.7 million which represents 64 per cent of total expenditure in the sector (Barfe, 1998). All the major retailers are in the process of providing value added services for their customers. These services include:

- differential pricing and products to suit all parts of the market;
- order and collect (available at some branches of Sainsbury's);
- easily accessible customer service facilities;
- help in packing for shoppers with children;
- an Internet ordering service (being trailed by a number of retailers);
- the use of loyalty cards with discounts relating to amount spent;
- celebrity endorsements (for example, Asda signed the Spice Girls in 1997);
- all-night and Sunday opening, offering more flexibility to customers;
- self-scanning to speed the process (at Safeway);
- joint money-off schemes with other retailers;
- new-format smaller inner city stores, e.g. Tesco Metro.

Economists usually distinguish further between those oligopolies that sell homogeneous products, for example oil companies, and those producing differentiated products. In reality all oligopolists try to differentiate their products, either in substance or by marketing, advertising and image creation. In markets where products are differentiated by advertising, for example the cigarette market, it is possible to erect substantial barriers that new entrants cannot overcome. In 1996 Gallaher and Imperial, the two leading manufacturers, each held around 38 per cent of the United Kingdom market and marketed eight of the ten most popular brands (Mintel, 1997), leaving very little room for new entrants.

The concentration ratio in this sort of market is typically high, with each organisation holding a substantial share of the market. Market share figures for the top five car manufacturers in the United Kingdom are shown in Table 2.8.

TABLE 2.8   New registration of cars in the UK by leading manufacturers (number and percentage share), 1996

Manufacturer	Number of vehicles sold	% market share
Ford	405 386	20
General Motors	298 875	14.7
BMW (includes Rover)	278 498 (221 658)	13.7 (10.9)
Peugeot Group	229 727	11.3
Volkswagen Group	171 258	8.5
Renault	132 374	6.5
Nissan	94 408	4.6
Fiat	91 662	4.5
Toyota	60 503	3.0
Others	264 248	13.2
Total	2 026 939	100

Source: *Motor Industry Market Review*, 5th edn (1997),
ed. S. Howitt, Keynote, Hampton

The top five retain a substantially larger market share than their smaller niche rivals.

It is in the interest of firms to erect barriers to entry to make it difficult for new organisations to enter the market. Barriers can be created in many ways (see below). In some markets it may be possible for organisations to enter and exit at no cost, increasing the effect of competition greatly. One way organisations can manufacture barriers to entry is by entering into agreements, known as collusion.

Collusion

Organisations in an oligopolistic market may have much to gain from some form of collaboration or collusion. This can be implicit or explicit. The aim is to jointly reduce uncertainty, prevent entry into the market and maximise profits. Collusion has a distorting effect on the market. It tends to raise prices and control output, both of which adversely affect the consumer. A case was referred by the OFT suggesting that 20 premiership football clubs are restricting choice and acting as a 'cartel' by negotiating a collective television deal with BSkyB and the BBC (*Guardian*, 1997).

Because of the likely impact on consumers, both explicit collusion (the operation of cartels) and implicit collusion are illegal. One of the roles of the Competition Commission and Directorate General (DG) IV, the Competition Directorate of the European Commission (see Chapter 7), is to ensure that markets do not operate against the public interest.

Explicit collusion

Under this form of collusion, usually referred to as a cartel, prices are fixed and output or sales are allocated to each member of the cartel. The cartel is able to act as a monopolist. Allocation decisions are usually the result of negotiation between the organisations. Often decisions are made in relation to the sales each organisation has had historically, or on a geographical basis. Exhibit 2.5 shows a cartel in action.

Cartels are evident across a wide range. The All Pakistan Cement Manufacturers' Association has assumed the shape of a cartel in the face of substantial

---

EXHIBIT 2.5

Organisation of Petroleum Exporting Countires (OPEC)

The OPEC cartel operated successfully from 1973 until 1986. The oil price rises instituted by the cartel in 1973 and 1979 resulted in a huge boost in the income of the countries within the cartel and caused severe problems in all non-oil-producing nations. Price rises caused significant inflationary pressures throughout the world. Oil producers outside OPEC also benefited from increased prices. Marginal fields, in the North Sea, belonging to Norway and the United Kingdom, and in the USSR, deemed too expensive to exploit, became viable propositions for development as the price of crude oil rose. It is unlikely that these fields would have been developed as quickly had it not been for the action of OPEC.

The latest collapse in the cartel was one of many such failures since the organisation was founded in 1960. During 1998 oil prices fell to levels previously seen in 1973. The causes of this dramatic fall were attributable to both sides of the market equation. On the supply side, technological advances have pruned the cost of oil exploration and recovery and enabled more reserves to be discovered and exploited. Secondly, members of OPEC undermined prices by increasing production quotas in November 1997, supplying more oil to the market. Lastly, because around 60 per cent of world output of oil comes from non-OPEC producers, there is an over-supply on world markets.

As supply has risen demand has declined. Asian 'tiger' economies have experienced significant downturns and Western European economies have shown little sign of growth. Consumers are demanding ever greater fuel efficiency and the northern winters have been unusually warm in the 1990s.

At the beginning of 1997 crude oil was around $20 per barrel; only a few months later it stood at approximately $12 per barrel. A further twist to the tale occurred in March 1998 when an agreement was reached between OPEC and non-OPEC producers to restrict supplies of oil in an effort to shore up prices. However the price had fallen to below $10 per barrel by the end of the year.

This case offers evidence that cartels are extremely difficult to control as individual members of a cartel can increase their revenue by ignoring the agreement and so have an incentive to cheat.

losses for twelve of Pakistan's nineteen cement companies (Bokhari, 1998). In the United States a fine of $29 million (£17.3 million) was levied on Showa Denko Carbon for anti-competitive practices. The organisation was said to have fixed prices and allocated market share for electrodes which distorted prices (Suzman, 1998).

Implicit collusion

In the case of implicit collusion a price leader may materialise within an industry and other organisations tacitly follow. Alternatively, agreements may have some form of official sanction. The price of transatlantic air fares from European destinations is fixed through IATA. It has been suggested that the existence of this type of system will encourage anti-competitive behaviour. Evidence seems to suggest that airlines have colluded through IATA to block cut-price fares. Understandings over fares also prompted the Civil Aviation Authority, in 1994, to suggest that collusion and price fixing on transatlantic air routes had blocked competition and held those fares at artificially high levels. Because agreements are often tacit rather than explicit it is difficult to find evidence of such arrangements. The European Commission may be forced to take action to stop this kind of price fixing.

An example of the role of competition policy and how difficult it is to identify implicit collusion can be seen in Exhibit 2.6.

EXHIBIT 2.6

The car cartel

Increasingly evidence seems to suggest that car prices are higher in the United Kingdom than in other parts of the European Union. The European Commission, on behalf of the UK government, has been looking at prices in the market since March 1998.

Out of 72 best-selling models covered by a study, 61 were found to be most costly in the United Kingdom (Butler, 1998). For example the price of a VW Golf is:

Holland	£6500 pre-tax;
France	£7000 pre-tax;
Great Britain	£9250 pre-tax.

KPMG suggest that when all factors, such as the need for right-hand drive in the United Kingdom and the strength of sterling, are taken into account, prices are still 6.6 per cent higher in the United Kingdom than the rest of Europe. Here we explore the reason for this by examining three car manufacturers.

Volvo

Indications are that the majority of dealers charge the same price for their cars, based on a Volvo price list. That is, 186 dealers are providing no price competition.

The inquiry shows 20 out of 23 dealers offer a Volvo S40 for £17 025 (1998). It seems that strict guidelines are in force at Volvo, no discounts are allowed. Competition law states that it is illegal for manufacturers to dictate prices. Because dealers do not have the power to set their own prices it seems, on the face of it, that competition law is being breached.

Competition amongst Volvo dealers used to exist. Some dealers used to discount up to 20 per cent. A meeting held in Volvo's training centre in Daventry in March 1995 seems to have been a prelude to price fixing. Dealers agreed to limit discounts. A network of cartels has been established at similar meetings across the country. Sanctions for dealers not following instructions include cars becoming difficult to obtain and the loss of monthly bonuses, which can make the difference between survival and failure.

Volkswagen

The study found eight out of twenty Golfs offered for sale at more than the list price, only two for less. VW can remove franchises and bonuses if discounts are evident. VW has set up profit clinics in the United Kingdom to discuss franchise development and strategy but agreements on prices and discounts are also on the agenda.

In January 1998 VW was hit with the biggest fine ever imposed on a company by the Commission, DM200 million (£67 million), for preventing German and Austrian consumers purchasing cut-price vehicles in Italy. The Commission believed that VW forced Italian dealers to turn away non-Italian customers and threatened to stop supplying vehicles. Seven dealerships were closed down by VW.

Mercedes

Mercedes suggest that discounts are not to be greater than 3 per cent of list price. In the study 19 out of 20 dealers were found to be within this limit. It is evident that the same type of sanctions apply to Mercedes dealers as to those elsewhere if guidelines are not followed.

Source: adapted from *The Car Cartel Panorama*, BBC1, 6 June 1998

The breakdown of collusion

A major problem associated with collusion is the temptation for organisations to 'cheat' and so ignore any agreement. By doing so it is possible for the organisation or country, in the short run, to increase profits at the expense of other parties to the agreement. As a result it may be difficult to sustain any agreement for a prolonged period, particularly if there are a large number of organisations. The Japanese construction cartel seems to have collapsed because of increasing competition in the market. The demise of OPEC was due largely to cartel members selling too much oil, that is, above their quota level (see Exhibit 2.5). The break-up of the cartel contributed to the increased tension between Iraq and Iran which culminated in war and later in Iraq's invasion of Kuwait.

Oligopoly is the dominant form of market structure found in all market economies. We have seen that in some oligopolistic industries competition is intense and organisations have to fight hard to maintain their market share. In others the nature of the industry, or the existence of agreements, means that organisations can come close to joint-profit maximisation. However, high profits will attract competitors, so organisations must devote a lot of time to maintaining and defending the barriers to entry. Competition authorities are also active in limiting the amount of collusive activity.

Monopolistic competition

Monopolistically competitive markets include a large number of organisations, with differentiated products, and no barriers to entry. There is, therefore, freedom of entry into a market where firms cannot make excess profits in the long run. Organisations act independently, because their market share is likely to be small and their actions are of little concern to others. If one organisation changes price, for example, this is unlikely to affect prices throughout the market. The large number of organisations, combined with their correspondingly small size, means that the concentration ratio will be low, which increases competitive pressures.

The retail trade is often cited as an example of this type of market. For example, a T-shirt is a product that no one has a monopoly on selling. They are not all the same, but differentiated by each seller. A price rise in one store will not result in price rises everywhere else (though it is suggested that neighbouring shops may respond).

One of the features of monopolistic competition is the high level of advertising as organisations attempt to maintain or improve their position in the marketplace. Product differentiation may exist because of imaginary differences in the mind of the consumer brought about through advertising, branding and the service provided by an organisation. Logos on T-shirts enable an organisation to sell the same material with a more desirable logo for a higher price.

Product innovation is also constantly sought after, as new products may provide a temporary competitive edge and an opportunity to raise prices and increase profit.

The health food industry is dominated by numerous small companies and a few large multinationals with health food interests. Because organisations are small, expensive forms of advertising, for example the use of television commercials, are avoided. Organisations concentrate on below-the-line advertising such as competitions and point-of-sale material. Advertising expenditure has increased substantially in the main sector of this market since 1988.

The real or perceived differences created by advertising and innovation mean that it is possible for an organisation to charge a higher price. If organisations in the market are seen to be obtaining high profits, new organisations can enter the market because of the low barriers to entry. The monopolistically competitive market is therefore liable to see high levels of competition between incumbents and entrants to the market. There will be enormous pressure on organisations to reduce their costs and improve their efficiency as a way of preserving margins and thus profitability.

Many economists maintain that this type of market is almost never found in practice. It is suggested that all organisations in the market have to take account of their competitors at some level.

Summary

We have now applied the traditional economic model of industry structure as a basis of analysing competition. To what extent is this model of use? Caves and Porter (1980) suggest that if structural change within an industry, particularly changes of concentration and entry, appears to be slow then the traditional model will be applicable.

However, in other circumstances the model may present only a partial view of the competitive conditions facing an organisation. In some industries the rate of change may be rapid with, for example, technology transforming the industry structure by changing both process and products. One only needs to look at the demise of products like electric typewriters and the changes forced on IBM to cope with the market for personal computers to see the influence of technology (refer also to Chapter 4). It is under these circumstances that the value of using industry structure as a basis for analysing competition may be diminished.

Other economists too have put the structure–conduct–performance approach under the microscope. The Chicago School has taken an alternative view that concentrated markets are not necessarily evil in themselves. Markets that exhibit extremes of concentration may gain benefits such as economies of scale or greater efficiency. The Chicagoans believe that barriers to entry are more apparent than real and that competition is powerful enough to prevent organisations from controlling markets. The conclusion is that conduct and performance of the market are not related to its underlying structure. Competition in a highly concentrated market could be fierce. This obviously has a significant impact on businesses operating in these types of markets.

QUESTIONS

1. In this section we have identified four dangers that might be associated with a monopoly. Using reports from newspapers and competition authorities identify, describe and analyse a monopoly situation.

2. What effect is the reduction in oil prices likely to have on the balance of payments of
   (a) oil-importing countries?
   (b) oil-exporting countries?

3. If companies have to pay less for their energy what is the likely impact on their business performance? Look at this question with reference to high and low energy users.

4. How does the grocery market outlined in the Exhibit 2.4 represent a typical oligopoly? How have retailers like Aldi and Netto been able to penetrate such a market?

CONTESTABLE MARKETS

A valuable addition to the theory of industry structure is provided by Baumol (1982). He suggests that it is possible for organisations to enter a market without incurring costs because these costs can be recovered when the organisation exits. There are no sunk or unrecoverable costs. This situation is known as a perfectly contestable market. Sunk costs can include the cost of building, advertising and R&D. If the sunk costs of entry are lower, then the market is more contestable or more competitive. Contestable markets are vulnerable to hit-and-run entry. Supermarkets have been able to establish a major market share in the cola market in three years (see Table 2.5). Manufacturing is carried out by a partner and shelf space is readily available. Own brands establish a market partly due to demand for the product being elastic – that is, it is price sensitive, and consumers will increase their demand for the product if the price is sufficiently low. Entry into the market was against a background of increasing consumption of soft drinks, from 6.6 billion litres in 1987 to an estimated 9 billion litres in 1996. This provides evidence of low barriers to entry and exit for supermarkets and low sunk costs.

It is doubtful whether a perfectly contestable market exists. In most cases some sunk costs are incurred in market entry. It is the scale of the sunk costs which may, or may not, dissuade a potential entrant from attempting a hit-and-run entry.

The risk that Virgin Atlantic took to start an air service from London to Japan was lessened because the sunk costs were relatively low. If the route proved to be unprofitable aircraft could be transferred to other routes, rental of terminal space could stop and ground equipment could be switched to another airport. In June 1995, Virgin Atlantic started a service on the London to Sydney route, the so-called kangaroo route, in partnership with MAS, using MAS aircraft – a strategy further designed to eliminate sunk costs of entry. The main block to contestability of the airline industry seems not to be sunk costs but regulation (see below). The service was still in operation in 1998! The construction of the Channel Tunnel presents a completely different story. If the operators fail to gain market share from ferry or airline operators then the whole cost of construction may represent a sunk cost, resulting in enormous losses to shareholders and the consortium of banks currently funding the business.

QUESTION

Using examples from published sources, investigate a situation, like the one for colas above, where the sunk costs of companies entering a market are low.

STRUCTURAL ANALYSIS OF COMPETITIVE FORCES

Despite criticism, the structure–conduct–performance model may still be a useful foundation for the analysis of a rapidly changing business environment. Porter

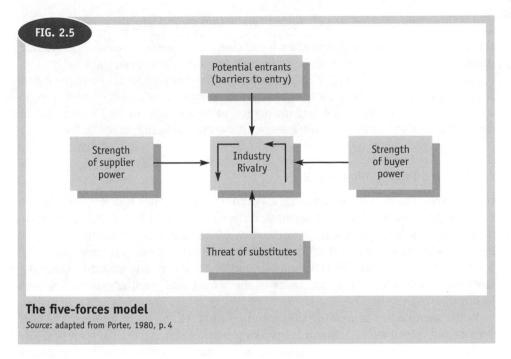

FIG. 2.5

The five-forces model
Source: adapted from Porter, 1980, p. 4

(1980) argues that 'understanding industry structure must be the starting point for strategic analysis'. Strategic analysis focuses on identifying the basic, underlying characteristics of an industry, which are rooted in its economics and technology. It is these characteristics that shape the competitive environment that the industry faces (Porter, 1980).

To enhance understanding it is advisable to examine Michael Porter's 1980 model more closely. The model illustrated in Figure 2.5 brings together many elements discussed above as it is based on the s–c–p paradigm.

Porter suggests that the collective strengths of five forces determine the state of competition and therefore the ultimate profit potential within an industry. The five competitive forces identified by Porter are:

- rivalry among competitors;
- threat of entry;
- threat of substitution;
- bargaining power of buyers;
- bargaining power of suppliers.

We will briefly explore each one.

Rivalry among competitors

This is Porter's central force. Increased rivalry will lead to increased competition and reduced profits. Intensity of rivalry between competitors will depend on several factors.

The number and relative size of competitors within an industry

If there are many organisations of a similar size, as in monopolistic competition, or oligopoly, then rivalry will be intense. Organisations in the industry are likely to try to gain market share through all possible means. Witness the situation in the petrol retail market where new deals to consumers are continuously being introduced. In industries with relatively few organisations, or where one or two organisations dominate, rivalry tends to be much less and the market much more stable.

The rate of growth in an industry

It is important to recognise that the growth rate of an industry is dependent upon a number of factors and that sectoral differences abound. Market growth in industries where product innovation and displacement are dominant is likely to be very different from that of the more traditional sectors, for example ship-building. Geographical differences also need to be taken into account. Cigarette smoking is increasing in some areas of the world and declining in others (see Exhibit 5.3).

When an industry is growing slowly competition will be more intense. The only way an organisation can expand is by taking market share from competitors. The early 1990s saw a fall in European car sales, a phenomenon referred to as negative growth. The only manufacturer to prosper in this cut-throat market was Rover, which managed to increase its market share, albeit from a low starting point.

It is important for organisations to be aware of the product life cycle that their products face, as competitive conditions can be very different at each phase of the life cycle. Figure 2.6 shows four stages in the product life cycle, each with its own characteristics.

Cost conditions

The relationship between fixed and variable cost is important. If organisations operate in a business with relatively high fixed costs it will be in the interests of that organisation to cut its prices in order to sell its output. The world steel industry, for example, saw savage price competition in the 1970s and 1980s as companies attempted to increase sales at the expense of competitors. Train operators are willing to reduce prices at certain times of the day and different days of the week to attract customers. Rail operators offer discounts for off-peak users and a range of discount cards for students, families and pensioners. Operators also use unconventional tactics to attract customers. The Penistone line in South Yorkshire runs some musical trains in the evenings, complete with folk music and real ale, in an effort to attract customers to use the line on a regular basis. The variable cost of selling a ticket is very low, the fixed cost of operating a railway high. Staff have to be employed and trains have to be in service. Organisations in this situation will seek additional business, that is, increased ticket sales, as long as the revenue from sales covers the variable costs of those sales.

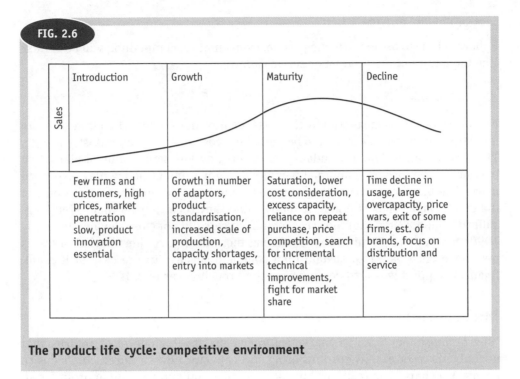

FIG. 2.6

	Introduction	Growth	Maturity	Decline
Sales	Few firms and customers, high prices, market penetration slow, product innovation essential	Growth in number of adaptors, product standardisation, increased scale of production, capacity shortages, entry into markets	Saturation, lower cost consideration, excess capacity, reliance on repeat purchase, price competition, search for incremental technical improvements, fight for market share	Time decline in usage, large overcapacity, price wars, exit of some firms, est. of brands, focus on distribution and service

The product life cycle: competitive environment

The battle to attract valuable inward investment from multinational companies is often augmented by substantial offers from governments that cover significant proportions of the start-up cost (see Exhibit 2.7).

EXHIBIT 2.7

UK foreign direct investment

The United Kingdom has been very successful, in the face of widespread international competition, in attracting this type of investment. In 1995–96 the Invest in Britain Bureau showed that almost 500 new foreign direct investment (FDI) projects had come to the United Kingdom. This investment created 48 256 new jobs and safeguarded over 50 000 existing jobs. The total investment attracted to the United Kingdom since the mid 1980s is over $200 billion which has generated in excess of 500 000 new jobs, with a substantial proportion in manufacturing.

Nissan, the Japanese car manufacturer, started in Sunderland in 1984 and now employs 4300 with a further 8000 local jobs in service firms and suppliers. Nissan have been followed by Toyota, Fujitsu, Honda, Siemens, Samsung and LG among others. However, the level of FDI from Asia is likely to fall substantially because of the problems in that part of the world since 1997 – some planned developments have already been shelved. See also Chapter 7 on regional policy.

Lack of product differentiation

If there is little to distinguish one product from another, competition will be intense (see the nature of the product or service above).

High exit barriers

Exit barriers can be measured by the costs organisations incur when they leave an industry. Exit barriers are said to be high if the cost of leaving an industry is high. These costs can include redundancy payments and low scrap value of plant. Exit barriers in the form of emotional barriers and government policy may also be in place. The fact that more football clubs have not been closed down owes much to the emotional as well as financial support that they receive from their often long-suffering supporters. That more car manufacturers did not close down in the early 1990s may reflect the high cost of leaving the industry. A short period of losses may have been easier to sustain than complete closure. In the case of Renault, financial support was forthcoming from the French government.

Threat of entry

New organisations enter a market, attracted by the high level of returns that incumbents receive. New entrants bring new capacity, new resources and a desire for market share. The result will be more competition and so a fall in profit for all organisations.

Threat of entry depends on the potency of barriers to entry. The higher the barriers, the lower the threat of entry. BT's repeated price reductions on some of its UK telephone calls is not only to satisfy its regulator, or to pressurise its main terrestrial competitor, Mercury, and various mobile phone companies, but also represents a higher barrier to others with ideas of entering the market. The main sources of barriers to entry are:

- product differentiation;
- economies of scale and absolute cost advantages;
- legal barriers;
- capital requirements;
- access to distribution channels;
- threat of retaliation.

Many of these have been discussed above. We will briefly explore those hitherto unmentioned.

Economies of scale and absolute cost advantages

Economies of scale were discussed in detail above. No matter what economies of scale exist, other cost advantages may also exist, so-called first-mover advantages, which cannot be replicated by potential entrants. These could include:

- access to raw materials – it is extremely difficult to establish a nuclear industry without access to raw material, as many countries have discovered (for example Iran and Iraq);
- favourable locations – it would be an almost impossible challenge for an overseas bank to set up a wide branch network to compete with the established networks of the home-based organisations, unless, like HSBC, it takes over a UK bank;
- product know-how and experience curve advantages (see above).

Government subsidies can be used to reduce absolute cost advantages. The launch aid received by Airbus Industrie helped it to compete effectively against America's Boeing. The support for sunrise industries, those emerging new industries of the future, may also be a legitimate use of subsidies.

Legal barriers

Legal barriers, such as government licence, charter or a patent, may also be used. A licence is required in many fields of business including the taxicab, banking and broadcasting sectors. The 1986 Financial Services Act requires that all sellers of investment products are authorised by the Securities and Investment Board, now the Financial Services Authority. Glaxo and other drug companies are able to protect their new products from competition by use of patents. Environmental and safety standards also place barriers in the way of new organisations entering some industries.

Inefficient public monopolies have in the past been accused of being protected from competition by government funding, especially the power, transport and telecommunications sectors in the UK and telecommunications and postal services in France and Germany respectively. The Japanese government has long been criticised in Europe and North America for imposing barriers that protect Japanese manufacturers and farmers and drastically limit the import of a wide range of goods, such as rice, cars and Scotch whisky, into the Japanese market. Action was taken in mid 1995 by the US government in response to Japan's conduct, and the increasing trade deficit between the United States and Japan, to limit the number of Japanese exports to the United States. Measures proposed included 100 per cent tariffs on Japanese cars entering the US market.

Capital requirements

The need for capital is linked closely to our earlier discussion of sunk costs. It may be too expensive for an organisation to enter a market. The London evening newspaper market has not had a successful new entrant for many years. One attempt at entry ended with the incumbent starting a price war and forcing its new rival out. The newcomer could not sustain its position.

Access to distribution channels

A barrier can be created by the inability of an entrant to gain access to a distribution channel. Mercury was given the right to rent access to BT's phone lines, otherwise it would have been impossible for them to enter the market. Manufacturers of designer/branded goods can prevent supermarkets from obtaining goods at a cheaper price on the 'grey market' outside Europe and selling them a lower prices to customers. This follows a decision on 16 July 1998 of the European Court of Justice. It is a blow for retailers like Tesco, who have successfully sold products like Levi jeans at substantially lower prices than regular Levi outlets, and their customers.

Threat of retaliation

The effectiveness of barriers may be in part reliant on the expectations that entrants have of the possible retaliation of incumbent organisations. Porter (1980) suggests that entrants into an industry can be deterred if

- there is a history of retaliation against entrants; e.g. it has recently proved difficult to establish new newspaper titles because of the aggressive nature of price cutting used by incumbents;
- established organisations with substantial resources fight back; e.g. the cross-channel ferry operators are very aware of the threat posed by the Channel Tunnel and are marshalling their resources in a bid to keep their market share;
- established organisations are heavily committed to the industry and have assets which cannot be employed in other sectors; e.g. British Steel have become one of the most profitable steelmakers in the world and it is in their interests to maintain barriers to ensure a continued growth in profits;
- the industry is undergoing slow or zero growth as new organisations cannot be absorbed so easily.

Threat of substitution

Substitutes are those goods or services, offered by another organisation, that can be used in place of the good or service that an organisation supplies. The American Express charge card, for example, faces competition from cash, traveller's cheques, chequebooks and credit cards. The threat of substitutes imposes a price ceiling as high profits will attract substitutes. The extent of the threat will depend on the propensity of the buyer to substitute, switching costs, and the relative price and performance of substitutes.

The propensity of the buyer to substitute

A critical factor is the propensity, inclination or tendency of a buyer to substitute. If the propensity of a buyer to substitute is high then substitutes will present a great threat. Some products have a low propensity of substitution because of the nature of the product. New car registrations in the United Kingdom are forecast to rise to over 2.2 million by 2000 (Howitt, 1997). It has proved and will continue to prove difficult to encourage people to switch from cars to other forms of transport.

The wider economic environment is also an issue in this case. Recession can bring job losses and lower real income which must have an impact on the buying patterns of individuals.

The situation is further complicated because substitutes may be difficult to identify and hence keep out. What is the substitute for a newly released CD? Is it not another CD from a different artist released by another label? That is an example of rivalry among competitors, Porter's central force. Substitutes come from outside the industry. Organisations compete for discretionary expenditure, the spare cash that people have. For example, the market for sports shoes is in turmoil in the USA. Consumers are not buying trainers at the same rate. There is a glut of products and consumers seem unwilling to spend. Major companies such as Nike, Adidas, Reebok and Fila are desperately trying to re-engineer their brands. LA Gear filed for chapter 11 bankruptcy protection and laid off 60 per cent of employees. Companies have also suffered from bad publicity over accusations of abuse of foreign workers (Cruickshank, 1998). The UK jeans market has suffered also, with 4 million fewer pairs sold in 1997. In 1999, Levi Strauss in the United States announced factory closures and the loss of over 6000 jobs. Clearly, consumer spending is being directed elsewhere. The problem for the manufacturers is to identify exactly where!

Switching costs

The one-off cost that faces a buyer when switching from one supplier to another is important. Where the switching cost is high then transfer of allegiances is less likely and vice versa. A consumer can quite easily switch to buying a health food product rather than potato crisps, thus reducing the sales of the snack manufacturer. However, the cost of switching from using a car to another form of transport may involve substantial cost and inconvenience to the driver and so discourage change.

The relative price and performance of substitutes

The ability of some of the Japanese high-volume car manufacturers to gain market share in the sports car segment of the car market, for example Mazda with the MX5, largely reflects the relatively lower price of the Japanese vehicles in comparison to their performance and the value that they offer in comparison with competitors.

Bargaining power of buyers and suppliers

Suppliers are those individuals or organisations from whom an organisation purchases items that are needed to carry out business activities. These are the inputs to the organisation and include raw materials and components. Supplier power can reduce prices, increase quality and increase service level demands, all of which will reduce margins.

Buyers are those individuals or organisations who purchase an organisation's outputs. Bargaining power of buyers can reduce prices, increase quality and increase service level demands. It could be argued that the fall in price and higher level of service offered by some of the recently privatised utilities, for example the regional electricity companies, is a direct result of buyers gaining more power from increased choice.

The examination of supplier power is analogous to that of buyer power (the factors that contribute to greater buyer power will decrease supplier power) and so we will concentrate on buyer power in this section.

Buyers depend a great deal on the quality and timeliness of information they receive. Full information means that a buyer is in a better position to negotiate a price. Buyers are powerful and more sensitive to price if:

- their switching costs are low – it is easy to go for a drink to the pub next door, no costs are involved;
- the product is important to the buyer. This could be the case if:
  - the product represents a high proportion of total costs – buyers of major pieces of capital equipment are likely to have a strong hand when it comes to contract negotiations;
  - the product is purchased in high volume (see below);
  - the profitability of the buyer industry is low which may mean that the buyer will want to reduce the price of goods that are bought in to protect its own margins.

Products are undifferentiated and substitutes are available

We have already outlined the problems that firms face if products are homogeneous and easily substituted. Buyers can simply play one company off against the other. Competition between suppliers of office stationery is intense. The homogeneous nature of the product means that buyers can shop around for the best prices and, consequently, reduce the sales and profit of their suppliers.

Buyer concentration is high

If your product is bought by only one buyer then concentration is at 100 per cent. In this case buyers have total power, not only over price but all other aspects of the relationship, including quality and delivery time. Toyota in Japan are able to gain almost 100 per cent reliability on the light bulbs for their cars because many are provided by a network of small family companies who rely on Toyota for all of their sales. Marks & Spencer have many exclusive agreements to buy the whole of the output of an organisation. If they withdraw their order then plant closure may be the result.

Threat of backward integration

In some cases a buyer has the ability to move into that particular business themselves. Typically, car manufacturers in the past reduced their dependence on their suppliers by taking them over. In 1995 Rover, the UK car manufacturer, was involved in a bid to regain control of Unipart, its former parts subsidiary. The big food processors have recently seen their sales hit because of moves by their buyers, the big grocery chains – for example, Tesco and Sainsbury – into cheaper own-brand labels which have displaced some of the better known branded products.

Porter's five forces model provides organisations with a model for analysing their competitive environment. Unless a company can analyse its competitors it will never be in a position to compete effectively. The benefits to be gained from having an intelligence-gathering system are immeasurable. A capable system may ultimately ensure survival. Exhibit 2.8 illustrates the use of the model.

EXHIBIT 2.8

A brief structural analysis of UK pharmaceutical retailers

Background

In 1996 the total sales of UK pharmaceuticals were £6.8 billion. This was split between ethical medicines (branded or generics), which are those drugs that are prescription-only medicines (POMs), and over-the-counter (OTC) medicines, which include those from a pharmacy only (e.g. Benilyn) and those on the general sales list (GSL) (e.g. paracetomol). Any analysis must take into account these product categories.

Products	Million	%
Ethical branded	4705	68.4
Ethical generic	830	12.1
OTC medicines	1341	19.5
Total	6876	100

The retailing of medicines is controlled by the Royal Pharmaceutical Society of Great Britain (RPSGB), whose members work in a variety of places including hospitals; industry; independent community pharmacies (6000 outlets); pharmacy multiples, such as Boots (1300), Lloyds (1400), Moss (900) and Superdrug; and grocery multiples, such as Tesco (400), Safeway, Sainsbury and Asda. The sale of drugs is governed by Retail Price Maintenance (RPM), whereby manufacturers set a minimum retail price for each drug. This practice is under review, as it is viewed by some as anti-competitive.

▶

Exhibit 2.8 continued

Competitive rivalry

The three large pharmacy multiples have 25 per cent of the market for ethicals and 39 per cent of OTCs. The major recent growth in the market has been by the grocery retailers, many of whom are currently redesigning stores to incorporate a pharmacy. The long opening hours of supermarkets, their loyalty cards, and specific clubs such as Tesco's baby club with special offers for members and Safeway's baby club that entitles the consumer to 10 per cent discount on the shopping bill until the baby is 6 months old mean, that smaller pharmacies are finding it harder to compete.

Supermarkets have also used a number of tactics to win permission for new or relocated NHS contracts. At present there is no price competition because of RPM and little product differentiation for generic drugs. Should RPM be abolished, competition is likely to intensify and a large number of independent pharmacies may face closure. Exit barriers are relatively low. They may find it difficult to compete given the economies of scale, advertising power (£198.3 million spent in 1996) and perhaps the use of predatory pricing that the large grocery multiples can bring to bear. On 10 February 1999 the Office of Fair Trading, backed by the supermarkets, brought the RPM case to court.

Power of suppliers

Ethicals are supplied direct from the manufacturer (25 per cent) or via wholesalers (75 per cent). The wholesale market is dominated by Unichem and AAH who control 81 per cent of the market. Numark and Nucare are owned and run by independent pharmacies. They were established to help regional wholesalers compete and support the independent pharmacist. Boots has its own distribution system.

There is evidence of forward integration. AAH and Unichem have acquired Lloyds and Moss chemists respectively. Suppliers are likely to have no power over grocery multiples.

Power of buyers

Power of buyers is generally low due to a lack of substitutes and RPM. Switching costs are low so if RPM is abolished consumers may be inclined to buy from the large multiples because of lower prices, especially for GSLs.

Threat of substitutes

Alternatives may include surgical intervention, and the use of alternative medicines. This may be particularly evident when switching costs are low and, for example, new homeopathic medicines perform well.

Threat of entry

Legal barriers are in place that require each pharmacy to register with the RPSGB in order to dispense an NHS prescription or hold an NHS contract. To obtain an NHS contract the premises must be in a neighbourhood and be both desirable and necessary. Many existing pharmacies have relocated to new health complexes, limiting the opportunity for new entrants. New housing estates or towns offer some scope for future development. However, the capital cost of entry is high. Main requirements are buildings, stock and labour. Returns are also limited by RPM.

Thanks to Jonathan Harte at UCN for his help.

QUESTIONS

1. Identify and comment on the costs that are likely to by faced by a car driver when switching to a motorcycle.
2. Use Porter's five forces model, along with the other key concepts raised in the chapter, to analyse the competitive environment of a particular industry.
3. What was the outcome of the court case brought by the OFT referred to in Exhibit 2.8? What impact has the decision had on retail pharmacists?

COMPETITOR ANALYSIS

The proliferation of different types of washing detergents, such as, enzyme-rich, enzyme-free, liquid, automatic, biological and non-biological powders, is not simply a tactic used by the two major manufacturers to put in place a barrier to entry, as described earlier. The multiplicity of types arises from the need of one company to match the innovation of the other. If the companies in the market are unaware of their competitors' direction then a rival may be able to increase its market share.

Competitor analysis is another way of achieving an insight into the activity of competitors. This type of behaviour exists in industries as diverse as the car industry and software design.

Competitor analysis involves an investigation of competitors' goals, assumptions, strategy, and capabilities (Porter, 1980). Not only do existing competitors need to be examined but there is also a need to put potential competitors under the microscope. Add to this a dose of self-analysis and a picture of the behaviour of the market comes into focus. Figure 2.7 shows the competitor analysis model.

Porter (1980) proposes that competitor analysis can answer questions such as the following:

- What are the implications of the interaction of the probable competitors' moves?
- Are organisations' strategies converging and likely to clash?
- Do organisations have sustainable growth rates that match the industry's forecast growth rate, or will a gap be created that will invite entry?
- Will probable moves combine to hold implications for industry structure?

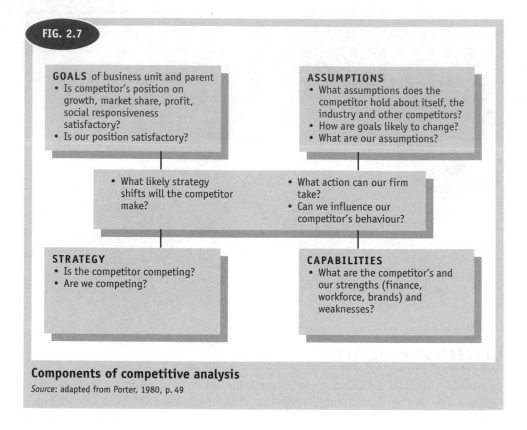

FIG. 2.7

GOALS of business unit and parent
- Is competitor's position on growth, market share, profit, social responsiveness satisfactory?
- Is our position satisfactory?

ASSUMPTIONS
- What assumptions does the competitor hold about itself, the industry and other competitors?
- How are goals likely to change?
- What are our assumptions?

- What likely strategy shifts will the competitor make?

- What action can our firm take?
- Can we influence our competitor's behaviour?

STRATEGY
- Is the competitor competing?
- Are we competing?

CAPABILITIES
- What are the competitor's and our strengths (finance, workforce, brands) and weaknesses?

Components of competitive analysis
Source: adapted from Porter, 1980, p. 49

Exhibit 2.9 provides an illustration of how competitor analysis can help the market entry strategy of an organisation.

EXHIBIT 2.9

Honda's penetration of the UK and US motorcycle markets

In 1959 Honda made its first moves into the US motorcycle market. Initially they targeted large cubic capacity (cc) machines. Honda failed to gain a foothold in this market segment as there were no customers for these machines. According to Pascale (1984) Honda had not carried out any market research prior to this move. Expansion into the United States was not even part of Honda's long-term plan. Honda were keen to assess why their attempt to sell in the US had failed and sent a team to evaluate the lack of market success. The team noticed that people were interested in the small machines that they were using for their own transport. One particularly important person was a buyer for Sears, a large US retailer. In response Honda decided to focus on selling at the smaller end of the market, and entered that segment with their 50 cc Super Cub range. This range found buyers immediately.

Honda's success went a long way in redefining the image of the motorcycle in the US to a practical, inexpensive mode of transportation for the urban commuter. With new US volume Honda was able to reap substantial global economies of scale in motorcycle production (Porter 1980, p. 289). By 1964 Honda was making inroads into the small machine market in both the United Kingdom and the United States.

Honda used its established position in one segment of the market to establish a dominance in the large-capacity segment and also used competitor analysis to investigate the competition and concluded that

- both BSA in the United Kingdom and Harley-Davidson in the United States pursued medium-term financial goals rather than market share goals;
- both organisations were benefiting from an upsurge in motorcycle demand (Grant, 1995).

Therefore the companies would not be unduly alarmed at forfeiting market share as

- both organisations believed that due to their own customer loyalty and brand image, the Japanese producers were not a serious threat in the big bike market;
- even if their rivals did act aggressively, the effectiveness of their response would be limited by their weak financial positions and by their lack of innovation and effective manufacturing capabilities.

The result, as we know, was the domination of the world motorcycle market by Honda and the other Japanese manufacturers.

QUESTION

Using the models that have been developed in the chapter examine how Honda were able to successfully enter the motorcycle market in the late 1950s and early 1960s.

CONCLUSION

We have seen, in this chapter, that the structure of the market has a direct impact on the competition that an organisation faces. It is, however, evident that market structure does not remain static. Today's monopoly could be tomorrow's competitive cockpit. Organisations face a dynamic and changing competitive environment. International competitors are becoming the barometer by which we measure the success of all organisations.

Organisations cannot rest and remain satisfied with their past achievements. It is important to develop and maintain mechanisms with which to sense environmental change. In this chapter we have introduced you to some of the tools and models that can assist organisations in understanding their own position and that of their competitors. We have also shown that there is a role for government at all scales.

Markets left to their own devices may become anti-competitive, so intervention may be needed. Governments can also provide support for new, fledgling industry to allow them to grow and become competitive in the international arena.

The next chapter explores the macroeconomic environment.

SUMMARY OF MAIN POINTS

Competition is influenced by a wide range of factors. In this chapter we have investigated a range of these factors and introduced you to models to aid your analysis of the competitive environment. The chapter has shown that:

- The basic economic problem, of allocation of resources, is resolved in quite different ways within the command and market economies.

- Competition is influenced largely by the nature of the product, the number of firms and their concentration, and the market entry conditions.

- Some organisations are protected from competition by barriers to entry and may be capable of making above-normal profits in the long run.

- A strong competitive position is likely to be eroded by, for example, the use of technology and innovation.

- Oligopolists are interdependent and must consider the actions of rivals when making business decisions; because of the lack of freedom of manoeuvre, competition is based largely on quality, branding, advertising and service.

- Some organisations act to reduce uncertainty by entering into agreements which may be anti-competitive. Regulations need to be in place to monitor such agreements and to protect the public interest.

- Contestable markets exist where there are no sunk costs of entry. In such markets competition will be intense.

- Porter's five forces are
  - rivalry among competitors
  - threat of entry
  - threat of substitution
  - bargaining power of buyers
  - bargaining power of suppliers.

- The collective strengths of the five forces determine the state of competition and therefore the ultimate profit potential within an industry.

- Competitor analysis involves the investigation of organisations' goals, assumptions, strategies and capabilities.

NET SEARCH

http://www.open.gov.uk
The Treasury site here is worth a look.

http://www.bubl.ac.uk/
BUBL provides a subject-based service. Subjects can be chosen from a subject tree. Includes discussion lists, news pages and access to other sources. It is designed for use by the higher education community.

http://www.dis.strath.ac.uk/business/index.html
A list of business information sources from Strathclyde University. Includes access to company directories, and profiles, news and economic data. Access through this site to many other sites.

http://www1.ifs.org.uk/
Site of the Institute of Fiscal Studies. Includes:

- what's new;
- the Budget;
- surveys;
- publications;
- links to web servers on economics and social sciences.

http://biznet.bris.ac.uk:8080/
Business education on the Internet, access to economics and business resources including:

- company reports;
- data sites, e.g. Central Statistical Office for UK economic data;
- media sites, e.g. *The Economist*;
- government, political and special interest groups, including political parties and Greenpeace;
- key word search facility.

http://netec.mcc.ac.uk/WebEc.html
WebEc is the virtual economics library. The site gives access to a huge number of areas of economics.

http://www.finweb.com/finweb.html
The financial economics web site. It provides access to many journals and data sources.

Newspapers

Newspapers are a good source of information on many topics. They can be found on the following sites:

Financial Times	**http://www.ft.com.**
Telegraph	**http://www.telegraph.co.uk.**
Times Higher	**http://thesis.news.co.uk.**
Guardian/Observer	**http://www.guardian.co.uk.**
The Times	**http://www.the-times.co.uk.**
Sunday Times	**http://www.sunday-times.co.uk.**

REFERENCES

Alexander, G. (1997) 'BT blown out', *Sunday Times*, 5 October.

Barfe, L. (ed.) (1998) *Supermarket and Superstores Market Report 1998*, 15th edn, Hampton: Keynote Ltd.

Baumol, W. (1982) 'Contestable markets: an uprising in the theory of industry structure', *American Economic Review*, March.

Beardshaw, J. (1992) *Economics: A Student's Guide*, 3rd edn, London: Pitman.

Begg, D., Fischer, S. and Dornbusch, R. (1994) *Economics*, 4th edn, London: McGraw-Hill.

Bokhari, F. (1998) 'Cracks emerging in Pakistan's cement industry', *Financial Times*, 17 March.

Bromley, R. and Thomas, C. (1993) *Retail Change*, London: UCL Press.

Butler, K. (1998) 'British cars are dearest in Europe', *Independent*, 14 February.

Caves, R. and Porter, M.E. (1980) 'The dynamics of changing seller concentration', *Journal of Industrial Economics*, 19, 1–15.

Cruickshank, J. (1998) 'Trainer firms get a kicking on Wall Street', *Sunday Times*, 8 March.

Fishwick, F. (1993) *Making Sense of Competition Policy*, London: Kogan Page.

Grant, R.M. (1995) *Contemporary Strategy Analysis: Concepts, Techniques, Applications*, Oxford: Blackwell.

Griffiths, A. and Wall, S. (1997) *Applied Economics*, 7th edn, London: Longman.

Guardian (1997) 'Court to examine TV cartel', *Guardian*, 13 November.

Hamilton, K. (1998) 'Store wars', *Sunday Times*, 22 February.

Howitt, S. (ed.) (1997) *Motor Industry Market Review*, 5th edn, Hampton: Keynote.

Langton, J. (1998) 'Lifestyle police sink teeth into burgers', *Sunday Telegraph*, 24 May.

Mansfield, E. (1994) *Applied Microeconomics*, New York: Norton.

Marshall, S. (1997) 'Virgin goes for bust', *Marketing*, 20 February.

Mintel (1997) *Cigarettes: The Supply Structure*, January.

Pascale, R.T. (1984) 'Perspectives on strategy: the real story behind Honda's success', *California Management Review*, 14 (3), 23–31.

Porter, M.E. (1980) *Competitive Strategy: Techniques for Analyzing Industries and Competitors*, New York: Free Press.

Suzman, M. (1998) '$29m anti-trust fine levied', *Financial Times*, 24 February.

Thompson, A.A. and Strickland, A.J. (1995) *Strategic Management: Concepts and Cases*, 8th edn, Chicago: Irwin.

Wrigley, N. and Lowe, M. (1996) *Retailing, Consumption and Capital*, London: Longman.

3

THE INTERNATIONAL ECONOMIC ENVIRONMENT

Mark Cook

LEARNING OBJECTIVES

On completion of this chapter you should be able to:

- appreciate the changing nature of production in the major international economies;
- appreciate the role of government in influencing macroeconomic activity;
- recognise the changing nature of growth in the major international economies and the implications that flow from this;
- consider the methods of control and impact of inflation;
- understand the reasons for the changes in unemployment within Europe;
- understand the development of trading blocs;
- recognise the importance of international trade between countries and trading blocs;
- understand the interrelatedness of the major European economies;
- appreciate how exchange rate regimes have developed and their possible implications;
- consider the impact of the Single European Market on countries inside and outside of the European Union;
- consider the implications for the European economies of the development of a single currency;
- consider the development of EU enlargement and its impact on the European Union.

KEY CONCEPTS

- macroeconomic goals
- the circular flow of income
- growth and structural change
- economic growth
- the costs of growth
- inflation and deflation
- the role of the state

- economic cycles
- unemployment
- international trade
- the Single European Market
- the single currency
- enlargement of Europe

INTRODUCTION

On one level it is possible to consider organisations as having control over their own actions. They can decide upon the kinds of resources they require, relate these to forecasts of demand, the current goals of the organisation and the organisation's long-term strategy. However, organisations do not exist in a vacuum. They are affected by and respond to changes in both short-term and long-term economic and business conditions. This chapter concentrates on the economic factors which impinge upon business behaviour. This not only includes changes in the domestic economic environment, but more importantly changes that have taken place in the international economic environment. These changes, such as those in trading relations, international competitiveness, the growing impact of the European Union, and the globalisation of markets affect organisations whether they are involved in international markets or not.

What are the international forces at play and what is their impact on organisations? It is fairly easy to see how interest rates, the level of inflation and competition policy have an effect on organisations, but there are other economic forces at play. For example, changes in government policy towards training will have a direct impact on organisations both in the short term and the long term and could lead to a shortage of skilled workers, reducing the organisation's productivity and allowing competitors to gain an increasing share of a previously safe market.

Changes in the external environment with regard to the development of trading blocs can affect the ability and desire of organisations to be involved in export markets. Economic problems in the home economy can result in government policies to alter its expenditure leading to a downturn in general economic activity. Poor underlying strength in an economy can lead to changes in interest rates and exchange rates, both of which may inhibit the performance of the organisations in an economy. This chapter therefore considers the changes that have occurred in both the domestic and international macroeconomic environment. It will consider the structural changes that have taken place in the major economies of the world, the move towards growing international integration, the development of trading blocs, and the role and evolution of international capital flows. In addition, the chapter will address issues such as growth, the co-ordination of macroeconomic policy and the changing power structures of the major macroeconomic economies. Throughout the chapter it is important to bear in mind the impact such macroeconomic environmental changes have upon the organisations that lie therein.

Any account of the macroeconomic environment needs to be selective. We have included those features which are believed to be most relevant. It should also be borne in mind that although the macroeconomic environment can be viewed from a number of perspectives the emphasis taken here is on a two-tiered approach, concentrating on Europe and then on the international economy.

MACROECONOMIC ACCOUNTS

Governments and organisations are often concerned with the performance of international economies both in absolute and relative terms. But can the level of economic activity in the major economies of the world be compared? A standard approach is to consider Gross Domestic Product (GDP) or Gross National Product (GNP) figures of the different countries. GNP – a measure of the level of economic activity produced in a country in any one year – is a record of the income accruing to a country, some of which may have been produced in the domestic economy (GDP) and some of which may have been produced abroad (net property income from abroad). This net property income from abroad is made up from previous investments abroad and is income earned by citizens or commercial organisations. GDP can be measured in a number of ways, but the following have come to be accepted as the traditional approaches:

- all the expenditures that are made on final products during the year – National Expenditure;
- all the output of final products/services produced in that country during the year – National Output;
- all the incomes received by the factors of production in the making of the final products during the year – National Income.

Tables 3.1, 3.2 and 3.3 show the GDP figures for the United Kingdom measured by the three approaches in 1997, each gives approximately the same result.

Larger countries tend to have higher total GDPs, therefore GDP per head or GDP per capita is a better inter-country comparison of performance. As Table 3.4 indicates, some of the smaller countries, such as Switzerland, have the highest GDP per head.

TABLE 3.1   UK Gross Domestic Product (1997) measured at market prices: expenditure approach

	£ million
(a) consumers' expenditure	500 616
(b) central government final consumption (G)	165 890
(c) gross domestic capital formation (I)	136 592
(a + b + c) give total domestic expenditure	803 098
(d) exports of goods and services (X)	228 708
d + total domestic expenditure equals total final expenditure	1 031 806
less imports of goods and services	−229 334
statistical discrepancy	−494
Gross Domestic Product at market prices	801 978

Source: National Income and Expenditure Blue Book, 1998

TABLE 3.2   UK Gross Domestic Product (1997) measured at market prices: income approach

	£ million
gross operating surplus, non-financial corporations – public	4 070
gross operating surplus, non-financial corporations – private	165 500
gross operating surplus, financial corporations	17 661
gross operating surplus – adjustment for financial services	−26 564
gross operating surplus – general government	12 434
gross operating surplus – households and non-profit institutions serving households	44 438
gross total operating surplus	217 539
mixed income	42 623
compensation of employees	432 280
taxes on production and imports	115 572
less subsidies	−8 035
statistical discrepancy	993
Gross Domestic Product at market prices	800 972

Source: National Income and Expenditure Blue Book, 1998

TABLE 3.3   UK Gross Domestic Product (1997) measured at market prices: output approach

	£ million
agriculture, hunting, forestry and fishing	10 820
mining and quarrying	18 137
manufacturing	146 522
electricity, gas and water supply	16 227
construction	36 491
wholesale and retail trade; repairs; hotels and restaurants	106 068
transport, storage and communication	59 694
adjustments for financial services	−26 564
financial and business activities	185 851
public administration, national defence and social security	38 940
education, health and social work	85 129
other services	33 955
value added taxes on products	55 686
other taxes on products	43 051
less subsidies on products	−8 035
Gross Domestic Product at market prices	801 972

Source: *National Income and Expenditure Blue Book, 1998*

TABLE 3.4   GNP and GNP per capita, various countries

Country	GNP 1997 (billions US$)[1]	GNP per capita 1997 (US$)
Austria	225.9	27 980
France	1526.0	26 050
Germany	2319.5	28 260
Italy	1155.4	20 120
Japan	4772.3	37 850
Spain	570.1	14 510
Sweden	232.0	26 220
Switzerland	313.5	44 320
United Kingdom	1220.2	20 710
United States	7690.1	28 740

[1] Current prices and exchange rates

Source: adapted from *World Development Report, 1998/9*, Table 1

There are a number of factors to consider when a comparison is made of different countries' GDP figures:

1. GDP needs to be considered in real terms – that is, taking account of inflation – rather than nominal or money terms. Account should be taken of the varying rates of inflation between countries.

2. GDP figures need to be converted into a common currency, for example American dollars, to facilitate comparison. There may be times when one currency is weak against the American dollar, whilst others are strong. This will lead to overvaluing or undervaluing some countries' GDP figures. For example, the exchange rate between Japanese yen and US dollars has varied between 139 and 110 yen to the dollar during 1998.

3. GDP figures can only include factors on which there is information. For some activities in the economy, data is not collected, since these are not measured in monetary terms. Housework is an example. Many products in less developed countries may not actually be exchanged for money but rather be bartered, and these transactions will not be included in any figures on expenditure.

4. Quality of information poses a problem; a country's GDPs may be understated. For the developed countries one major source of information is the tax authorities. Data is collected from companies and individuals report incomes. How certain can we be of the accuracy of these figures? Often income is not reported, being part of what has become known as the hidden or underground economy – activity which does not come to the market for tax purposes (see Table 3.5). In addition, we need to consider the time factor. Data from the tax authorities is subject to a level of time delay and estimates need continual revisions as more accurate information comes to hand. The inaccuracy of data can pose significant problems for policy makers.

5. GDP figures do not make reference to the distribution of income. The unequal distribution of income and wealth can lead to changes in the overall expenditure patterns of a country's citizens and this has implications for the business communities both within and outside of that country.

6. Finally, GDP figures make no reference to the social costs of production. Thus changes in perceptions about environmental damage and the resulting policies that may follow can have important implications for organisations.

In some countries, GDP has grown at a faster rate than others. This tendency for unequal growth between countries and within trading blocs has implications for

TABLE 3.5 Estimates of the underground economy (as percentage of the economy)

Canada	France	Germany	Italy	Netherlands	Norway	UK	USA
3–8	4	4–24	5–52	6–16	4–17	2–15	2–26

Source: Economie et Statistiques. Nov. 1989

government policy, interest rates, exchange rates and the optimal conditions for the growth of businesses within those countries.

QUESTIONS

1. GDP is often criticised as a measure of well-being since some public goods are inherently difficult to price. Which goods fit into this category and how can the GDP data be improved or adjusted to account for this problem?

2. How do changes in the level of GDP affect the performance of domestic organisations?

MACROECONOMIC GOALS

In general, most countries have a range of economic goals, not all of which are mutually compatible. These include:

- a high level of economic growth;
- a strong balance of payments;
- a low level of inflation;
- a low level of unemployment.

Some of the goals may be conflicting. For example, it may not be possible to have a low level of inflation together with a low level of unemployment. Higher levels of economic growth can lead to increases in the rate of inflation. Thus in achieving one goal, governments may have to forego others.

Governments have a raft of economic policies which they can use to achieve their targets. For example, a government which wishes to improve the sales of its domestic industries could try and stimulate its domestic economy by:

- reducing taxes (fiscal policy);
- increasing the amount of money available or lowering interest in the economy (monetary policy);
- erecting trade barriers to encourage domestic consumers to buy more home-produced goods.

These policies may result in a short-term increase in business activity in the domestic economy, but the long-term impact may be different. Reducing interest rates may lead to higher levels of inflation in the domestic economy, which then encourages domestic consumers to purchase substitute foreign goods since these products appear to be relatively cheaper. The introduction of trade barriers may lead to other countries imposing retaliatory trade barriers on the country's exports and so damage business sales abroad. What the above indicates is that policies can be implemented to achieve a particular short-term goal, but the long-term side-effects may well be different.

> **QUESTION**
>
> What do you consider to have been the main economic goals of the economy over the last
> (a) five years, and
> (b) twenty years?

THE CIRCULAR FLOW

The circular flow of income is a useful model to use to appreciate the impact of changes in economic activity. It is illustrated in Figure 3.1.

At the centre of Figure 3.1 are two groups, households and firms. Households provide services to firms in exchange for wages, and firms sell products to households in exchange for income. Figure 3.1 also indicates that there are some leakages from and injections into the circular flow. Both firms and individuals are subject to taxes, and this money is withdrawn from the circular flow. Much, if not all, of this will be put back into the circular flow through general government expenditure on, for example, road building and social security payments. Savings undertaken by firms, individuals and governments also represent leakages from the model, and corresponding to this are inflows into the circular flow from investment. Finally, very few economies are 'closed', that is, not involved with

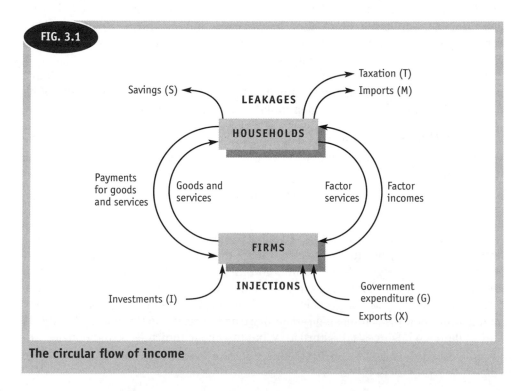

FIG. 3.1

The circular flow of income

international trade and capital flows, thus exports are seen as foreign money entering the domestic economy and are a further injection into the circular flow, whilst imports can be viewed as money leaving the national economy and thus a further leakage.

The circular flow model indicates, amongst other things, the role of the government in the economy. The government steers the economy through the Budget, delivered, in the United Kingdom, annually in March. It is a reflection of the government's income and expenditure. If the government has expenditure which exceeds income then it needs to borrow money from external sources such as the International Monetary Fund (IMF). Money can also be raised from the sale of government securities (gilts). In the United Kingdom the amount that the government borrows is called the Public Sector Borrowing Requirement (PSBR).

Alternatively it is quite possible that government revenue exceeds the level of expenditure. This surplus on the government account is called a Public Sector Debt Repayment (PSDR). Such a situation occurred in the United Kingdom during the 1980s. Revenue rose from the increased tax paid by more individuals in work and from receipts from the sale of privatised industries. The move away from a PSBR and to a PSDR is expected once again in the UK economy during the early part of the next millennium. Some European countries, such as Luxembourg, have consistently run surpluses on their government account whilst others such as Italy and Belgium usually have very high levels of government debt and borrowing.

QUESTIONS

1. Why do some countries appear to run surpluses on their government account whilst others appear to run consistent deficits?
2. If there is an increase in the amount of injections entering an economy what effect may this have on the organisations?

STRUCTURAL CHANGES IN THE MAJOR ECONOMIES

The circular flow depicts, in a clear way, the flows between two groups in the domestic economy – households and firms – and the external forces that impinge upon them. In macroeconomics there is a tendency to treat all firms as one and the same yet, over time, there have been important changes in the structure of industry. By structural change we mean how the sectors in an economy have changed. It useful to give some broad definitions of these sectors.

- The primary sector includes activities directly related to natural resources, for example, farming, mining and oil extraction.
- The secondary sector covers production industries in the economy such as manufacturing, the processing of materials produced in the primary sector and construction.

- The tertiary sector includes all private sector services, for example, banking, finance, computing services and tourism as well as public sector services such as health and defence.

Generally there has been a convergence of economic activity in structural terms. That is, the developed economies have become more orientated towards the service sector. As Table 3.6 indicates, in many countries, 60 per cent or more of economic activity is in the service sector. In Belgium, Denmark, the United Kingdom, France, Norway, Sweden and the United States it accounts for around 70 per cent of economic activity. In other European countries, such as Ireland, Spain, Portugal and Greece, agriculture plays a bigger part in the economy.

Consideration of the sectors overall may hide important changes within sectors. For example, the decline in the primary sector in the United Kingdom is almost entirely attributed to changes in mining during the 1960s and 1970s and to the subsequent rise and fall in activity in oil and gas production (see Cook and Healey, 1995). Within the secondary sector it is manufacturing which has felt the full force

TABLE 3.6 Sectoral contribution to GDP and employment, 1996, percentages

	Agriculture		Industry		Services	
	GDP	Employment	GDP	Employment	GDP	Employment
Belgium**	1.4	2.5	27.3	26.7	71.4	71.4
Denmark	3.0	4.0	24.0	27.0	73.0	69.0
Germany***	1.1	3.3	31.9	37.5	67.0	59.1
Greece	12.0	20.4	23.8	23.2	64.2	56.4
Spain	3.7	8.7	33.2	29.7	63.1	51.6
France**	2.6	4.6	27.6	25.9	68.8	69.5
Ireland	–	10.7	–	27.2	–	62.3
Italy**	3.4	7.0	33.0	32.1	63.6	60.9
Luxembourg	1.0	2.8	25.0	30.7	76.0	66.1
Netherlands	2.8	3.9	27.6	22.4	69.6	73.8
Portugal	5.3	12.2	37.8	31.4	56.9	56.4
United Kingdom	1.2	2.0	29.0	27.4	69.8	71.0
Austria*	1.0	7.2	30.0	33.1	68.0	59.6
Finland	2.8	7.1	24.0	27.6	73.2	65.3
Norway	2.9	5.2	35.5	23.4	61.6	71.5
Sweden	2.4	2.9	28.4	26.1	70.0	71.0
Switzerland	3.0	4.5	33.4	27.7	65.2	67.4
US**	1.6	2.8	28.4	23.8	70.0	73.8
Japan	2.1	5.5	39.8	33.3	58.1	61.2

* 1994 figures;   ** 1995 figures;   *** 1997 figures

Source: OECD economic surveys, various countries

of any structural change, though once again there are differences by country, as Table 3.6 indicates.

These changes in employment between the various sectors of the economy are, to some extent, overstating the problem faced by the manufacturing sector since many manufacturing firms undertake service sector activities themselves and when asked to provide information on employment in manufacturing would have included under the manufacturing heading some service sector jobs undertaken by the manufacturing company itself. More recently these firms have begun to contract out this type of activity (such as marketing) as they 'spin-off' part of their operations, so that these 'manufacturing jobs' now appear as service sector employment. Although the data in Table 3.6 indicates important differences between countries it also shows that a number of countries are alike in terms of their economic structure. Some countries appear to stand out from the others as having less developed service sectors, in particular Germany and Japan.

Industrial structure

The United Kingdom has seen a fall in its share of world manufacturing exports and a fall in manufacturing employment, a factor which will be considered later in this chapter. For other countries, like Japan and Germany, the picture is somewhat different. In fact, between 1964 and 1994 Japan continued to see its manufacturing employment grow, whilst at the same time Italy lost 15.2 per cent, the Netherlands 10.2 per cent and the United Kingdom over 46 per cent. Consideration of such a long time period also disguises other changes that have taken place. Since 1979 the Netherlands has actually gained in industrial employment, as have Austria, Switzerland and Japan.

Not only has the overall structure of economies changed, but within the various economic sectors, countries have tended to specialise in producing certain products. The United Kingdom is more specialised in extractive industries, chemicals and financial services, France in food products, Germany in engineering and chemicals, and Italy in clothing, textiles and footwear. Of the smaller European countries, Sweden specialises in wood products, paper and furniture, Spain in leather goods and tourism and Belgium in iron and steel. These differences may explain some of the variances in trading patterns, which will be considered later. It is useful to note that if we disaggregate the various areas of manufacturing into slow, medium and fast growth sectors, as noted by Sharp (1992), then the majority of countries in the OECD had equal proportions of these. There were exceptions, however: Germany, Japan and the United States had a higher concentration of manufacturing in the high-growth sector, particularly in capital goods. Conversely, countries such as Spain, Portugal and Greece have traditionally had a higher proportion of their manufacturing industries in slow-growth sectors of the economy, such as textiles. This suggests that when there are upturns in economic activity these countries will have improvements in growth which are less than in those countries which have sectors that exhibit high-growth performance.

QUESTIONS

1. Examine your own economy. Has there been a movement away from primary and secondary production to the tertiary sector? Provide illustrations of these changes.

2. What explanations can you give for the structural changes that have occurred in your economy?

ECONOMIC GROWTH

As we have seen already, GDP figures differ between the various nations; if these are considered not just in a particular year but over time, this provides an estimate of the long-run growth of the various economies. Growth brings improvements in real incomes and a greater variety of goods and services to all sectors of the economy. The generation of growth may follow from a highly motivated, highly skilled and highly productive workforce, coupled with innovation, quality capital investment, and a high level of skill training and education.

Table 3.7 describes growth in real output per worker, a good proxy for growth in real income per person, of five of the world's major industrial countries, and provides a comparison of the post-war years with earlier eras.

The United Kingdom has a long-standing peacetime tendency for a slower growth in labour productivity and, therefore, slower growth than its major competitors. Moreover, the table reveals that there has been a general slow-down in productivity growth since 1973 compared with the two decades after World War II. Reasons cited for slower UK growth performance are:

TABLE 3.7   Growth rate of real output per worker employed (% per annum)

	UK	USA	France	Germany	Japan
1873–1899	1.2	1.9	1.3	1.5	1.1
1899–1913	0.5	1.3	1.6	1.5	1.8
1913–1924	0.3	1.7	0.8	−0.9	3.2
1924–1937	1.0	1.4	1.4	3.0	2.7
1937–1951	1.0	2.3	1.7	1.0	−1.3
1951–1964	2.3	2.5	4.3	5.1	7.6
1964–1973	2.6	1.6	4.6	4.4	8.4
1973–1979	1.6	0.3	2.9	3.1	2.8
1979–1997	1.7	0.9	2.2	1.2	2.3

Sources: Matthews, R.C.O., Feinstein, C.H. and Odling-Smee, J. (1982), *British Economic Growth, 1865–1973*, Stanford University Press, p. 31; Organization for Economic Co-operation and Development (OECD) (1988) *Historical Statistics, 1960–1987*, OECD, Paris; *OECD Economic Outlook*, June 1998

- the short-termism of UK industry – industry favouring projects which give large short-term returns rather than investing for the long term;

- the poor labour relations between unions and management;

- its less skilled and qualified workforce;

- the role of North Sea oil, as noted by Forsyth and Kay (1980), which served to drive up the United Kingdom's exchange rate during the early 1980s making its exports less competitive and imports more attractive to purchase;

- its poor record on non-defence research and development.

Table 3.7 further indicates that after 1979 there was a relative improvement of the United Kingdom in the growth league, although in absolute terms productivity growth did not regain the level of the 1960s.

The pattern of growth has been very uneven since the second oil shock of 1980/81. If we take the early part of the 1980s through to 1985, the overall growth rate of the European Union was very slow at around 1.4 per cent per annum (economies are said to require a growth rate of at least 2 per cent per annum to keep unemployment from rising). Some countries, such as Denmark and the United Kingdom, did perform a little better, whilst in the latter part of the 1980s almost the reverse appeared to be true – that is, Germany, Spain, Ireland and Portugal had growth rates in excess of the EU average of 2.8 per cent, whilst the UK, Denmark, Sweden and Greece were the poorer performers. During the 1990s the growth performances of most Western economies have come more into line, though there were still indications of countries in the EU whose level of economic growth was out of phase with others. For example, in both 1993 and 1994 the UK registered significant improvements in its real GDP, whilst other EU members were slower to come out of recession. These differences in economic growth rates could indicate that some of the EU economies are in different phases of their economic cycles, and this has been put forward as one of the reasons why the UK has opted not to be among the first-wave entrants into European monetary union.

What factors affect growth rates?

If countries knew precisely which were the important factors affecting economic growth then remedial action could be taken and we would notice a large number of countries with extremely high and similar growth rates. The factors that are believed to influence growth may have an individual country dimension, or constraints to growth might involve policies at a wider level, such as that of the trading bloc (for example, the North American Free Trade Association) or economic bloc (the European Union).

Cook (1996) has suggested a range of factors which can be growth-enhancing or growth-suppressing. The growth-enhancing factors are:

- schooling and education investment;

- capital savings and investment;

- equipment investment;
- the level of human capital.

The growth-suppressing factors are:

- the level of government expenditure;
- political and social instability;
- trade barriers;
- the political nature of the ruling party.

Growth and structural change

The 1950s and 1960s saw the growth rates of the European economies at unprecedented levels. There was an abundant supply of labour, moving from agriculture into other sectors of the economy. Oil discoveries in the Middle East ensured cheap oil supplies, particularly as oil production was in the hands of a few major Western European companies. Further, technology transfer from the United States enabled the relatively backward industries of post-war Europe to make rapid improvements in productivity. Increasing real incomes improved market sizes and coupled with the removal of trade barriers through the development of the European Free Trade Area (EFTA), the development of the European Community (EC) and the successes of the General Agreements on Tariffs and Trade (GATT), conditions were ripe for high levels of sustained growth.

By the early 1970s conditions were beginning to change. The movement of labour from agriculture to manufacturing had begun to decline; labour relations deteriorated. The 1973/74 oil price rise led to a period of more expensive and less secure energy, and exchange rate movements led to European commodities losing some of their competitiveness. In addition, there was increasing competition from Japan and the newly industrialised countries (NICs) – Singapore, Hong Kong, South Korea and Taiwan – in shipbuilding, steel and car manufacture – areas in which the Europeans had regarded themselves as pre-eminent.

At the same time Japan, in particular, had begun to adopt different working practices which implied that the old labour rules needed adjusting, a feature which was heavily resisted by the trade unions in Europe. In other words, inadequate adjustment of its industry had reduced Europe's ability to compete in global markets. Free marketeers believe that the weakness of governments and the strength of trade unions allowed real wage rates (the amount that take-home pay will purchase) to soar. Thus, products became more expensive within Europe and government policy only served to safeguard jobs rather than improve output. The much more laissez-faire approach adopted by the UK government since the early 1980s has attempted to address the problem of the high price of labour through legislation designed to limit the power of trade unions and encourage private sector involvement through its privatisation policy.

Another factor linked to the slower growth rates of the European economies was the level of government involvement in the economy, a subject to which we will return later in this chapter. A high level of government expenditure, Bacon and Eltis (1976) argued, has tended to 'crowd out' private sector investment – high levels of government expenditure had diverted resources to the government and away from the private sector. Thus one reason for the slower growth rates in Europe during the 1970s and 1980s was that the private sector had experienced rationing of investment funds. In addition the actual behaviour of the welfare state was deemed to have stifled innovation by providing a 'cosy safety net' for some groups. Government involvement may also have propped up ailing industries, led to lower efficiency, through the spread of state-run enterprises, and increased both consumer and industry tax burdens. As a result public spending took an ever-larger share of GDP during the 1980s, a part of which can be related to the growing underlying upward trend in European unemployment. The period of retrenchment during the 1980s saw governments unwilling to increase their fiscal deficits in order to reflate their economies, relying instead on export-led strategies to improve their growth records. There may be individual problems faced by some countries which constrain their growth performances. Exhibit 3.1 indicates areas which 'New Labour' see as important to address.

EXHIBIT 3.1

Competing in the new economy

The white paper on competitiveness published by Peter Mandelson, the trade and industry secretary, commits the government to the ambitious aim of reversing a century of relative economic decline in the UK.

It contains a raft of policy announcements ranging from action to promote science and engineering to financial help for entrepreneurs and limited protection from creditors for small companies in difficulties.

But the most important element of the bundle of papers released by the Department of Trade and Industry may be the economic analysis of the role of knowledge in economic growth, set out in a separate 32-page report. The report, which explains the thinking underlying the white paper, shifts the perspective of the DTI away from any lingering attachment to interventionism and towards facilitating knowledge transfer.

This approach, the 'big idea' with which Mr Mandelson hopes to make his mark at the DTI, is not new. Friends say he was deeply impressed shortly after replacing Margaret Beckett at the DTI by an article on the subject written in 1994 by Peter Drucker, the management guru.

The idea had also been floated as long as 1995 by Tony Blair. Nor is Mr Mandelson the first industry minister to come to the job with a big idea. For George Brown and Douglas Jay, the economic team in Harold Wilson's first government in 1964–66, it was the National Plan, which was supposed to raise gross domestic product by 25 per cent over six years. For Tony Benn the big idea was industrial planning agreements; Keith Joseph started a free market crusade that ended in mass

Exhibit 3.1 continued

privatisation of state assets; Lord Young tried to turn the DTI into a department for enterprise; Nicholas Ridley wanted to close it. And Michael Heseltine promised a bonfire of controls, yet vowed to intervene 'before breakfast, lunch and dinner'. Government worries about competitiveness are nothing new, either. The issue surfaced in 1963 in a report from the National Economic Development Council calling for action to improve education and skills if Britain was to remain able to compete with overseas rivals.

That idea was resurrected by Mr Heseltine with a 1994 white paper – the first of three annual reports produced by the Conservatives that contained a wealth of detail, but achieved little.

Mr Mandelson, however, can legitimately claim to have produced a new and coherent way of looking at the role of the DTI that is capable of providing a framework for most of the policy making it has to do.

The core of the argument is that knowledge is becoming more important as a factor in economic growth because of four mutually reinforcing developments: rapid developments in information and communications technology, the increased speed of scientific and technological advances, greater global competition, and more sophisticated demand patterns caused by growing prosperity. This is changing the way businesses compete, the analysis says, increasing the importance of innovation and increasing the returns to products with a large knowledge component.

These developments lead to a crucial role for entrepreneurs – in identifying and exploiting the economic opportunities presented by rapid change – and for investors – who may find companies' wealth-creating potential increasingly tied up in intangible assets such as the knowledge of the workforce.

Generating economic prosperity in future, it says, will require the capacity to exploit science and technology, enterprise and innovation, people and skills; collaboration between companies operating in networks and clusters; and greater competition to increase innovation and consumer choice.

The paper says the UK is in a strong position in many areas of the knowledge economy because of the strength of its media, entertainment and financial services. The composition of UK output is already changing to reflect the importance of knowledge, reflected in increases in knowledge-based employment and exports.

However, the analysis blames a relatively low level of gross domestic product per head on a labour productivity gap of between 20 and 40 per cent with the United States, France and Germany. The DTI approach, it says, 'must not be one of heavy-handed intervention, nor can the development of the knowledge-driven economy be left entirely to the market. There is a clear role for government in addressing market failures to promote science and technology, foster enterprise and innovation, develop education and skills, facilitate collaboration and promote modern competitive markets'.

Source: Brown, K. (1998) *Financial Times*, 17 December, National News: competing in the global economy: 'Knowledge is power' emerges as big idea for the economy: reversing the decline.

Finally, within the Western economies, we need to consider how external shocks – factors which affect businesses but have their origin outside the domestic economy – affect growth. The oil price rises of 1973/74 and 1980/81 resulted in very tight monetary policies coming into operation, making investment expensive. Fiscal policy (the use of government expenditure changes or tax changes) was an option, but many policy-makers believed that either expanding government expenditure or reducing taxes would only serve to drive up the inflation rate rather than have any long-term effect on production and output. Having success-fully reduced their debts during the 1980s, governments were loath to push them up again by borrowing more. There is an extensive belief that only export-led growth is an acceptable means by which growth can be re-established.

Although these factors may underlie the poor growth performance of the major Western industrialised nations, not all countries have experienced slower growth rates during the 1980s and early 1990s. South-East Asian countries (the 'tiger economies') performed remarkably well until 1997, as we can see from Table 3.8. Some saw this as result of a much more laissez-faire approach by governments – allowing markets to operate without government interference – and unfettered, cheap labour. However, all this was to change during the later part of the 1990s. Their growth performances have been severely dented following the banking and financial crisis that has hit South-East Asia. In fact both Indonesia and Thailand registered negative growth performances in 1998.

Later in this chapter we discuss the crisis in South-East Asia and the way in which it has spilled over into the rest of the global community.

The costs of growth

It may be assumed that growth brings only benefits. However, there is a view that growth has a number of negative aspects in terms of environmental damage

TABLE 3.8 Estimates of real GDP growth rates for selected South-East Asian countries

Country	Annual average growth rate 1984–91	GDP growth rate (%) 1992	GDP growth rate (%) 1994	GDP growth rate (%) 1998
Hong Kong	6.9	6.3	5.5	3.0
Singapore	6.8	6.0	10.1	3.5
Taiwan	8.4	6.7	6.5	5.0
China	9.8	13.2	11.8	7.0
Indonesia	6.0	6.5	7.4	−5.0
Malaysia	6.2	7.8	8.5	2.5
Philippines	1.1	0.3	4.3	2.5
Thailand	8.9	7.9	8.5	−3.1

Source: World Bank, *The World Bank Atlas 1995*; Asian Development Bank, *World Economic Outlook*, May 1998 (IMF)

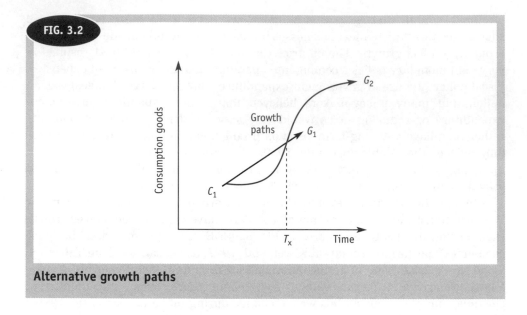

FIG. 3.2

Alternative growth paths

and that the process of achieving higher growth may not be worth the effort. First, to achieve a higher growth rate some consumption expenditure may have to be foregone today and resources switched to investment goods so that future consumption may be higher. We can illustrate this concept using Figure 3.2.

The initial consumption level is shown as C_1 and the growth path as G_1. Suppose the government wishes to push the economy on to a higher growth path, shown as G_2. To enable this growth path to be reached requires more investment, which could be financed through more savings or higher taxes, both of which reduce current consumption. As Figure 3.2 indicates, it takes until time T_x before the two growth paths coincide. Whether or not the sacrifice is worthwhile depends upon the amount of extra consumer goods produced in the future and how long it takes to make up for the sacrificed goods.

Secondly, growth may cause negative externalities, where the actions of producers or consumers affect not only themselves but also third parties, other than through the normal workings of the price mechanism. It is the developed countries which produce the greatest amount of pollution, including 45 per cent of greenhouse gases, and consume around 70 per cent of all resources; see Chapter 6 for a discussion of environmental costs. Many of these costs are likely to be understated, since precise measurements are not available. If, as Meadows *et al.* (1992) suggest, the costs of growth are included in the estimates of real national income then the benefits of economic growth may be overstated.

Growth also has an impact on resources, particularly non-renewable ones. If growth is stimulated today we are just bringing the day forward when non-renewable resources will disappear. Growth also brings technical progress, which may create jobs but, at the same time, destroy others by making skills redundant.

People may be forced to take low-paid, unskilled work or migrate. The results of this process can be seen in the structural changes outlined earlier.

Whether governments should pursue the goal of growth depends, therefore, on the costs and benefits of growth and how much weight individual groups in society attach to them. Perhaps constrained growth is the solution, where growth is sought, but subject to, for example, levels of environmental protection, minimum wages, and maximum rates of resource depletion.

There are individuals who suggest that we do not have to worry about using up finite resources. In their view as the resource is depleted so its price will rise and consumers will purchase less of it. It is possible too that resources which were not profitable at the old price will come into use, as was the case in the development of North Sea oil and gas reserves. These marginal resources may be used efficiently if technology can provide a means of increasing the capacity usage. Suppose, however, that there comes a point when technology cannot make marginal resources as effective as those that have been depleted. It follows that the prices of materials would rise; this would feed through to inflation, and a wage price spiral would ensue, reducing everyone's standard of living. Alternatively resources could be rationed.

Although these arguments seem a little improbable on first viewing, the notion of resource depletion did receive support at the Earth Summit in Rio de Janiero in May 1992 and was considered further at the environmental conferences at Montreal (1996) and Tokyo (1998). The call was for controlled growth. A constrained growth rate is easier to bear for the developed countries, but for many less developed countries (LDCs) or newly industrialised countries (NICs) the development of indigenous natural resources is seen as a prerequisite for escape from low levels of GDP per capita. The acceptability of this constrained growth scenario to those countries depends upon whether the developed nations provide increased aid to finance any difference between sustainable growth and their 'normal' level of growth. Even without consideration of the environmental impact of growth, on a macroeconomic level growth can have an important impact on prices. High levels of growth which are coupled with resource constraints can lead to inflation.

QUESTIONS

1. What factors are seen as the prominent drivers in the growth process?
2. What can governments do to stimulate growth in their economies?

INFLATIONARY PRESSURES

Inflation may be defined as a persistent increase in prices over time, in other words, the rate of inflation measures the change in the purchasing power of money.

There are a number of ways in which inflation can be measured. One method is by measuring changes in the Retail Price Index (RPI) (sometimes called the headline rate). The RPI measures the change in prices from month to month in a representative 'basket' of commodities bought by the average consumer. The commodities in the basket are weighted differently to indicate the proportion of expenditure made by the average consumer on various items. As Table 3.9 indicates, the weights change over time as goods change in relative importance in the average basket of commodities purchased by consumers. Thus in the United Kingdom since 1987, food, fuel and light (due to privatisation and the growth in competition) and clothing and footwear account for smaller proportions of the average expenditure of consumers, whilst housing costs have increased.

In the UK, mortgage interest payments are included in the RPI. This means that higher rates of interest will push up mortgage rates and increase the rate of inflation. So if it is the government's intention to reduce inflation by increasing interest rates and thereby reducing consumer expenditure, the opposite effect will occur. Since the RPI was the index usually used as a basis for wage claims, workers and trade unions could be encouraged to pursue higher wage claims if the RPI increased through increased mortgage rates. These would then increase the costs of industry, causing further price rises.

Other European countries, for example France and Italy, exclude owner-occupation from their consumer price index, whilst other countries, because of the small size of their home ownership sector compared with their rental sector, will exhibit different changes in their retail price index for an equivalent change in interest rates.

TABLE 3.9   General index of retail prices: group weights

Category	1987	1994	1998
Catering	46	45	48
Food	167	142	130
Alcoholic drinks	76	76	71
Tobacco	38	35	34
Housing	157	158	197
Fuel and light	61	45	36
Household goods	73	76	72
Household services	44	47	54
Clothing and footwear	74	58	55
Personal goods and services	38	37	40
Motoring expenditure	127	142	136
Fares and other travel costs	22	20	20
Leisure goods	47	48	46
Leisure services	30	71	61
	1000	1000	1000

Source: *Labour Market Trends* (1988, 1994, 1998)

In the United Kingdom a measure of inflation has been developed which does not include the costs of mortgages, RPIX, now called the underlying rate of inflation. A further method for measuring inflation has also been developed, called RPIY. This measure of inflation excludes both mortgage interest rate payments and indirect taxes such as VAT and excise duty. This is a measure, therefore, of the true underlying rate of inflation.

Why the concern about inflation?

From 1950 to 1970 prices were fairly stable in Western nations. The first oil price rise in 1973/74 changed this. The increase in the price of oil pushed up energy prices and transportation costs, and increased the prices of goods which were oil-related. The response of the Western nations was to try to squeeze inflation out of the system. Figure 3.3 shows how inflation has changed in the United Kingdom over the years since 1972, and indicates the price rises following the 1980/81 oil shock and the further rise in inflation towards the end of the 1980s.

Inflation is said to have redistribution effects. If money wages rise at the same rate as inflation, then real wages remain constant. However, if tax bands and tax thresholds do not rise in line with inflation a greater proportion of income is subject to tax. Inflation also reduces the real value of the debt to the government, thus redistributing income from the people to the state.

The redistribution effects of inflation not only take place from individuals to governments but also affect individuals and businesses. Inflation favours debtors rather than creditors, as it erodes the value of debt.

Inflation also has external consequences, making domestically produced goods more expensive and less competitive on world markets and imported goods

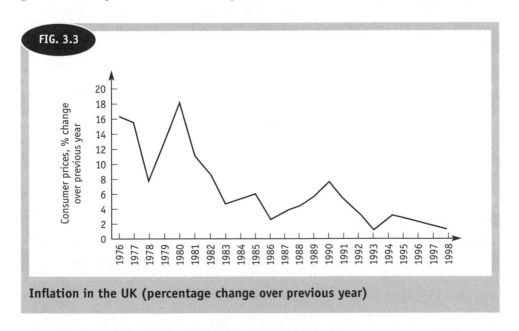

FIG. 3.3

Inflation in the UK (percentage change over previous year)

cheaper on the home market. In this case the balance of payments position will worsen and pressure will mount for the exchange rate to fall. As the exchange rate falls it will make imports more expensive and reduce the price of exports, thereby restoring equilibrium in the balance of payments. Governments, however, may pursue a policy of managed exchange rates which prevents the market from restoring equilibrium in the balance of payments. In these cases, controlling the effect of inflation by other means rather than letting the exchange rate do the correction may be a better approach.

Government policies throughout Europe shifted, during the 1980s, from reducing unemployment to controlling the rate of inflation. Policy-makers argue that this is the correct approach since, once inflation is beaten, unemployment will fall. The arguments are stated as follows. High and variable inflation makes future income streams from investment projects uncertain. Thus firms may reduce investment or may only consider undertaking investment projects which yield a high rate of return in the short term. However, the positive link between inflation and unemployment is somewhat tenuous; Friedman (1977) supports the relationship, while Higham and Tomlinson (1982) find no general evidence.

High inflation may lead to governments imposing wage and price controls which inhibit the working of the market mechanism. Some firms, which may be relatively more efficient or in markets where the demand for their products is rising, may be prevented from offering their employees better rewards because of the controls put in place by government. In addition, the more efficient firms may be unable to offer rewards high enough to entice staff from other sectors of the economy. High inflation may also lead to industrial unrest as unions seek money wage increases in order to prevent a deterioration in their real wages. It may also be expected that high inflation depresses saving, as consumers purchase products from organisations before their price increases once again.

Inflationary expectations also take time to adjust downwards. A reduction in current inflation may not lead to an improvement in the amount invested since it is possible that investors may feel that the inflation rate will remain high in the future.

Given the problems that can arise from inflation it would be easy to suggest that countries which have relatively higher rates of inflation perform less well than countries with lower levels of inflation. As Figure 3.4 indicates, this is not always the case. Thus a government which pursues a policy of low inflation as a means of improving the economy's growth performance cannot always be guaranteed this outcome.

The causes of inflation

Inflation can be damaging both internally and externally and it is not surprising that governments have used a variety of means to control inflationary pressures. The more traditional view was that inflation could be due either to 'cost–push' or 'demand–pull' factors. In the former it may be due to:

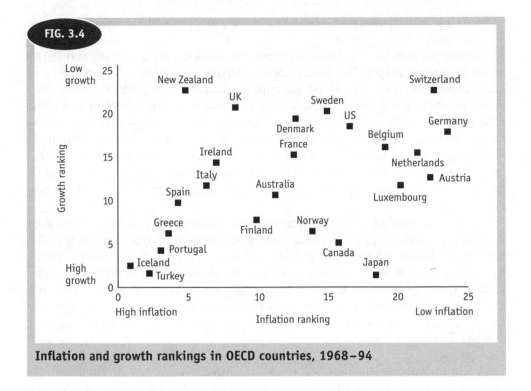

FIG. 3.4

Inflation and growth rankings in OECD countries, 1968–94

- increases in costs of labour that are not linked to increases in labour productivity;
- increases in the costs of raw materials which could come about in buoyant stages of the economic cycle, where the demand for raw materials may outstrip supply in the short term;
- a deterioration in exchange rates, which tends to cause import prices to rise.

In the demand–pull scenario, it is the excess demand for goods that pulls up prices. If aggregate demand increases, the increased demand for labour would bid up real wage rates. If unions in other sectors of the economy attempted to keep their members' wages in parallel, then it is possible that, even with an excess labour supply in these other sectors, unions would be able to force up wage rates. The overall general increase in wage rates then feeds through into the costs of industry and is subsequently passed on in price increases. This causes real wages to fall, with the possibility that further wage demands could follow. In such circumstances a damaging wage–price inflationary cycle is likely to be established.

Inflation can also be caused by governments 'accommodating' price increases. In this instance, whenever aggregate demand falls, leading to higher levels of unemployment, governments step into the economy directly through changes in either government expenditure or taxation to stimulate the economy. This increase in economic activity would increase national income but can also cause the price level to rise.

Monetarists saw the excessive role of governments during the 1960s and 1970s as being directly responsible for the rise in inflation and argued that this type of intervention would have no long-term impact on output and unemployment. They suggested that the economy would return to some natural level of economic activity, but at a higher level of inflation. Does this mean that government activity in the economy may not be worthwhile since it cannot increase output or employment in the long term? From a governmental perspective the long term may extend beyond the lifetime of an elected government; it still might be possible, therefore, to increase employment during the government's term of office! See Figure 3.5(a).

Monetarists argue that if real output and employment is to be increased then governments should intervene not in the demand side but in the supply side of the market. As Figure 3.5(b) indicates, the level of output can be increased not only by shifting the aggregate demand curve to the right from AD_1 to AD_2 but also by shifting the aggregate supply curve to the right from $SRAS_1$ to $SRAS_2$. Thus the monetarists advocated the use of policies to shift the supply curve to the right, so-called 'supply-side measures'. These policies are designed to reduce government involvement and so reduce the frictions they perceive exist in markets (see also Chapter 2).

In addition monetarists see the need to control the amount of money in the economy, so would suggest that governments control either the quantity of money (the money supply) or the price of money (the interest rate).

Since government expenditure often exceeds the revenue from taxation, the consequent deficit, the Public Sector Borrowing Requirement (PSBR), was often

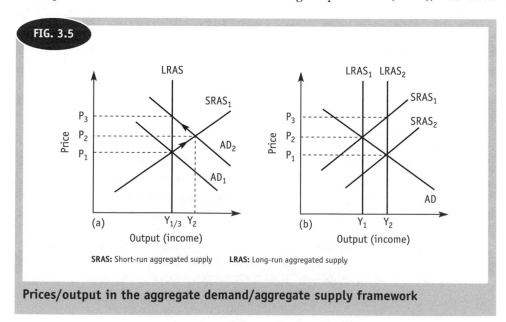

FIG. 3.5

SRAS: Short-run aggregated supply   LRAS: Long-run aggregated supply

Prices/output in the aggregate demand/aggregate supply framework

financed via government printing the extra money. Seigniorage – the printing of money to finance government expenditure – alleviates the government's need to borrow. However, this growth in the money supply increases the amount of money in circulation and could have inflationary consequences. Monetarists suggested that governments seek to reduce the amount of borrowing they undertake. If the monetarists are to be believed then all governments need to do is control the money supply and introduce a series of supply-side measures – policies aimed at improving the quantity and quality of supply – as a means to reduce the level of inflation. It has been notoriously difficulty to control the money supply. This is for two main reasons. First, we need to define what we mean by the money supply. Is it notes and coins in circulation (this is defined as M_0), is it notes and coins in circulation plus bank deposits (this is known as M_1) or is it some other definition? The Federal Reserve Bank, in the United States, has over twenty definitions of the money supply. Second, it was found that, when the UK government targeted a particular measure of the money supply during the 1980s, it had the habit of going out of control, that is exceeding its target rate of growth.

The monetarist approach of using higher interest rates to control inflation can damage business confidence and increase the costs to industry. In addition, if government expenditure is controlled then this subsequently affects consumer expenditure and business sales. The difficulties experienced by the UK government encouraged it to abandon direct controls over money supply in 1985.

Non-monetarist views of inflation

It has been argued that monetarist approaches to inflation have not been responsible for bringing inflation under control, and that other forces have played a more dominant role.

As Table 3.10 indicates, the United Kingdom's anti-inflation strategy appeared to be succeeding during the early part of the 1980s and in the 1990s, but was less satisfactory at other times. Beckerman (1985) suggests that much of the fall in inflation in the early 1980s can be attributed to the fall in commodity prices that followed from the world recession. The very tight fiscal stance taken by the government also had an influence. Soteri and Westaway (1993) suggest that for the UK, world inflation, the exchange rate and its effect on import prices have both played an important part in explaining the changes in its inflation record. We should also consider the UK's 'temporary' membership of the Exchange Rate Mechanism (ERM). Under fixed exchange rates organisations cannot rely on the exchange rate to restore competitiveness in their prices if their relative inflation rates are too high. In the short term, if labour seeks too high a wage claim, then the loss of competitiveness that follows from any increases in prices would lead to job losses. Thus, the ERM was seen as providing discipline for the labour market. During the later part of the 1990s we have seen inflation at low levels once again. Some consider that inflation is now very much under control and is not the major concern of the developed nations. Part of the reason as to why governments attach less significance to inflation in the 1990s is that many Western developed nations

TABLE 3.10   The UK and world economy since 1979

	Inflation (% rate)		Unemployment (% level)		Real GDP (% growth rate)	
	UK	OECD	UK	OECD	UK	OECD
1979	13.4	8.7	5.0	5.0	2.8	3.5
1980	18.0	11.3	6.4	5.7	−2.2	1.5
1981	11.9	9.5	9.8	6.6	−1.3	2.0
1982	8.6	7.2	11.3	8.0	1.7	0.1
1983	4.6	5.5	12.5	8.5	3.5	2.8
1984	5.0	4.9	11.7	8.0	2.1	4.7
1985	6.1	4.3	11.2	7.8	3.7	3.5
1986	3.4	2.7	11.2	7.7	3.6	3.0
1987	4.2	3.4	10.3	7.3	4.7	3.4
1988	4.9	3.3	8.6	6.7	4.5	4.4
1989	7.8	4.3	7.1	6.2	2.3	3.6
1990	9.4	4.7	6.8	6.1	1.0	2.8
1991	5.9	4.5	8.9	6.8	−2.0	1.0
1992	3.7	3.5	9.9	7.4	−0.5	1.9
1993	1.6	2.9	10.3	8.0	2.1	1.2
1994	2.5	2.4	9.4	7.9	4.3	2.9
1995	3.4	2.5	8.6	7.6	2.7	2.2
1996	2.4	2.3	8.0	7.5	2.2	2.8
1997	3.1	2.1	6.9	7.2	3.3	3.1
1998*	2.7	2.1	6.8	7.1	1.7	2.4

* estimated

Source: *OECD Economic Outlook*, June 1998

have been following anti-inflationary policies and the level of economic activity has not been allowed to grow so rapidly. The out-turn of this policy approach is to have unemployment higher than it should be. The pursuit of targets for entry into the European single currency, where low inflation was one of those targets, has also led to lower inflation. At the same time the UK government has given control of its interest rates to the Bank of England which may have adopted a stronger grip on squeezing inflation out of the system.

For some countries, notably a number of those in South America which have had historically high levels of inflation, an approach adopted was to fix their exchange rates against the US dollar, and this has successfully reduced their inflationary spiral. It is also worth noting that while inflation has been reduced within Europe, the UK still has a higher inflation rate than many of its major trading partners.

At this stage let us consider the arguments. Inflation is costly both domestically and internationally. Many reasons have been put forward to explain why inflation occurs, and almost as many remedies. For the latter there does not appear to be

TABLE 3.11   Consumer price inflation (% per annum) in selected
Eastern European countries

Year	Bulgaria	Czech Republic	Hungary	Poland	Romania	Slovakia
1989	5.6	1.4	17.0	251.1	1.1	1.3
1990	23.8	9.7	28.9	585.8	5.1	10.4
1991	338.5	56.6	35.0	70.3	174.5	61.2
1992	79.4	11.1	23.0	43.0	210.9	10.0
1993	59.1	25.2	22.5	35.3	256.1	23.2
1994	121.9	10.0	16.8	30.7	62.0	15.5
1995	32.9	9.1	28.3	26.8	28.0	7.2
1996	311	8.8	23.5	20.2	57.0	5.0
1997	1089	8.4	18.3	15.9	150.0	6.0
1998*	35	11.8	15.0	12.5	25.0	5.0

Sources: Employment Observatory, Cental and Eastern Europe, No. 6, 1994, European Commission; Barclays Bank Country Reports

any consensus. However, in seeking to bring down inflation countries have often deflated their economies and in doing so worsened the conditions for business. For Eastern European countries the scenario is somewhat different. By Western standards, inflation has remained high in most parts of the region, as Table 3.11 indicates.

Part of the explanation for the relatively poor inflation performance of many Eastern European countries has been the introduction of market forces into many sectors and the reduction in state management of prices. Nonetheless, there are signs that inflation is being controlled, especially in Slovakia, the Czech Republic and Poland, though high levels of inflation probably have affected business formation and development.

Dealing with deflation

Whereas the 1970s and parts of the 1980s were associated with relatively high levels of inflation, the 1990s have been denoted as a period of not only low levels of inflation but also with negative price increases (deflation). Although for many consumers the RPI is still positive, the reason for it being that way is that some heavily weighted commodities in the average consumer's basket are still rising but many other commodities, less heavily weighted, are falling. For some countries such as Germany and Japan, even the more heavily weighted goods whose prices are rising cannot outweigh the falls in other commodities, thus at the end of the 1990s they are actually showing negative inflation figures.

Deflation sounds like a consumer paradise. In the United Kingdom we have seen mortgage rates falling, the price of a loaf of bread at 7 pence (March 1999), and prices of goods considered as luxuries, such as television sets, video recorders and hi-fi systems falling in price to just over half the 1987 price. Computers continue to fall in price, and in the UK in March 1999 it cost 3 per cent less to clothe a child than it did in February 1998. The fall in these prices can be explained by

- the fall in commodity prices as the global economy slows;
- the opening up of markets such as telecoms and electricity to competition;
- the role of technology increasing productivity;
- the behaviour of organisations which are being threatened by investigation into their pricing practices (supermarkets, over-the-counter medicines etc.).

Living in more deflationary times may be good for consumers but it is not easy for businesses. If consumers believe that prices will fall in the future then they will wait longer to make purchases. This reduces current demand and this in turn drives down prices. The economic crisis in South-East Asia has resulted in lower prices for UK imports, both through absolute price falls in commodities/goods and through the devaluations that have taken place in South-East Asian currencies. Both these factors are leading to increased competition for domestic producers. Exporters too are facing similar problems. In order to sell products abroad in markets in which there is competition from South-East Asian companies, businesses in the developed world are having to reduce their prices too.

For some industries deflation is not bad – industries with rapidly improving technologies and productivity, such as computers. It is mature industries which have more problems, as they face reduced demand and overcapacity. Low demand leads to lower prices and perhaps lower levels of investment. This, through the circular flow, leads to further demand and so the cycle continues. So long as global demand remains relatively sluggish, we may have to get used to living with deflation for some time to come: see Exhibit 3.2.

EXHIBIT 3.2

Deflation

Everyone in chemicals is doing it. Pulp and paper is following suit. Oil is starting to move the same way. Steel is teetering on the brink. Cars are joining in too. For basic industries – the ones that powered the world's industrial transformation over a century and a half – there's no escape. No longer the stars of their domestic economies, they are undertaking cross-border rationalisation to survive.

The chemicals industry is the most visible example. Hoechst's merger talks with Rhone-Poulenc bring together two companies that have already taken big steps to escape from their chemicals roots. They follow hard on the heels of ICI's transformation, the planned merger of Clariant and Ciba Specialty Chemicals, and the purchase by Shin Etsu of Japan of Rovin, a Shell/Akzo Nobel joint venture, to become the world's biggest PVC producer.

Other traditional manufacturing industries have also seen the writing on the wall. In steel, Usinor of France is taking over Belgium's Cockerill-Sambre, and British Steel has acquired control of Sweden's Avesta. In pulp and paper, Sweden's Stora and Finland's Enso have come together. In oil, British Petroleum is taking over Amoco. In cars, Daimler is merging with Chrysler.

One way of looking at this cross-border merger frenzy is to see it as part of globalisation. With the world now a single market for many basic products, a pattern of production and ownership that reflects traditional national boundaries no longer makes sense. So industries are settling down into new constellations of power and scale, crossing national boundaries as easily as they once crossed local ones.

That is only part of the story. True, globalisation would have shaken up traditional patterns of ownership – eventually. And without a recent willingness on the part of governments, managers and shareholders to accept overseas ownership without complaint, many of these deals would have proved difficult. But the urgency with which these companies are coming together derives from something else. It's one of those invisible economic trends we all know is happening but find it hard to pin down: deflation.

Stable prices, which now reign across the developed world, are a statistical illusion. Those unmoving consumer price indices do not reflect what is really happening to businesses. In the words of a hoary old statistical joke, they are the average temperature of a man with his head in the freezer and his feet in a bucket of hot water.

Some businesses, especially in the service sector and other high-growth areas, are comfortably warm, with prices for their products rising. For others, chilled to the marrow, prices are relentlessly falling. The industries that find themselves at the freezer end of the body corporate are the ones rushing towards cross-border mergers.

For industries supplying the basic ingredients of manufacturing – chemicals, steel, oil, paper – the freeze has got much worse in the past year. The Asian tigers provided almost all the growth in demand for these products, as they turned themselves into the workshops of the world. With Asian manufacturing in deep recession, prices of industrial building blocks have been tumbling.

In other industries, such as cars, there is not the same demand-side pressure on prices. Their Achilles heel is overcapacity, a surplus of plants built on the back of cheap capital. In some cases, this capital was artificially underpriced – in Japan or Korea, for example. In others, it is the result of low long-term interest rates or booming stock markets.

Industries that do not face the same pricing pressures would do well to learn a lesson from those that do. The impact of deflation seems set to get worse, if anything, rather than better. Real interest rates remain high all round the world, even after the recent easing in the United States and elsewhere.

Consumers have been conditioned to expect bargains – and are sufficiently apprehensive about the macroeconomic outlook to seek them out. Asian exports will recover fast enough to keep downward pressure on finished-goods prices, but

Exhibit 3.2 continued

not fast enough to ease the squeeze on suppliers of basic ingredients. And in Europe, the increased transparency that follows the euro will help push prices down.

These are all reasons to think that even those businesses currently basking at the warmer end should think hard about how to cope with falling prices. Product differentiation, extra service, internal cost-savings, the creation of parallel 'bargain' brands – these are all familiar weapons in this struggle. Only when these remedies are exhausted should companies contemplate cross-border acquisitions. Such deals are inherently risky. They are riskier still when produced by fear rather than greed. Defensive mergers of equals, in which the distribution of power is unclear and the unspoken shared motive is a desire to shelter from the cold, are the riskiest of all.

Cross-border mergers are likely to succeed only when their motivation is aggressive and the victors in the internal struggle for power are identified at the outset. Some of the recent deals in basic industries (such as BP/Amoco) fit this pattern. Many do not.

The 1970s taught us how inflation damaged business decisions and the allocation of resources. We will soon be learning, the hard way, that deflation has an industrial price too: botched mergers and unworkable combinations.

Source: Martin, P. 'Chain reaction: It is not just globalisation which is forcing companies into cross-border mergers. Deflation is also playing a big part', *Financial Times*, 17 November 1998

QUESTIONS

1. How does monetary policy affect the behaviour of organisations?
2. Since 1997 the United Kingdom has given its central bank control over its interest rates. Do you consider that inflation will be kept more under control?

THE ROLE OF THE STATE IN THE ECONOMY

Table 3.12 indicates that government expenditure by European Union governments is, in total, around half of EU GDP. The six top-spending governments are Finland, Denmark, France, Belgium, Austria and Italy, all of which spend between 50 and 55 per cent of GDP.

Government spending by all European Union governments exceeds that of both the United States (32 per cent of GDP) and Japan (35 per cent of GDP). There is no single reason to explain why some countries have higher proportions of GDP devoted to government expenditure than others.

TABLE 3.12   Government expenditure 1997

Country	Total government expenditure as percentage of nominal GDP
Belgium	52.2
Denmark	54.2
France	54.1
Germany	47.7
Greece	41.8
Ireland	36.1
Italy	50.6
Netherlands	49.1
Portugal	45.9
Spain	42.2
United Kingdom	39.7
Austria	50.7
Finland	54.2
Norway	44.7
Sweden	42.6
EU-15	48.2
Japan	35.2
USA	32.0
Korea	21.9

Source: OECD National Accounts

These different levels of government activity occur for a variety of reasons. Part of the spending represents a redistribution of income amongst citizens. Governments may also play an active role in macroeconomic stabilisation of the economy, using government spending to prevent excessive fluctuations in income and unemployment, thus smoothing out business cycles.

Government expenditure is a very important part of total expenditure in most economies. Governments are big consumers, spending around a third of the total that all households spend on goods and services. Like many households they are prone to over-expenditure and are forced to borrow money from the private sector or from abroad. The level of this debt can reach almost unmanageable amounts and, as Table 3.13 indicates, for some countries, such as Greece, Italy and Belgium, this burden of debt can be in excess of a full year's domestic product.

Interest payment on these debts is an important problem for countries, particularly those with debts in excess of 100 per cent of GDP. In these countries higher taxes, both on the business sector and on consumers, may have to be levied, for a long period, to finance the interest payments and to repay the debt.

TABLE 3.13   Government debt as a percentage of nominal GDP (Maastricht definition)

Country	1988	1993	1996	1998
Belgium	132	139	136.4	118.4
Denmark	61	80	68.4	57.3
France	34	46	60.9	58.9
Germany	44	48	62.5	60.7
Greece	80	115	120.2	108.2
Ireland	118	96	79.1	57.0
Italy	93	119	120.5	118.5
Luxembourg	10	8	6	–
Netherlands	79	81	79.5	99.5
Portugal	75	67	64.0	63.4
Spain	42	60	68.7	68.5
United Kingdom	50	48	52.8	52.1
Austria	58	57	61.4	64.8
Finland	17	62	71.4	53.4
Norway	43	45	46.5	–
Sweden	54	84	86.3	74.5

Source: *European Economy, Supplement A*, 11/12 November 1998;
European Commission, OECD, *Economic Outlook*, various years

Another way to hold down the rise in government debt is to curtail government expenditure. However, this may be difficult, since as unemployment rises there is often a concomitant rise in state benefits and reduction in tax revenue. It may, of course, be possible to reduce the deficit through increasing tax revenues. Table 3.14 shows the main sources of revenues for governments in the European Union as a percentage of GDP.

The proportion of revenues obtained from the various sources differs from country to country. For the European Union as a whole the proportion of revenue raised by direct taxes matches that from indirect taxes. However, in the UK, Portugal, Greece, and France, indirect taxes are a more important source of revenue, while in Belgium, Denmark, Finland, Italy and the Netherlands the reverse is true. These differences between the burdens of the various forms of taxation can have an impact on company location, level of profits, consumer behaviour and the incentive to work harder. All these have important consequences for business.

Economic cycles

It could be argued that one role of government is to reduce the fluctuations that occur in the economy. Often these fluctuations are not random but follow a cyclical pattern. There are long and short cycles in the economy. The long cycle

TABLE 3.14   Receipts as a percentage of GDP (1995 figures)

Country	Indirect taxes	Direct taxes	Social security contributions	Other	Total
Belgium	12.8	18.0	17.3	1.8	50.0
Denmark	18.3	27.4	6.2	5.5	57.4
France	15.1	9.5	20.9	3.8	49.3
Germany	13.1	11.9	19.1	2.8	47.0
Greece	15.5	5.3	13.1	2.6	36.4
Ireland	15.7	14.7	5.0	1.7	37.0
Italy	12.1	15.0	14.8	3.8	45.6
Luxembourg	14.4	14.2	11.7	3.5	43.9
Netherlands	13.0	13.5	19.4	3.7	49.6
Portugal	14.0	8.8	10.9	3.8	37.5
Spain	11.4	11.5	13.7	4.1	40.7
United Kingdom	16.1	13.2	6.2	2.2	37.7
Austria	16.0	13.1	15.9	3.1	48.1
Finland	14.3	15.7	15.2	7.0	52.2
Sweden	14.4	22.0	14.7	9.2	60.3

Source: Commission of the European Communities

(Kondratief cycle) is estimated to have a period of 50 years and to be associated with technological breakthroughs. Other cycles are observable, such as the business cycle (trade cycle), a seven- to ten-year economic cycle, and political cycles, cycles of four or five years coinciding with elections. We would expect to find that in the boom periods of the cycle economic activity is buoyant and organisations find it much easier to sell their goods and services. At the same time there may be pent-up pressures beginning to appear which serve to drive up prices. At this stage the government may seek to dampen economic activity. Conversely, at the bottom of a cycle, economic activity is subdued; there may be high levels of unemployment and less pressure on prices, and the government may perceive a need to step into the economy more directly and stimulate the level of economic activity.

Over time markets have become more internationalised and countries have increasingly been involved in closer trading groups so that the phases of their cycles are more concurrent. Thus, when one trading bloc or area goes into recession, it may cause other trading blocs to do the same. One national government cannot, on its own, stimulate its economy whilst others in its trading bloc do nothing. It is now necessary for groups of countries to co-ordinate economic intervention. This co-ordination of economic policy can be seen within Europe as individual nation states have striven to meet the entry criteria for monetary union within the European Union. Co-ordination also takes place on an international level. For example, the global community has moved together towards stimulating the global economy following the financial crashes in South-East Asia.

We should recognise that governments sometimes attempt to drive their economy out of its normal business cycle for political reasons, such as re-election. Alesina (1989) suggests that it is politically risky for governments to approach an election with deteriorating economic conditions.

It is relatively easy to see the impacts of economic cycles on international economies, but explaining why they occur is much more difficult. The political cycle can be explained, though not fully, by the behaviour of domestic governments, but the trade cycle is much more difficult to interpret. The development of the South-East Asian crisis, described below, might supply us with some insights into the way problems in one area of the global community can get transmitted throughout other areas of the globe.

The South-East Asian crisis

The financial crisis in South-East Asia began in July 1997 following a speculative attack on the Thai baht. The Bank of Thailand, after defending the currency as it had done earlier in May 1997 and losing foreign exchange reserves, finally let the baht float on 2 July 1997. The baht immediately depreciated by 15 per cent and this was followed by the floating of the Indonesian rupiah, the Malaysian ringgit and the Philippine peso. By January 1998 the rupiah had depreciated by 80 per cent, the baht by 53 per cent, the ringgit by 42 per cent and the peso by 36 per cent. The South Korean currency also suffered and this too depreciated by 42 per cent by January 1998.

But what led to this crisis? The traditional currency crisis does not really fit the Asian experience. There was not monetary or fiscal profligacy, unemployment was not high, and although current account deficits were large they were not overly so and were easily offset by foreign capital inflows. These capital inflows made South-East Asian countries' real exchange rates appreciate. Due to pegged exchange rates and high interest rates money flowed into South-East Asia. The risk that could follow from this was reduced by the perception that governments guaranteed financial institutions. However, the structural weaknesses in financial institutions resulted in over-investment in excessively risky projects.

Export growth began to falter due to a downturn in the demand for electronics, the falling value of the yen gave Japanese exporters a competitive advantage and interest rates were required to rise. Faced with the need to get greater inflows of foreign capital and the bad debt issued by a number of financial institutions, confidence in the tiger economies began to wane. Investors began to move money rapidly out of South-East Asia. A net inflow into the region of $95 billion in 1996 changed to a net outflow of $15 billion in 1997. A number of South-East Asian currencies began to collapse. Because investors realised that there were going to be no government guarantees for investment, asset prices in the area burst. Falling asset prices resulted in insolvency of a number of financial intermediaries, leading to a fully-fledged financial crisis. The problems for South-East Asia are further compounded by the importance of intra-country trade between the tiger economies.

The fall in raw material prices which affected the South-East Asian economies was also felt in Europe. In 1998 Russia imposed a moratorium on some of its international debt payment and was forced to devalue the rouble. For Western European countries the impact of the South-East Asian crisis was being felt by exporters and through the freezing of FDI from a number of South-East Asian economies, such as that by Hyundai and Samsung of South Korea in the UK. The repercussions then moved on to South America. Countries such as Argentina and Brazil had, during the 1990s, reduced their inflation-prone economies by pegging their exchange rates to the US dollar. The net outflow of speculative capital that was seeking to leave the tiger economies was placed by speculators in what they considered a more safe haven, the US dollar. This caused the dollar to appreciate in value. To continue to peg their exchange rates against the US dollar, both Brazil and Argentina were forced to raise interest rates. The rise in interest rates and the depreciation of the tiger economies' currencies meant that domestic producers in both Argentina and Brazil found trading opportunities difficult. The result of increased pressure in Brazil forced the Brazilian peso to be devalued in January 1999.

Both the United States and the Europeans have responded to the global slowdown by reducing interest rates, and Japan, which has had its financial system mauled by bad debt provision, has also slowed. Thus what the South-East Asian crisis has shown is that changes in one area of the global economy can have major effects in other countries on the other side of the world.

QUESTIONS

1. Why did fiscal policy (the use of government budgets to control the level of economy activity) go out of favour during the 1980s?
2. How is the crowding-out effect likely to impact on organisations?
3. 'If different types of cycles exist in the economy then the government are powerless to affect the overall level of economic activity.' Discuss.

UNEMPLOYMENT

From the end of World War II until the 1970s control of unemployment was the main goal of most European governments. During the 1970s and 1980s control of inflation assumed greater importance. Phillips (1958) argued that low inflation is not compatible with low unemployment. Nonetheless, a number of governments saw that low relative inflation could lead to higher competitiveness and provide the conditions for improvements in employment.

Although unemployment has fluctuated with the general level of economic activity there has been a slow upward trend in the natural level of unemployment – the level of unemployment which is consistent with overall equilibrium in the labour market – since World War II. The OECD's estimate for the UK for 1996 is about 8 per cent. Although this is slightly lower than a decade ago, suggesting some progress on supply-side measures in the labour market, it does suggest that the UK economy is getting dangerously close to full capacity.

So why has there been a general rise in the natural rates of unemployment in Europe in particular?

1. There is some evidence from Burda and Wyplosz (1997), though not conclusive, that where the safety provisions, such as benefits, for the unemployed are more extensive then unemployment levels are higher. Benefits may allow some people to stay out of the labour market. Their skills become inappropriate for the needs of the labour market and they become part of the long term unemployed.

2. Trade unions have been more militant in Europe.

3. Labour costs consist of more than wages; they include labour taxes (social security and retirement contributions), and these too have risen steeply.

4. Regulation of the use of labour, for example length of the working week and dismissal procedures, is also of importance.

5. Productivity – output per person – must also be examined. As labour becomes more productive fewer employees are required to produce a given quantity of output.

6. Sectoral changes have taken place in a number of European economies as they have moved from labour-intensive manufacturing based industries to service-orientated ones.

Job creation in the United Kingdom is possible. This is unlikely to come from a simple boost in demand but rather from a longer-term emphasis on investment in infrastructure, training and education (Begg, 1995).

For more than a decade the UK government has been acutely aware of the lack of training taking place, a shortage of skills and a general failure to keep pace with the rapidly changing world of work. The world of education has seen the development of a new National Curriculum and vocationally-orientated qualifications. The government's response to the skill shortages that have appeared in UK industry, even though unemployment has been relatively high, include, for example, NVQs, Investors in People, Modern Apprenticeships and the New Deal (see also Chapter 5).

Some employers, during the recessionary period, have cut their training budgets and sought to obtain new employees from the unemployment register who already possess the skills they need.

To emphasise the situation, Studd (1996) finds the UK

- 18th out of 25 in the world prosperity league, with an identified skill shortage;
- 18th out of 48 in overall competitiveness;
- 40th out of 48 in motivation of the workforce;
- 35th out of 48 in the adequacy of its education.

Therefore, although the UK has successfully tackled some its supply-side problems such as state ownership and trade union issues, it has still to get to grips with deficiencies in the skill base of its workforce.

QUESTIONS

1. Why has there been a general upward trend in average unemployment levels within Europe over the last 15 years?
2. How do skill deficiencies lead to unemployment?

INTERNATIONAL TRADE

Since World War II, markets have become increasingly internationalised, and it follows that economies have become more 'open', that is, more heavily involved in international trade. But why do countries trade? Clearly, much trade takes place because one country is better able to produce particular products and services than its trading partners. For example, a country situated closer to the equator than the United Kingdom is better able to produce tropical fruit, whilst it is possible that, because of its manufacturing base, the UK is better able to produce some manufactured goods. Countries, by specialising in the products in which they are more efficient, can gain by trading these products for other products produced more efficiently elsewhere. These concepts of efficiency and specialisation lie behind two of the oldest theories of international trade, those of Absolute Advantage (Adam Smith) and Comparative Advantage (David Ricardo).

These two theories tell us why trade takes place but perhaps do not provide us with the complete picture as to why there has been a growth in international trade. The role of mutual benefit is certainly one driving force. Businesses and governments are unlikely to engage, voluntarily, in international trade if they do not expect either to improve their economic situation or to achieve any material gain in return. Variations in the costs of production constitute another incentive for international trade to occur. In particular, international trade may lead to domestic firms achieving economies of scale which were not available in their domestic markets alone. Changes that have taken place in international markets are of great importance. Many markets have recently become deregulated with reductions in the barriers to trade, and this has enhanced trading opportunities. New patterns of organisation and business location have emerged, including using foreign suppliers, foreign direct investments, joint ventures, and international co-operation. These have arisen to obtain better access to markets and to enhance competitiveness by exploiting specific local production factors such as favourable labour costs, labour skills and tax situations.

If trade is encouraged, the world may be better off in terms of total production of goods and services and in terms of the efficiency with which resources are used. However, countries taking this 'specialisation' route could end up being dependent upon a small range of products or services. In this case, if another country is able to produce one of these items more cheaply then the former country may see a large reduction in demand for its good or service. This could lead to balance of trade problems, reductions in sales and increases in unemployment. Countries may therefore consider producing items which they are less efficient at providing by using trade barriers.

Before we consider barriers to trade and the attempts made to reduce trade restrictions, let us appraise the importance of trade in the international arena.

Exports by country

The importance of international trade continues to increase. Trade in goods from European OECD countries increased from 14.3 per cent of GDP in 1962 to 23.6 per cent of GDP in 1995. There is increasing evidence of the Europeanisation of international trade. This intra-European trade rose from 37.2 per cent in 1958 to 58.4 per cent in 1994. Table 3.15 shows evidence of the growth in intra-European exports of the European Union (12) countries.

The main target markets for European Union exporters are other European Union markets and, in particular, those of neighbouring countries. This is especially true for the relatively smaller countries within the European Union such as the Netherlands and Portugal. Larger EU members are more likely to possess a greater number of large-scale enterprises which can address global markets, thus their proportion of intra-EU trade tends to be lower. Other smaller EU countries such as Denmark, by being on the periphery of the EU, will have a greater proportion of their trade directed to countries fringing the EU. During recent years countries situated closer to Central and Eastern Europe, for example

TABLE 3.15 Destination of exports by EU-12, 1958 and 1994 (%)

Country	Intra-EU-12, 1958	Intra-EU-12, 1994
Belgium/Luxembourg	55.4	25.0
Denmark	59.3	45.0
France	–	64.0
Germany	37.9	48.9
Greece	50.9	54.2
Ireland	82.4	70.0
Italy	34.5	53.4
Netherlands	58.3	74.7
Portugal	38.9	75.1
Spain	46.8	64.5
United Kingdom	21.7	54.1
EU-12	37.2	58.4

Source: *European Economy*, No. 65, 1998, Table 45, Annex

Germany, have also seen an increasing proportion of their trade directed towards Hungary, Poland and the Czech Republic, for example out of total EU exports to these countries Germany accounts for approximately 40 per cent. Trade figures are in a constant state of flux. A strong situation in one year can often be overturned by factors beyond the control of individual organisations.

Composition of international trade

In the United Kingdom there has been increased emphasis on trade with continental Europe. But what of the composition of its trade outside of Europe? Trade with North America has remained relatively constant, but this hides the fact that the majority of trade is now with the United States, with only a small proportion now with Canada. The share of trade with Australia and New Zealand has also fallen, but trade with Japan has increased, particularly exports from Japan. There has been a rapid fall in the United Kingdom's percentage of trade with the rest of world, most notably with other Commonwealth countries and with the Latin American states. However, there is growing evidence of increased trade with the newly industrialised countries (NICs) such as Hong Kong, Singapore, Malaysia, South Korea, Taiwan and Thailand.

The United Kingdom imports less food and beverages, basic materials, minerals and fuel, as a percentage of all imports, in 1997 than it did in 1960. However, imports of manufactured goods or semi-manufactured goods represent a much higher share of imports.

This decline in the United Kingdom's manufacturing sector can be seen more starkly when we examine the decline in United Kingdom's share of exports of manufactures (see Table 3.16), which does not appear to have been replicated by any of its major competitors. But is the decline sector-specific? Table 3.17 indicates that, in terms of exports, the United Kingdom is the only country to have fared worse in all export market segments. Increased import penetration (the increased flow of imports), particularly in high- and medium-technology sectors, may indicate a lack of competitiveness on the part of UK manufacturers (see OECD, 1994).

TABLE 3.16 Share of world exports of manufactures of major OECD countries (%)

Country	1960	1969	1979	1993	1995
United States	22	19	16	19	20
Japan	7	11	14	18	14
France	10	8	10	11	10
Germany	19	19	21	10	18
Italy	5	7	8	8	8
United Kingdom	17	11	9	9	8
Others	21	23	22	21	22

Source: National Institute of Economic and Social Research, OECD

TABLE 3.17 Export market shares and import penetration in manufactures

Country	High technology		Medium technology		Low technology	
	1970	1990	1970	1990	1970	1990
France	7.7	8.8	8.5	10.0	10.7	12.1
	(21.6)	(31.6)	(19.7)	(34.1)	(10.7)	(21.4)
Germany	17.7	16.2	23.1	24.7	15.0	17.9
	(14.9)	(37.0)	(17.2)	(29.5)	(11.1)	(20.9)
Italy	5.5	5.1	7.1	7.7	8.5	12.8
	(16.2)	(22.8)	(23.6)	(28.9)	(11.8)	(15.7)
United Kingdom	10.5	10.2	11.9	8.5	8.9	8.5
	(17.4)	(42.2)	(22.1)	(39.4)	(12.4)	(19.8)
Japan	13.2	21.1	8.5	16.9	13.2	7.1
	(5.2)	(5.4)	(4.5)	(5.9)	(3.0)	(6.6)
United States	31.1	26.3	21.7	15.4	13.4	13.3
	(4.2)	(18.4)	(5.6)	(18.5)	(3.8)	(8.8)

Note: Figures in brackets refer to import penetration
Source: OECD (1994)

United Kingdom manufacturers are, therefore, responding less well to changes that are taking place in the international business environment.

Trade barriers

The evidence indicates that

- there has been a growth in trade, especially over the last five decades;
- trade has become increasingly focused on particular trading blocs;
- there should be specialisation through trade;
- some countries may lose from trade as their particular historic advantages are eroded.

With regard to the last factor in particular, and because of the costs of economic change, countries have sought to protect their industries, using such devices as

- subsidies – payments to reduce domestic prices down to, and sometimes below, world competitive levels;
- tariffs – taxes placed on imports to raise prices up to, and above, domestic prices;
- quotas – limits on the supply of imports into the domestic market;
- Voluntary Export Restraints (VERs) – agreements by an exporter to limit exports into a foreign market.

All prevent the free flow of goods between countries. These types of measures may appear to protect a country's domestic firms but may not bring long-term advantage as other countries may respond. Table 3.17 shows that Japanese market import penetration is low. This could imply that the Japanese do not wish to buy foreign imports, but it could suggest that there are various barriers to entry into the Japanese market. Trade barriers also proliferate when the global economy slows and international trade tensions rise.

EXHIBIT 3.3

FT

The risks for world trade

Keeping world markets open and the international trade system functioning smoothly is essential to global economic recovery. Yet just when stability is most needed, it is being called into question by increasing strains, caused by slower world growth and big shifts in trade flows.

United States and European steel makers are screaming for protection from cheap imports, particularly from Asia. The United States is castigating Europe and Japan for restricting access to their markets, while last week a Pacific rim trade liberalisation initiative ended in acrimonious failure. To cap it all, the US and EU are at daggers drawn over trade in bananas.

So far, serious economic damage has been avoided. But the threats to free trade could increase next year, if growth slows sharply in the United States, while its trade deficit mounts. That prospect is alarming Bill Clinton's administration. While enjoining the rest of the world against closing markets, it appears increasingly unsure about keeping its own open. Mr Clinton and his officials now say that unless other countries shape up, the United States may turn protectionist.

The temperature seems set to rise as the US presidential election campaign gets under way. Vice-president Al Gore, the Democratic front-runner, is vulnerable to an economic slowdown and rivals' accusations that he is soft on foreigners. He also needs the support of protectionist-minded unions. His response is to talk tough on trade, in terms which recall Mr Clinton's tirades against Japan a few years ago.

Fortunately, United States freedom to resort to unilateral trade measures has been curtailed by the World Trade Organisation's strengthened authority to enforce multilateral rules. That has deprived United States threats of sanctions on unco-operative trade partners of much of their force. Washington has acknowledged as much by increasingly pursuing trade complaints in the WTO.

The United States is also pressing for strict compliance with WTO rulings, notably in the case of the European Union's banana regime. But its tough stance is a two-edged weapon. If a WTO ruling ever requires the United States to change its laws, it will face equally strong pressure to comply. Yet it is far from certain that Congress, in its current mood, would oblige. Failure to do so could undermine the whole basis of WTO rules – an outcome no responsible government wants. That danger makes it even more vital to reduce international trade tensions.

One key is to recognise that many are unrelated to trade policy. Border barriers do not explain sluggish demand and low import absorption in continental Europe

▶

Exhibit 3.3 continued

and Japan. A much more important reason is slow deregulation and restructuring of their economies.

Europe's cross-border merger wave suggests parts of industry may be rising to the challenge. The euro may add impetus. But the message has yet to get through to many European governments – in particular Germany's – and still eludes Japan. United States impatience at their failure to reform aggressively underlies much of the friction with its main trading partners. The longer they delay action, the greater the risk that United States frustration will stoke up the pressure for protectionism.

Source: 'The risks for world trade', Leader, *Financial Times*, 23 November 1998

The growth of tariffs leads to economic inefficiency, companies find it difficult to export their products and world activity levels fall. The General Agreement on Tariffs and Trade (GATT) was set up in 1946 in an attempt to reduce tariffs which had been ratcheted upwards between the two world wars.

There have been eight rounds of GATT trade talks which have become increasingly complex, given the rise in membership from 23 countries in 1946 to 125 in 1995. Moreover, the original trade talks focused on reducing tariffs, particularly those on manufactured goods since manufactured goods were those more likely to be traded, whilst the last GATT round, the Uruguay Round (1985–93), considered much wider trade issues including the trade in services and agricultural products. Whilst GATT has been successful in reducing tariffs generally, countries have still sought to limit the free flow of trade via other means. In particular barriers such as quotas, voluntary export restraints and non-tariff barriers – the use of red tape, government legislation, and health and safety factors – have come increasingly into play.

A final conclusion to the Uruguay Round was agreed in December 1993 and involved 28 separate accords devised to extend fair trade rules to agriculture, services, textiles, intellectual property rights and foreign investment. Tariffs on industrial products were cut by more than a third and were eliminated entirely in eleven sectors. Non-tariff barriers were to be converted into tariff barriers and these would subsequently be removed. Table 3.18 shows the subjects covered in the various GATT rounds.

GATT itself was wound up and replaced by the World Trade Organisation (WTO) on 1 January 1995. The WTO differs from the GATT in a number of respects.

- The WTO has a greater global membership, comprising over 132 member countries with 34 observer governments (May 1998).
- It has a far wider scope than GATT, considering, for the first time, trade in services, intellectual property protection and investment.
- It is a fully-fledged international organisation in its own right, while GATT was basically a provisional treaty by an ad hoc Secretariat.

TABLE 3.18   The GATT trade rounds

Year	Place/Name	Subjects covered	Countries
1947	Geneva	Tariffs	23
1949	Annecy	Tariffs	13
1951	Torquay	Tariffs	38
1956	Geneva	Tariffs	26
1960–61	Geneva (Dillon Round)	Tariffs	26
1964–67	Geneva (Kennedy Round)	Tariffs and anti-dumping measures	62
1973–79	Geneva (Tokyo Round)	Tariffs, non-tariff measures, plurilateral agreements	102
1986–93	Geneva (Uruguay Round)	Tariffs, non-tariff measures, rules, services, intellectual property, dispute settlement, textiles, agriculture, creation of the WTO, etc.	123

- It includes a package of instruments and measures to which all members are agreed, whilst GATT included a number of policy measures agreed to by a limited range of countries.
- It contains a much improved version of the original GATT rules.
- It reverses policies of protection in certain sensitive areas such as textiles and clothing and voluntary export restraints which had been tolerated under GATT.
- It is to be the guardian of international trade, making sure that the agreements at the Uruguay Round are adhered to. It will also examine on a regular basis the trade regimes of individual member countries and try to reduce the level of trade disputes.

Members of the WTO are also required to supply a range of trade statistics. Perhaps more importantly, it has a speedier trades dispute settlement mechanism, encouraging parties to go for arbitration rather than resorting to their own domestic trade policies.

Trading blocs

The GATT rounds were a series of multilateral trading agreements – trade agreements between different countries at the same time but in different geographical areas of the global community – and these have been paralleled by a process of regional trade agreements. These trading agreements can be of various types such as

- those that involve reducing tariffs between member countries;
- those that involve reducing tariffs among member countries together with a common external tariff against non-members;

- those that are similar to the second but promote much more commonality than trading arrangements and can cover other rules and regulations, such as common currencies and defence/social policies.

Table 3.19 indicates those regional trading agreements operating as at January 1995.

TABLE 3.19 Reciprocal regional integration agreements notified to GATT and in force as of January 1995

Europe

- European Community (EC): Austria, Germany, Netherlands, Belgium, Greece, Portugal, Denmark, Ireland, Spain, Finland, Italy, Sweden, France, Luxembourg, United Kingdom
- EC Free Trade Agreements with Estonia, Latvia, Norway, Iceland, Liechtenstein, Switzerland, Israel, Lithuania
- EC Association Agreements with Bulgaria, Hungary, Romania, Cyprus, Malta, Slovak Republic, Czech Republic, Poland, Turkey
- European Free Trade Association (EFTA): Iceland, Norway, Switzerland, Liechtenstein
- EFTA Free Trade Agreements with Bulgaria, Israel, Slovak Republic, Czech Republic, Poland, Turkey, Hungary, Romania
- Norway Free Trade Agreements with Estonia, Latvia, Lithuania
- Switzerland Free Trade Agreements with Estonia, Latvia, Lithuania
- Czech Republic and Slovak Republic Customs Union
- Central European Free Trade Area: Czech Republic, Poland, Slovak Republic, Hungary
- Czech Republic and Slovenia Free Trade Agreement
- Slovak Republic and Slovenia Free Trade Agreement

North America

- Canada–United States Free Trade Agreement (CUFTA)
- North American Free Trade Agreement (NAFTA)

Latin America and The Caribbean

- Caribbean Community and Common Market (CARICOM)
- Central American Common Market (CACM)
- Latin American Integration Association (LAIA)
- Andean Pact
- Southern Common Market (MERCOSUR)

Middle East

- Economic Cooperation Organisation (ECO)
- Gulf Cooperation Council (GCC)

Asia

- Australia–New Zealand Close Economic Relations Trade Agreement (CER)
- Bangkok Agreement
- Common Effective Preferential Scheme for the ASEAN Free Trade Area
- Lao People's Democratic Republic and Thailand Trade Agreement

Other

- Israel–United States Free Trade Agreement

Source: WTO, *Focus*, Newsletter, May–June 1995, No. 3, p. 9

The European Union is one of the oldest and best known trading blocs. More recently the United States has become increasingly focused on the issue with the development of the North American Free Trade Agreement (NAFTA), signed in 1993, which includes the United States, Canada and Mexico. Chile has also opened negotiations with the United States and by the year 2010 it is forecast that a free trade area will exist which will cover the whole of the Americas.

A further, ambitious project is under way to create an Asia–Pacific Economic Cooperation Forum (APEC) to include America, Japan, China, Taiwan, Malaysia, Australia and other countries with Pacific coastlines. The European Union is looking for closer ties with its Eastern European neighbours and there is even talk of a free trade area being set up between the European Union and North America.

To what extent do free trade areas affect companies? We need to consider the concepts of trade creation and trade diversion. When a free trade area is set up it encourages trade between member countries. This is trade creation, and it occurs because previous barriers to trade will be reduced, giving each of the countries' industrial sectors reduced costs and therefore encouraging inter-country trade within the free trade area. Countries now outside of the free trade area may find it more difficult to sell their products to countries which used to be outside the free trade area but are now inside the free trade area, since they often face external tariff barriers. Thus trade is diverted away from the countries outside the free trade area because the price of their products will increase as they face external tariffs, and countries inside the free trade area which do not face any of these external tariffs are more likely to trade between themselves.

There are also problems with rules of origin. Is a Japanese car made in Europe Japanese or European? The definition may depend on the proportion of parts that are provided by the European country. If it is European then it can be exported within the free trade area subject to no additional tariffs.

What appears to be happening gradually is the development of trading areas or zones. These might lead to significant reductions in trade barriers which then get transmitted throughout the rest of the world in a kind of domino effect, the result of which is that many firms are likely to be winners. On the other hand trading blocs can lead to some firms being excluded from markets thereby damaging exports.

Exchange rate systems

Within the context of the growth in trade we should consider how different exchange rate regimes affect business behaviour.

Fixed exchange rate

A fixed exchange rate is one which fixes the value of one country's currency against another. The advantages of a fixed exchange rate are twofold. First, the stability that it provides for businesses encourages long-term contractual arrangements between businesses. Second, since the exchange rate cannot be altered to restore a country's competitiveness, if it runs a balance of payments deficit, it imposes a disciplined fiscal and monetary policy, which means a tight grip on inflation.

Floating exchange rate

At the other end of the possible set of exchange rate regimes lies the floating exchange rate – an exchange rate which responds to the market demand and supply of the currency. If there are differences between the demand for and supply of the domestic currency, the price of the currency, the exchange rate, should automatically adjust. Thus one of the great advantages of this type of exchange rate is that it does not require any government intervention; market forces undertake the adjustment. The problems with floating exchange rates are that there are increased uncertainties for traders which may lead to a greater proportion of short-term contracts. In addition, if import prices rise then the balance of payments deteriorates, leading to a depreciation in the value of a currency. This restores the competitiveness of exports but further raises the price of imports, and these increased import costs can feed through into domestic inflation levels.

The history of exchange rates since the end of World War II is one of movements between relatively fixed and relatively floating exchange rates. But what about the impact of the various exchange rate regimes on businesses? Evidence suggests that fluctuations in the exchange rate are more likely to have harmful effects on investment. That is, both international investment and domestic investment may be reduced, with concomitant effects on exports, in general, and output in particular. It follows that any move to a fixed exchange rate system within Europe reduces this uncertainty and improves businesses expectations. With regard to whether flexible exchange rates lead to more imported inflation it was notable that when both Italy and the United Kingdom left the European Exchange Rate Mechanism (ERM – a fixed exchange rate system operated by the European Union since 1980) in 1993, the depreciation in the value of their currencies did not lead to higher inflation and higher interest rates as might have been believed. In fact it had quite the reverse effect.

The decision, therefore, to adopt one exchange rate system in preference to another may not be taken purely on economic grounds, but may be the result of the need for closer political ties. It is to this area of closer integration and commonality of policy within Europe that we turn next.

QUESTIONS

1. Give examples of the various forms of non-tariff barriers countries use to limit the free flow of trade. How successful has GATT been in tackling these various forms of non-tariff barriers?

2. Consider the advantages and disadvantages of both fixed and flexible exchange rates for organisations.

3. What are the implications of the growth in trading blocs for export-orientated businesses? Are the implications the same for companies which do not export commodities?

EUROPE AS ONE

The establishment of the European Economic Community in the 1950s was a major step towards helping trade within the European 'six' at the time. The widening of membership to the twelve member states by the early 1980s, the further reductions in trade barriers and the setting up and development of pan-European forums appeared to move the major Western European countries to a stronger economic position. In the 1980s there were, however, signs to suggest that the EU twelve were experiencing some difficulties. First, their growth rates had begun to slow and, second, unemployment levels had begun to rise. There was also a distinct lack of co-operation between Community members and a weakness of common policies. Since a number of countries appeared to be pulling in different directions, the European Community appeared to be paralysed. In addition, the massive technological changes that had taken place in the world had, to some extent, left Europe behind. It was importing increasing amounts of high-technology products. The Community's external position, to some extent, was weakening and it was becoming increasingly dependent on foreign suppliers. The fragmented home market in the Community was seen as a main reason for this development and there was a desire to speed up integration between the various member countries. It was argued that a single European market would stimulate the scale of production, marketing, and R&D, and also strengthen competition, enhancing the efficiency and competitiveness of European industry. However, to get to this stage the European Union needed to tackle the various barriers that existed within the EU market. These included:

- physical barriers such as form-filling and the cost of keeping frontier posts to govern goods and people;
- fiscal barriers – differences in VAT and excise duties distorted trade patterns;
- technical barriers – obstacles to the free movement of goods, services, labour, and capital; throwing open to competition the bidding for local or national government contracts (public procurement).

Once the shackles on markets within the European Union had been reduced this could lead to increased social problems. Therefore, to deal with the social element of the SEM programme, a social charter was drawn up. This was approved in December 1989 by eleven of the European Union states – without the United Kingdom. The Social Chapter of the social charter was originally set to cover a range of social issues including employment rights, minimum wages, the right to training, collective bargaining, freedom of association, and health and safety. Because of the controversy this raised the final proposal was much watered down, leaving many of the social issues to be decided by the individual nation states, rather than the Commission. In 1998 the United Kingdom signed up to the Social Chapter.

A further condition deemed as necessary for the successful creation of the 'internal market' was a change in the Community decision-making procedures, which until then required unanimous decisions in the Council of Ministers. This condition was met by the adoption of the Single European Act in 1987 whereby in matters concerning the internal market qualified majority voting was permitted. The SEA included the provision that the internal market should be completed before the end of 1992.

Mergers and acquisitions in the Single European Market (SEM)

Assessing the outcome of the Single European Act is difficult, since, as Kay (1993) and Swann (1992) note, it is likely to have effects in the long term as well as in the short term. The removal of barriers between markets was expected to encourage competition, yet there was an upsurge in merger and acquisition behaviour as firms previously in protected markets sought to reduce the competitive edge in the Community by merging or taking over their rivals.

Figure 3.6 indicates that the SEM does appear to have led to a major restructuring of industry from merger and takeover activity. This is particularly the case for cross-border mergers between EU companies (18.7 per cent of all mergers and acquisitions). Between 1986 and 1995 the number of mergers and

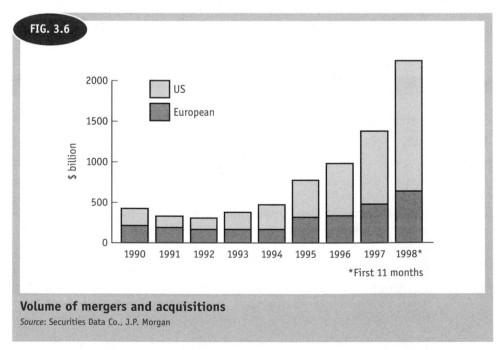

FIG. 3.6

Volume of mergers and acquisitions
Source: Securities Data Co., J.P. Morgan

takeovers increased from 720 to 2296 in manufacturing and from 783 to 2602 in services. However, over 60 per cent of these mergers and acquisitions were between domestic companies, suggesting that the SEM has also led to restructuring in the national market due to the greater level of competition.

Other impacts of the SEM

The European Commission made an evaluation of the SEM in their report, *The Impact and Effectiveness of the Single Market*, in October 1996. It should be noted when considering the results from this report that a number of the pieces of legislation pertaining to the Single Market did not come into force until 1994 or 1995. Having noted this, the report noted the following effects:

- Both intra-EU trade (trade between EU countries) and extra-EU trade (trade between the European Union and the rest of the world) have been boosted. Despite predictions that the SEM would lead to 'fortress Europe', this does not appear to have taken place. In addition the SEM appears to have accentuated intra-industry trade.

- There has been an increase in both domestic and across-border mergers and acquisitions. There is some indication of increasing concentration ratios across Europe, but on a national level the growth in some European countries' industries appears to be much greater relative to other countries. This is particularly the case in Germany and France compared with the UK. Thus the SEM appears to have reinforced different industry structures in some countries rather than equalising it between member countries.

- There has been a growth of FDI into the European Union, rising from 28.2 per cent of world FDI in the mid 1980s to over 44 per cent in the 1990s.

- On a macroeconomic level, investment appears to have risen by 1 per cent more than it would have done without the SEM, inflation is 1 per cent to 1.5 per cent less, and income between 1.1 per cent and 1.5 per cent higher. Employment is estimated to have grown by somewhere between 300 000 and 900 000.

- For businesses, the view was that the SEM had removed a number of obstacles to cross-border transactions and that greater opportunities were apparent. This level of approval was stronger for manufacturers than services, and larger companies compared with smaller ones.

At this stage, although the SEM has removed a number of barriers, there are still barriers that exist through culture, tradition and consumption patterns. At the same time there are still gaps in the legislation such as the issue of European company law and the harmonisation of taxation. In addition, some of the legislation has still to be enforced, adopted or implemented. One area where the SEM has had an impact is that of duty-free shopping, as Exhibit 3.4 indicates.

A further obstacle to a single market is that of different national currencies and it is to this issue that we now turn.

EXHIBIT 3.4

Industry counts cost of losing duty-free sales

FT

The abolition of duty-free shopping on journeys between European Union countries will lead to the loss of about 19 000 jobs in the UK travel, tourism and drinks industries, according to a study by the Centre for Economics and Business Research.

The centre, an economic consultancy, says the loss of income from selling duty-free goods after June 30 1999 will force ports, airports and transport companies to raise charges for travellers. It calculates the abolition of the duty-free concession will add an average of £14 to the cost of journeys between the UK and other EU countries. This will cut the number of UK travellers visiting other parts of the EU by 635 000 by 2005, and reduce the number of EU visitors to the UK by 115 000. 'There will be a very significant disruptive effect to the UK economy,' said Professor Douglas McWilliams, the centre's chief executive. 'It will do a lot of damage in particular areas and to particular industries.'

The study forecasts nearly 5000 jobs will go in Kent, around the Channel ports, and more than 1000 jobs are at risk in the Scottish Highlands, heartland of the Scotch whisky business. The hardest hit sectors will be travel (8591), tourism (2236) and the supply industries (8180). Across the whole European Union, the study estimates the job losses will be 127 000, 90 per cent of which will go in the two years after abolition.

The impact of next year's abolition was already being felt in the travel industry, according to George Ryde, the Transport and General Workers' Union's national officer for the civil aviation industry. KLM UK, formerly Air UK, had already decided to reduce cabin staff on intra-EU flights by one member – a loss of around 100 jobs. He added that some of the United Kingdom's regional airports, which relied heavily on flights between the United Kingdom and European destinations, would put development projects on hold if they lost the income from duty-free sales. This would damage economic regeneration in the Midlands and the north where the airports were magnets for inward investment. John Prescott, UK deputy prime minister, had recently called for a review of the decision.

Source: Willman, J. 'Industry counts cost of losing duty-free sales: Economic consultancy suggests that 19 000 jobs could be lost.', *Financial Times*, 27 February 1998

Maastricht and beyond

The SEA can be viewed as a major step towards an economically united Europe, but it is not the ultimate step. If Europe is to be truly united then some argue that there is a need for both political and economic union. The move towards economic union was further developed through the proposal for a Europe-wide single currency. The move towards monetary union (EMU) seeks to co-ordinate both monetary and economic policies. Monetary policy, presently the jurisdiction of each country, would be transferred to a European central bank and national currencies would be replaced by a single currency. Fiscal policy would be in the hands of national governments, but subject to common policies and restrictions. The move towards monetary union, as enshrined in the Treaty of European Unity 1992 (the TEU or Maastricht Treaty), was to proceed in three stages (a useful outline of this process is given by Arrowsmith, 1995). The TEU also included a number of other important issues, detailed in Chapter 7.

EMU Stage 1 (July 1990 to 31 December 1994)

Completion of the internal market, including totally free movement of goods, capital and persons (before 31 December 1992). Countries will begin their economic convergence programmes and are expected to enter the narrow band of the Exchange Rate Mechanism.

EMU Stage 2 (1 January 1994 to between 1997 and 1999)

The Establishment of a new European Monetary Institute (EMI) to enhance co-operation between European Union central banks, co-ordinate monetary policy and prepare for the setting up of a European Central Bank. The EMI will seek to establish the convergence of the European Union member economies. The convergence criteria as set out under Maastricht were as follows:

- price stability: the inflation rate should not exceed the average inflation rate of the three countries with the lowest price increases by more than 1.5 percentage points;
- currency stability: the exchange rate should not have been subject to de-valuation within the narrow band of the exchange rate mechanism of the European Monetary System during the last two years before the date of entry in EMU;
- public deficit: the budget deficit must not exceed 3 per cent of GDP;
- national debt: the public debt must be lower than 60 per cent of GDP;
- interest rates: the nominal long-term capital interest rates should not deviate by more than two percentage points from the average of the long-term interest rates of the three countries with the lowest interest rates.

The TEU dictated that the EMI should specify, by the end of December 1996, the regulatory, logistical and organisational framework for the European System of Central Banks. It also set a date for the beginning of the third stage.

EMU Stage 3 (between 1997 and 1999)

Founding of the European Central Bank (ECB) and the European System of Central Banks which incorporates the ECB and the national central banks, responsible for the implementation of the monetary policy set by the ECB; replacement of national currencies of the member states admitted to the EMU by the Euro.

There are two other important dates to note also. On 1 January 2002 ('E-Day'), circulation of Euro banknotes and coins will be started. National currencies will be completely replaced by the Euro within six months after the introduction of Euro notes and coins. On 1 July 1 2002, the legal status of national banknotes and coins is cancelled.

Many commentators felt that a number of countries would find it difficult to meet the criteria. However, the drive towards meeting the targets for entry into a single currency surprised many observers and by 25 March 1998, 11 out of the 12 countries which sought entry in the first wave, i.e. 1 January 1999, were deemed to have satisfied the entrance criteria, as shown in Table 3.20.

The only country failing to meet the criteria was Greece. Although Sweden, Denmark and the United Kingdom meet most, if not all, of the criteria, they chose not to be members of the first wave.

There is no doubt that some element of fudging has occurred. Critics suggest that taking the less strict interpretation of the entry criteria will weaken the Euro and it will come increasingly under speculative attacks. Moreover, it is not whether countries meet the entry criteria in March 1998 that is important – the real issue may be to ensure sustainable convergence over the longer term.

Given that European monetary union will go ahead, what are the main advantages and disadvantages for Europe and European business of a single currency?

Impact of EMU on policy

Monetary policy has become the concern of the European Central Bank rather than being the responsibility of each nation's monetary authority. This means that an individual country will not have the ability to use interest rates for any other economic requirement such as to reduce domestic unemployment or control domestic inflation. Conversely, to what extent would a country which is not within the single currency have the ability to set interest rates which diverge greatly from those set by the single currency bloc? It was notable that during the ERM crisis in the early 1990s UK interest rates were forced to respond to those being set at that time in Germany. Thus even if a member of the European Union stays out of a single currency its interest rates may need to respond to those being set by the ECB.

Although monetary policy would be lost as a management tool, for each of the individual monetary authorities this would leave fiscal policy as the only form of discretionary economic policy available. The Maastricht Agreement set out targets for fiscal policy expenditure as a prerequisite for joining the single currency and the worry about fiscal mismanagement resulted in 1996 in a proposal to establish a new European Union 'Stability Council' – a council set up to monitor individual nations' fiscal policy expenditure after entry into a single currency – to make sure that fiscal policy guidelines were not breached. If these fiscal policy guidelines were breached then the Stability Council would have the power to impose fines on

TABLE 3.20 Countries satisfying the EMU entrance criteria

Country	Inflation HICP (a) January 1998	Government budgetary position						Exchange rates ERM participation March 1998	Long-term interest rates (c) January 1998
		Deficit (% of GDP) (b) 1997	Debt (% of GDP)						
			1997	Change from previous year					
				1997	1996	1995			
Reference value	2.7	3.0	60.0						7.8 (d)
Belgium	1.4	2.1	122.2	−4.7	−4.3	−2.2	yes	5.7
Denmark	1.9	−0.7	65.1	−5.5	−2.7	−4.9	yes	6.2
Germany	1.4	2.7	61.3	0.8	2.4	7.8	yes	5.6
Greece	5.2	4.0	108.7	−2.9	1.5	0.7	yes (e)	9.8 (f)
Spain	1.8	2.6	68.8	−1.3	4.6	2.9	yes	6.3
France	1.2	3.0	58.0	2.4	2.9	4.2	yes	5.5
Ireland	1.2	−0.9	66.3	−6.4	−9.6	−6.8	yes	6.2
Italy	1.8	2.7	121.6	−2.4	−0.2	−0.7	yes (g)	6.7
Luxembourg	1.4	−1.7	6.7	0.1	0.7	0.2	yes	5.6
Netherlands	1.8	1.4	72.1	−5.0	−1.9	1.2	yes	5.5
Austria	1.1	2.5	66.1	−3.4	0.3	3.8	yes	5.6
Portugal	1.8	2.5	62.0	−3.0	−0.9	2.1	yes	6.2
Finland	1.3	0.9	55.8	−1.8	−0.4	−1.5	yes (h)	5.9
Sweden	1.9	0.8	76.6	−0.1	−0.9	−1.4	no	6.5
United Kingdom	1.8	1.9	53.4	−1.3	0.8	3.5	no	7.0
Europe average	1.6	2.4	72.1	−0.9	2.0	3.0		6.1

Notes:
(a) Percentage change in arithmetic average of the latest 12 monthly harmonised indices of consumer prices (HICP) relative to the arithmetic average of the 12 HICP of the previous period.
(b) A negative sign for the government deficit indicates a surplus.
(c) Average maturity 10 years: average of the last 12 months.
(d) Definition adopted: simple arithmetic average of the 12-month average of interest rates of the three best-performing member countries in terms of price stability plus 2 percentage points.
(e) Since March 1998.
(f) Average of available data during the past 12 months.
(g) Since November 1996.
(h) Since October 1996.
Source: European Commission

any individual country if it takes more than a year to address its fiscal policy difficulties. Without such a stability pact it is possible that excessive borrowing by one or more of the members of EMU could force up interest rates for all other members.

A third problem with a single currency is that a member country faces a loss of discretionary exchange rate policy – the ability of a country to set its own competitive exchange rate. Before a single currency comes into existence a country could use its exchange rate as a 'safety valve' if its economy became uncompetitive, say, due to some internal shock, such as a rapid decline in competitiveness of one sector of its economy. Under a single currency an internal shock of this type could only be solved by the use of massive European Union fiscal transfers (regional policy).

Impact of EMU on business

The impact on business can be looked at from a number of perspectives: first, from the point of view of businesses in countries within EMU; second, from the perspective of businesses in European countries which stay outside of EMU, such as UK or Swedish businesses; third, it can be considered from the position of businesses from countries which are non-European but which are active in European markets.

Impact on businesses inside

From a purely economic standpoint, a single currency appears to be attractive for at least some of the larger countries within the European Union. It is anticipated that there would be low inflation and interest rates, participation in setting of these interest rates and belonging to a currency area which may have more equal power with those of Japan and the United States.

In addition, a single currency removes transaction costs (the costs of converting one currency into another), which are estimated to average at 0.4 per cent of EU GDP. This may be especially important for small and medium-sized businesses. The United Kingdom may find that it benefits less from transaction cost savings as it undertakes a higher proportion of its trade with the United States and the Commonwealth. Competitive pressures will increase due to price transparency. This will almost certainly lead to more bids and mergers both within and between countries in the Euro bloc. Price transparency will also lead to organisations reviewing their business strategy and could encourage innovation as companies try to stave off competition. Moreover, price transparency will force companies to put an end to differential pricing across the European Union. For the airline industry and travel firms there will also be greater price transparency of air fares and hotel rates. At present the same airline often charges more for flying from, say, Frankfurt to London than in the opposite direction. It may also charge different fares on two routes of similar length. The travel industry will see some elements of price instability reduced with the development of the Euro. Tour operators who booked hotel rooms without knowing the conversion rate of the local currency and therefore the impact on package holiday prices will have this problem diminished. However, ECTAA (European Association of Travel Agents and Tour Operators) puts the changeover costs from investment in new technology and finance at between 1.8 and 3 per cent of a travel company's turnover. This is a significant cost for a low-margin industry. In fact it is also possible that destinations such as Spain and Italy, which have had relatively weak currencies in Europe, could find themselves at a competitive disadvantage compared with Turkey, Greece and North Africa, if the Euro is strong.

Along with price transparency there will also be wage transparency. Therefore, employees will know whether companies in the same sector but in different countries are offering higher wages.

One of the main benefits from a single currency comes through the greater development of intra-EU trade and through its greater certainty this could boost investment (FDI and domestic), growth and jobs. In the case of FDI a single currency should lead to greater market size/potential and this should encourage larger amounts of FDI.

Set against the benefits outlined above are a number of potential costs following from the establishment of a single currency. First there are the costs of transition. Machines and other appliances (such as cashpoints and parking meters) which take money will have to be adapted to take the Euro. Staff need to be trained and customers educated. During this transition period 'double bookkeeping' or dual currency price tags and invoices will be required. This could be administratively expensive. For example in Germany more than half the accounting software cannot deal with more than one currency (DIHT, 1995).

The Euro could also alter things such as the basic design and size of a product. A marketing price of say, £45.99, when changed into, say, 55.73 Euros, may make the product unattractive psychologically. Should the product be rounded up or rounded down? To achieve an acceptable price point, retailers may have to ask suppliers to alter the way the product is manufactured.

Impact on businesses outside

In terms of merger and acquisition behaviour, because the UK is not in the first wave of countries entering monetary union there may be important consequences for foreign acquisition activity in the UK. Marsh (1997) suggests that while many US executives stress concern about Britain's lack of entry in the first wave, they expect the UK to join eventually and therefore this is not affecting their behaviour on acquisitions of UK firms. However, for some investors the greater costs of being outside the Euro bloc could lead to some FDI being switched to countries within the Euro bloc. This has been mooted as being one of the factors which has led to Toyota undertaking new investment in France rather than expanding its activities in the UK. British companies will also face exchange rate risks not experienced by those in countries with the Euro area. In fact it is possible that the pound may become more volatile.

Even though the UK is not in the first wave, some foreign companies, notably Siemens and Daimler-Benz, are planning to force their UK suppliers into accepting the Euro as the sole means of payment. UK bankers too are expecting that the Euro will be pushed through the supply chain, as the affected suppliers might hedge against the resulting currency risk by forcing their own suppliers to accept Euros. Marks & Spencer will even accept the Euro at its cash desks, which means that they will accept cheques denominated in Euros. Thus non-participation will not shield the UK from the effect of EMU. So companies will prepare irrespective of the UK government's strategy – in terms of their technical systems, financial systems and even corporate strategy. Moreover, UK companies will be affected by the way in which their European competitors change their strategy. For example, if Ford Europe or BMW change their pricing strategy so that cars carry a single pre-tax price tag in Euros, this will have major effects on the UK car market.

The single currency is meant to provide lower interest rates, thus companies in countries outside the Euro bloc may face a competitive disadvantage in the cost of borrowing. The Euro is also meant to encourage better integration of national markets and in some industries this will mean restructuring.

Once the Euro is in operation there is likely to be further co-ordination of economic policies, most likely in the areas of tax harmonisation – the bringing into line of the different tax rates operated by the European Union countries. Corporation taxes, indirect taxes and excise duties would be the most likely cases. This may not result in unified rates of tax, but is likely to lead to common tax bands and rules. Thus the UK would be expected to adopt whatever the prevailing rules are among the Euro-11. The development of a single currency for Europe, therefore, poses many opportunities and threats for businesses, the outcome of which will not be equally borne by all sectors of the business community. For countries such as the UK, Sweden and Denmark, the costs to industry of remaining outside the single currency may dent competitiveness.

Finally, major concerns have been expressed regarding the whole process of moving towards EMU. Concern has been voiced that the financial and monetary elements of the economy have been prioritised and very little emphasis has been given to unemployment. In fact, as mentioned above, in an attempt to hit the targets set out at Maastricht, the European economies have been operating tight fiscal policies which have resulted in growing levels of unemployment and labour unrest, an example being the general strike in Greece in 1997. In addition, for some countries the role of privatisation has taken on a higher profile as they seek to balance their government accounts. If countries need to be more convergent in their performances as expressed through the Maastricht criteria then any fudging of the criteria for entry will make the member countries of a single currency less convergent and thereby weaken the strength of the Euro. As Desai (1997) notes, the Euro could be a severely deflationary currency. Countries may have to continue tight fiscal stances and if entry is too broad in the first instance then the Euro will be seen as a weak currency. It is this view, and the notion that the United Kingdom will not be amongst the first wave of countries into the single currency, which has led to a large revaluation in the pound sterling during 1997/98. It is hoped that, for everyone's interest, the Euro bloc is made up of strongly convergent countries. It is certain that the run up to and working of the single currency provides a big challenge for the European Union nations in their attempt to strengthen their trading position.

Further enlargement of the European Union

Although the European Union has agreed that enlargement will not be considered until economic and monetary union has been securely established, the European Union sees its expansion to include a number of the Central and Eastern European countries (CEECs) as being a natural progression. In the light of this, the European Union set out, in Agenda 2000 in July 1997, the criteria for future membership. The criteria included a number of political and economic 'hurdles':

- political issues: the stability of democratic institutions, the rule of law, the respect of human rights and the protection of minorities;

- economic issues: the Copenhagen European Council suggested that these economic issues required the existence of a functioning market economy as well as the capacity to cope with competitive pressures and market forces within the Union. Included here was that significant barriers to market entry and exit should be absent, that there should be adequate price stability and sustainable public finances and external accounts, and that the finance sector should be sufficiently well-developed so that savings could be channelled towards productive investment;

- the ability to take on the obligations of membership (the *acquis communitaire*), including adherence to the aims of political, economic and monetary union.

After consideration of these criteria, the European Commission deemed that Hungary, Poland, the Czech Republic, Slovenia and Estonia would be in the first wave of new entrants in the next millennium (2005/6). In addition Malta (if it so wishes) and Cyprus have also been included in the first wave. This leaves Slovakia, Romania, Bulgaria, Latvia and Lithuania as countries in the second wave (2010/11).

These new entrants bring a number of costs and benefits to the European Union. The CEECs' economies are at present twice as agricultural as the EU15 and two and a half times poorer in terms of GDP per head. In addition the five Eastern European economies taken together amount only to approximately 6 per cent of the EU15 economy. Thus East–West integration should expand the CEECs' opportunities much more than those for the EU15. Trade with the CEECs is dominated by Germany from the European Union, but overall export trade with the CEECs accounts for around 5 per cent of total EU15 exports. Of total exports from the CEECs, the EU15 account for approximately 60 per cent of export trade.

Further costs to the EU15 can been seen in terms of the level of agricultural and regional support which the CEECs hope to gain from the current members. However, proposals put forward by the EU15 in March 1999 are seen as, first, a way to reduce agricultural expenditure as part of the total European Union budget and, second, a way to cope with the costs the new entrants will bring with their large agricultural sectors. The CEECs will also require large amounts of regional funding given that many, if not all, of their regions have GDPs per head lower than 75 per cent of the EU average. There will be, therefore, many problems to overcome in the further expansion of the European Union, but if all proceeds to plan, by the year 2010/11, the European Union will be seen to cover a region from the Arctic to the Mediterranean and from the Atlantic to the Baltic. The costs of this expansion may be high for the big four countries of the EU15 but this may be a price worth undertaking to reduce the political risks of having the CEECs outside of the European Union.

QUESTIONS

1. What could be the advantages, to organisations, of a country joining a single currency? What may be the costs for those countries which join and those which opt to stay out?

2. What are the implications for organisations in the current EU15 from widening the membership of the European Union?

CONCLUSION

Business has always been aware of the impact of the economic environment on its performance and behaviour, but whereas businesses would have paid heed to changes in their own domestic economy, the post-war years have seen markets becoming increasingly internationalised so that it is now changes in the international economic environment which may have more impact. Some of these changes, such as alterations in environmental legislation, agreements about the provisions for labour and corporate tax changes, have a direct impact on organisations; other changes alter the environment in which the firm exists and, although not aimed at organisations directly, potentially have greater influence on their behaviour. Here we would include on an international level the Single European Market legislation, the South-East Asian crisis, monetary union and external trade policies.

Over the last two decades closer co-operation between countries in pursuing macroeconomic policies and the internationalisation of markets has been evident. Such moves require co-ordinated actions amongst countries. Of course, not all industries are uniformly affected by international macro policy changes – companies which undertake much of their business in the domestic market are perhaps less affected by exchange rate changes than those which are exporting a proportion of their output abroad. In addition, as discussed in other chapters, the impacts of technology are not equally borne by the different sectors in our society. Nonetheless, businesses cannot ignore the changes that are taking place in their domestic, European and international environment. If they do so it is highly likely that in the longer term their position in the market will be weakened to such an extent that their businesses are placed at a competitive disadvantage.

SUMMARY OF MAIN POINTS

We have seen that organisations are influenced by the many forces at play in the wide economic environment and therefore need to be aware of these forces and to be able to react to any changes. The main points made are that:

- GDP can be used as a measure of economic growth and it can be used to compare the performance of countries.
- Governments have four main economic goals: a high level of growth, a strong balance of payments, a low level of inflation and low unemployment.
- The goals of the government may conflict.
- Governments may steer the economy and smooth economic cycles through the use of fiscal and monetary policy.
- The industrial structure of an economy is not static but open to continual change.
- Generally, Western industrial economies are seeing a shift to the tertiary sector.
- Growth can bring with it improvements in real incomes and a greater choice of goods and services.
- Growth in the European Union has been under pressure.
- Growth also brings with it costs to society.
- Inflation can be caused in a number of ways – through excess demand in the product market, through increased costs of the factors of production, and through slack monetary policy.
- Inflation causes both internal and external problems. It may make exports less competitive and therefore imported goods more competitive with domestically produced goods. Internally to the economy it harms those groups on fixed incomes, can cause disruption in the labour market, can lead to even higher levels of expected inflation and favours debtors rather than creditors.
- Government expenditure plays a key role in the functioning of all countries.
- In the pursuit of the targets for monetary union, unemployment is higher than it would have been in the 11 single currency countries.
- The UK economy still has a number of skill gaps which prevents the economy operating efficiently.
- Countries have become more open, and this has stimulated international trade.
- Evidence suggests an increasing Europeanisation of trade and the establishment of trade blocs which could both create and divert trade.
- Exchange rates affect trade and competitiveness.
- The Single European Market provides opportunities to businesses.
- The process of integration arising from the TEU is likely to continue and gather pace.
- The European Union will seek to expand its membership during the next millennium to encompass a number of Central and Eastern European countries.

NET SEARCH

See Chapter 2 (p. 77).

REFERENCES

Alesina, A. (1989) 'Politics and business cycles in industrial democracies', *Economic Policy*, 8.

Arrowsmith, J. (1995) 'Economic and monetary union in a multi-tier Europe', *National Institute Economic Review*, May.

Bacon, R. and Eltis, W. (1976) *Britain's Economic Problem – Too Few Producers*, London: Macmillan.

Beckerman, W. (1985) 'How the battle against inflation was really won', *Lloyds Bank Review*, 15 January.

Begg, D. (1995) 'The anatomy of a recovery: the UK since 1992', *The Begg Update*, McGraw-Hill, No. 5, Summer.

Burda, M. and Wyplosz, C. (1997) *Macroeconomics: A European Text*, 2nd edn, Oxford: Oxford University Press.

Cook, M. (1996) 'Economic growth and the UK economy', *Economics and Business Education*, Summer.

Cook, M. and Healey, N. (1995) *Growth and Structural Change*, London: Macmillan.

Desai, M. (1997) 'Better late than never: strong enough to cope', *Observer*, 17 August, p. 2.

DIHT (1985) Survey among 733 German Companies, September.

European Commission (1996) *The Impact and Effectiveness of the Single Market*, Communication to the European Commission, EU.

Forsyth, P. and Kay, J.A. (1980) 'The economic implications of North Sea oil revenue', *Fiscal Studies*, 1, 1–18.

Friedman, M. (1977) 'Inflation and unemployment', *Journal of Political Economy*, 85 (3).

Higham, D. and Tomlinson, J. (1982) 'Why do governments worry about inflation?', *National Westminster Bank Review*, May.

Kay, N. (1993) 'Mergers, acquisitions and the completion of the internal market', in Hughes, K.S. (ed.) *European Competitiveness*, Cambridge: Cambridge University Press.

Marsh, P. (1997) 'US engineers invest in EMU', *Financial Times*, 31 December.

Meadows, D., Meadows, D. and Randers, J. (1992) *Beyond the Limits*, London: Chelsea Green Publishing.

OECD (1994) *Manufacturing Performance: A Scoreboard of Indicators*, Paris: OECD.

Phillips, A.W. (1958) 'The relationship between unemployment and the rate of change of money wages in the United Kingdom', *Economica*, 25, November.

Sharp, M. (1992) 'Technology and dynamics of integration', in Walker, W. (ed.) *The Dynamics of European Integration*, London: Francis Pinter.

Soteri, S. and Westaway, P. (1993) 'Explaining price inflation in the UK: 1971–92', *National Institute Economic Review*, 144, May.

Studd, S. (1996) 'The training challenge', *Leisure Opportunities*, May.

Swann, D. (1992) *The Single European Market and Beyond: A Study of the Wider Implications of the Single European Act*, London: Routledge.

4

THE TECHNOLOGICAL ENVIRONMENT

Stephen Swailes

LEARNING OBJECTIVES

On completion of this chapter you should be able to:

- explain the differences between technology and innovation;
- understand how different business sectors use technology;
- describe some of the generic technologies that are affecting organisations;
- outline how different countries support research and development;
- explain how technology affects organisations, people and jobs;
- describe how technology can be managed in an organisation.

KEY CONCEPTS

- technology
- knowledge
- innovation
- research and development

- change
- competitiveness
- organisational implications
- managing technology

INTRODUCTION

Elsewhere in this book, the effects of other macroenvironmental forces on organisations are explained. Economic forces impact upon the organisation through factors like exchange rates, interest rates and consumer spending. Social forces affect the availability and skill levels of labour and the demand for products. Political forces set a broad framework for all organisations and have a strong influence upon public sector organisations.

This chapter introduces the business end of the biggest story of the twentieth century – the proliferation of technology. Unlike political, economic and social forces which are mostly beyond the influence of organisations, managers have much more control and influence over technological forces. After all, technology is developed by organisations for use by organisations, but, as we will see, its pace can outstrip society's ability to cope with it.

Technology adoption can be affected by the attitudes and behaviour of employees and some organisations are unable to respond to technological shifts and eventually fail because of this.

Technology growth and adoption are linked to other macroenvironmental forces such as the health of the economy which influences the funds that organisations invest in developing and implementing new technology. Political decisions can have a strong bearing upon government-sponsored research and development targeted at particular sectors or upon assistance programmes for industry. In contrast, governments have to respond to the changes that new technologies bring to society. Political control over news and information is now harder to achieve in an era of satellite communications and powerful media.

While all the primary macroenvironmental forces discussed in this book wax and wane in their intensity and impact over time, the technological environment is currently witnessing a 'new wave' of information-based change. Recent trends towards deregulation in Western markets and intense cost-centred competition have highlighted the central role of technology in helping to maintain and build competitive advantage.

WHY IS TECHNOLOGY IMPORTANT?

What is technology?

We need a definition of technology if we are to understand the relationship between organisations and their technological environment. Technology is not the same as knowledge or innovation. Knowledge is a theoretical or practical understanding of a subject such as chemistry, mathematics, sociology or language. Knowledge and understanding about a subject are usually added in very small increments, usually following continuous improvements to existing products and manufacturing processes.

Technology is the application of knowledge into some practical form, typically applied to industrial and commercial use.

There can be a prolonged period between the early development of technologies and their evolution into widely usable formats. Galbraith (1967) defines technology as 'The systematic application of scientific or other organized knowledge to practical tasks'. Monck *et al.* (1988) developed this view: 'Technology is both a body of knowledge concerned with the solution of practical problems, what we might term know-how, and also the tools and artefacts which are used to achieve those solutions: it is both software and hardware.' Gillespie and Mileti (1977) define technology as 'the types and patterns of activity, equipment and material, and knowledge or experience to perform tasks'. This latter definition suggests that all organisations use a technology and that only the intensity varies. A useful summary of some of the definitions of technology can be found in Berry and Taggart (1994).

Innovation is the spread and diffusion of technology into society and organisations.

Freeman (1982) saw technical innovation as the introduction and spread of new and improved products and processes in the economy. This definition includes the design, manufacturing, and management activities involved in the marketing of a new or improved product. Three examples of the links between between knowledge, technology and innovation are shown in Table 4.1. A knowledge of genetic structure, for example, has led to the development of tests for specific genes and, possibly, will lead to the proliferation of gene modifying drugs.

A historical perspective

Technology has been both attractive and problematic to entrepreneurs and managers for at least the past two hundred years. Throughout the nineteenth century businessmen and workers did not see science as being applicable to their world and treated new machinery simply as labour-saving devices (Coleman and MacLeod, 1986). The British synthetic dye and electronics sectors declined in the face of German and American competition because British attitudes to management stood in the way of businesses responding to technological innovation from competitors (Shiman, 1991).

TABLE 4.1 Examples of knowledge, technology and innovation

Knowledge	The accumulator (late nineteenth century)	Hydrocarbon chemistry (early twentieth century)	Identifying particular genes (1980s and 1990s)
Technology	Alternator and electric turbines	Internal combustion engine	Tests for specific genes, gene-sensitive compounds
Innovation	Power stations	Automobiles, aircraft	Gene-modifying drugs and genetically modified foods

In the nineteenth century the British cotton textile industry had no international competitors although domestic competition was intense. When corporate economies such as America and Japan became serious threats, British cotton textile companies were unable to respond with appropriate technologies because of the particular industry structure that had evolved (Lazonick, 1981, 1983). This example highlights a link between industry structure and technological change. Structure can impede change, yet we will see later that technology can be a driver of structural change.

A study of Japanese companies from 1929 to 1984 identified that the Japanese economy shifted from mining and light industries to heavy and chemical industries and (after World War II) to automotive and electronics industries. Companies able to absorb Western technology into efficient production systems quickly established market dominance (Yamazaki, 1988). Hence, technology can help create industries but can also be instrumental in their decline.

Technology and modern organisations

While some technologies are associated with harmful effects such as pollution and exploitation of the earth's resources, the overall benefits of technological change to mankind are well documented. Indeed, technologies are now being sought to break the link between economic growth and pollution. Governments are anxious to raise national competitiveness and living standards which, in turn, requires a sound economy in terms of job availability, working conditions and public spending. Technology impacts on these factors. It has a large influence on productivity and, in the same way that products pass through a life cycle, so do companies and industries. Sometimes technology accelerates the decline of an industry, as word processors signalled the end for mechanical typewriters. Technology also adds new sectors – the new biotechnology industry, for example, now employs around 40 000 people in Britian.

Faced with intense competition from low-cost countries, some sectors decline in terms of output and employment levels although often a core of efficient producers remains. Leather manufacture is an example where, faced with intense competition from southern Europe and South America, output in North America and northern Europe has fallen as a consequence. In this example, tanners in high-cost countries have access to manufacturing technologies that improve both the efficiency of the company and working conditions. The long-term problem, however, is that, when the manufacturing infrastructure (a network of machinery and component suppliers and distributors) of low-cost producers is more developed, they will also be able to install the same technologies. Thus a cycle occurs in which developed countries attempt to stay ahead of competing nations through continual renewal of their technological base and in which the less technologically advanced organisations can catch up through investment.

Thus technology can help to extend the lifetime of certain industries facing strong competition from less developed producers. It also contributes to economic development through new sector growth, which may arise because technology contributes to achieving competitive prices in world markets, for example in the telecommunications sector. This could arise from technologies that allow quick response to orders, consistent quality and cost reduction, but to support regeneration, growth and competitiveness companies need to invest. The amount of spending on technology is huge, for instance, about 40 per cent of all capital spending in the United States is on technology (Courtenay, 1995).

One of the biggest trends affecting business organisations is globalisation, that is the convergence of consumer tastes and product designs on a worldwide scale and the formation of organisations with global or multinational scale operations. Consider, for example, the world automobile market, where manufacturers seek scale economies by marketing the same designs across many countries. This reduces costs and so makes good business sense. As newly industrialised countries (NICs) such as Thailand and Indonesia develop their economic and social infrastructures, technology greatly assists the process. Technology is a major change agent in world markets and the pace of technological change is rising.

It is widely believed by managers that investment levels go some way to explaining productivity levels and, in turn, the ability to be competitive in world markets. Arguably the most successful business product ever, the photocopier first introduced by Rank Xerox, was the foundation for that company's domination of the copier market for upwards of twenty years, until patent protection expired. Investment by Canon in copier technology later allowed them to develop their own strong position in the copier market.

We can build a picture of technological development underpinning national growth and consumer living standards. While the British are often stereotyped as being good inventors but poor innovators, the problem may not be as bad as is sometimes made out (Edgerton, 1987). Emerging technologies present some thorny problems for society as illustrated by the case of genetic science (see Exhibit 4.1).

EXHIBIT 4.1

Genetic science

Recent advances in genetic knowledge mean that it will soon become possible to develop self-administered screening tests for faulty genes, in the way that pregnancy or blood cholesterol levels can now be tested for with over-the-counter kits. These tests will be applicable to unborn babies and to adults to see if there is a gene defect or an increased likelihood of developing a particular condition such as Alzheimer's disease or Huntingdon's Chorea. Furthermore, our improved understanding of genetics will accelerate the production of new drugs to treat conditions such as cystic fibrosis.

Genetic technologies pose some fundamental questions for certain types of businesses, as well as society in general. When each person's genetic fingerprint is identifiable to the extent that their health and even personality can be predicted

Exhibit 4.1 continued

then how much of this information will be available to employers? How might insurance companies react to the widespread availability of gene testing? Would persons identified as having an increased risk of developing a particular condition in life be able to get insurance? Under present arrangements they may not, so insurers will need to re-evaluate long-held views about personal eligibility for policies with inevitable consequences for the portfolio of policies offered.

The spread and use of genetic information will need tight control by responsible agencies such as the police and by government. At the moment, scientists are ahead of society in the understanding and use of genetics. The political and media interest in genetically modified foods in early 1999 illustrated, despite assurances from the scientific community, that there can be a long lag between society's acceptance of technology and state-of-the-art science. Society needs to catch up so that restraints and restrictions are enforced and acceptable uses of genetic science become clear.

QUESTIONS

1. To what extent do you agree with the statement that British engineers and managers are not as effective at exploiting new technology as those in other industrialised countries?

2. Can Europe and North America sustain a technological lead ahead of newly industrialising countries? Will the NICs eventually catch up?

FUNDING OF RESEARCH AND DEVELOPMENT IN INDUSTRIAL COUNTRIES

National differences

Technologies do not simply evolve by accident: they are the fruits of dedicated research projects that had clear objectives. In our look at the technological environment we need, therefore, to examine how research and development (R&D) is organised in industrial nations. Research spending in the European Union from public funds was 53 billion ECUs in 1994, equivalent to 144 ECUs per capita. The European Union publishes details of the research it wants undertaken to meet particular social and technical objectives and organisations are free to bid for contracts. At national level, individual governments operate a structure for managing and funding R&D. The Department of Trade and Industry in the UK manages the funding of government-held research laboratories and non-profit-making research and technology organisations. Funding for projects is also provided through Research Councils such as the National Environmental Research

TABLE 4.2   Types of research and development

- *Basic or fundamental research* is experimental or theoretical work undertaken mainly to acquire new knowledge. Such work would be undertaken without a particular end use in mind. An example would be the synthesis of new chemical compounds but without any notion of what use they might have.

- *Applied research* is undertaken with some application in mind, for example, investigating the usefulness of innovations to medicine or materials technology.

- *Experimental development* is the use of both basic and applied research in the development of materials, processes and synthesis and would typically extend to the prototype or pilot stage.

Source: Adapted from Research and Experimental Development (R&D) Statistics 1996, *Economic Trends*, 537, August 1998, HMSO

Council and the Economic and Social Research Council. The main types of research activity are indicated in Table 4.2.

The main sources of R&D funding are government and business enterprises. Universities and non-profit organisations also carry out some of the work. Expenditure on R&D changes along with the general state of the economy. When an economy is buoyant, central government's revenues from taxation support public spending, a small part of which goes towards R&D. In a buoyant economy, business enterprises may enjoy relatively higher profits which, in turn, can be invested in R&D. Table 4.3 shows gross expenditure on R&D in the UK in 1996 at £14.3 billion, up 3 per cent on the recession-hit 1991 but still down on the peak year of 1990 when total spending was at its highest level for some years. Note that Table 4.3 shows spending by the sector performing the R&D, not the sector funding it. There are some important differences between the two.

In 1996, universities provided 1 per cent of funding for research and development but performed 19 per cent of the work (by value) because of the funding they get from the government and business enterprise. Business enterprise funded 47 per cent of R&D but carried out 65 per cent of the work because it too is receiving funding from the government and from private sponsors such as charities and medical foundations. Government funding of British enterprise R&D fell from 23 per cent in 1986 to 14 per cent in 1992 and to 9.4 per cent in 1996. This is partly caused by cutbacks in expenditure on defence-related R&D. Companies have compensated for the fall by attracting funding from abroad which now represents about 22 per cent of funding.

TABLE 4.3   Gross expenditure on R&D in the UK

Performed by	1988	1990	1992	1994	1995	1996
Business enterprise	9779	10171	9364	9719	9511	9301
Higher education	2225	2290	2349	2770	2771	2792
Government	1921	1915	2037	2166	2043	2070
Non-profit	252	286	247	178	182	177

Note: Figures show expenditure by the sector performing the research, and are given in £m, at 1996 price levels. Government spending includes Research Councils.

Source: *Economic Trends*, No. 537, August 1998 (Crown Copyright 1998; reproduced by permission of the Controller of HMSO and the Central Statistical Office)

TABLE 4.4 Gross expenditure on R&D as percentage of GDP

	UK	Germany	Japan	USA
1988	2.2	2.9	2.7	2.8
1989	2.2	2.9	2.8	2.8
1990	2.2	2.8	2.9	2.7
1991	2.1	2.7	2.9	2.8
1992	2.1	2.5	2.8	2.7
1993	2.2	2.4	2.7	2.6
1994	2.1	2.3	2.6	2.5
1995	2.0	2.3	2.8	2.6
1996	1.9	2.3	–	2.5

Source: *Economic Trends*, No. 537, August 1998
(Crown Copyright 1998; reproduced by permission of the
Controller of HMSO and the Central Statistical Office)

Table 4.4 shows the gross expenditure on R&D from 1988 to 1996 for several countries expressed as a percentage of each country's GDP. The UK spent 2.0 per cent of GDP on R&D in 1995 compared to 2.3 per cent for France and Germany, 2.6 per cent in the USA and 2.8 per cent in Japan. The UK, Germany and the United States have all reduced the share of gross national product given over to R&D during the period 1988–1996, whereas France and Germany have maintained their levels of spending.

At first glance, the percentages appear very similar, but it is important to recall that gross national product values are huge, e.g. £4680 billion for the United States in 1996 compared to £1043 billion for Germany and £739 billion for the UK. Small changes to the percentage of gross national product spent on R&D thus translate to large sums in absolute terms. For instance, 0.01 per cent of the USA's GDP is around £468 million. Table 4.5 shows gross domestic expenditure on R&D for European Union countries. For Mediterranean countries it is less than 1 per cent of gross national product.

Countries also differ in the way they fund and perform R&D. The governments of the UK, Germany, France and Japan typically fund over twice the amount spent in their own research centres. The United States funds about four times as much. Business enterprise typically funds about 70 to 80 per cent of the R&D it performs whereas Japanese companies fund virtually all of the R&D that they undertake. Also worth noting is that, despite overall reduced spending on defence-related R&D, the US, British and French governments still spend a large proportion of the funding on defence-related research. The United States spent 55 per cent of government-funded R&D on defence-related work compared to 37 per cent in the UK and 29 per cent in France. Germany and Japan spent less than 10 per cent. While it is impossible to make any causal link between defence spending and industrial competitiveness – indeed, United Kingdom defence spending secures many jobs in aerospace for example – these figures provide a good discussion point.

TABLE 4.5   Gross domestic expenditure on R&D in the European Union, 1993

	Percentage of GDP
EUR 15	1.99
France	2.45
Germany	2.43
United Kingdom	2.19
Netherlands	1.89
Denmark	1.79
Belgium	1.60
Italy	1.20
Eire	1.08
Spain	0.92
Portugal	0.62
Greece	0.50

Source: *Basic Statistics of the European Union*, 33rd Edition, 1996, Table 2.11b

An examination of R&D spending by socio-economic objective sheds more light on this point. Table 4.6 shows the main objectives for government-funded R&D in 1996. While some allowance should be made for the difficulty of categorising R&D projects to particular socio-economic objectives, Japan and Germany appear to target around 50 per cent of government-funded R&D at the advancement of knowledge, i.e. without necessarily having clear practical applications for the research in mind. The British in particular seem less comfortable with the notion of 'blue sky' research. This might reflect political and cultural norms in the United Kingdom such as the Anglo-Saxon capitalist tradition, pushing funders into a pragmatic mindset in which R&D funding is largely allocated to projects with commercial short-term objectives. While this outlook prevails in the United States also, their capital market is more willing to invest in technology companies. In the

TABLE 4.6   International comparison of government-funded R&D by socio-economic objective, 1996 (percentages)

Objective	UK	Germany	France	Italy	Japan	USA
Defence	37	10	29	5	6	55
Advancement of knowledge	30	52	35	53	49	4
Industrial development	2	13	5	9	3	0.6
Energy	0.7	3	5	3	23	4
Health	15	3	5	9	3	18

Source: *Economic Trends*, No. 537, August 1998 (Crown Copyright 1998; reproduced by permission of the Controller of HMSO and the Central Statistical Office)

United States, about two-thirds of venture capital is channelled into growth based on new technology compared to less than a quarter of European investment (Galley, 1998).

Another factor to consider is the cost of borrowing money. In the United Kingdom the cost of capital is high, compared to Germany and Japan, and businesspeople are pushed towards a short-term outlook on investment and risk-taking (Rassam, 1993). In contrast, UK companies regularly pay out higher percentages of net earnings to shareholders than German and Japanese businesses (Foster, 1993). Cheaper borrowing is thought to encourage longer-term planning horizons.

Comparing countries on the basis of percentage of gross national product spent on R&D is a crude but useful measure and to give us a clearer comparison we need to take into account the nature of industry in a country, the extent to which it is labour or capital-intensive, and the average size of companies.

As noted elsewhere in this chapter, some industrial sectors are less research-intensive than others. In a labour-intensive business the main vehicle for value added is labour. In a capital-intensive business, plant and machinery are the main vehicles for value added. Labour-intensive sectors such as footwear and clothing manufacture tend to have low fixed costs and high variable costs. Capital-intensive sectors like electronics and chemicals have, in comparison, high fixed costs and low variable costs and tend to spend proportionally more on research and development than labour-intensive sectors. Average company size could also play a part in explaining the differences in national spending patterns as large companies spend more on research than small companies.

Research on sector differences (e.g. Small and Swann, 1993) suggests that large UK companies perform adequately and in some cases above average when compared to other countries in terms of R&D/sales ratios, but less well when R&D per employee is compared. However, ratios based on employee numbers do not make the best indicators with which to compare companies or countries. In reporting the size of their workforce, organisations may or may not include part-time employees, and they may not include persons employed in subsidiary organisations. Comparison on a per capita basis also does not account for the differing skill levels that may exist between organisations.

Value-based ratios are much better indicators of performance but are still vulnerable. Since sales revenues from an organisation's many business units are aggregated into a single group turnover figure it would be problematic to compare a single-product organisation, where all R&D supports all sales, with a multi-product company where R&D might only support some of the product lines. Furthermore, some sectors, e.g. the labour-intensive footwear and clothing industries, find it more efficient to channel much of their R&D activity through an industry research and technology organisation rather than conduct it in-company.

One of the strongest figures to use in inter-firm comparisons is added value, rather than sales. This is a more robust measure of an organisation's performance and can be related to R&D spending to get a good measure of R&D productivity. Added value is more complex to calculate, however. R&D to sales turnover

TABLE 4.7   Research and development expenditure as percentage of turnover for selected companies

Company	1994	1997
Glaxo Wellcome	15.2	14.4
Zeneca	11.6	12.6
GEC	4.0	7.0
Volkswagen Group	3.5	3.9
Volvo Group	3.0	4.7
Courtaulds	1.8	2.0
British Telecom	1.9	1.9
Anglian Water	0.7	0.8
Microsoft	–	16.9
British Petroleum	0.6	0.3

Note: Data relate to financial years which do not always represent calendar years
Source: Calculated from Annual Reports

ratios are given for selected companies in a range of sectors in Table 4.7. The highest-spending company, a computer software supplier, devoted about 17 per cent of turnover to research in 1997. Auto manufacturers spent about 4 to 5 per cent and an oil company spent less than 1 per cent.

Expenditure by business enterprises on research has increased overall for the past two decades. According to Dussauge *et al.* (1994) there are three possible reasons for this increase in corporate funding of R&D.

1. The Crisis hypothesis asserts that major technologies such as petrochemicals have life cycles. The oil shocks of 1974 and 1979 signalled the end of this major technology, and increased R&D spending by petrochemicals companies could be a search for cost reductions in the face of rising cost of oil-based products, or searches for replacement technologies.

2. The Sustained Progress hypothesis suggests that the time lag between discovery of new knowledge and commercial application is shortening, thus the funds needed to generate new technologies have increased.

3. The Global Competition hypothesis suggests that newly industrialising countries (NICs) compete strongly in low-technology industries, for example, textiles, clothing and footwear, and that some technologies are easily transferred to NICs.

Thus organisations in the industrialised countries such as Japan, the United States and northern Europe have been forced into funding high-technology programmes as a way of competing.

Table 4.8 shows the world's top 200 R&D spenders in 1997 grouped by country. The dominance of the United States and Japan in the table reflects the number of large companies in those countries. The highest-spending company in each country is also identified in the table along with its R&D expenditure.

TABLE 4.8   National breakdown of the top 200 companies by R&D expenditure, 1997

USA	91	General Motors	(£4984m)
Japan	42	Hitachi	(£2353m)
Germany	17	Siemens	(£2749m)
UK	15	Glaxo Pharmaceuticals	(£1216m)
France	14	Alcatel	(£1113m)
Switzerland	5	Asea Brown Boveri	(£1615m)
Sweden	4	Ericson Telefon	(£1857m)
Other countries	12		

Note: The R&D expenditure of the highest-spending company in each country is shown in the last column.

Source: adapted from *The UK R&D Scoreboard 1998*, Department of Trade and Industry

Sectoral differences

Not all business sectors use technology to the same extent, and technology is not equally important to all sectors. Some sectors such as small local service providers or organisations providing care services may use little or no technology in meeting their customers' needs although such organisations require considerable know-how to underpin their business operations, for example the know-how needed to provide care to persons with special needs.

Table 4.9 shows research and development expenditure as a percentage of turnover for leading companies in several high spending sectors. Some sectors, such as textiles, clothing and footwear manufacture, invest relatively small amounts of turnover in research, and that particular sector accounts for about

TABLE 4.9   Average R&D expenditure as a percentage of sector turnover, 1997

Pharmaceuticals	12.8
Computer software	12.0
Health care	11.5
Electronics and electricals	6.5
Chemicals	6.3
Engineering	4.1
Telecommunications	3.9
Vehicle manufacture and engineering	4.2
Food manufacture	1.2
Oil exploration and refining	0.7

Note: Percentages calculated by dividing total R&D expenditure by total turnover for companies in the top 300 international list.

Source: adapted from *The UK R&D Scoreboard 1998*, Department of Trade and Industry

0.3 per cent of R&D undertaken by businesses. This is not to say that they are somehow worse off than sectors with higher spending levels. Labour-intensive sectors are characterised by small companies which individually are not large enough to justify their own research and development department. They have tended to centralise their R&D efforts in industry research centres as this has been the most efficient way of conducting research and development for the sector. Developments then transfer from the research centre to individual companies. Technology remains important to labour-intensive sectors but on a different scale. Technology tends to be used for incremental process improvements such as combining two or more operations so that labour can be released from the production process, automating some processes such as cutting garment sections and cutting multiple layers of fabric, and developing new fabrics or polymers that can be cut and moulded to give enhancements to the manufacturing process or the final product.

It is partly because of the difficulty of achieving radical technological break-throughs that some sectors remain labour-intensive. In sectors such as clothing and footwear manufacture, some of the manufacturing operations needed to assemble the products require manual manipulation and joining of parts. Until solutions are found to the immensely complex problems of manipulating irregu-larly shaped components in three-dimensional space and joining them to very high accuracies such sectors will continue to await breakthrough technologies that will alter the cost structure of the industry.

By contrast, in pharmaceutical manufacture, it is by the development of a new drug or of new ways of synthesising a compound that companies can gain a distinct advantage over their competitors. Developments of this complexity require dedicated in-house research, for two reasons: first, to keep control over very complex projects so that research spending is managed effectively; second, to keep industrial secrets (intellectual property) within the organisation to retain a competitive advantage.

However, we will see later that collaboration with other organisations is an important way of supplementing in-company activities. About 20 per cent of R&D performed in UK businesses takes place in the pharmaceutical sector. Pharma-ceutical research has a large appetite for new molecules with medical applications. Finding these molecules among the millions of potential molecular structures is costly. Even when drugs have been trialled and approved for use, damaging side effects can be identified. Boots Pharmaceuticals had to withdraw their Manoplax treatment for heart conditions for this reason.

An emerging technology to identify the likely properties of different compounds is known as combinatorial chemistry. The UK pharmaceutical company, Glaxo Wellcome, purchased a US company specialising in this technique for $533 million in 1995 as a way of rapidly integrating the new technology into its operations (Cookson, 1995). Mergers and acquisitions are widely used ways of acquiring technology. Glaxo Wellcome itself was formed in 1995 from the merger of Glaxo and Wellcome. Part of the rationale for the merger was a drive for greater economies of scale in R&D in an increasingly competitive sector.

QUESTIONS

1. To what extent are low defence budgets in Germany and Japan and their high spending on pure research linked to their status as leading economic powers?

2. If you were comparing companies in different countries in terms of their spending on R&D, what indicators could be used? (Hint: think of company financial statements and link certain figures to R&D spending.)

3. What indicators could be used to measure the effectiveness of a company's R&D department?

SOME GENERAL TECHNOLOGIES

It is not the purpose of this chapter to explain individual technologies in detail. They are well covered elsewhere and are so many and varied that to focus on any one would be of little use. However, there are some technologies that are having a big impact on many business sectors. These are highlighted below along with examples of some specific technologies in different sectors.

Information-based technologies

Information-based technologies have had a tremendous impact upon financial services such as banking, insurance and mortgage services. In this case technology is applied to the capture, storage, manipulation and retrieval of information. Much of the impact of technology in this sector has been to accelerate processing times, to replace labour and to change the nature of work that employees need to do. Technology's impact on financial organisations has arguably been revolutionary when compared to the more incremental impact seen in other sectors. Job losses have been severe and the technology has de-skilled the decision processes such that junior staff can be trained quickly to take responsibility for complex customer enquiries. An interesting question about these relatively recent changes, however, is to what extent the extensive labour cutbacks have caused a loss of organisational knowledge that will have negative effects. In the short term, the quality of decision making will diminish, staff loyalty and trust will stay low and customers will be unable to differentiate between providers (see Dopson *et al.*, 1998).

In addition to labour substitution, information technologies have blurred the boundaries between formerly distinct sectors (Porter and Miller, 1985). Developments in information technology, coupled with deregulation of financial markets in the 1980s, have allowed building societies to enter the market for insurance services and high street banks to offer mortgage products. Because of trends towards longer working hours and busier social lives, the banking service First Direct was set up to offer people 24-hour telephone banking.

Decision making in organisations is another broad area bolstered by information technologies. Corporate databases allow storage of product-market data on a massive scale and the idea of an organisation's data 'warehouse' and the concept of data 'mining' have arrived (Gooding, 1995). Because sophisticated IT systems have been used by organisations for perhaps ten to fifteen years, longer in some sectors, some organisations have created a data archive concerning sales, costs and operations management. An example would be to identify the demographic profile of a retailer's customer base and the way different products appeal to customers according to their position in the profile. Trends within the data archive are explored so that managers can make short-term decisions, for example, whether to withdraw a product or to extend a product into new outlets; and make long-term decisions about the best location of a new outlet, for example, a new supermarket site, or optimum timing and content for a forthcoming promotion or campaign.

Information technologies allow much closer scrutiny of individual products in retail outlets. Traditionally profit margins were thought of in terms of the difference between sales price and purchase price. But products come in different sizes, weights and pack quantities. These variables, and others, affect the actual cost of ordering, transporting and stocking products and thus actual profit margins can be less or more than simple selling price and purchase price would suggest. This concept, Direct Product Profitability, is brought to life with database software and is now important to retailers selling many different lines in a wide range of weights and sizes.

Advanced manufacturing technology

Historically, a manufacturing production line contained a sequence of processes arranged to add to or change a partly made item in some way. Machines were not connected or integrated and often performed only one process or, at best, only a few processes. When a new product passed down the line, each machine might have required substantial time to change settings. For example, changing the die in a press to stamp out body parts for cars might have taken up to a day.

Manufacturers have always preferred long production runs of the same product since the unit cost of producing the product falls as volume rises. This occurs through

- buying materials and supplies in bulk at lower unit costs;
- gaining experience of making a single product so that problems and breakdowns can be quickly overcome;
- operators becoming more skilled and efficient at making the product.

Collectively, these factors combine to produce an experience curve, on which unit costs continually fall as volume output rises. This experience curve effect (see Chapter 2) lies behind some decisions made by organisations when they take over or merge with another organisation. By integrating with another organisation's experience, the total experience of making a product is increased and, in theory, unit production costs will fall. However, there are many reasons why mergers and takeovers may not be as successful as originally intended, and the experience curve benefits do not always accrue.

Pressures for change that start in consumer markets often conflict with the production department's desire for long runs of the same product as it requires product innovation and renewal to be a key part of an organisation's marketing strategy. Companies that rely on long production runs to minimise costs may find their cost structures compromised by consumer demand for product innovation. Shorter production runs are required and some organisations are unable to respond to the challenge. Flexible manufacturing systems have helped manufacturers make that response by making shorter production runs more cost-effective, by reducing both set-up costs and changeover times for machines. Decision-making and tooling-up times are also reduced. For example, to tool up for a new product traditionally involves manual design drawing, making patterns for new components or tools, manufacture of tools to cut or mould a new component, and re-tooling of machines to cope with new products or components.

Advanced Manufacturing Technology (AMT) has opened up new possibilities.

1. Machines can be easily re-programmed so that a single machine can cope with changes to processing requirements of different components as they pass through a production line. For example, on a car production line, different fixings are tightened to different levels by the same machine depending on the model of car being worked upon.

2. Machine re-setting is faster.

3. Machines can share and exchange information about the specification and processing needs of different products so that a machine informs the next process in the sequence.

4. Many different processes can be combined and undertaken by one machine.

AMT typically involves computer-aided design (CAD) and computer-aided manufacturing (CAM). CAD allows clothing or engineering patterns, for example, to be designed on a computer screen and stored for easy alteration and re-use. CAM systems receive and interpret CAD data to co-ordinate the production process.

Designs are now commonly built on a computer screen. When the design is confirmed the digital information is fed into the next stage so that components are generated from the computerised design and the information used to engineer, for example, new tools or moulds. Designs can be transmitted from European or North American headquarters to offices and factories in low-labour-cost countries where the product is manufactured. Processes that once took several weeks have been reduced to a few days.

Technological initiatives vary widely between different industrial sectors. Some of the key initiatives currently being followed are shown in Table 4.10.

TABLE 4.10   Some current technological initiatives

Chemical industry

- waste reduction
- recovery of chemicals used in manufacturing processes (intermediate chemicals)
- reduction of harmful emissions
- formulation of novel pesticides and fungicides
- more ecologically friendly fuels and lubricants
- replacements for harmful products such as CFCs
- water-based rather than solvent-based products

Energy

- developing clean technologies
- recovery and recycling
- control systems for energy production

Information technology and electronics

- mobile communications
- novel optical fibres and optoelectronic communications
- development of new services, e.g. video on demand
- semiconductor services
- printed circuit board design
- imaging technologies (image scanning, storage and retrieval)

Manufacturing and materials

- high-speed manufacturing coupled with precision and automation
- innovations in joining technologies (adhesives, welding)
- new polymeric materials with enhanced processing and properties

Source: adapted from *The Industry File*, Oakland Consultancy, Cambridge, with permission

Supply chain management

Installation of AMT has also coincided with a major remodelling of the manufacturer's supply chain. Traditionally, buyers dealt with many suppliers of materials who tended to be treated in an adversarial way. Suppliers were often switched to enable the buyer to obtain the lowest cost for an item. This relationship evolved in the time of long production runs and relatively long product life cycles. When market changes pushed in the other direction, retail and industrial buyers pushed manufacturers to find ways of making smaller quantities of more items and to deliver them much more quickly. This was made possible with AMT and IT. Point-of-sale data capture in retailers is analysed to identify the quantity of stock items to reorder. This data can be transmitted to a manufacturer who is able to tool up rapidly to make the item.

Manufacturers have similar links with suppliers so that the materials needed to make a product can be ordered and delivered. Thus time has been eliminated from the total supply chain. Meeting customer needs in a just-in-time (JIT) environment has also altered the relationship between organisations in the chain. Because of the need to share information and better understand the customer's needs (customers are all those in the supply chain, not just the final consumer), organisations have tended to be much more careful about how they select suppliers. Supplier selection is a much more rigorous procedure with customers seeking assurances that suppliers can consistently meet price, quality and delivery targets. However, once selected, the relationship between suppliers and customer is more secure, organisations work for mutual benefit and long-term relationships are sought. This is in stark contrast to the adversarial, stand-off, type of relationship that commonly used to exist. The automotive sector is a good illustration of where supply partnerships have been forged. Life in the garden is not all roses, however, as supportive relationships do not exist in all sectors.

Business use of the World Wide Web

A survey of business use of the WWW (Ng *et al.*, 1998) shows that 50 to 60 million people use the Internet, and the number is growing fast. Airlines can make reservation systems open to passengers who book their flights and purchase tickets on-line. Companies can put their entire product catalogue on the Net and create a virtual showroom. Universities can place teaching modules on the Net and make distance learning more accessible and enjoyable. Communities of people who share common interests, for example doctors specialising in a particular medical condition, can share knowledge and information among themselves. The benefits to organisations of maintaining web sites include

- helping to establish a presence, e.g. a small company's web site could be more attractive and efficient than that of a well-known large competitor;
- the Internet acts as a distribution channel for electronic products (software, music, images) and thus lowers the cost of transactions;
- as transactions are one-to-one, the Net is suited to the advertising and sale of 'embarrassing' or personal products;
- business-to-business transactions are simplified;
- electronic business with small companies becomes viable.

The current limitations of web use include

- insecurity of financial transactions and the need for new forms of electronic payment to be developed (despite this, the value of e-commerce is growing fast);
- unacceptable connection times;
- the demographic profile of current web users restricts the potential for using it as a marketing medium;
- vulnerability of servers to 'hacking';
- virtually unrestricted and uncensored access to materials that much of society finds unacceptable which might, in the long run, alter society's attitudes to such materials.

Other types of communication between organisations are also boosted by the Internet. International and global companies require extensive communications between decision-makers in various countries. Travelling to meetings is costly and yet alternatives such as video conferencing have achieved only limited use. The Internet offers an alternative through posting information on a web site. Functional areas in global businesses, for example R&D or design, can communicate ideas, concepts and drawings quickly. Technical and scientific conferences can be held on the Internet if authors post their papers on a web site for browsers to read and respond to. While this is an important breakthrough, travel to face-to-face meetings will not stop. Humans are social animals after all.

Potentially, the Internet could revolutionise shopping habits by enabling customers to compare and scan a store's product range and order for home delivery. This seems likely to appeal to professional and managerial classes more than to other groups who might have lower motivation to shop electronically and who, conversely, could be motivated to adhere to more social shopping habits. We should take a cautious view of such possibilities, however, as our desire to rationalise the future often fails to foresee other trends that have a bearing on the issue. When computers began to proliferate in businesses there was much talk of the paperless office. In fact, the opposite happened because computers made editing and printing much easier and because business trends moved towards greater documentation to support business objectives, for example in quality management systems.

The Internet can also be seen as an early development in what is potentially a revolutionary transformation of business communications. Governments of advanced nations are encouraging the development of information superhighways as potential wealth creators and a series of initiatives at European and G7 level exist.

QUESTIONS

1. If trading on the Internet becomes secure, what would the implications be for suppliers of goods and services?

2. How could close ties between manufacturers be affected if a buyer is easily able to identify cheaper suppliers of components with the same quality and delivery times?

3. What are the barriers to major expansion of the Internet as a business medium?

TECHNOLOGY AND ORGANISATION

While technology, particularly IT, is often seen as a solution to an organisation's problems, the view that IT for its own sake will yield benefits is receding (Coffey, 1995). Managers need to be clear about the total impact that will come from investment in technologies. Understanding the impact is a complex task because cost-benefit analysis needs to account for much more than changes to incomes and expenditure, yet the non-financial costs and benefits are difficult to estimate. The difficulties of managing the best out of technology are illustrated by two particular problem projects. The TAURUS project, a computer system for the London stock exchange, was abandoned after about £500 million had been spent. The UK government reportedly became very concerned about a defence contract being handled primarily by GEC-Marconi (Gray, 1995). The Phoenix low-flying, unmanned reconnaissance aircraft was six years late in 1995 because of technical problems after over £200 million had been spent on the project.

A key problem in managing large technology projects is their vast size and the high numbers of people and organisations involved. Adcock *et al.* (1993) note that managers can have expectations of IT that exceed its capabilities. Technology installations need to be backed up by strategies for other critical factors, such as customer service and product delivery.

Information technology in particular has been linked to workplace stress levels (Cooper and Payne, 1990) caused by job and workstation redesign, worries about job losses or worries about retraining needs. As well as directly affecting individual jobs, changes caused by the introduction of new technology can indirectly affect other employees. Managers and supervisors, for example, have to plan and implement change and deal with the human issues arising, including their own fears about loss of control (Hughes, 1995). Because improvement policies are ongoing in organisations, they lead to continuous change and the pressure on employers and managers can seem never-ending. Simons (1986) identifies several human resource issues that need reviewing as a result of technical change:

- job evaluation and grading;
- career development and training;
- remuneration policies and working conditions;
- personnel planning; and
- labour relations.

Technology and organisation structure

According to Souder (1991), the vehicle for innovation is the organisation, and the organisation of the company 'has not kept pace with demands of modern technology'. He argues that classical management philosophies, which can be summarised as managers planning, organising and controlling the work of others through a hierarchical chain of command in which people from different specialisms have been organised into separate departments, are not conducive to innovation.

An assumption of the classical approach is that organisational efficiencies are best achieved through specialisation of tasks and subdivision into specialist units. This notion extended to individual jobs being clearly defined and distinct. Many people might have done the same job, but there was little overlap between jobs.

TABLE 4.11 Characteristics of organic and mechanisatic organisations

Organic	Mechanistic
No rigid rules	Many rules/low individual freedom
Participative/informal	Bureaucratic/formal
Views aired openly	
Face-to-face communication	Writtten communication
Interdisciplinary teams	Functional separation
Creative iteration	Long decision chains
Outward-looking	Slow decision making
Flexible adaptor	
Non-hierarchical	Hierarchical
Information flows up and down the organisation	Information flows up the organisation
	Directives come down the organisation

Source: adapted from Rothwell (1992)

By the early 1960s this form of organisational structure was recognised as being a significant barrier to the innovation process. Burns and Stalker (1961), in one of the most influential books on innovation management, called the classical organisational structure 'mechanistic' and argued that a different, 'organic' organisational structure was much more conducive to innovation. The main differences between mechanistic and organic structures are shown in Table 4.11.

In essence, organic structures are less burdened by rules and restraints upon employees, tasks are less rigidly defined and creativity is assumed to come from co-operation and exchange of ideas and information, facilitated by a less hierarchical chain of command. Managerial control is present, of course, but the climate is one of involvement, participation and sharing, rather than close supervision and demarcation. Horizontal co-operation across an organisation, rather than vertical authority relationships, is stressed.

Burns and Stalker (1961), however, also related organisation structures to the organisation's environment. Where environments were essentially stable – that is, the past tended to repeat itself, and predictions could be made with high degrees of confidence – the mechanistic form of organisation could be successful. Confectionery and insurance companies, at the time, fitted this category. Where environments were more dynamic – that is, less easy to understand and harder to predict – organic structures were more successful at supporting innovation processes.

The finding that mechanistic organisation structures could be successful in stable environments is probably still true today. However, far fewer sectors still enjoy a stable business environment. The first oil shock of 1974 signalled the vulnerability of Western oil-based product markets including transport, energy and plastics. Higher energy costs resulted thereafter and the search for non-oil-based energy sources began in earnest.

Political deregulation of the financial services market in the United Kingdom in the early 1980s had major impacts upon the stability of business environments for banks and insurance companies. Privatisation of the UK water, gas and electricity utilities has dramatically increased the rate of change and degree of uncertainty in those sectors.

The increasing complexity of markets evidenced through continuing cost pressures and pressure for internationalisation or globalisation of products and activities has affected once stable professional partnerships. Accounting and legal partnerships, for instance, which formerly operated in a stable environment have seen their clients' environments become more complex. KPMG, one of the world's largest financial consultants, found that it could no longer function with a structure based on historic lines, for example, separate audit and tax divisions. Clients' business affairs were becoming more complex through mergers, acquisitions and internationalisation, and so 'complete' consulting packages for business growth were sought. These complete solutions required integration of previously distinct business areas and in general a shift towards the organic organisation (Johnson, 1993).

We might now begin to expect that organisation structure needs to change with the business environment, to continually evolve to cope with fresh demands upon it. This idea of constant metamorphosis has been advocated by Greiner (1972). Whether environmental change is driven by new technology or not, Greiner's notion is worth remembering. Over short periods (up to a few years) organisational restructuring may be small and incremental in nature. During this time there will be periods when structure will not change at all. Every few years, however, a major transformational change is needed to realign the organisation with its fast-moving environment.

Technology and jobs

It is true that technological change does lead to loss (or displacement) of jobs. Yet this statement is too simple since it is the net effect of job losses and job creation that is more important. Job loss does occur but, simultaneously, new jobs are created in companies making and supplying new technologies.

The market for semiconductors, for instance, is worth around $250 billion and most of the growth occured in the 1990s. Double-figure growth is predicted. The world market for business software is worth around $14 billion and is growing. The multi-billion-dollar biotechnology industry is also only a few years old. Readers should be able to appreciate that the knowledge and skills required to work in these industries are very different to those needed in declining sectors such as mining, shipbuilding and textiles.

Studies of the impact of IT on organisations point to very little job displacement in manufacturing caused by innovation in production processes (Campbell, 1993). Job losses from organisational change have much more impact across all occupations than losses from technological change. Production and professional workers have mostly not been badly affected although clerical staff have proved more vulnerable. These findings have been supported by Matzner and Wagner (1990), who found that diffusion of new technology favours better quality labour, although there is a small net negative loss when considering jobs in both technology providers and adopters. It seems likely that there are several variables that can intervene between technological change itself and job change. The attitude of management to the job security of the workforce is one, the ability of workers to negotiate protection from job loss another.

In large publicly-owned organisations, technology, until recently, has consistently displaced labour from specific jobs, but public funding allowed the displaced workers to be absorbed elsewhere. Given the tightening of public spending now evident, and the threat of privatisation to public sector organisations, capital expenditure can now only be justified if savings can be demonstrated. Because future budgets are set on the basis that savings will be realised, it is no longer possible for displaced labour to be reallocated. If this stricter regime affects other organisations, then the belief that technology is not, on balance, a thief of jobs may have to change.

Technology and productivity

Conventional wisdom holds that technological change is a driver of productivity although it is not the only one. The USA is usually placed at the top of international productivity leagues, with the UK some distance behind. Such global comparisons, however, obscure the fact that in certain sectors, such as pharmaceuticals and agriculture, the UK is as competitive as any nation. Overall, however, the UK has some embedded features of its business environment that appear to impede progress (Lorenz and Smith, 1998). These include:

- a naturally smaller market than the United States and Japan, which both enjoy large domestic markets which make capital investment more attractive;
- a national culture which is thought to devalue manufacturing and production in favour of services, and which inhibits the training and development of engineers who can compete internationally;
- relatively poor management skills that fail to capitalise on creativity and productivity of employees;
- insufficient development of companies operating in high-growth sectors, such as electronics and electronic engineering, and reluctance to cast off declining and low-growth sectors, such as brewing and textiles.

Even when technology is available to a sector, organisations may not enjoy fully all the potential benefits from it. A study of the footwear manufacturing industry found that while technological change was a source of productivity growth, the industry had been slow to exploit the gains available to it (Guy, 1984) and technology had not diffused fast enough. Footwear is historically a low-profit industry, and a brief consideration of the sector using Porter's five forces model (see Chapter 2) shows why. Barriers to entry are small, scale economies occur at low volume, and there are many competitors who use price as the basis of competition. Much of the output is purchased by large retail chains with high power. In contrast, supplier power is weak and there is no substitute for foot-wear. The continuing low profit levels that this position brings to most footwear manufacturers acts as a brake on investment which tends to be sporadic, following relatively good profit years, rather than part of a long-term investment strategy. The returns on investment in these circumstances are limited (Guy, 1985).

Technological change is a major agent of productivity growth in the food and drink sector although other causes are returns to scale and an excess of workers in the short term (Clark, 1984). In chemicals, a highly research-intensive sector, both technology and the state of demand for chemicals are major productivity drivers (Clark, 1985). A study of paper manufacturing found three main ways of raising labour productivity – intensification, technological change, and rationalisation. Intensification refers to the reorganisation of workers into a more efficient arrangement and does not necessarily involve technological change.

Teleworking

Teleworking, or telecommuting, is a system in which an employee uses IT or telecommunications to perform work some distance away from the organisation for which it is carried out. It is prevalent in many sectors; typical teleworking jobs include information analysis, data processing, financial services, sales and journalism.

Sparked off by the recession of the early 1980s and 1990s, organisations began to look very closely at the cost of overheads like personnel services and data processing departments. There was a general trend to eliminate these functions from corporate structures and to buy in the services as needed. Often, displaced employees would establish a bureau and work for their former employer. When savings from overhead reduction had mostly been achieved, organisations turned their attention to the remaining employees. Organisation structures were 'flat-tened' by moving away from pyramid-like structures. Layers of management were eliminated, remaining managers had larger spans of control, and there were fewer grades of employees. Job security declined as the number of fixed-term and part-time contracts grew. The trend was towards a core of decision-making managers and a platform of flexible employees. The latest focus for cost-cutting is the cost of occupancy, that is, building costs, rents, rates and maintenance. Where employees are able to telework, the need for permanent office space is reduced. An organisation of 400 employees could exist with space for 100, knowing that 300 will be working at home, with customers or travelling.

Such changes though bring with them changes to the relationship between the teleworker and the organisation that need careful management (Chapman *et al.*, 1995; Teo *et al.*, 1998). These include:

- reduced promotion prospects caused by the employee's 'marginalisation', i.e. falling victim to the 'out of sight, out of mind' problem;
- reduced opportunity for peer interaction and professional development;
- reduced job security;

- confusion over the boundaries between home and work that influence social relationships;
- greater feelings of social isolation that can lead to low motivation;
- the need for a particular management style which is task-focused and relies on trust and shared responsibility.

These and other issues need to be managed if teleworking is to spread. Managers will have to manage without close control and this will require a revolution in the mindset of many. Employees will need to take responsibility for their own careers and act as if self-employed, looking after their own pension and sickness arrangements, as there will be little likelihood of reliable employment with a single organisation for more than a few years.

QUESTIONS

1. What factors might intervene to minimise the impact of technological change on job losses in an organisation? What other factors could cause job losses?

2. What are the factors that explain a nation's levels of international competitiveness?

3. How might teleworking affect the relationship between employee and employer? What could be the possible upsides and downsides?

4. How might delayering of organisations affect their ability to innovate?

MANAGING TECHNOLOGY

Technology development

Before the industrial revolution and the growth of the large organisation, important developments in, for example, metalworking and milling evolved over many hundreds of years and some came about by chance. People of independent means pursued life-long interests which gradually advanced understanding and occasionally led to a new exploitable technology. Several people worked independently, but simultaneously, on the steam engine, yet it is Stephenson's *Rocket*, of 1829, that is remembered. Accidental or random discoveries of important new knowledge such as Alexander Fleming's discovery of antibiotic behaviour are now very much the exception. In the main, discoveries and the innovations resulting from them are not random processes. Scientific and engineering know-how are usually deliberately focused on a problem in response to societal pressures or needs (Ayres, 1991). This is certainly the case today when business and government research funding is clearly targeted on, for example, specific social, industrial or agricultural problems.

Yet we should not expect technological progress to be in simple proportion to the amount of R&D invested. Barriers exist to advances which can prove particularly troublesome to overcome. Nuclear fission reactors were developed soon after the first fission (atom) bomb was exploded in 1945. The controlled nuclear fusion reactor once thought to be imminent after the invention of the fusion H-bomb in the early 1950s is still thought to be at least several decades ahead (Ayres, 1991, p. 32).

The state of related and supporting technologies also affects the rate of progress in an area. Consider for instance the growth in computerised travel booking systems and the increase in demand for air travel. This simple example shows how progress in one area can accelerate progress in another. Recently motor manufacturers have used advances in electronics to produce engine management systems to help maximise fuel economy. Catalysts are now commonly used to detoxify exhaust gases. But we may consider that the limits of efficiency and cleanliness from the internal combustion engine are being approached. Breakthroughs in vehicle technology await possible advances in fuel systems or radically new engine designs. Arguably, advances to automotive engines have held back the development of alternative drive units like electric motors.

Thus significant technological breakthroughs are not random happenings, nor are they purely dependent upon the amount of research and development by companies and nations. Ayres (1991, p. 41) suggests that important innovations occur in clusters after a scientific breakthrough that opens up new territories for process and product development. Researchers can be imagined pushing on a particular door until it begins to open. They may need to push for years, even decades, until the breakthrough emerges. If this simple vision of the technical environment is representative, then it raises some important questions for managers of research-dependent organisations:

- How do we determine how much money to invest in an area?
- What is the best organisation structure to get results?
- What collaborative or co-operative research is needed?
- How do we measure progress with particular research projects?
- When should we stop supporting a project?

The clustering of innovations was one of five causes of innovation identified by Rothwell and Wisseman (1991). They noted the connections between social, economic and technological developments as follows:

- There is a need for technological change – simply stated this says that technologies are developed when there is a need for them, as with the development of radar in the late 1930s.
- Very often, major inventions are not single advances, but rely upon clusters of related technologies to make them work. There may be a time lag between one breakthrough and a breakthrough in an important related area.
- Social resistance to change is well known, though it varies between nations and between age groups. America is associated with entrepreneurship and risk-taking and is open to change. Countries in Eastern Europe are not associated with such a spirit of invention. Satellite TV receiver dishes were prohibited in Iran to stop the spread of Western ideas and images (Temourian, 1995).

- In addition to technical capability (including expertise, finance, and organisation), driving force and dogged perseverance are needed to see projects through to marketable ends, such as new processes or products. The very short time between President Kennedy's announcement of a space programme and Neil Armstrong's lunar walk testifies to a national driving force.

- Social objectives are important. At any point in time, a society will have objectives for its development. These objectives in turn influence the direction of technology development. Volvo's pioneering work with semi-autonomous work teams in the 1970s may well reflect a general Scandinavian preference for group decision making.

Rothwell and Wisseman (1991) argue that there is a reciprocal relationship between technology and culture; technology follows culture and culture follows technology. Both statements seem to be true.

Integrating technology in the organisation

When business environments were mostly stable and the rate of technological progress was slow, technology could be integrated into production processes with minimum disruption to an organisation. That said, adopting new technology has never been easy. Think of the English Luddite movement of 1811–13, when organised gangs smashed machinery in cotton mills in a reaction to the threat posed to jobs, in a time of general economic depression.

Environments are no longer stable; they are turbulent, dynamic arenas. While technology, for some organisations, represents small incremental improvements to tools and equipment, it increasingly involves complex interactions between people and information-based systems. Complex systems cannot easily be integrated into organisations. In technology-intensive sectors, managers can no longer devise a strategy and a structure for an organisation and then seek technologies to make the strategy work. Advanced technologies need careful management if they are to make maximum contribution to organisations. They should not be seen as obedient servants to their masters. Technology choice needs to evolve at the same time as decisions are made about strategy and structure, not afterwards (Parthasarthy and Sethi, 1992). This is illustrated in Exhibit 4.2.

EXHIBIT 4.2

Managing technology

Scandinavian Airlines Systems (SAS) was a profitable airline throughout the 1960s and 1970s. But in 1979–81 SAS reported a small loss equivalent to about 0.6 per cent of turnover. The company was fundamentally sound, however, as revenues still exceeded operating costs. The accounting losses were made after adjusting for depreciation.

> **Exhibit 4.2 continued**
>
> The problem was largely caused by the climate and culture that existed within the organisation. Over the years SAS had invested in new routes and new aeroplanes and the prevailing internal culture was of a technology-driven company with rigorous operating procedures in both technical and customer domains. This preoccupation with technical issues had focused SAS away from the customer and had spawned a middle management bureaucracy to maintain it.
>
> A new chief executive appointed in 1981 recognised these problems and set about a transformational change process in which the customer took centre stage and technology was seen, properly, as the servant not the master of the company.
>
> *Source*: adapted from Ghoshal, S. (1994)

The organisation of research and development

There are several ways of organising successful R&D. The simplest approach is to manage in-house facilities under the control of an R&D director. This is the traditional approach. It gives full control over projects, and sensitive information is relatively secure. Problems with this approach have surfaced, however, as it can be slow and inward-looking. Given the trend towards shorter product life cycles and expanding legislation covering products, working conditions and the environment, shorter development times are needed. For instance, over 70 per cent of products sold by German electronics company Siemens are less than five years old (Wood, 1998). To accelerate idea generation and development, organisations actively seek collaborative projects, spin-offs, joint ventures, mergers and acquisitions to supplement in-house research.

Growing concerns about water and effluent qualities led Yorkshire Water to set up a partnership with the University of Manchester Institute of Science and Technology (UMIST) to develop an on-line biosensor to monitor the toxicity of water. Further development of the sensor is under way with the electronics company Siemens. Once installed, biosensors will allow faster detection and response to pollution incidents. Zeneca, a pharmaceuticals and agrochemical company formed by the ICI demerger, developed a new antibiotic with Sumitomo Pharmaceuticals of Japan. In an effort to keep ahead of emerging technologies, organisations seek collaboration or sometimes take over another organisation to gain access to their R&D know-how.

Organisations enter formal alliances to manage the transfer of technology between them. Rolls-Royce and Westinghouse Power Generators of the United States formed an alliance to cover the joint development of turbine technology and power plant. Rolls-Royce agreed to transfer aeroengine technology for incorporation in Westinghouse's industrial turbines for power generation (Tighe, 1995).

When large-scale development takes place, as with, for example building a major industrial complex, the client, possibly a government department, may want a turnkey project, that is, one where contractors supply and install all the

EXHIBIT 4.3

Managing technology – collaboration

Leading nations agreed through the Montreal Protocol to end the production of harmful chlorofluorocarbons (CFCs) by the end of 1995. CFCs are thought to interact with ozone in the upper atmosphere causing a depletion in the ozone layer which protects us from the extremes of the sun's radiation.

CFC producers were already seeking replacements for CFCs following research that pointed to their harmful ecological role. To accelerate commercialisation of alternatives, the chemicals group ICI and pharmaceutical company Glaxo signed a joint venture. Under the venture, Glaxo provided funds to build a new plant to produce CFC alternatives on one of ICI's sites and took all the production for use in its inhalable asthma drugs. ICI earned a 'generous management fee' reflecting the value of its proprietary technology.

ICI held about a third of the world market for CFC replacements and was determined to 'capitalise on its technology as the market expands'. Expansion was assured by the Montreal Protocol and the continuing need for industrial-grade CFC replacements for use in factories as well as purer pharmaceutical grades.

Source: 'ICI & Glaxo join forces to replace CFCs', *The Times*, 16 January 1995

EXHIBIT 4.4

Managing technology – 'eat my shorts!'

The market for soap powders is aggressively fought over by two companies in particular: Unilever, the Anglo-Dutch group, and Procter & Gamble. In an effort to boost sales of its Persil brand, Unilever spent over £200 million developing and launching a new formulation containing a manganese-based accelerator.

A new Persil Power brand was launched along with claims that it would remove the most 'stubborn' stains. Arch-rival Procter & Gamble quickly attacked the new brand, alleging that it damaged fabrics. Several months later the new brand was withdrawn from the market.

In February 1995, Unilever's chairman admitted that the Persil Power brand was defective. It had been introduced to the market without being fully tested. On top of the £200 million development and launch costs, Unilever also suffered £57 million in write-offs.

Source: 'Persil Power tears £57 million hole in Unilever profit', *The Times*, 22 February 1995 necessary technology. In turnkey projects, one supplier might be unable to provide all the expertise needed and so alliances with other organisations are essential to win contracts and for project completion. Alliances could also be necessary to begin trading with a particular country. For example, a company with no experience of trading with a country might need to form an alliance with another company already established in that country.

In response to constant competitive pressures an organisation may look to acquire another and by combining the two R&D departments create a more effective R&D unit. Glaxo, which spent about £850 million on R&D in 1994, acquired Wellcome, which spent around £350 million. One outcome of the new company was job losses among scientists. Here, a predator company, Glaxo, sought and identified a takeover target, Wellcome.

In contrast, occasionally an organisation comes unstuck in a product area. This happened to Boots Pharmaceuticals in 1993 when clinical trials of their heart drug Manoplax indicated that people taking it had a higher chance of returning to hospital or dying than people not taking it. Boots' drug portfolio was small by comparison to other pharmaceutical companies and the failure of Manoplax, which had attracted hopes of boosting Boots into a more dominant market position, was instrumental in bringing about the division's sell-off. Boots' pharmaceutical division was later sold to the German chemical company BASF. This suited BASF since Boots' portfolio was largely in the UK, the USA and Commonwealth countries. BASF was mostly focused on continental Europe (Jackson, 1993).

EXHIBIT 4.5

Managing technology – the elk test

German car producer Mercedes unveiled its new A-class small car to expectant journalists in October 1997. The car was a much-heralded move by Mercedes into the small-car market and included radical design aspects. With an engine slung underneath the car, instead of the usual front or back, the space inside the car would comfortably hold four people. This was the most advanced small car since the Mini was introduced forty years earlier.

Now, in Sweden, the docile elk causes thousands of motor accidents a year and motor testers use an 'elk test' on all new cars. This involves swerving sharply from side to side as if to simulate sudden elk avoidance. Unfortunately for Mercedes, the A-class flipped over when attempting the elk test and in front of the assembled media. Mercedes were faced with an immediate public relations crisis given their reputation for vehicle safety and engineering excellence.

The car's launch was delayed to give time to modify the chassis and Daimler's share price fell by over 20 per cent in a couple of months. In the long run, Mercedes' reputation was not harmed and the car was successfully introduced – but the story does highlight the highly unpredictable nature of new product development.

QUESTIONS

1. How might scientists and engineers differ from unskilled and semi-skilled employees in their attitudes to work, to their managers and to their organisations?

2. How might the inter-personal skills of scientists and engineers differ from those of non-scientific employees?

CONCLUSION

Technology represents an environmental force so strong that it can affect the competitive advantage of entire nations and shape the attitudes of whole societies. The days of R&D departments pushing their ideas sequentially through design, development, production and into markets have gone. Technology management today involves scientists and engineers working with suppliers and early adopters of products and processes to learn from each other. Although scientists and engineers will continue to work at the leading edge of technological development, managers must understand how emerging technologies could affect their organisation so that it responds to threats and opportunities in the best way. Information technologies look set to affect organisations, society and even entire economies in a revolutionary way. Managing technology into the organisation is a skill that must be acquired. This calls for a sound understanding of the benefits technology can offer and of the people management issues created inside the organisation.

SUMMARY OF MAIN POINTS

This chapter introduces the technological environment in which organisations operate. We have sought to identify key areas of technology as it applies to business organisations. Specifically:

- Technology evolves, usually in a series of small incremental steps but occasionally in large jumps. We are experiencing such a jump in information-based technologies at present.

- Information technologies are having revolutionary impacts upon some types of organisation, and there are grounds for predicting major shocks to social, political and economic enviroments.

- For optimum performance, organisations need to find the best fit between technology available to them, the socio-economic environment and their choice of strategy.

- Where technology is a factor in determining organisational performance (there are many organisations and sectors where it is not a factor) it must be seen as central to organisational decision making.

- Wealth creation through the exploitation of information superhighways is an important aim for developed nations.

- Technology should not be seen as something to put in place when 'big decisions' about a firm's strategy and structure have already been made. Technology choice is now a part of those big decisions.

NET SEARCH

It is likely that any net search concerning this chapter will focus on a particular technology or issue outlined in the chapter. Students should look directly for the particular issue that is of interest.

http://tbe.mit.edu/
The Technology, Business and Environment programme at MIT. Details technological issues that link business success to environmental excellence. Provides access to a publication list and other web sites.

http://cep.lse.ac.uk/
Site for the centre for economic performance at the London School of Economics. The site provides access to papers on many topics including technology and jobs.

http://bizednet.bris.ac.uk:8080/
Check bizednet and ask companies how technology is used in their company. Some of the responses are quite useful.

REFERENCES

Adcock, H., Helms, M. and Jih, W.-J.K., (1993) 'Information Technology: can it provide a sustainable competitive strategy?', *Information Strategy – The Executives Journal*, 9 (3), 10–15.

Ayres, R.U. (1991) 'Barriers and breakthroughs: an expanding frontiers model of the technology industry life cycle', in Rosseger, G. (ed.) *Management of Technological Change*, Oxford: Elsevier Science.

Berry, M.M.J. and Taggart, J.H. (1994) 'Managing technology and innovation: a review', *R&D Management*, 24 (4), 341–53.

Burns, T. and Stalker, G. (1961) *The Management of Innovation*, London: Tavistock.

Campbell, M. (1993) 'The employment effects of new technology and organizational change: an empirical study', *New Technology, Work, and Employment*, 8 (2), 135–40.

Chapman, A.J., Sheehy, N.P., Haywood, S., Dooley, B. and Collins, S.C. (1995) 'The organizational implications of teleworking', in Cooper, C.L. and Robertson, I. (eds) *International Review of Industrial and Organizational Psychology*, Chichester: John Wiley, vol. 10, pp. 29–248.

Clark, J. (1984) 'Food, drink and tobacco', in Guy, K. (ed.) *Trends and Employment, 1: Basic Consumer Goods*, Aldershot: Gower.

Clark, J. (1985) 'Chemicals', in Clark, J. (ed.) *Technological Trends and Employment, 2: Basic Process Industries*, Aldershot: Gower.

Coffey, P. (1995) 'How the risks of IT failure are making business re-assess IT strategies', Unpublished Combined Honours Dissertation, Nene College, Northampton.

Coleman, D.C. and MacLeod, C. (1986) 'Attitudes to new techniques: British businessmen', *Economic History Review*, 39 (4), 588–611.

Cookson, C. (1995) 'Breakthrough in mixing the molecules', *Financial Times Survey*, Chemical Industry, 27 October, p. 1.

Cooper, C.L. and Payne, R. (1990) *Causes, Coping and Consequences of Stress at Work*, Chichester: John Wiley.

Courtenay, A. (1995) 'Oracle points to the masters of technology', *Sunday Times*, 29 October, Section 6, p. 10.

Dopson, S., Ruddle, K. and Stewart, R. (1998) 'From downsizing to revitalisation', *Financial Times*, 27 February, p. 12.

Dussauge, P., Hart, S. and Ramanantsoa, B. (1994) *Strategic Technology Management*, Chichester: John Wiley.

Edgerton, D.E.H. (1987) 'Science and technology in British business history', *Business History*, 29 (4), 84–103.

Foster, G. (1993) 'The innovation imperative', *Management Today*, April, 60–3.

Freeman, C. (1982) *The Economics of Industrial Innovation*, London: Frances Pinter.

Galbraith, J.K. (1967) *The New Industrial State*, Harmondsworth: Penguin Books.

Galley, C. (1998) 'An investor's perspective', in *The UK R&D Scoreboard 1998*, Department of Trade and Industry, pp. 7–9.

Ghoshal, S. (1994) 'Scandinavian Airlines Systems (SAS) in 1988', in Dewit, B. and Meyer, R. (eds) *Strategy: Process, Content, Context – an International Perspective*, West Publishing.

Gillespie, D.F. and Mileti, D.S. (1977) 'Technology and the study of organizations: an overview and appraisal', *Academy of Management Review Symposium: Organizations and Technology*, 4 (1), 7–16.

Gooding, C. (1995) 'Boosting sales with the information warehouse', *Financial Times*, 1 March, Supplement p. 15.

Greiner, L.E. (1972) 'Evolution and revolution as organizations grow', *Harvard Business Review*, July, 37–46.

Gray, B. (1995) 'MoD issues GEC-Marconi ultimatum on deal', *Financial Times*, 6 April, p. 10.

Guy, K. (1984) 'Footwear', in Guy, K. (ed.) *Technological Trends and Employment, 1: Basic Consumer Goods*, Aldershot: Gower.

Guy, K. (1985) 'Paper', in Clark, J. (ed.) *Technological Trends and Employment, 2: Basic Process Industries*, Aldershot: Gower.

Hughes, K.L. (1995) 'Stress at work – is there a link to IT strategy?', Unpublished Combined Honours Dissertation, Nene College, Northampton.

Jackson, T. (1993) 'Boots withdraws heart drug after 2 year study', *Financial Times*, 20 July.

Johnson, G. (1993) 'A strategy for change at KPMG', in Johnson, G. and Scholes, K. *Exploring Corporate Strategy*, Hemel Hempstead: Prentice Hall.

Lazonick, W. (1981) 'Competition, specialisation and industrial decline', *Journal of Economic History*, 41 (1), 31–8.

Lazonick, W. (1983) 'Industrial organization and technological change: the decline of the British cotton industry', *Business History Review*, 57 (2), 195–236.

Lorenz, A. and Smith, D. (1998) 'Britain fails to close competitiveness gap', *Sunday Times*, 11 October, Section 3, pp. 10–11.

Matzner, E. and Wagner, M. (eds) (1990) *The Employment Impact of New Technology*, Avebury: Gower.

Monck, C.S.P., Porter, R.B., Quintas, P. and Storey, D.J. with Wynarczyk, P. (1988) *Science Parks and the Growth of High Technology Firms*, London: Routledge.

Ng, H.I., Pan, Y.J. and Wilson, T.D. (1998) 'Business use of the world wide web: report and further investigations', *International Journal of Information Management*, 18 (5), 291–314.

Parthasarthy, R. and Sethi, S.P. (1992) 'The impact of flexible automation on business strategy and organizational structure', *Academy of Management Review*, 17 (1), 86–111.

Porter, M.E. (1979) 'How competitive forces shape strategy', *Harvard Business Review*, March/April.

Porter, M.E. and Miller, V.E. (1985) 'How information gives you competitive advantage', *Harvard Business Review*, July–August, 149–60.

Rassam, C. (1993) 'Science in crisis', *Management Today*, June, 60–3.

Rothwell, R. and Wisseman, H. (1991) 'Technology, culture and public policy', in Rosegger, G. (ed.) *Management of Technological Change*, Oxford: Elsevier Science.

Shiman, D.R. (1991) 'Managerial efficiency and technological decline in Britain 1860–1914', *Business and Economic History*, 20, 89–98.

Simons, G.L. (1986) *Management Guide to Office Automation*, National Computing Centre.

Small, I. and Swann, P. (1993) 'R&D performance of UK companies', *Business Strategy Review*, 4(3), 41–51.

Souder, W.M. (1991) 'Organising for modern technology and innovation: a review and synthesis', in Rosegger, G. (ed.) *Management of Technological Change*, Oxford: Elsevier Science.

Temourian, H. (1995) 'Iran bans Baywatch with purge on Satan's dishes', *Sunday Times*, 23 April, p. 18.

Teo, T., Lim, V. and Wai, S. (1998) 'An empirical study of attitudes towards teleworking among IT personnel', *International Journal of Information Management*, 18 (5), 329–44.

Tighe, C. (1995) 'A productive marriage', *Financial Times*, Survey of Power Generation Equipment, 11, 16 May.

Wood, A. (1998) 'An industry perspective', in *The UK R&D Scoreboard 1998*, Department of Trade and Industry, pp. 3–5.

Yamazaki, H. (1988) 'The development of large enterprises in Japan: an analysis of the top 50 enterprises in the profit ranking table (1929–1984)', *Japanese Yearbook on Business History*, no. 5, pp. 12–55.

CHAPTER

5

THE SOCIAL AND DEMOGRAPHIC ENVIRONMENT

Ian Brooks
and Jamie Weatherston

LEARNING OBJECTIVES

On completion of this chapter you should be able to:

- understand the complex and dynamic nature of social, cultural and demographic forces;
- appreciate that organisations operate in a cultural context;
- understand that national cultural differences influence managerial and organisational activity and have consequences for the organisation–environment relationship;
- interpret key population statistics and diagrammatic representations (e.g. population pyramids);
- appreciate some of the prime differences in demographic characteristics at local, regional, national and international scales;
- recognise the characteristics of an ageing population and assess the prime influences on organisations of this trend;
- appreciate the influences upon organisations and geo-political areas of population migration;
- discuss some of the political, social and economic consequences of demographic changes;

Learning objectives continued

- recognise characteristics of, and trends in, a number of key social forces (such as the family, crime and health) and assess their impact on organisations;
- assess recent changes in the role and significance of the trade union movement in the UK, and European developments and alternatives.

KEY CONCEPTS

- national culture
- demographics
- society
- convergence and divergence theory
- individualism/collectivism
- power distance
- uncertainty avoidance
- masculinity/femininity

- age/sex population structure
- migration
- ageing and age/sex segmentation
- social issues
- changing roles
- the hidden economy
- trade unionism
- life-long learning

INTRODUCTION

Organisations operate in a dynamic and multifaceted social environment. They experience a complex interactive relationship with a social community or society. This chapter takes a closer look at a number of crucial social phenomena which profoundly influence organisations and their activity. We examine the cultural context of organisations before exploring demographics. Finally, the chapter focuses on the dynamic nature of the environment with a examination of some key issues.

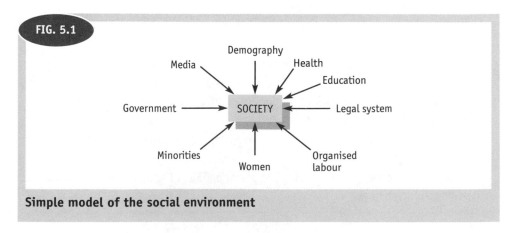

FIG. 5.1

Simple model of the social environment

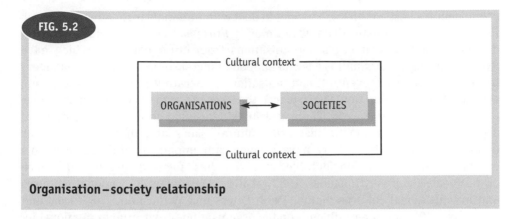

FIG. 5.2

Organisation–society relationship

Figure 5.1 illustrates a diverse array of social phenomena which individually and collectively both shape, and are shaped by, society. Figure 5.2 illustrates the broad two-way relationship between organisations and society, that is, the social community in which organisations operate. This relationship takes place within a local, national and regional cultural context. Each societal force will not exert the same influence over all organisations. For example, a society's changing health expectations may have little direct relevance for a consumer electronics company yet will assume great importance for many food manufacturers.

This chapter will investigate demographic (population) issues at a local, national and international scale and assess their influence upon organisations. We will then take a closer look at a number of critical social phenomena and identify many of the key consequences of social dynamism for commercial and other organisations. Issues such as crime, health, the family and the changing face of organised labour will be considered. However, the chapter opens with a discussion of national culture which, it is argued, influences all organisational and environmental activity.

NATIONAL CULTURE

Organisations interact with the social community within a cultural context (see Figure 5.2). As such, culture itself acts as a pervasive force influencing all organisations, whatever their nature and sphere of operations. What is more, companies are seeking an international presence as a means of diversifying their markets, helped by the development of trade blocs. In the European Union, for example, the single market programme sought to remove a range of barriers that had previously inhibited trading and business across borders. Despite the slump in the mid to late 1990s, the economies of South-East Asia have attracted massive investment from other countries and have also, in turn, invested heavily in Europe and the Americas. These developments mean that an increasing number of organisations are operating in several countries and, thus, managers of the organisation's host country are having to deal with nationals from other countries. From a European perspective it is not merely European companies investing and developing overseas; it is also organisations from other countries which have invested in Europe. Again there is a likelihood of increased contact with managers from other countries, even if the organisation is operating predominantly in one country. These developments have placed the issue of national culture much higher on the organisational agenda. There is clear evidence that an increasing number of organisations are having to deal with cultural issues and that the success or otherwise of their efforts may have a significant impact on the organisation's overall effectiveness. Considerable research has focused on the influence of national cultures (Hofstede, 1983; Adler, 1991, 1997), regional cultures and organisational cultures (Sathe, 1983; Peters and Waterman, 1982; Deal and Kennedy, 1982) and their influence on the organisation–environment relationship. Argenti (1974) suggests that there is a need to understand the dominant values of society. With this in mind we will explore the work of key researchers in that field, as their findings have a bearing on international business activity.

Culture refers to the collectively held values, beliefs, attitudes, assumptions and behaviours of a group. The most deep-rooted element of culture is the set of values held by the group. Such values may manifest themselves in particular beliefs and attitudes and also in people's behaviour. Often surface behaviour is 'driven' by a much deeper belief, for example, in the difference between right and wrong, which is itself a product of national cultural conditioning. What is considered to be right or wrong differs between cultures. For example, people of a particular country may cherish their personal right to freedom of speech, while another culture may feel that such a right should be subordinate to the best interests of society as a whole. The United States of America typifies the former category while the Singaporean culture adopts a more societal orientation.

Culture is shared; however, that is not to say that everyone in a particular culture thinks and acts in the same way. Individual differences are significant. When describing cultures we look for 'typical' values, beliefs and attitudes and 'norms' of behaviours.

Many countries have a distinct national culture; nevertheless, subcultures exist within many countries. For example, in the United Kingdom there are certain regional groups, such as the Welsh and the Scottish, who possess some cultural characteristics which partly differentiate them from the English. There are also differences between the regions in England. Similarly, there are significant, and politically critical, differences between the French-speaking and English-speaking Canadians. Additionally, different subcultures exist based on other criteria, such as social class, gender, age, religion, and occupational group. As a consequence all organisations operate within a complex, often multi-tiered, cultural context. Figure 5.3 illustrates some of the features which contribute to the national cultural environment.

The assumption of cultural convergence dominated business, organisational and management studies up to and including the 1960s. Theodore Levitt (1983) argued that national cultures were converging such that culture was becoming an

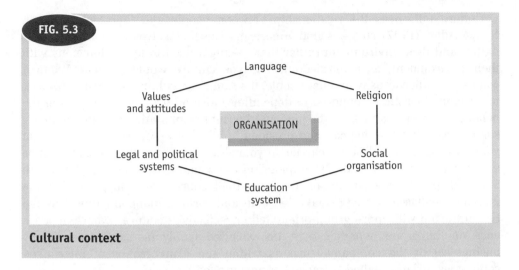

FIG. 5.3

Cultural context

unimportant variable for business to consider. The convergence hypothesis argues that management is a universal phenomenon, and that 'good practice', which usually emanated from the USA or Europe, could and should be applied throughout the world. However, in recent decades, and especially since the 1980s, considerable attention has been paid to cultural differences between nations and there is growing acceptance that 'good' managerial practices may be those which best fit and are in keeping with a particular culture. Additionally, differences between countries have been increasingly recognised, so that the 'divergence hypothesis' is now given considerable credence. The European Union, a supranational organisation which was founded on the convergence belief, has had to recognise significant national differences. It is now more widely accepted that national differences are here to stay and that they pose crucial management problems for global organisations.

National culture is important politically, sociologically and psychologically. Hofstede (1983) argues that 'nations are political units, rooted in history, with their own ... forms of government, legal systems, [and] educational systems'. Nationality is also symbolic to citizens who derive part of their identity from it. These national differences are very real to people. Our thinking is conditioned by national culture through the mechanism of the family, our education and the workplace, our friendship groups and the media.

Culture is dynamic and continually evolving; however, fundamental change in cultural values is rather slow. Behaviours may change more rapidly and transparently. Nevertheless, for most observers within any country cultural changes can be noted. For example, most citizens of the UK recognise that societal norms, values, attitudes and behaviours have slowly changed throughout the 1990s, so that they are now quite different in many respects to those found in the 1980s. Culture continues to change, so that organisations have to be sensitive to new and growing social values such as concern for the natural environment or, more specifically, for animal welfare.

Culture influences the relationship between people and their environment. Nancy Adler (1997) suggests that Americans see themselves as dominant over nature and their environment rather than feeling a need to live in harmony with their environment, as a more Confucian-type culture would suggest. When it comes to relationships with other people, the American culture can clearly be seen to be individualistic as opposed to depending more on groups. There is still the belief that anyone can rise to the top with the right combination of skill and drive, sometimes called the 'log cabin to president' philosophy. Americans believe that your birthright should be no barrier to your development within society. People who achieve are seen as the 'champions' of the country, whether Bill Gates with Microsoft or Michael Jordan on the basketball court. Adler suggests that the individual will be expected to make decisions and perform independently. This can be contrasted with more group-orientated or collectivist cultures where dependence on the group, whether it is the extended family (as in Chinese family businesses) or the company (such as within the giant groups of interlinked companies in Japan called *keiretsus*), is encouraged.

We will now look at the work of Geert Hofstede, who has identified work-related values in fifty world countries on four dimensions. Although methodologically some of the findings may, in detail, be questionable, what they do show is significant and crucial differences between countries. These differences have important implications for all organisations that operate in, have dealings with, or employ people from more than one country. Unilever, for example, operates in more than ninety countries and employs nearly 270 000 people. Hofstede (1983) found that cultures differ according to the degree people exhibit

- individualistic or collective tendencies,
- large or small power-distances between one another,
- strong or weak uncertainty avoidance tendencies, and
- masculine versus feminine characteristics.

People in the USA, Australia and Great Britain, for example, are shown by Hofstede to value individualism, while many Latin American and Asian countries value collectivism, that is, they possess a group or societal orientation. Knowledge of this may influence an organisation's marketing practices and advertising focus. It may influence people's motivation to work and how they decide to utilise their leisure time.

In many countries a large power-distance exists between workers and management or between social classes. This is true of many Latin American and Asian countries and France. In France management tends to be highly stratified, and considerable deference is expected by superiors. In Scandinavian countries, Israel, Australia and Great Britain, for example, power-distances are smaller.

Countries also differ in their cultural ability to cope with uncertainty. As uncertainties create anxiety, some cultures attempt to organise everything carefully in order to reduce uncertainty of outcome. Hence in Germany, Japan and France, for example, trains run on time and organisation and detail are considered highly important, whereas Hofstede argues that in Scandinavia, Great Britain, Singapore and Hong Kong, for example, people are more accepting of uncertainties. In a business environment context this may mean that countries with high uncertainty avoidance (e.g. France, Germany, Japan) may undertake more environmental scanning in an attempt to gather information which may reduce uncertainty and facilitate organisational planning. Evidence of this may be found in the meticulous preparation of Japanese companies when looking at foreign investment opportunities and the rather more haphazard approach of Ikea, the Swedish retailer, as it attempted to expand into both the USA and China.

Some cultures make a clear and strong distinction between the nature and role of men and women. In Scandinavia and Holland men and women experience similar values, beliefs and attitudes. Additionally, 'macho' behaviours are less common than in Australia, Ireland, much of Latin America, the USA and Great Britain.

Whilst Hofstede's findings indicate four areas of potential difference between cultures, it is now commonly accepted that a fifth variable exists. This resulted from the Chinese Values Survey carried out by the Chinese Culture Connection Group (1987), which sought to evaluate the effectiveness of Hofstede's cultural dimensions in a specific Asian context where there would be significant influence of Confucianism. What did emerge from the study was the evidence of a fifth dimension which seemed particularly applicable to Asian cultures and which identified that most Asian countries had a long-term perspective about work and organisations. This was labelled 'Confucian dynamics', but Hofstede called it 'long-term orientation' (LTO). This may be useful to explain different behaviour between, say, Japanese organisations and Western organisations: the Japanese may be much more influenced by long-term market share than immediate short-term factors, such as dividends. It may also explain why Asian companies are keen to build long-term relationships with Western companies rather than attempt takeovers or other short-term activities.

There have been some criticisms of Hofstede's model. One of the most obvious is that although a substantial number of countries were involved, there were none from Eastern Europe, and Russia and many Asian countries were ignored. This can be explained by the fact that the survey was explicitly based on IBM, and in 1980 and 1984 IBM did not have a significant presence in these countries. This has to some extent been corrected by the Chinese Values Survey and more recent work applying the work of Hofstede to Eastern Europe. However, this leads to a second criticism, in that the results were based on an organisation with a very strong corporate culture which may have distorted the findings. Despite this, most subsequent research has upheld the validity of his analysis and it remains the most popular model which is used worldwide to evaluate cultural differences between countries and assess their implication on organisational behaviour.

It is crucial that each of these cultural dimensions is appreciated by managers within multinational, multiethnic and global organisations. There are many cases of American and European companies, for example, who have failed to 'acclimatise' to cultural conditions in other countries and suffered financial losses as a consequence.

Ronen and Shenkar (1985) built upon Hofstede's work and identified clusters of countries based on certain cultural commonalities, such as religion and language. Some of these groups are illustrated in Table 5.1. It is interesting to note that member countries of the European Union (shown in italics in Table 5.1) fall into five separate cultural groups (nine were identified in total). It is not surprising that there are differences in perception and in substance between EU members' national governments.

Trompenaars (1997) has identified seven dimensions which differentiate cultures. These are:

- universalism versus particularism,
- collectivism versus individualism,
- affective versus neutral cultures,
- specific versus diffuse relationships,
- achieving versus ascribing status,
- time as sequence versus time as synchronisation, and
- inner-directed versus outer-directed.

It is the last of these which is of particular interest to those studying the relationship of an organisation and its environment.

The inner-directed versus outer-directed dimension contrasts countries like the USA and Switzerland, where there is a belief that the individual should seek to control the natural and human environment, with nations like China where people aim to be in harmony with nature. The latter is central to both Confucianism and Buddhism. This may explain why, in countries like Japan, organisations are seen holistically as operating in harmony with their surroundings and with the people within the organisation, and could further explain why direct conflict or confrontation is often resisted.

Adler (1991) suggests that cultures vary in the extent to which people adopt particular problem-solving styles. People may perceive problems in the business environment quite differently depending on their cultural orientation. They may also gather data and manage solutions to those problems quite differently.

TABLE 5.1   Groupings of national cultures

Anglo	Australia, Canada, New Zealand, Ireland, South Africa, USA, UK
Far Eastern	Malaysia, Hong Kong, Singapore, Philippines, South Vietnam, Indonesia, Thailand, Taiwan
Nordic	Sweden, Denmark, Norway, Finland
Latin-European	France, Belgium, Italy, Portugal, Spain
Near Eastern	Turkey, Iran, Greece
Germanic	Germany, Switzerland, Austria

Source: Ronen and Shenkar, 1985

Adler identifies two types of culture (or personality), 'problem-solving' and 'situation-acceptance' cultures. Problem-solving cultures, which dominate in the UK and in the USA, will identify numerous issues as problems which need to be solved by gathering facts, changing people, making decisions and generally acting decisively and with authority. Situation-acceptance cultures, on the other hand, which are more common in Latin and Asian countries, will accept many issues rather than attempt to change them. They may, for example, see certain environmental factors as given. They tend to gather ideas and perceptions rather than just hard facts. Decisions tend to be made slowly and only after consultation. When looking at the time dimension of their activities, Adler (1997) found the Americans to be future-orientated in that they believed you should look at issues and assess the potential future benefits that could be produced, although they would tend to look at these benefits very much in the short term rather than the long term. Past-orientated cultures are more likely to be found in Europe and Asia. This might partly be a result of a greater sense of history or a belief that actions should fit in with beliefs and traditions. It is also noticeable that many Asian companies adopt a longer-term perspective and this may explain Japanese companies' preference for long-term market growth rather than short-term profits.

The field of cross-cultural or inter-cultural management is now blossoming as the relevance of national culture to the success of business ventures is increasingly being recognised.

QUESTIONS

1. How might national culture influence organisational activity?
2. Explore the ways in which global companies might adapt their marketing effort to better 'fit' a national culture. Use Hofstede's dimensions and the work of others in the field as a guide.

DEMOGRAPHIC FORCES

Demography is the study of human populations. It is often a prime area of focus for those undertaking courses in geography and some other social sciences. Our concern here is the particular insight organisations can gain from analysing population dynamics. Consequently, this section will illustrate how demographic forces can pose both opportunities and threats to all types of commercial, not-for-profit and public enterprise. It takes a closer look at various critical population characteristics, at a variety of geographical scales, and assesses how changes are likely to influence organisations both now and in the future.

First, however, we will explore some demographic characteristics and patterns at a variety of geo-political scales.

Population structure and life expectancy: a small-scale comparison

We are all aware from personal experiences that the age/sex structure of any given population varies between one place and another. By way of example we will examine two similarly sized but quite different towns in England. The observations we will make could apply equally to contrasting towns in any European country.

Eastbourne, on the south coast of England, is a favourite destination for retired people who seek an attractive environment away from the bustle of city life. On or near retirement, many people sell their city homes and buy a retirement home in a quieter, more picturesque environment. This outward migration from urban areas such as London has been common for at least fifty years. Between 1981 and 1994 9.2 million people went to live in the seven biggest cities in the United Kingdom, but 10.5 million moved out (Pearman and Nuki, 1996). This phenomenon has led to an increase in the numbers of older people in towns such as Eastbourne. Hence such favourite retirement destinations have a skewed population structure with large numbers of older residents. This pattern is often compounded by the fact that few retirement or dormitory towns have many worthwhile employment prospects for the young. Consequently there is often a net outward migration of younger age groups (e.g. 16-to-30-year-olds) seeking employment. This loss of young people, some with small children, further increases the average age of the population.

Figure 5.4 compares the population structure of Eastbourne with that of Kettering, a small and rather typical town in Northamptonshire in the Midlands of England. In terms of size alone the two towns are similar, with Eastbourne having a population of 85 200 (1991, i.e. the last full census date) and Kettering 76 150 (1991). Further observation, however, reveals significant differences in the

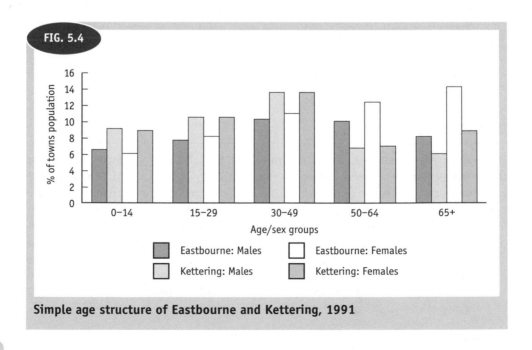

FIG. 5.4

Simple age structure of Eastbourne and Kettering, 1991

TABLE 5.2   Life expectancy in selected countries

Country/region	Life expectancy in years at birth	
	Males	Females
Sub-Saharan Africa	49	52
Asia Pacific	60	63
United Kingdom	72	78
OECD average	72	78
USA	72	79
France	72	80
Holland	74	80
Sweden	74	80
Norway	74	80
Japan	75	81

Source: *The Economist Annual Yearbook, 1990*

age/sex make-up of the two towns' populations. Over 40 per cent of Kettering's population is under 30 years of age. The comparable figure in Eastbourne is just 30 per cent. However, it is in the older age groups where the differences are most pronounced. In excess of 45 per cent of people in Eastbourne are aged over 50 years of age compared to just 31 per cent in Kettering. Eastbourne has nearly 13 per cent of its population over the age of 75 compared to a national average of less than 7 per cent.

The relatively small proportion of young male adults in Eastbourne may suggest that employment opportunities in Eastbourne were largely in service activities.

Another factor which further distorts population structure and accounts for differences between the two towns is the male/female ratio. The average life expectancy at birth varies significantly between males and females, between different socio-economic groups and between countries and regions in the world (see Table 5.2). Women, being physiologically more resilient, live longer. This pattern is more or less universal. It accounts for the considerable imbalance in the male/female ratio in both Eastbourne and Kettering among the older age groups. The imbalance becomes increasingly apparent with age as approximately two out of every three people over 75 years of age are female while less than 20 per cent of over-90-year-olds are male.

Population structure: European Union comparisons

Variations in population structure are not confined to the small-scale examples discussed above. Differences in structure become even more apparent on a global scale. However, two particular contrasts are worthy of consideration here. First, we will look at the current difference between two European Union countries – Denmark and the Republic of Ireland – before analysing the predicted changes in population structure in the whole of the European Union to the year 2020. The consequences of these changes, which will have important and far-reaching implications for business and government in the EU, will be discussed later.

The Republic of Ireland and Denmark have been selected as they illustrate different population structures. In scale terms, both countries are dwarfed by many of their European partners. Denmark's population, showing virtually zero growth in recent years, was 5 135 000 in 1990, making it a little larger than the Republic of Ireland with 3 507 000 in the same year. The United Nations estimates that the population of Denmark will remain around 5.1 million in 2020 while Ireland's will grow to around 4 million. In many ways Denmark's population structure – its age/sex make-up – resembles that of the UK, Germany and many other Western European countries, while Ireland's is somewhat unique in the European Union.

Ireland has a larger proportion of its population in the younger age groups and fewer older people when compared to Denmark. This is in part a result of differing fertility rates (the number of babies born per 1000 women per year) between the two countries. To put it simply, Irish families have tended to be larger than those in Denmark. More precisely, the birth rates for the two countries between 1985 and 1990 were 18.1 in Ireland and 10.7 in Denmark – that is, the birth rate in Ireland was 69 per cent higher than that in Denmark (although the scale of that difference is now reducing). The birth rate represents an annual figure indicating the number of live births in a country for every 1000 of its population. It is a useful, although slightly crude, comparative measure.

Another cause of the different population structures between the two countries is the relative life expectancy of their people, with the figure for Denmark being a little higher than that of Ireland. However, a third, more pervasive reason for the observed differences exists. Ireland, unlike its Scandinavian partner, has for well over a century 'suffered' from a mass exodus of its people. Despite its high natural increase in population, outward migration has been on such a scale that the total population of Ireland has barely grown over the last 150 years. However, for the first time for well over a century, due to rapid growth and prosperity in Ireland, emigration is declining, and in fact Ireland is attracting skilled workers from overseas. Traditionally, the majority of emigrants have been young adults, many of whom have never returned on a permanent basis. The particular economic, political and social issues surrounding migration are discussed below. Many of the consequences for organisations and governments may become apparent to the reader.

Demographic dynamism and ageing

In addition to geographical differences within the European Union, significant changes take place over time. Figure 5.5 shows the change in structure predicted within the European Union between 1990 and 2020. In many ways the pattern indicated resembles that which may be seen when comparing the current structure of Denmark and Ireland. However, what is clear is that the EU's population is ageing. There is a decreasing proportion of young people and a growing number of old people, especially of those over the age of 80.

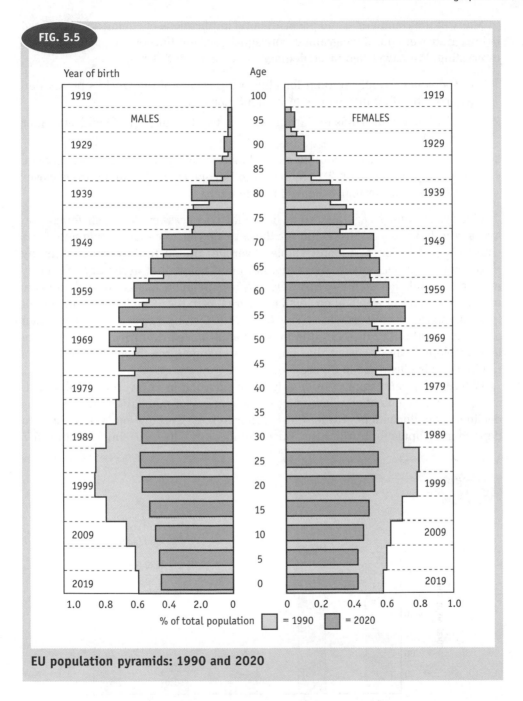

EU population pyramids: 1990 and 2020

The trend illustrated in Figure 5.5 has been apparent for many years in the United Kingdom, Germany and Denmark, for example, but it is now the southern European countries, particularly Greece, Italy, Spain and Portugal, where the rate of ageing is most rapid as birth rates have plummeted during the last two decades.

Many of the commercial and governmental implications of ageing are discussed below; however, the demographic consequences, for Europe in particular, are interesting. We have listed three demographic 'facts' in this respect:

1. Europeans currently account for almost 9 per cent of the world's population whereas by 2050 they will be less than 3 per cent.

2. The number of over-65s in Europe will outstrip the number of children under 15 by 2020.

3. In order to replace or maintain a population each woman of child-bearing age needs to produce about 2.1 children – in Europe currently the figure is closer to 1.7, while in Germany the rate is below that.

Clearly, assuming zero migration, it would be necessary for each female on average to have two children, and for these to survive to child-bearing age, for a country's population to remain stable. Average annual fertility rates in many European countries, notably Germany, are often below that necessary to merely maintain population stability. Yet Germany's population has continued to grow until recently, a fact which in no small measure has in recent years been due to net inward migration. Nevertheless, low birth and fertility rates in Europe, when compared to those in the USA, the newly industrialised countries or most of the less developed world, ensure that population change (growth or decline) will be minimal, as is illustrated in Figure 5.6.

Whereas this may appear to be a healthy situation in an overcrowded world, there are many potentially damaging consequences of population stagnation or decline. The dependency ratio (the proportion of working-age population to dependent population) will also vary significantly through time. Figure 5.7

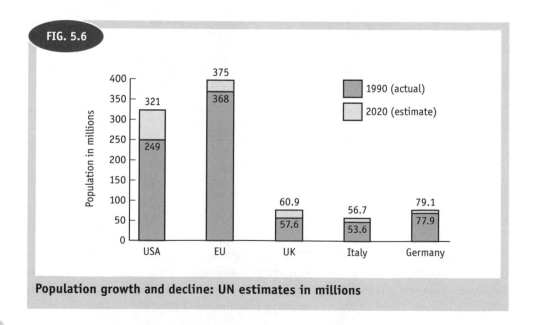

FIG. 5.6

Population in millions

1990 (actual)
2020 (estimate)

USA: 321 / 249
EU: 375 / 368
UK: 60.9 / 57.6
Italy: 56.7 / 53.6
Germany: 79.1 / 77.9

Population growth and decline: UN estimates in millions

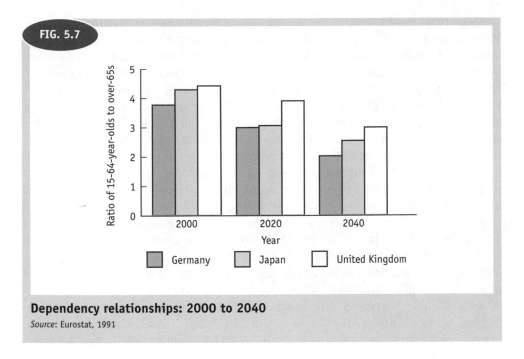

FIG. 5.7

Dependency relationships: 2000 to 2040

Source: Eurostat, 1991

indicates the ratio of working-age population (15-to-64-year-olds), in Germany, Japan and the UK, to over-65-year-olds. As can be seen, the dependency ratio is set to deteriorate rapidly over the next forty years, especially in Germany where by 2040 there will be just two 15-to-64-year-olds for every over-65-year-old. This 'switch' from young to old has important policy, social and organisational implications.

There are a number of contributory reasons for this changing structural pattern. Life expectancy has been gradually increasing and fertility rates slowly decreasing over the last fifty years in Europe. However, birth rates in particular are not stable but fluctuate in unpredictable cycles. They are influenced by a variety of short-term factors such as the state of a national economy and government family policies as well as by longer-term socio-economic trends. Life expectancy figures should continue to creep upwards rather slowly while fertility rates will be unlikely to increase significantly.

International migration: the cases of Germany and the Republic of Ireland

Migration of people across national boundaries has been a burning issue of political, social and economic debate for many centuries. It has facilitated the demographic and economic growth of many nations and the decline of some. For example, mass migration to the USA, Canada, Australia and New Zealand have enabled these 'new world' countries to enjoy enormous economic growth and prosperity, particularly in the twentieth century.

Mobility of labour is vital for the successful functioning of economic activity. With structural and geographical changes in industry it is essential that skilled labour is prepared to move to find opportunities in other regions or countries. Without such mobility, either within countries or across national boundaries, economic growth would undoubtedly be stifled in the more prosperous regions while conditions of high unemployment would be further exacerbated in declining areas. In the European Union, for example, rates of unemployment vary significantly between different regions. In some parts of Germany and Scandinavia there has long been a labour shortage, while in many peripheral regions of Europe unemployment rates commonly exceed 15 per cent. The problems involved in migration, however, tend to be rather acute when considered at the international level, that is, involving cross-national migration.

As outlined above, the Republic of Ireland has long experienced significant outward migration. The UK and the USA have been the main beneficiaries of these migrants, although many Irish people live and work all over the world. It is said that there are more Irish in New York than there are in Ireland. It is believed that there are 44 million Americans of Irish decent, that is, twelve times the population of Ireland. The horrific potato famine in 1845/46 was a significant spur to migration, primarily to the 'new world' and the United Kingdom. Ireland experienced a large decline in population size as a result of this first major wave of migration.

Unfortunately for Ireland many of those who left the country were young, fit adults, often skilled, ambitious and willing to work hard. Such migrants have been an asset in England where the construction industry in particular has long benefited by having such a flexible workforce. One country's gain is another's loss.

Ireland has a disproportionate school-age population when compared to its EU counterparts. As stated above, birth rates are high and family sizes tend to be large. However, once educated, many Irish are keen to succeed and traditionally have seen the opportunities offered overseas as substantial. The Irish government have, particularly in recent decades, invested a great deal in terms of eduction and health expenditure on its young people, many of whom emigrate, often permanently.

Figure 5.8 compares birth, death and migration rates in Ireland, Germany, Denmark and the United Kingdom. Of particular interest is the migration rate of each country. Ireland, in 1991, had a net outward migration rate of 47, indicating that for every 1000 people in the country 47 emigrated – almost 5 per cent of the entire population each year. So, despite a sizeable birth rate (the highest in the European Union) Ireland's population in 1991 declined by almost 2.5 per cent. Meanwhile Germany's population growth only remained positive due to a net inward migration of almost half a million people.

Economically, the prosperous German economy has encouraged high levels of immigration and has benefited from an influx of predominantly low-cost labour from Turkey and, more recently, Eastern European countries. However, socially and politically all is not rosy. Many migrants in Germany have been subjected to sometimes horrific racial attacks, prejudice is rife and large-scale political unrest is

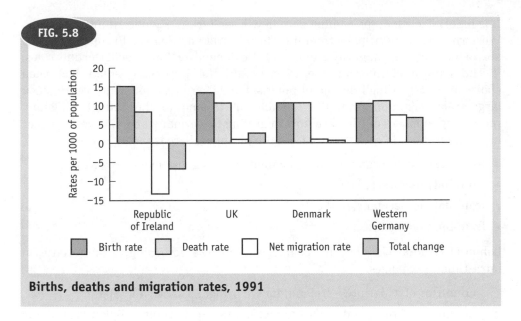

FIG. 5.8

Births, deaths and migration rates, 1991

simmering. The extreme right in Germany have made little secret of their feelings towards foreign migrants, leading to scenes somewhat frightening to outside observers and the majority of German citizens.

Many migrants face other social and economic difficulties. Some find themselves 'ghettoised', frequently in low-cost, poorly-maintained housing. Education standards are often below average for the host country and employment prospects poor. So, whereas a fluid mobility of labour across national boundaries facilitates economic growth and restructuring, it is not without social, economic and political consequences.

Migration patterns within the European Union

Paul White (1993) notes that in addition to the more predictable movements of migrant populations within the European Union over the past decade there have been a number of unforeseen developments. These include

- the political transformation of Eastern Europe and consequent increases in immigration from former Communist countries, e.g. from the former East Germany to the West and from Albania and the former Yugoslavia to the European Union, notably Italy and Germany;

- Third World migration into Italy and, to a lesser extent, Spain;

- a rapid decline in fertility rates among many established minority groups within the European Union (e.g. the West Indian population in England) and above national fertility rates for other minority groups (e.g. the Indian, Pakistani and Bangladeshi populations in the UK);

- a reduction in internal mobility rates of European Union migrant populations.

It is highly likely that the coming decade will see further significant migration into Western Europe, principally from the Third World and Eastern Europe, while the size of many existing minority groups will also depend on their specific fertility rates.

The pattern of internal migration within the European Union has been characterised by a high degree of polarisation. There has, for many years, been large-scale migration from the Republic of Ireland to the United Kingdom. Increasing numbers of Irish are now migrating to Germany and vice versa. Other major migrations in recent years from the peripheral areas include

- from Portugal to France (about one million Portuguese live in France),
- from Italy to France,
- from Italy to Germany, and
- from Spain to France.

Lebon (1990) has classified EU countries as follows according to their status in intra-Union exchanges:

1. Countries of departure – Ireland, Italy, Portugal, Greece and Spain.
2. Countries of reception – Luxembourg, France, Germany, Belgium and the United Kingdom.
3. Countries with balanced exchanges – Holland and Denmark.

In broad terms it seems likely that these patterns will prevail for the foreseeable future, although Ireland, for example, is likely to become a country with a balanced exchange. The extent to which new patterns are likely to develop is largely unknown, for there remain many obstacles to migration. Whereas legally European Union citizens are more or less free to work in any community country, mobility is hampered by problems of language, lack of job-related skills, housing, information and prejudice.

Another migration trend of particular interest is the movement of people within any Western industrialised country away from large urban areas. This pattern of migration contributes to unique problems in both the receiving localities and the cities of origin. Increased congestion, environmental problems, high house prices and urban sprawl are but a few of the issues facing receiving areas. Meanwhile major urban areas continue to suffer from poor housing and education, declining services, increasing crime and general social and economic hardship. The very old, the unskilled and certain ethic minority groups are less likely to find migration to the 'affluent' semi-urban areas an option. This contributes to increasing inner-city difficulties, such as high unemployment, crime and deprivation, for organisations and governments. Additionally, migration of this kind tends to create a divided society – divided economically, socially and geographically.

The global pattern of population growth

The demographic features discussed above comprise a selection of the interesting and relevant patterns emerging in Europe. On a global scale, population growth and distribution add complexity to the organisational environment. Population growth remains a prime concern. At current rates of growth, world population will double in about 36 years. It has more than doubled in the last 36 years. If this rate of growth were to continue, by the year 3000 there would be 2000 people piled on every square metre of the earth's surface!

Population growth in the developing world averages about 2.5 per cent per year. When compared to the minimal growth in Europe it is clear that global population distribution is shifting towards, for example, South-East Asia, and away from Western countries. Despite the efforts of many Asian governments to curb their population growth, this pattern continues. However, some countries recognise the economic and political benefits of a growing population. In fact the Malaysian government plans to increase its indigenous Malay population rapidly. In the United Arab Emirates, indigenous population growth is encouraged in attempts to increase the proportion of 'local' to expatriate workers, making the country relatively less dependent on overseas personnel.

There is little doubt that the continued population growth in China and South-East Asia has acted as a spur to economic growth. This is in part due to the need to maintain and improve living standards, increasingly difficult in the current deep recession in such countries which in turn 'demands' that governments strive for economic growth. South-East Asian countries are fighting poverty through industrialisation and development; a consequence of economic growth in the 1980s and early 1990s is a small decline in the rate of population growth.

It is a thought-provoking fact that both the total income and population of Europe comprise, in the long term, a declining proportion of global totals. The changing global patterns of economic development, growth of new power blocs and the prospects for Europe have been discussed in Chapter 3.

DEMOGRAPHIC RESTRUCTURING

For many organisations, demographic trends and social issues are of little apparent concern. This may be a short-sighted view, although it is true to say that for some organisations there is a very tenuous link between changes in population patterns and their well-being. However, at the local, national and continental level of government the changes discussed above are highly significant. So too are they for many commercial organisations which, for example, employ a large labour force, sell their goods or services to specific segments, or are considering relocation or growth. Population provides organisations with one of their most important resources, labour, and also the markets for their goods and services.

Changing demand

Ageing, or demographic restructuring, has many implications for commercial, non-profit-making and public sector organisations. Restructuring may alter patterns of consumption, production, employment, savings, investment and innovation. Many goods and services are targeted at specific age/sex segments of a population. The brewing industry is just one example of this. Exhibit 5.1 illustrates the relevance of demography as an important market consideration.

EXHIBIT 5.1

The brewing industry

The table below shows the market share (in the European market) of the main players in the European brewing industry.

Heineken (Holland)	10.1%
Carlsberg (Denmark)	8.2%
Danone (France)	7.0%
Bass (UK)	5.3%
Courage (UK)	5.3%
Interbrew (Belgium)	4.8%
Guinness (Ireland)	4.6%
Oetker (Germany)	3.2%

Patterns of manufacturing and consumption of beers are changing rapidly in Europe. For example, in part due to differential rates of tax on alcohol, an estimated 10 per cent of beer for consumption at home in the UK is purchased overseas (often in Channel port supermarkets). Drink-drive laws and social habits are also changing consumption patterns as is the development of innovative new alcoholic drinks and alternatives to beer.

Brewers, such as Bass, Carlsberg-Tetley and Scottish Courage depend for a significant proportion of their beer sales on males aged between 18 and 25. An

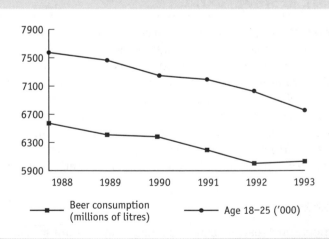

Declining beer consumption and youthful population

average European male in his twenties consumes 70 per cent more beer than one in his forties. With an ageing population, brewers in the UK have had to target other age groups and promote sales of many other products and services to compensate for the relative decline in this age-specific consumption group. Hence there has been an increase in the sale of food in pubs, catering for more mature adults and families, while brewers have diversified into the broader entertainment business (e.g. hotels, gambling, recreation facilities). This is in no small way because of demographic changes, although more general societal change has also contributed. There is now considerable overcapacity in the UK brewing industry.

Most European brewers face similar problems. In Germany, for example, which has the highest beer consumption per capita in Europe, it is estimated that the decline in the male population in their twenties may be as much as 38 per cent between 1987 and 2000. The equivalent figure for the United Kingdom is 20 per cent.

In the last fifteen years there has been a rapid growth in the financial services sector, with many companies, for example Virgin, offering numerous 'products' aimed at the retirement/redundancy market. Life assurance, pension funds and single-sum (e.g. redundancy payment) products have flourished. This has been sustained by the progressive growth in both the numbers and affluence of middle-aged and older people in the UK and in many of the Western developed nations. It is evident that people currently in their forties and fifties expect a different lifestyle from earlier generations. Those who grew up in the 1950s, 1960s and 1970s have different cultural values and lifestyle expectations than those of their parents. These people are seen by marketing departments as a prime target group for certain leisure products.

Most Western countries have an ageing population and demand has gradually switched in relative terms away from products and services for the young and towards catering for more mature tastes. The tourist industry has seen a steady and unrelenting growth in business from middle-aged and older people, often in search of day trips and short break travel and hotel-based vacations. Airlines and other carriers frequently offer off-peak special concessions to the elderly in order to attract this increasingly affluent and 'adventurous' market segment. Exhibit 5.2 illustrates how one successful company has turned demographic ageing into an environmental opportunity.

There has been a large increase in the number of registered nursing and retirement homes catering for the older citizen. Similarly, numerous building companies, such as McCarthy & Stone, have flourished by constructing specially designed retirement homes and sheltered accommodation. Many elderly people, often single widows or widowers, sell their home after the family has left and seek the more manageable and safer environment offered by sheltered accommodation. The demand for this type of housing looks set to increase significantly in the next decade.

EXHIBIT 5.2

Saga holidays

In the mid 1950s, entrepreneur Sidney De Haan decided to offer cheap holidays to retired people at off-peak times. He took advantage of the low prices offered by hoteliers who were only too willing to see their poor occupancy rates rise. Forty years on, the Saga group, with a turnover in excess of £150 million, offers holidays, financial services and magazines to the over-50s. Saga recognised that the special needs of older customers represented a market opportunity.

Retired people have grown progressively wealthier and Saga now offers holidays trekking in the Himalayas and round-the-world cruises costing up to £30 000 per head. They have expanded in the lucrative US market. They have also developed their 'product' portfolio to include financial services such as insurance brokering. They can negotiate many preferential rates for their low-risk customers, since, for example, older people tend not to drive great distances hence reducing the probability of being involved in a car accident. They also spend more of their time in their houses, so reducing the opportunity for burglars to strike.

About half of Saga's 750 staff employed in Folkestone, Kent, now work on the financial services side of the business. What is more, they find their business is virtually recession-proof as a decline in a national economic cycle has little influence on the income of retired people. What is damaging, however, is a decline in interest rates which does adversely influence the incomes of their clients.

Manufacturers and retailers of children's clothing and other infant products have had to operate in an increasingly competitive marketplace as birth rates across Europe have been depressed since the late 1960s. Sales of baby foods in Europe's largest market, Germany, have hardly risen in volume terms. However, the pattern of fertility decline is not consistent; birth rates fluctuate over time, adding further complexity and uncertainty to organisational players in these market segments.

Even as the population gets older it is still vital for companies to maintain a stream of products to satisfy the needs of diverse consumer groups. Alcopops originated in Australia and came to the UK when Merrydown started importing Two Dogs in 1995. Brewers quickly recognised a change in the market. Bass introduced Hoppers Hooch. The alcopop craze took hold, particularly with young drinkers, and the market, previously dominated by cider, became a battleground. In 1996 some companies were caught out by a change in taste. Matthew Clark, the makers of Babycham and Diamond White and K ciders, saw sales in July and August fall by 40 per cent because young drinkers switched to alcopops. The market for alcopops peaked at £350 million a year.

The labour force

Changes in population structure will not only affect market demand but will also influence labour availability and other, less tangible, aspects of society. Compared to previous decades, there are now far fewer young people in the 16-to-25 age group who require employment. In many respects this is not, for the time being at least, a serious problem. In fact, considering the larger than average unemployment rates among young people, it may be a blessing in disguise. Figure 5.9 shows the typical unemployment pattern by age. Of course, if conditions of near full employment do re-emerge, labour shortages may result. However, it is likely that problems of skill shortages will be more acute, as is currently the case in nursing and teaching in the UK.

It is often argued that younger populations are more willing to embrace technological and social change while the tendency towards ageing may reduce workforce flexibility and dynamism. Additionally, it is traditionally believed that the young have greater geographical and occupational mobility, qualities which many argue contribute to workforce flexibility. The decline in the number of young workers has led may organisations to adjust their recruitment and staffing policies. For example, the Tesco supermarket chain and B&Q DIY stores have actively encouraged women with families and other more mature personnel to re-enter the workforce. It is moves such as this which have led to the large rise in the number of part-time jobs in the 1990s (see below and Chapter 9). Women returners are seen

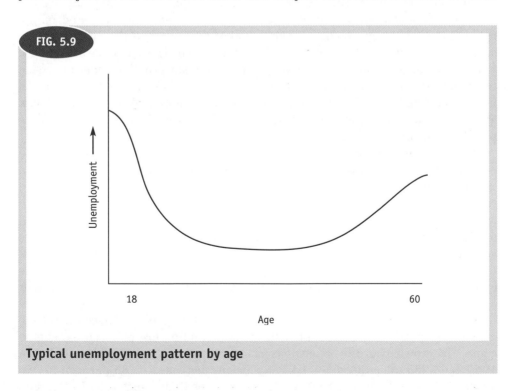

FIG. 5.9

Typical unemployment pattern by age

by many employers as offering a broader array of skills and experience than many school-leavers.

Although the recession of the late 1980s and early 1990s created a large body of unemployed labour for companies to draw upon, many stable or growing organisations have made every effort to retain their skilled and experienced workforce rather than rely on a shrinking number of young people from whom to select (and train) to fill available posts.

Problems for the government?

An ageing population creates many issues for governments and society to address. Some have argued from an intuitive as opposed to a 'scientific' basis that as average age increases society will more readily take on board the concerns and attitudes of the old as opposed to the young. There is little evidence that this is the case, although it is worthy of debate. It is difficult to assess whether the UK has become, for example, more past-orientated, security-conscious, wise or reflective – characteristics one might associate with more mature people. Perhaps the UK has always been past-orientated, at least in our lifetimes, and not particularly reflective or overflowing with wisdom, especially when it comes to major economic and social policy decisions!

There are further implications for society and governments of an ageing population. Pierre-Jean Thumerelle (1993) argues that 'ageing populations will become a profound structural handicap in the twenty-first century and only a marked revival in reproduction is likely to alter the course of this particular age structure'. The nature of this 'handicap' is multifaceted. There may be an increase in the dependency ratio, that is, larger numbers of people (mainly elderly) outside the working age group who are supported by those in employment. Pension benefits will be required in increasing quantities to support this enlarged group, and health care and other social benefits will be increasingly demanded as the population continues to age.

It is quite possible that the universal benefit of a state pension in the UK may be phased out or scaled down or provided only to the really needy. In New Zealand the universal right to a state pension, whatever one's economic status, has been removed. Hence those who have significant alternative sources of income in retirement receive a reduced benefit even though they may have fully contributed to this during their working lives. Certainly, one contributory reason for the government decision in the United Kingdom to increase the female age of retirement from 60 to 65 years old, in line with that of men, is recognition of the enormous cost implications of realigning male and female retirement ages at 60 or even 63 years of age.

All major political parties in the UK are considering the implications of the changing population structure for both the scale and nature of social benefits to come. The growing burden of pensions has been apparent for some time. Between 1960 and 1985 expenditure on old age pensions increased by 85 per cent in real terms in the four largest European Union countries (Italy, Germany, France and the UK) combined. It now stands at about 12 per cent of the gross domestic product of these countries. This upward trend is continuing, although not at quite the same pace.

The retirement/pension entitlement age may still be increased in the future; however, paradoxically, many companies across Europe are encouraging older employees to take early retirement. A great deal clearly depends on the state of the economy and the ability of individual nations to pay the increasing price of retirement pensions. Again, it is no coincidence that the basic state pension in the UK has merely been tied to the Retail Price Index (a measure of inflation) since 1979 despite the fact that average real earnings have risen by more than 60 per cent above the RPI since that time. Relative to average salaries in the United Kingdom, state pensions have declined significantly since 1979.

The problem of ageing is also acute for a number of key government services, notably the UK's National Health Service and other hospital and health organisations across the world. In simple terms, the elderly, being more prone to illness, impose considerably greater costs on the NHS than any other age group. More complicated and expensive medical techniques have become available to prolong human life and improve the quality of that life. It is a rather thought-provoking fact that an average over-75-year-old accounts for as much health and social service expenditure as ten adults in the 20 to 60 age group. It is also worthy of note that it is this same age category, that is, the over-75-year-olds, which has increased in numbers significantly in the UK and in other developed countries in recent years.

It is estimated that there will be a further increase of over 20 per cent in the numbers of 'very old' (over 75 years) between 1990 and 2020 in the UK. Most European Union countries are estimated to have had, by 1999, over 7 per cent of their population aged over 75. In Germany, the EU nation with the most rapid natural decline in population, it is estimated that the under-15s will represent just 12 per cent of the country's population in the first decade of the twenty-first century – just half that of the over-64s.

Of course it must be stressed at this juncture that most citizens in the United Kingdom have made regular contributions to the NHS, through taxation and National Insurance. It is also a recognised and strongly supported belief that society has an unconditional obligation to provide quality medical care to all its citizens. It could be argued that the standard and sincerity with which that care is provided, irrespective of cost, acts as a barometer of the state of advance of society. With increasing advocacy in many EU countries of market forces and individual responsibility the problem of an ageing population is one which warrants considerable debate within organisations and governments in order to address the inevitable issues and problems that lie ahead.

It is also worthy of note that rising life expectancy is a desirable state. However, if it is combined with continuing low levels of fertility, the elderly population of the European Union will comprise, by the middle of the next century, as much as one-third of the total. By that time it is likely that these people will be more affluent, better educated and housed, and both able and willing to contribute to the rich fabric of society. It is far from proven that the old will be a 'burden' from either a fiscal or sociological perspective.

SOCIAL DYNAMICS

In this section we will look more closely at some of the other social issues highlighted in Figure 5.1, focusing specifically on health, changing family and individual roles, crime, the changing face of organised labour, skills shortages and life-long learning.

Health

Health concerns have been high on most people's agendas for a number of years. It is evident that health consciousness, for many, is not a passing fad, but rather is stimulating a change in lifestyle. It is having an impact in many communities and across major business sectors. Exhibit 5.3 illustrates how health consciousness may influence the fortunes of a major global industry and promote changes of direction.

The situation described in Exhibit 5.3 illustrates a dynamic situation, with many forces acting upon the industry. A similar problem to that experienced by the tobacco business may also be occurring in other sectors. Health concerns and changing social attitudes to drinking alcohol have meant a decline in alcohol consumption in the major northern European markets. This has necessitated brewers taking action to protect their profits. This has included moving to southern European markets and moves by some UK brewers to diversify from their reliance on the sale of beer. Scottish Courage, for example, have interests in the wider leisure sector including hotels and holiday complexes.

Health scares regarding the consumption of chicken and beef, the animal welfare debate and the popularity of a vegetarian diet have all contributed to a fall in consumption of meat since the late 1980s. The uncertainty over the cattle-infecting disease bovine spongiform encephalopathy (BSE) served to further

EXHIBIT 5.3

The tobacco story

The tobacco industry has been the subject of considerable debate for many years. It is widely accepted that there are life-threatening consequences for those who smoke. Increasing research evidence also shows links between secondary or passive smoking and smoking-related diseases. These health issues have contributed to the situation that the industry finds itself in.

The market for tobacco products in the four major European markets (France, Germany, Italy, and the UK), which in 1993 accounted for two-thirds of the European market, declined by around 4 per cent annually, in value, between 1993 and 1996. Volume sales in the UK market have fallen steadily since the peak of 1973, when around 50 per cent of the adult population were regular smokers. From 1992 to 1996 sales fell 9 per cent by volume (source: Mintel). The European advertising ban will make it harder to establish new brands. The situation in the United States was also worrying for the industry. In 1977, Americans smoked 617 billion cigarettes; by 1993 it was down to 485 billion; the proportion of adults who smoked fell to 25 per cent. In 1993 the US Environmental Protection Agency blamed passive smoking for an estimated 3000 lung cancer deaths a year. The American Food and Drug Administration asked Congress whether it should ban cigarettes or regulate them as a drug. Legal action against the tobacco industry is aggressive, particularly in the United States.

As the market matured and declined competition became more intense as manufacturers fought to maintain sales. The result was acute price competition, often a feature of mature markets. This was intensified by the introduction of cut-price own-brand cigarettes. An unmistakable manifestation of this price competition was witnessed in 1993 when American tobacco giant Phillip Morris severely marked down the price of its leading brand, Marlboro, in an effort to recoup lost market share. This episode became known as 'Marlboro Friday'.

In response to the decline in the cigarette market many tobacco companies sought to diversify away from their core tobacco business. British American Tobacco's 'tobacco turnover' fell to below half of its total business activity, with its expansion into the financial services and insurance sector.

The situation facing the industry may be changing. The legal battle in the United States may be drawing to a conclusion. The major British manufacturers, BAT, Imperial and Gallaher are again independent tobacco companies. The cigarette market may well be in a mature or declining stage of its life cycle in many developed countries. However, because nicotine is a drug and the habit is hard to kick, sales levels in the developed nations now look fairly secure. 1998 saw the number of adults smoking increase by 1 per cent to 23 per cent.

These companies are cash-rich and looking to grow on the continent by buying local rivals and building plants (Rushe, 1998). The tobacco industry has targeted different geographical areas, particularly those where increasing industrialisation

> **Exhibit 5.3 continued**
>
> together with higher disposable incomes may create an extended market. Manu-facturers have expanded sales particularly in Africa, the Middle East, Asia Pacific (including the biggest market, China) and Eastern Europe, particularly the former Soviet Union. The latter is becoming important as demand for Western cigarettes, to replace those produced by the government, is increasing (Mintel). The industry has also targeted specific groups more clearly in their drive to maintain sales. Advertisers are targeting women and younger age groups in particular. ASH (Action on Smoking and Health) have accused manufacturters of targeting nightclubs.

emphasise the risks associated with the consumption of meat in the minds of some consumers. Although these health scares are of primary concern to farmers, the effects of the changing pattern of consumption are likely to spill over into the meat-processing industry.

Governments and health care professionals all over the world are becoming increasingly strident in their calls to protect the health of the population. In 1995, the British government launched the Health of the Nation initiative, which focuses largely on targets for reducing illnesses, which, in part, are caused by poor diet, smoking and other 'self-inflicted' causes. The role of the Food Standards Agency, which should be in place in 2000, will be to monitor many aspects of the food eaten in the United Kingdom. The voice of professionals is being heard, increasingly, in the media as they strive to bring health issues to the attention of the public. This media coverage will increase public awareness and give more power to pressure groups like ASH (Action on Smoking and Health). In 1999, a number of scientists called for a moratorium on genetically modified foods so that further assessment could be made of the impact they may have on consumers and the environment. This type of coverage is likely to further encourage governments to take action to limit the more undesirable health problems.

It is important that organisations are aware of likely health-related issues concerning their products so that responses can be co-ordinated and action taken to protect profits. Some organisations have been quick to respond to concerns. In the autumn of 1997 many alcopops were withdrawn from the market, partly due to the mounting concern that they were encouraging young people to drink. The government also took steps to reduce their popularity by introducing higher excise duties and a pub chain, J.D. Weatherspoon's, stopped selling them in their outlets.

Increasing awareness of health has had a number of positive results and provided opportunities for business. Individuals have been encouraged to change to a 'healthier' lifestyle. A bonus for firms should be a healthier workforce and reduced absenteeism. Food producers have responded to the health campaign and created profitable market niches. Low-fat spreads, lean cuisine menus and natural foods have attracted a following because of their perceived health qualities. Sales of fruit and pasta increased substantially between 1988 and 1995. Many leisure activities, including aerobics and gardening, have also benefited from increased participation. Sales at UK garden centres managed to buck the down-ward retail trend in the recession of the early 1990s, rising by 30 per cent to over £1 billion. The plethora of new health clubs and gyms is evidence of a dynamic and burgeoning market in that sector.

As people have become more health-conscious, the demand for sporting facilities has increased. It has been recognised that facilities are required by older age groups; this is in response to the changing demographic patterns. The general rise in life expectancy and a healthier older population has had a large impact throughout the business world.

A changing family and new roles

The role of individuals and the structure of the traditional family have been transformed in the last twenty years. Across Europe there has been a significant increase in the number of private households (see Table 5.3). The situation in the United Kingdom follows a similar pattern. Figure 5.10 shows the number and composition of UK households in 1998. The growing number of households is partly due to the growth of the number of one-person households and partly due to the growth of one-parent households.

As well as changes in the composition of households, there have clearly also been changes in the role and activities of individuals. In the past decade the British have become the hardest-working people in Europe (Craig and Grice, 1996), moving ahead of the Swedes (see Table 5.4). Almost 30 per cent of men and 12 per cent of women in Britain work at least 48 hours a week (ONS, 1998a).

The rise in hours is partly due to 'downsizing' by organisations in the face of global competitors, partly the result of declining trade union power (see below) and partly due to the office culture which demands attendance. The advantage for business organisations is measured in increased output, better productivity and increased profits. However, there is also a cost, notably accidents at work, the impact on family and poor health, particularly for women who, as they play an even greater role in the workplace, are affected by the same pressures (ONS, 1999). The UK population is said to suffer from the highest levels of stress in the

TABLE 5.3 Number of private households (figures in thousands)

Year	1988	1989	1990	1991	1992	1993
France	21305	21482	21542	21614	21736	21883
Germany	33821	34477	35170	34570	34510	34186
Italy	18081	18113	18174	19766	20306	21472
United Kingdom	21050	21145	21196	21198	21290	21337
Holland	5935	6026	6069	6112	6185	6230
Ireland	875	874	873	869	869	867
Euro total	141471	142652	143930	145262	146264	147592

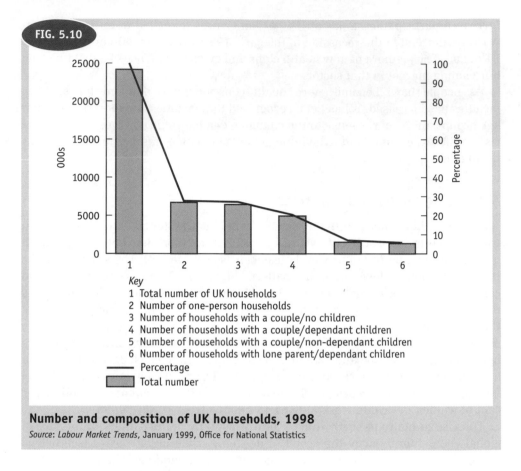

FIG. 5.10

Key
1 Total number of UK households
2 Number of one-person households
3 Number of households with a couple/no children
4 Number of households with a couple/dependant children
5 Number of households with a couple/non-dependant children
6 Number of households with lone parent/dependant children
—— Percentage
▨ Total number

Number and composition of UK households, 1998

Source: *Labour Market Trends*, January 1999, Office for National Statistics

TABLE 5.4   Average weekly hours of work in selected European countries

Country	Hours worked per week
Britain	43.7
Portugal	41.2
Sweden	40.7
Spain	40.5
Greece	40.5
Ireland	40.0
France	39.9
Luxembourg	39.8
Netherlands	39.5
Germany	39.5
Denmark	39.1
Italy	38.5
Belgium	38.2

Source: adapted from the European Commission (1998)

European Union. The working time directive, which sets a maximum 48-hour week for many workers, is designed to make a positive contribution to these health and safety problems (see Chapter 7).

New job opportunities and patterns of employment are also bringing a change to traditional family roles with greater employment of women, who comprise 45 per cent of the workforce (ONS, 1998b), in part-time, semi-skilled and professional jobs. The UK has a far higher proportion of part-time jobs than its main European Union competitors. From 1971 to 1994 the number of jobs for part-time employees increased by 2.6 million, and by 1998 over 25 per cent of employees worked part-time. The government defines part-time workers as those who work less than 30 hours per week. The European Union definition includes all individuals who work less than full-time hours. About 86 per cent of part-time employees are women and more than half of these are over 40 years of age (Naylor, 1994). There has also been a further decline of traditional full-time male occupations. The regions that relied on the old staple industries like heavy engineering, shipbuilding and the iron and steel industry, such as the north-east of England, have seen a continued demise of jobs in these traditional sectors.

The projected rise in the labour force between 1993 and 2006 will be accounted for solely by women (Ellison, 1993). Employers are keen to employ women on a part-time basis, originally partly because part-time workers had fewer employment rights, but also because they are cheaper to employ and traditionally are non-unionised.

Figure 5.11 shows that the industry sectors in which many women work are likely to be low-pay sectors, that is, those where pay is under the national

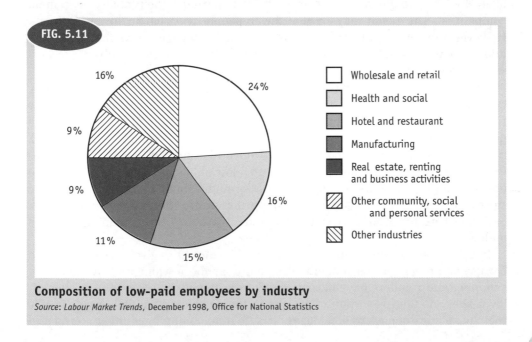

FIG. 5.11

16%
24%
9%
16%
9%
11%
15%

- Wholesale and retail
- Health and social
- Hotel and restaurant
- Manufacturing
- Real estate, renting and business activities
- Other community, social and personal services
- Other industries

Composition of low-paid employees by industry
Source: Labour Market Trends, December 1998, Office for National Statistics

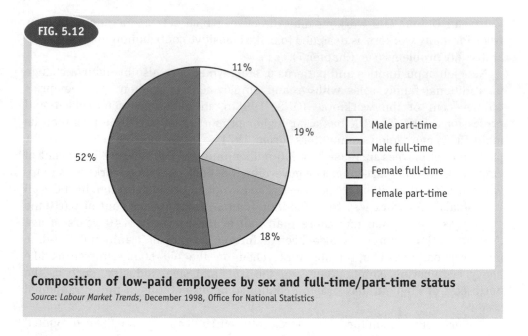

FIG. 5.12

11%

19%

52%

18%

Male part-time

Male full-time

Female full-time

Female part-time

Composition of low-paid employees by sex and full-time/part-time status
Source: Labour Market Trends, December 1998, Office for National Statistics

minimum wage level of £3.60/hour. Further, Figure 5.12 shows that 52 per cent of those workers who receive less than the national minimum are women working part-time.

Organisations, particularly those in sectors identified in Figure 5.11, may be concerned about this situation. The introduction of a national minimum wage is likely to have an impact on their costs, and perhaps their ability to remain competitive. The result may be that fewer people will remain in employment. However, this need not be the case. International evidence shows that a national minimum wage need not cause a significant adverse effect on jobs if set at a sensible level (ONS, 1998c).

The dynamic social situation has had enormous consequences for business. One of the results of the change in household composition can be seen in the retail sector, where there has been an increase in demand for convenience products: for example, a number of companies have promoted easy-to-cook ranges and 'one-person' products. Shops have also had to respond to changes in shopping habits. The change, in 1994, to allow shops in England and Wales to open for up to six hours on Sundays, was brought about by pressure from the stores prompted by consumers pushing for more flexible opening times. Supermarkets have gone even further and provide 24-hour opening at some outlets.

Increasing employment opportunities and affluence have given rise to increased car use and much greater mobility. People are far more willing to travel for their shopping and retailers have decentralised from the city centres to new edge-of-town sites. As the proportion of women in the workforce has increased, people seem to be more conscious of the use of leisure time. Shopping is either considered as a leisure pursuit or as something to be conducted quickly. The large out-of-town complex can meet both expectations.

Marketing and selling to different types of households represents a task that is very different to satisfying the needs of the typical nuclear family of popular mythology. It is also clear that the change is not consistent throughout Europe, and this brings problems for organisations as they struggle to cope with the disparate needs of Europe's 350 million consumers.

The change in working patterns and family structure has other consequences for organisations. Child-care facilities are of great importance to working and single parents. A commitment to universal nursery school places for 4-year-olds was a central part of the Labour party's general election campaign as it sought to win votes from the growing numbers for whom child care and pre-school education are important concerns. The government had plans to support 30 000 out-of-school clubs and pledged part-time nursery places for all 4-year-olds. Local authorities were instructed to draw up Early Years Development Plans. However, there is still a lack of child-care places. Only 700 000 regulated places are available for over 6 million children under 8. The situation in the private sector is even worse. Only 2 per cent of employers offer workplace nurseries (Roberts, 1998). Increasing provision will inevitably increase costs for organisations, but, as the proportion of working mothers with children under 5 has increased to 45 per cent, they may have to consider it.

Crime is a constant feature of every modern society and is a product of that society. As such, changing social conditions will affect the incidence of crime. In the next section we will explore some of the key issues.

Crime

Heidensohn (1991) suggests that the quite dramatic change that continues to affect family life and gender roles may have an impact on crime. She points out that a growing number of children are being raised in one-parent households, often poorly housed in the worst areas. It seems that these children may be more likely to be 'pushed' into criminal activity.

UK government statistics show that crime increased throughout the 1980s and into the 1990s. Although the rate of increase has declined, and most recently reported crime figures have actually fallen, it is likely that the numbers of crimes committed will continue to increase. Of equal importance to government and the business community is people's perception and fear of crime even though they are unlikely to be direct victims of serious crime.

Unemployment is thought by many academics to be linked to crime (Svindoff and McElroy, 1984; Farrington *et al.*, 1986), so the rising unemployment experienced in the European Union may be a contributory factor to higher levels of crime evident in some countries. Unemployment is likely to stay at historically high levels throughout the Western world.

Drug abuse has also been linked with crime, unemployment and social deprivation. The easy availability of crack cocaine and so-called designer drugs –

that are highly addictive and extremely profitable – is highlighted as a major contributory factor to the upsurge in crime in the United States and in a number of European countries including the UK.

The hidden economy

The continuation of old forms of crime, such as the hidden economy, which has been described as 'the illicit buying and selling of cheap, usually stolen goods among ordinary people in honest jobs', is likely to continue and expand, particularly with the introduction of new and improved consumer durables. The scope of the hidden economy has also increased from its traditional roots to include counterfeiting of perfumes, spirits, branded clothing and vital products such as pharmaceuticals, brake pads and engine turbines. The failure of such products can have serious consequences for the consumer and damage the reputation of the company whose name the product bears. Counterfeiting is said to account for 15 per cent of world GDP. The International Chamber of Commerce in 1998 estimated sales in excess of $250 billion per year. Much of the trade is under the control of criminal gangs who employ cheap and child labour and use the trade to launder profits from the sale of drugs.

The hidden economy can be stimulated by the actions of the legislative authorities or simply because legitimate suppliers are unable to meet demand. In Canada the hidden economy accounts for over 50 per cent of spirits consumed (Gibbens, 1995). This is in response to the high level of taxes levied by the Canadian government. The differences between tax and VAT rates amongst European Union members has led to the growth of large amounts of 'smuggling' across national borders. The situation is problematic for UK drink retailers, especially off-licences in the southern part of the country. From there access to the continent is relatively easy, and the large amounts of cigarettes and alcohol coming through the channel ports have affected profits. This has led to demands for the UK government to reduce excise duties on alcohol and tobacco in line with other EU countries.

Computer crime

The 9th United Nations Congress on the Prevention of Crime and the Treatment of Offenders (Cairo, May 1995) identified computer crime as a major concern. A 1995 study of 1200 American companies by the management consultants Ernst & Young confirms the growing problems of computer crime. Over half the companies in their survey had suffered financial losses related to computer security. The theft of computers and computer parts, rather than the theft of information, seems to be a problem for small businesses in particular. It is estimated that computer theft in the United Kingdom more than doubled from 1992 to 1994 and is now worth over £175 million a year. No one is exempt from the risks associated with computer crime. Bloombecker (1986) and the US National Center for Computer Crime Data describe victims as commercial users, banks, telecommunications authorities, government, individuals, computer companies, retail firms and universities. As with any activity there can be positive effects as market niches can be created that offer business opportunities.

The changing face of organised labour

For many European countries the three decades after World War II seemed to herald a move toward industrial democracy. In Sweden, for example, trade unionists have, since the 1970s, taken seats as members on company boards and were able to bargain with management over strategic decisions. Union membership has been maintained in Scandinavia, Germany and Belgium (Clarke and Bamber, 1994).

However, the picture is variable. Italy and France have seen sharp falls in membership. In the USA, union density (the proportion of employees who are members of a union) has fallen from 25 per cent in the late 1970s to 14 per cent in the late 1980s (Wever, 1998). In the UK the position of trade unions has radically changed between the late 1970s and the 1990s. There is little agreement between academics on the causes of the lessening of trade union power. Metcalfe (1990) argues that the decline in union membership is the result of an interaction of five factors:

- the macro-economic environment;
- the composition of jobs and the workforce including the relative decline in manufacturing industry;
- the policy of the state;
- the attitudes and conduct of employers; and
- the stance taken by employers.

It has been suggested by Freeman and Pelletier (1990) that the vast bulk of the observed 1980s decline in union density in the UK was due to the changed legal environment for industrial relations. It is clear that the Thatcher government of the 1980s was intent on curbing union power to remove this perceived constraint upon the operation of the 'free' market. The industrial relations environment in which organisations operate was transformed within just eleven years.

The main trade union legislation was the 1980, 1982, 1988 and 1990 Employment Acts, and the 1984 Trade Union Act. Marsh (1991) outlines the six major elements of this legislation.

1. The blanket immunity enjoyed by unions, as distinct from unionists, was removed by the Employment Act 1982.
2. The definition of a legitimate trade dispute has been successively narrowed so as to reduce the immunities enjoyed by unionists and unions.
3. The legal basis of the closed shop was initially restricted by the 1980 and 1982 Employment Acts and subsequently removed in the Employment Acts of 1988 and 1990.

4. Under the Trade Union Act 1984, unions are required to hold secret ballots for the election of officers. Unions are also required, under this act, to conduct political fund ballots.

5. The Employment Act of 1988 gives individual unionists a series of rights vis-à-vis their unions.

6. The 1990 Act makes unions responsible for their members' unofficial action, unless the unions repudiate the strike, or make it official, after a ballot.

The harsh political and economic climate of the 1980s and 1990s had a significant impact on union power and contributed to the decline in union membership and density. Exhibit 5.4 explores some of the recent trends in trade union membership.

EXHIBIT 5.4

Trade unionists today

The number of trade unions in Britain has declined along with membership, which fell from 13.3 million in 1979 to 9.0 million in 1992. By 1996 only 7.9 million employees were union members.

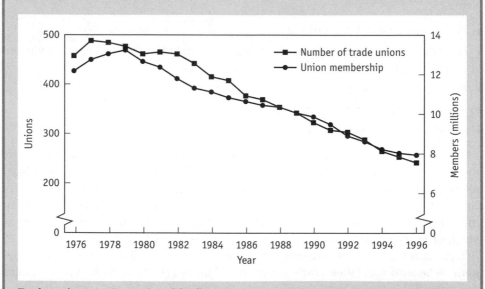

Trade unions and membership figures
Source: *Labour Market Trends*, July 1998, Office for National Statistics

Trade union density (or unionisation rate) fell from 39 per cent in 1989 to 30 per cent in 1997 (see Table 5.5).

These global figures hide some large variations in unionisation rates of which organisations may need to be aware. Union density is higher for permanent, full-time staff and tends to be concentrated in managerial, professional and

TABLE 5.5 Trade union density (percentage)

Year	1989	1990	1991	1992	1993	1994	1995	1996	1997
All employees	39	38	37	36	35	33	32	31	30
Men	44	43	42	39	38	36	35	34	32
Women	33	32	32	32	31	30	30	29	28
Full-time	44	43	42	40	39	38	36	35	34
Part-time	22	22	22	22	22	21	20	20	20
Production	45	43	42	38	37	36	34	32	31
Service	37	37	37	35	35	33	33	32	31

Source: adapted from *Labour Market Trends*, July 1998, Office for National Statistics

associate professional jobs and in companies employing more than 25 people. Men account for 55 per cent of total employee membership. Unionisation rises as length of service in the job increases and further rises with age, with the highest union density recorded in the 40–49 age group. Regional differences are also evident with high unionisation rates in northern England, Scotland and Wales and substantially lower rates in the south-east of England. Trade union membership is fairly evenly split between the private and public sectors; but union density figures for the private and public sectors in Autumn 1996 were very different – 21 per cent and 61 per cent respectively. Manufacturing unionisation rates vary from 54 per cent for motor vehicles to 19 per cent for electrical equipment sectors.

These figures represent a dynamic situation. Because individuals are likely to change jobs a number of times, the result is a rapid turnover in membership. The stereotypical union member of a generation ago, a man in a full-time, manual job, is out of date. Unions need to reach into new sectors such as fast food, high technology and small businesses to recruit the member of the new millennium.

Source: based on Trade Unionists Today, http://www.tuc.org.uk

The mid 1990s heralded concerns within the European Union about the UK gaining 'unfair' competitive advantage through 'social dumping', a consequence of the British government's anti-union stance and its decision to opt out of the Social Chapter and so undercut workers' rights and create a lower-cost environment for companies. Evidence suggests that international investment may seek out those European countries where union legislation is most severe and imposed social costs on employers are minimal. This was highlighted by Hoover's decision in 1995 to shift some of its production from France to Scotland. Hoover was determined to take advantage of the lower costs that production in Scotland would involve, prompting protest from France. The situation showed little change from the position summed up by Kavanagh (1987), who stated that 'the balance of advantage has changed since 1979, the election of a Conservative government, from union to employers and managers and from the consultative role granted to the unions to one in which they are virtually ignored by the government'.

By 1997, and the election of a New Labour government, change was percept-ible. Although the government had no plans to repeal any of the trade union legislation passed by the previous government, they signalled acceptance of the European Union Social Chapter and many EU directives. This has resulted in the introduction of European Works Councils, a national minimum wage (from 1 April 1999), new rights for part-time workers and parental leave laws. Furthermore, employees will be able to agree to be represented by a trade union even if they are not members of the union. New laws have also been proposed which will allow workers to join a union if over 50 per cent of employees approve.

Newly unionised companies may face stiff competition if their competitors decide to remain non-union. Works Councils in Germany and Belgium, for example, have the right to be consulted over closures and redundancies. There is only one EU-wide redundancy rule in operation. This requires worker representat-ives to be given 90 days' notice and proper consultation over large-scale redundancies. The likely extra costs imposed on organisations by these moves will have to be shared between prices, productivity and profit margins. Sutcliffe (1998) suggests that while large companies may have the resources to deal with the new legislation many small businesses are not likely to have such resources and some will not be strong enough to survive.

One benefit of the convergence of workers' rights and union status may be that it makes the task of managing across national borders less problematic. The differences in industrial relations between countries make it difficult for multi-national corporations to operate.

Employer–employee relationships do not have to be overtly confrontational. There are other approaches to employer–employee relations, and many com-panies have made great progress towards developing a more sensitive and creative relationship. Exhibit 5.5 illustrates one such case.

EXHIBIT 5.5

Scania Production Angers S.A., France

Built on the river Loire in northern France, Angers is the location for Scania's large new truck assembly plant. Scania, a Swedish company, manufactures heavy goods vehicles. Trucks from this plant are distributed across France, Spain and Italy.

Within the plant there are just four levels or grades of personnel from the Chief Executive to the individual operatives. The senior management team is mainly from Sweden, apart, that is, from Bernard Proux, the French HRM manager. The vast majority of the working people within the factory are grouped into clusters. In 1995 there were nine clusters, each with between 20 and 25 staff. These clusters concentrate on building a significant part of the trucks, for example, the cab. Each cluster has one manager. In addition to a part of the production line, clusters are also responsible for budgetary control, quality, routine maintenance of machinery and even the tidiness of the shop floor. Considerable responsibility and account-ability is thus devolved to the cluster mangers and ultimately to the team.

The cluster managers negotiate, individually, the salaries of all personnel within their team. The manager holds an annual performance review with each worker in his cluster. Discussion covers such topics as training needs, performance since last review and salary negotiations. The HRM department issues broad guidelines for such negotiations.

Members of each cluster work co-operatively with their colleagues. Morale appears to be high. Workers are given ample training opportunities and the resultant multi-skilling is rewarded through salary enhancements. Absenteeism in the plant is considerably below the national average at just 2 per cent and labour turnover is virtually non-existent.

The ideas encompassed within this system are in part unique. They reflect innovative Swedish thinking. The Swedish are renowned for their desire to build consensus in the workplace and for their liberal, non-hierarchical approach to social organisation generally.

This cultural force clearly influences organisational activity in Angers, where traditionally (rather like the UK) a more adversarial relationship between workers and management existed and where mutual antagonism was rife. As a result, collectivisation of labour was a natural mechanism to combat the power of the employer.

The dynamic nature of the environment makes it very difficult for organisations and their employees. Companies require knowledge so they can estimate the demand for their goods and services and the number of workers that they need. In some situations organisations may not be able to obtain the skilled labour that they need and so may face labour shortages. As the pattern of employment changes, with more part-time jobs, a distinction between core and peripheral workers, less trade union support, global competition and changing technology, it is becoming more important for individuals to plan their own development to gain more relevant skills.

Skills shortages

In February 1998 the British Chambers of Commerce (BCC) and the Institute of Management both published surveys reporting that skills shortages were harming businesses. According to the BCC 75 per cent of manufacturers were having problems recruiting staff (Browne, 1998). This problem is not new, but the impact on the rate of growth of the economy can be quite severe.

Information technology and computing was identified as a shortage sector. The Computing Services Association estimated that the number of people employed in IT rose by a third to over 1.3 million in five years, with over 30 000 vacancies (Brierley, 1998). This situation is the consequence of quickly outdated skills and the millennium bug. Skills shortages have prompted organisations to use some novel initiatives. The Construction Industry Training Board set up a web site for job seekers. The initiative was prompted by predictions that the industry would need 240 000 extra employees in 1998 (Pandya, 1998). Other possible remedies that are open to business include; using less well-qualified people, using more sub-contractors, recruiting abroad or offering more overtime to existing staff (Browne, 1998). The shortage of nurses has prompted many NHS trusts to recruit staff from overseas to make up the shortfall. While this may help in the short term, with fewer nurses being trained and an ageing population of those in post it is unlikely to provide a long-term solution.

While there are some predictions of shortages some bodies, for example the Confederation of British Industry, do not agree. It has been suggested that life-long learning and improvements in the education system and the greater take-up of training have increased labour flexibility and skills (see below).

Life-long learning

Every country needs educated people in all walks of life. The ability of a nation to develop and harness new ideas contributes to international competitiveness and hence raises standards of living in the country. Employers require individuals with ideas and those who are willing to take responsibility and be flexible at work and to meet the demands of new global markets. What are the forces pushing the need for life-long learning? Hillman (1996) suggests that the new millennium will coincide with a transformation of social and economic life whose key features are

- increasingly footloose economic activity;
- fierce global competition, fuelled by advances in information and communications technologies;
- shifts in occupational patterns in favour of managerial, professional and technical jobs in the service sector;
- growth in the importance of small and medium-sized enterprises, reflecting changes in the nature and organisation of work;
- more flexible labour markets in many countries, with part-time and temporary work, weaker relationships between employers and employees and the threat of recurrent unemployment and underemployment;
- fractured career patterns and work/leisure boundaries, with training increasingly the responsibility of individuals themselves;
- increasing dangers of exclusion for socially and economically disadvantaged groups.

Edwards (1997) makes similar observations; he identifies economic changes, demographic change and changes in technology as the most important factors. Employers now require employees to be flexible and multi-skilled. This enables companies to respond quickly to market changes as workers have the capacity to switch from one task to another. The challenge to the individual is clear. Competition for employment will escalate. People can no longer rely on stable employment in one organisation. Transferable skills and competence are crucial. Those with skills and qualifications will witness an expansion of opportunity, while those with the fewest will experience a contraction of employment (Glyn, 1996).

Technology has had an impact on the nature and quantity of employment. New technology has increased production and encouraged cultural change through the use of personal computers, satellites, jet aeroplanes and the Internet (see Chapter 4). The multi-skilled will have a distinct advantage in this environment, ensuring that life-long learning needs to continue.

The demographic time bomb was discussed earlier. The older population may result in a shortage of labour and gives rise to concerns regarding economic competitiveness. Longer retirement also gives the opportunity for individuals to take advantage of learning opportunities.

Life-long learning is also important because companies need consumers who need to be re-educated to fuel their desire to consume. Learning can create new markets for info-tainment and cultivate tastes for new lifestyles (Edwards, 1997). Post-compulsory education has a key role to play in helping to promote life-long learning. Since the early 1980s the higher education sector has doubled in size and merged into a single sector with common funding, quality assurance and support systems. Some of the most significant changes have included

- a major drive to expand and widen participation;
- a growing partnership with other agencies, especially FE colleges and employers;
- a steady growth of work-based learning;
- a co-ordinated national strategy to create an extensive technology infrastructure; and
- a widespread modularising of the curriculum to make it easier for individuals to meet particular needs (DfEE, 1997).

TABLE 5.6 Job-related training

Mode of training	Number in training (thousands)
Modern apprenticeship	118.9
National traineeships	11.9
Other training	145.7
Work-based training (young people)	276.5
Pre-vocational training	9.9
Occupational training	20.4
Work-based training (adults)	32.3

Source: adapted from Labour Market Trends, July 1998,
Office for National Statistics

The government also recognises the importance of training and has shown its support for it. A survey in the spring of 1998 found that 3.3 million employees (14.6 per cent) were receiving job-related training (ONS, 1999). The figures in Table 5.6 for July 1998 show the numbers undergoing different modes of training.

The role of government is that of a facilitator, providing the opportunities to train and re-train. A skilled, flexible workforce is important if a nation wants to attract international capital.

QUESTIONS

1. Changing health awareness has had a dramatic impact on the tobacco and farming industries. Using resources from your library and elsewhere, trace the impact of a health concern on another industry.

2. Utilising resources in your library and elsewhere, establish what may be the consequences for business and other organisations in the UK accepting the working time directive.

3. Identify and analyse the impact of the hidden economy on a chosen industrial sector.

4. Will trade union membership ever reach the levels seen in 1979? Discuss.

5. Analyse the impact that life-long learning is likely to have on businesses, individuals and the economy as a whole.

CONCLUSION

This chapter has explored some key aspects of the social environment. Although we could not hope to cover in detail the vast and complex issues which exist within the social community, and which influence organisational activity, we have attempted to explore a number of crucial areas. Some of the issues raised are further explored in Chapter 9.

SUMMARY OF MAIN POINTS

This chapter has focused on the social environment. More specifically it has looked at three broad aspects of that environment: national culture, demographic restructuring and various social changes. The main points made are:

- Organisations interact with society and operate within a cultural context.
- National culture varies considerably between countries on a number of key dimensions, each of which fundamentally influences an organisation's interaction with its environment.
- Population structure, life expectancy, birth rates and migration patterns vary both from place to place and through time, creating a dynamic demographic environment in which organisations operate.

- Population structures, and ageing in particular, have crucial implications for patterns of consumption, production, employment, savings and investment and for government and society as a whole.

- Changing health expectations have a substantial impact on all aspects of business.

- The traditional family structure and the role of individuals, in the UK and Europe, are rapidly changing, with social implications and consequences for patterns of consumption and employment.

- Crime of many types, such as theft, white-collar fraud, computer fraud and the hidden economy, appears to be a feature of the environment that requires a considered response from organisations.

- The power of trade unions, particularly in the UK, has been significantly reduced since the early 1980s.

- European Union directives and regulations may mean that trade unions have a more central role to play in the future.

- Life-long learning should support industry competitiveness and limit skills shortages.

NET SEARCH

http://www.sosig.ac.uk/
The social science information gateway gives access to over 900 resources on its database under subject headings.

http://europa.eu.int/en/comm/eurostat/eurostat.html
This is the site of the statistics office of the European Union. It provides a statistical information service on many relevant issues.

http://www.gov.uk/ons_f.htm
Site of the Office for National Statistics (ONS). This site is an excellent source of UK national statistics. Archives are available as well as new releases for the last 30 days.

http://dawww.essex.ac.uk
The data archive of social sciences and humanities. The site provides access to many other catalogues.

http://www.who.org
The website of the World Health Organization. The site covers many issues including environment and health.

http://www.open.gov.uk/
The government's website. This has access to a wide range of information on social issues, especially via the functional index.

REFERENCES

Adler, N.J. (1991) *International Dimensions of Organizational Behaviour*, 2nd edn, Kent: PWS.

Adler, N. (1997) *Organizational Behaviour*, 3rd edn, South-Western College Publishing.

Argenti, J. (1974) *Systematic Corporate Planning*, London: Nelson.

Bloombecker, J.J. (1986) 'Computer crime, computer security, computer ethics', *Statistical Report of the National Center for Computer Crime Data*, Los Angeles: NCCD.

Brierley, S. (1998) 'All systems go for IT jobs', *Guardian*, 5 September.

Browne, A. (1998) 'The skill lies in spotting shortages', *Observer*, 1 February.

Chinese Culture Connection Group (1987) 'Culture, contingency and capitalism in the cross-national study of organizations', *Journal of Cross-Cultural Psychology*, 18(2), 143–4.

Clarke, O. and Bamber, G.J. (1994) 'Changing management and industrial relations in Europe: converging towards an enterprise focus?', *International Journal of Human Resource Management*, 5(3), September.

Craig, O. and Grice, A. (1996) 'Rich rewards of the hard-working class', *Sunday Times*, 10 November.

Deal, T.E. and Kennedy, A.A. (1982) *Corporate Culture*, London: Addison-Wesley.

DfEE (1997) *The Contribution of Higher Education to the University for Industry*, Higher Education and Employment Division, Department for Education and Employment, HEE8, Sheffield.

Edwards, R. (1997) *Changing Places? Flexibility, Lifelong Learning and a Learning Society*, London: Routledge.

Ellison, R. (1993) 'British labour force projections: 1994 to 2006', *Employment Gazette*, April.

Farrington, D., Gallagher, B., Morley, L., St Ledger, R.J. and West, D.J. (1986) 'Unemployment, school leaving and crime', *British Journal of Criminology*, 26 (4).

Freeman, R. and Pelletier, J. (1990) 'The impact of industrial relations legislation on British union density', *British Journal of Industrial Relations*, vol. 28.

Gibbens, R. (1995) *The Financial Times*, 15 June.

Glyn, A. (1996) in Edwards, R. (1997) *Changing Places? Flexibility, Lifelong Learning and a Learning Society*, London: Routledge.

Heidensohn, M. (1991) *Crime and Society: Sociology for a Changing World*, Basingstoke: Macmillan.

Hillman, J. (1996) *University for Industry: Creating a National Learning Framework*, London: Institute for Public Policy Research.

Hofstede, G. (1983) 'The cultural relativity of organisational practices and theories', *Journal of International Business Studies*, Fall.

Kavanagh, D. (1987) *Thatcherism and British Politics*, Oxford: Oxford University Press.

Lebon, A. (1990) 'Ressortissants communautaires et étrangers des pays tiers dans l'Europe des Douze', *Revue Européenne des Migrations Internationales*, 6.

Levitt, T. (1983) 'The globalization of markets', *Harvard Business Review*, May/June.

Marsh, D. (1991) *Trade Unions in Britain: Union Power and the Thatcher Legacy*, Basingstoke: Macmillan.

Metcalfe, D. (1990) 'Union presence and labour productivity in British manufacturing industry: a reply to Nolan and Marginson', *British Journal of Industrial Relations*, vol. 28.

Naylor, K. (1994) 'Part-time working in Great Britain – an historical analysis', *Employment Gazette*, December.

ONS (1998a) *Labour Market Trends*, December, Office for National Statistics.

ONS (1998b) *Labour Market Trends*, November, Office for National Statistics.

ONS (1998c) *Labour Market Trends*, September, Office for National Statistics.

ONS (1999) *Labour Market Trends*, January, Office for National Statistics.

Pandya, N. (1998) 'Build a new career with a hand from the internet', *Guardian*, 14 February.

Pearman, H. and Nuki, P. (1996) 'High living', *The Sunday Times*, 1 December.

Peters, T.J. and Waterman, R.H. (1982) *In Search of Excellence*, Harper and Row.

Roberts, Y. (1998) 'Left holding the baby', *Guardian*, 27 January.

Ronen, S. and Shenkar, O. (1985) 'Clustering countries on attitudinal dimensions: a review and synthesis', *Academy of Management Review*, July, 445–54.

Rushe, D. (1998) 'Tobacco becomes financially correct', *The Sunday Times*, 22 November.

Sathe, V. (1983) 'Implications of corporate culture: a manager's guide to action', *Organisational Dynamics*, Autumn.

Sutcliffe, A. (1998) 'Flood of employment law brings chaos', *The Sunday Times*, 15 November.

Svindoff, M. and McElroy, J. (1984) *Employment and Crime*, New York: Vera Institute of Justice.

Thumerelle, P.-J. (1993) 'Age and sex structures', in Noin, D. and Woods, R. (eds) *The Changing Population of Europe,* Blackwell, pp. 76–81.

Trompenaars, F. (1997) *Riding the Waves of Culture*, London: Nicholas Brealey.

Wever, K.S. (1998) 'International labor revitalization: enlarging the playing field', *Industrial Relations*, 37 (3), 388–407.

White, P. (1993) 'Ethnic minority communities in Europe', in Noin, D. and Woods, R. (eds) *The Changing Population of Europe*, Blackwell, pp. 206–25.

6

THE ECOLOGICAL ENVIRONMENT

Alistair Sutton
and Jamie Weatherston

LEARNING OBJECTIVES

On completion of this chapter you should be able to:

- understand some serious ecological concerns affecting the earth;

- appreciate the basic economic arguments which underlie the operation of the marketplace (including the law of demand and supply and the concept of externalities) and which underpin any analysis of how business organisations are able to pollute the environment;

- outline the range of actions which can be taken by governments to monitor and regulate the output of pollutants from economic activity;

- appreciate the range of organisational responses to ecological issues in general and to environmental legislation in particular;

- recognise the impact of economic activity, and of different regulatory regimes, on consumers, and appreciate the extent of consumer power in respect of ecological issues;

- set the above outcomes in the context of actions taken at global, national and local scales.

KEY CONCEPTS

- environmental pollution
- climate change
- theory of demand and supply
- price determination

- equilibrium
- market failure
- externalities
- the principle that the polluter pays
- sustainable development
- BATNEEC

- environmental impact assessment
- environmental contexts
- environmental options
- the consumer and the environment
- ethics

INTRODUCTION

We are all aware of a range of environmental problems facing the planet. In this chapter we look at some of the most serious ecological concerns and the extent of their impact, investigate the economic arguments which help us analyse how organisations are able to pollute the environment and explore the range of actions which can be taken by governments to monitor and regulate the outputs from economic activity.

Over recent years the basis of much environmental regulation has been via market-based mechanisms. Therefore, the introductory part of this chapter examines the economic arguments which underpin the operation of market-based economies. The areas covered include the laws of demand and supply and the price mechanism. This section also has a wider purpose; it links to the coverage of competition in Chapter 2, as demand theory underpins much of the work related to market structure (please note that this section features general, rather than environment-related, examples to explain the ideas).

The chapter moves on to consider externalities and different approaches to regulation. We end the chapter by examining the different approaches adopted by organisations towards environmental issues, discussing the impact of these upon consumers and noting the extent of consumer power in respect of ecological issues. This analysis is set in the context of actions taken at a global, national and local scale.

Environmental pollution has an impact on a number of areas which affect us all. In order to assess the nature of this impact we need to distinguish between renewable and non-renewable resources. Renewable resources can be replaced, but non-renewable resources when used are lost forever.

There has been considerable concern about the effects of acid rain, loss of biodiversity, sea pollution, depletion of natural resources such as tropical rain-forests, and the destruction of the ozone layer. Since the end of the 1980s there has been much discussion of climate change, as nine out of ten of the warmest years on record have occurred since 1983 (Radford, 1997). A number of international conferences such as those in Rio in 1992, Berlin in 1995, Kyoto in 1997 and Buenos Aires in 1998 have taken place to discuss, amongst other things, the more changeable climate being experienced in recent times. This chapter explains the impact of these on organisations and government.

Without naturally occurring greenhouse gases like carbon dioxide, methane, nitrous oxide and water vapour, human life would not exist. However, industrial development has necessitated the burning of significant amounts of coal, oil and methane and the felling of more and more forests resulting in excessive carbon dioxide (CO_2) emissions. Carbon dioxide and chlorofluorocarbon (CFC) gases are said to contribute to the greenhouse effect. The greenhouse effect brings a rise in global temperatures. CFCs are being steadily banned due to their adverse effects on the earth's protective ozone layer.

The increase in the earth's temperature has, in turn, caused sea levels to rise. It has been predicted that, at current rates of increase, sea levels could rise by another 50 cm by the year 2100 (Radford, 1997). This would have a serious impact on coastlines, particularly those in East Anglia, Holland, Egypt, India and Bangladesh, as well as imperilling many small low-lying islands such as the Maldives in the Indian Ocean and the Marshall Islands in the Pacific Ocean (Brown, 1995). Effects would clearly be felt in communities near the coast and have severe consequences for agricultural areas such as the Ganges Delta in India, an area already prone to flooding.

Whatever one's view of the seriousness of the problems of global warming and destruction of the ozone layer, it is clear that environmental problems result from economic activity. The growth of business activity is often at the expense of the environment.

The balance of power between business organisations, particularly large multi-nationals, on the one hand, and individuals and environmental groups on the other, is grossly unequal. Government has a role to play regarding the potentially polluting activities of organisations. Regulation proceeds, essentially, from a knowledge of how markets operate. It is therefore appropriate to examine the theory of demand and supply and of externalities in order to appreciate the debate on environmental regulation and the role of government intervention. For the global economy to become ecologically sustainable, it may be necessary to organise business and industry along ecologically sound principles. This will require the transformation of corporations, their products, production systems and management practices (Shrivastava, 1995). In this chapter we will explore the role and activities of each of these actors and their effect, both positive and negative, on the environment.

THE IMPACT OF THE MARKETPLACE ON THE ECOLOGICAL ENVIRONMENT: AN ECONOMIC PERSPECTIVE

The two extremes of economic management, the free market (discussed in Chapter 2) and the command economy, are not evident in their purest form within any country. For example Hong Kong, which used to closely resemble a pure market economy, now has to follow the diktat of the Communist government in

China to some extent. The recent past has seen the demise of command economies in, for example, Poland, the Czech Republic, Bulgaria and the former Soviet Union. Market forces have been allowed to become more active in these economies to alleviate the worst excesses of state control.

Within all Western-style market economies government influences the allocation of goods and services. It does this for a number of reasons:

- to moderate the trade cycle by demand management and supply-side policies to promote such things as employment, investment and direct structural change (see Chapters 3 and 7);

- to restrain unfair use of economic power by, for example, monopolies (see Chapter 2);

- to correct inequalities through the redistribution of wealth via taxation or regional policy to support industry (see Chapters 3 and 7);

- to manage price levels, employment, balance of payments and growth rate in accordance with social objectives (see Chapter 3);

- to provide public goods, such as defence, law and order, roads and parks; such things are socially desirable, but unprofitable, and it is generally not possible to directly charge for them; and, of specific relevance to the subject of this chapter,

- to remove socially undesirable consequences of commercial activity. The private profit motive does not always ensure that public wealth will be maximised; it can create environmental problems, such as pollution and resource depletion.

Society has to find a way of resolving the primary economic issues of what to produce, and how, and for whom, to produce it. In many economies we have seen that these questions are now more commonly being answered by market forces (see Chapter 2). In this chapter we will explore the problems that industrial activity causes to the environment. However, in order to understand how market forces can result in environmental problems and to appreciate the viability of potential solutions it is necessary to understand the foundations of the market system, that is, the concepts of demand and supply.

The theory of demand

Demand is the quantity of a commodity which will be demanded at a given price over a certain period of time. By 'demand' we mean demand backed by money, or effective demand. For most goods (normal goods) the quantity demanded will rise as price falls (even if this increase in consumption leads to an increase in pollution or environmental damage). A lower price will mean that more will be purchased; at a higher price less will be purchased. This is the law of downward sloping demand. For any commodity it is possible to use market data to construct a demand schedule, showing how many units of the commodity would be demanded at various prices. Table 6.1 shows a fictitious demand schedule for CDs.

TABLE 6.1 Demand schedule for compact discs

Price/unit (£)	Quantity demanded/week (000s)
13	80
12	130
11	200
10	260
9	300

The data in Table 6.1 can be presented in the form of a graph. Price is plotted on the vertical axis and quantity on the horizontal axis. This is the demand curve as shown in Figure 6.1.

The demand curve tells us the quantities which would be demanded at each price. From the area of the rectangle $OXYZ$ we can calculate the total revenue at the given price, as the area of the rectangle is equal to price multiplied by quantity $(P \times Q)$. As price (P_x) changes there will be extensions or contractions of demand (changes in the quantity demanded) as shown in Figure 6.2.

As the price of CDs decreases from £12 to £11, demand extends along the demand curve to 200 000 units. The opposite effect is evident, as can be seen from Figure 6.2: as price rises there is a contraction of demand. In this example we see the effect of a price change only. However, it is not only price that determines or influences the demand for a product. The other determinants or conditions of demand are:

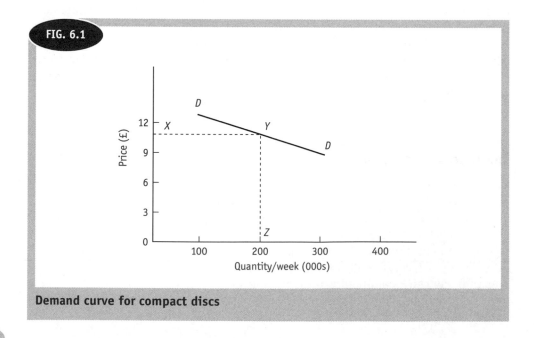

FIG. 6.1

Demand curve for compact discs

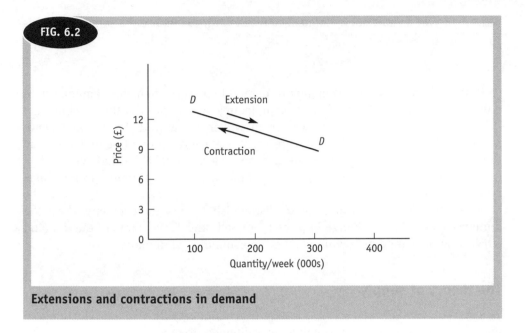

FIG. 6.2

Extensions and contractions in demand

1. *Price of other related goods* (P_r). Changes in the price of other goods will affect the demand for CDs, whether the goods are substitutes, such as pre-recorded cassette tapes, or complements, such as CD players. Substitute goods are competitively demanded. If the price of cassette tapes rises then demand for that product will fall. Some consumers will switch to the substitute product; in this case demand for CDs will rise. Complementary goods, in comparison, are jointly demanded: if the price of CD players falls, for example, then more people will buy them and demand for CDs will also rise. Demand for CDs trebled between 1988 and 1993, largely as a result of the increased affordability of compact disc players.

2. *Income* (Y). A rise in income will result in more goods demanded, whatever the price. Your spending on CDs is likely to increase when you begin to earn more money. A reduction in income will obviously have the reverse effect. However, in the case of inferior goods, an increase in income will result in a fall in demand. For example, your spending on baked beans is likely to fall as you earn more money and are able to buy higher quality items.

3. *Taste* (T). A change in taste or fashion (perhaps influenced by advertising) will alter the demand for that product. If mini-discs gain in popularity, and Sony, in particular, are marketing their mini-disc player energetically, then the demand for CDs is likely to fall off, perhaps in the same way that LP records have largely disappeared in the 1990s.

4. *Other factors* (Z). These include seasonal factors, government influences such as legislation limiting the sale of firearms, the availability of credit and changes in population size or structure.

Demand for a good can be influenced by all of these factors. We can express this by the demand function:

$$D_x = f(P_x, P_r, Y, T, Z)$$

If any one of these determinants of demand changes then the demand curve will shift to the right or the left. For example, in a spell of hot weather (a change of Z in the equation) demand for ice cream will increase and the demand curve moves to the right. As cold weather returns, less ice cream will be demanded so the demand curve will move to the left (see Figure 6.3). Note that we need to qualify this by stating that we expect this to happen *ceteris paribus* – other things being equal.

To summarise, it is important to distinguish between movement *along* the demand curve, due to change in price of a good, and movements *of* the demand curve, due to change in one of the other determinants of demand.

The theory of supply

The market for goods and services is determined not only by demand. The demand which consumers express, through their willingness to buy, needs to be met by the willingness of producers to supply a good. Supply is the propensity of producers to sell the commodity at a given price over a certain period of time.

More goods will be supplied at a higher than at a lower price. This law of the upward sloping supply curve can be explained by the aim of producers to

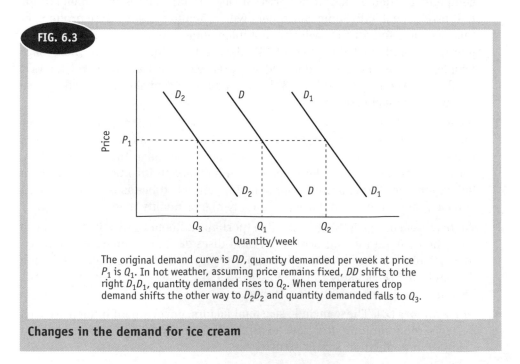

FIG. 6.3

The original demand curve is *DD*, quantity demanded per week at price P_1 is Q_1. In hot weather, assuming price remains fixed, *DD* shifts to the right D_1D_1, quantity demanded rises to Q_2. When temperatures drop demand shifts the other way to D_2D_2 and quantity demanded falls to Q_3.

Changes in the demand for ice cream

TABLE 6.2 Supply schedule for compact discs

Price/unit (£)	Quantity supplied/week (000s)
13	350
12	280
11	200
10	145
9	45

maximise their income. We know from our earlier discussion of the demand side that the data can be presented either in the form of a schedule or graphically, as shown in Table 6.2 and Figure 6.4.

As price changes there will be extensions or contractions along the supply curve (changes in the quantity supplied). For example, if the price of CDs moves from £11 to £10 the quantity supplied falls from 200 000 units to 145 000 units per week, as shown in Figure 6.5.

Also in this example we see the effect of a price change only. However, as with demand it is not only price that determines or influences the supply of a product. The other determinants or conditions of supply are:

1. *The objectives of the firm* (B). A firm aiming to achieve maximum profits will have a different level of output (lower) from one which is aiming to maximise sales.

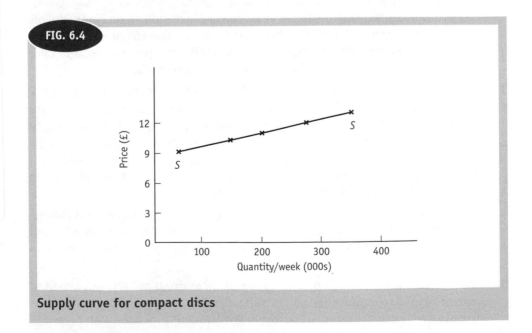

FIG. 6.4

Supply curve for compact discs

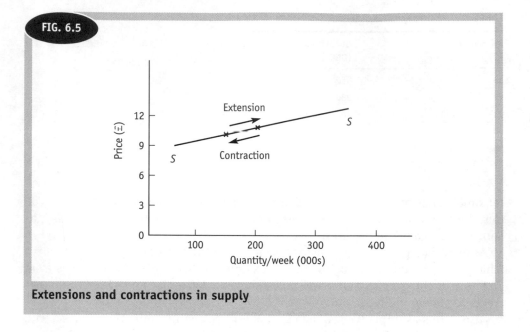

FIG. 6.5

Extensions and contractions in supply

2. *The price of certain other goods* (P_g). Where goods are jointly supplied, they are said to be complements in production, like beef and leather; a decrease in the price of one good will lead to a decrease in the quantity of the other good which will be supplied. If the price of beef falls then farmers are less likely to supply it to the market. This occurred during the BSE scare in 1996, discussed in Chapter 5. The result may be a reduction in the supply of leather. Goods that are substitutes, such as beers at a brewery, are said to be competitively supplied. A brewer could probably switch production from one brew to another, for example from bottled beer to draught if the price of draught beer were to rise while the price of bottled beer was unchanged.

3. *Price of the factors of production* (P_f). The cost of production will rise if the price of a factor of production increases. For example, if higher wages are demanded and the price of a good remains unchanged then its output becomes less profitable, and less will be produced. In this scenario it may be better for the workforce not to increase its wages in order to protect jobs. Other costs, such as raw materials and the cost of capital, are also important to companies and influence their output decisions.

4. *The state of technology* (T). Technology can be used to improve productivity. Part of the success of UK industry in the 1980s and 1990s has been achieved through introducing new technology which reduced costs and made some firms more competitive.

5. *Other factors* (Z). Although this heading acts as a 'catch-all' it is important in its own right. An organisation can be influenced by its expectations of what is likely to happen in the future. Changes in government practices with regard to

taxation, subsidies or regional policies have a substantial impact. This will be discussed below.

Supply of a good can be influenced by all of these factors. We can express this by the supply function:

$$S_x = f(P_x, B, P_g, P_f, T, Z)$$

The rules that apply to the demand curve also apply here. If there is a change in one of the conditions influencing supply, assuming price is held constant (*ceteris paribus*), then the supply curve may be shifted to the right or left. For example, a business organisation may seek to improve its competitive position by increasing its market share. This is a change in the objective of the organisation (B). As a result the supply curve will move to the right because the firm has increased its output. The reverse situation will also be true (see Figure 6.6).

To summarise, it is important to distinguish between movement *along* a supply curve, due to change in price of a good, and movements *of* the supply curve, due to change in one of the other determinants of supply.

Price determination

Economists use the term 'equilibrium' to describe a state in which internal forces, or variables, are in balance and there is no tendency to change. Market price is determined by the price at which consumers are willing to buy and producers willing to sell. This is called the equilibrium price. The corresponding quantity is

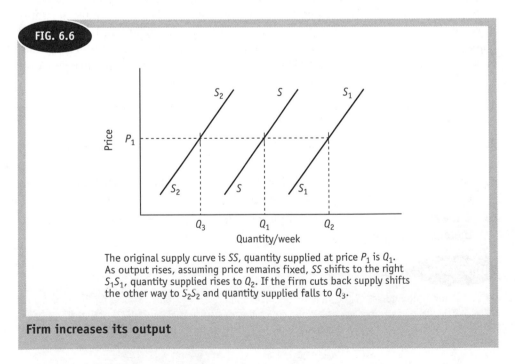

FIG. 6.6

The original supply curve is *SS*, quantity supplied at price P_1 is Q_1. As output rises, assuming price remains fixed, *SS* shifts to the right S_1S_1, quantity supplied rises to Q_2. If the firm cuts back supply shifts the other way to S_2S_2 and quantity supplied falls to Q_3.

Firm increases its output

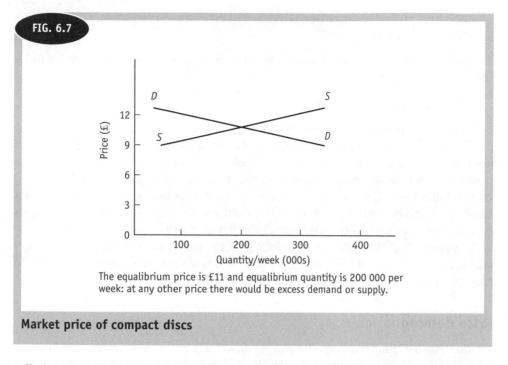

FIG. 6.7

The equalibrium price is £11 and equalibrium quantity is 200 000 per week: at any other price there would be excess demand or supply.

Market price of compact discs

called the equilibrium quantity. In the case of the market for CDs, in our example, the equilibrium price is £11 and the equilibrium quantity is 200 000 per week. The point of intersection is called the equilibrium point in the market (see Figure 6.7).

If there are changes in demand the demand curve moves and changes in supply result in the movement of the supply curve. Both market price and quantity will change. The extent of the changes depends on the price-elasticity of supply and elasticity of demand, that is, the extent to which demand and supply are sensitive to changes in price. However in general we can state that

1. An increase in demand causes an increase in the equilibrium price and quantity.

2. A decrease in demand causes a decrease in the equilibrium price and quantity.

3. An increase in supply causes a decrease in the equilibrium price and a rise in the equilibrium quantity.

4. A decrease in supply causes an increase in the equilibrium price and a fall in the equilibrium quantity.

QUESTIONS

1. Examine the figures for the sale of ice cream and draw up a graph. Do the figures reveal a particular pattern in demand? What are companies such as Häagen-Dazs trying to do to overcome this pattern of demand?

2. What happens to the equilibrium price and quantity if both the demand and supply curves shift?

3. Give reasons for and explain, using diagrams,

    (a) the fall of spirit sales in Thailand by 30 per cent during 1997;

    (b) the 15 per cent increase in cruise bookings by young couples in the United States in the spring of 1998.

4. (a) Using diagrams, show how the opening of the Channel Tunnel decreases the price of journeys across the Channel. What happens to the number of journeys?

    (b) What happens to the demand and supply curves for air and ferry journeys across the Channel?

MARKET FORCES AND THE ENVIRONMENT

When every person's standard of living is maximised, market forces can be said to be an efficient mechanism for the allocation of resources. In this case the market can operate free from any regulatory control. This scenario is unrealistic; it is unlikely that a market can ever achieve such an allocation and so be completely free from intervention. The release of CFCs from, for example, aerosol containers, was thought to be having a serious impact on the ozone layer (see above). Resources, in this case, were being used to the detriment of society in general. The market did not act to reduce the impact of CFCs and adopt less-polluting propellants until put under substantial consumer and political pressure (e.g. the Montreal Protocol). Even so, many refrigeration systems and car air-conditioning units still use CFCs. This example shows that, although the market may act to reduce the harmful impact that it has on the environment, it is often in response to stakeholder pressure, discussed later in the chapter, and frequently an incomplete response. Finally, governments had to play a role in reducing the use of CFCs; on 1 January 1995 the production and import of CFCs was banned in the European Union.

It is probable that market forces will not bring about the best or optimum allocation of resources. It is beyond the scope of this chapter to look in detail at all aspects of the failure of markets, but it is vital for us to assess how this failure can result in damage to the environment.

It is not only in market systems that high levels of pollution have been experienced. The former Communist states have also suffered. In east-central Europe considerable pollution may be the result of four decades of central planning by Communist parties, which failed to adhere to declared priorities for sound environmental management; instead, there was serious ecological damage of the sort previously attributed only to Western capitalist regimes (Carter and Turnock, 1993).

The production and consumption of goods and services can generate spillover effects that indirectly affect persons other than those who produce or consume them. These effects are known as externalities. Pollution may result from economic

activity. An organisation producing chemicals may discharge waste into a river, causing fish to die. In this case the producer, while undertaking its normal business, has harmed third parties such as the marine life and the fishing industry. It has created an external cost known as a negative externality (Lipsey and Harbury, 1992). Alternatively, positive externalities are created when there is an external benefit from economic activity.

Organisations do not, generally, fully consider the wider social costs or benefits of their business activities. For example, a company may argue that it is not in its economic interest to invest in anti-pollution systems and so may economise on the provision of anti-pollution controls (this will be discussed later in the chapter). In this case 'private costs' and shareholder returns are of uppermost concern to the organisation. This judgement may lead to higher levels of noxious emissions into the environment. We can show how this happens using a diagram.

Figure 6.8 shows the demand curve DD for a product x. SS is the supply curve which corresponds to the private cost of producing the product because the organisation only takes account of the private costs of production, ignoring the wider social costs such as pollution. Economists label this the marginal private cost (MPC) curve. In this case the market price for good x is P and the quantity is Q.

However, if the organisation were to take stock of all of the costs involved in its activities it would have to include external costs, that is, the cost to society of the externalities caused. Adding external cost to private cost gives us the social cost and shifts the supply curve or MPC curve to the left, labelled MSC in Figure 6.8. Price would rise from P to P_1, and quantity demanded would fall from Q to Q_1. The resulting lower output should reduce the externalities. This new level of output is the socially efficient level of output with no welfare loss to society.

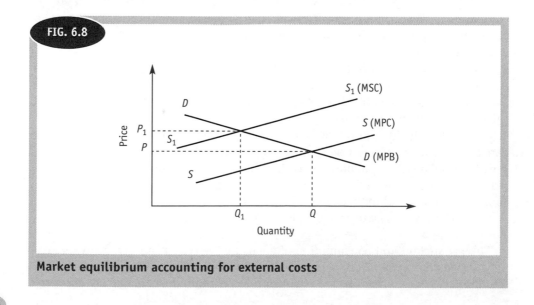

FIG. 6.8

Market equilibrium accounting for external costs

It is clear that negative (and positive) externalities arise under specific circumstances. Companies do affect individuals and vice versa. We can examine this situation under four main headings:

- actions by companies which affect other companies;
- actions by companies which affect individuals;
- actions by individuals which affect companies;
- actions by individuals which affect other individuals.

Actions by companies which affect other companies

It is best to illustrate this with an example. Industrial waste from production processes can enter the sea and so impact on commercial fisheries. The gradual pollution of Japan's inland sea, between Honshu and Shikoku, in the 1950s and 1960s severely damaged fish stocks. A similar situation can be seen in the North Sea and in many of Europe's rivers. In these cases private costs have predominated as it is not in the economic interests of those industries producing the waste to reduce pollution caused by their activities. In these cases a negative externality has arisen.

Positive externalities can be of great benefit. The success of some football clubs, especially the large Public Limited Companies, can enhance business activity in a town or city. With over 30 000 spectators at games the knock-on effect on shops, restaurants and pubs is substantial. The 'feel good' factor is also felt by supporters, who, as employees, may even bring benefits to their employing organisations. It has even been suggested that sporting success can help to attract inward investment.

Action by companies which affect individuals

Companies can affect individuals in many ways. A dramatic illustration of producers affecting individuals was illustrated by the Union Carbide disaster in Bhopal, India in 1984, when methyl isocyanate, a poisonous gas, was released from the plant causing 2600 deaths and many adverse long-term consequences for the surrounding community. However, international experience confirms that education and training is a positive externality. In 1997 Unilever's Elida Gibbs factory received an award for educational excellence from Brazil's Ministry of Education. The training employees receive has a strong environmental basis which can also applied to their attitudes outside the workplace and promote awareness of the environment.

Action by individuals which affect companies

Road traffic is likely to grow substantially over the next 20 years. Compared with 1996 it has been estimated that overall traffic volumes will rise by 9 per cent

by 2001, by 19 per cent by 2006, by 28 per cent by 2011, and by 38 per cent by 2016. The example of traffic congestion illustrates how individuals do not consider their full impact on road conditions. This increasing congestion raises transportation costs for firms and has direct repercussions on the price of goods in the shops.

There is a clear positive benefit to industry of a better trained and more highly qualified workforce. However, it is increasingly difficult for organisations, particularly in times of recession, to fund in-house training. This training gap is now being filled by individuals taking the initiative for their own training. Over 30 per cent of 18-year-olds are now enrolled on higher education courses. Through undertaking training and extending their education, often at their own expense, these students should provide a well-trained workforce for business organisations.

Action by individuals which affect other individuals

There are further, potentially serious, social costs which result from current levels of private motoring. Concerns have long been raised about problems to health from exhaust emissions. This is clearly an example of a negative externality where the activity of individuals affects other individuals. On the other hand, a positive externality was created in 1994/95 by the National Health Service in the United Kingdom when it immunised young school children against measles. Not only are those who have been immunised protected from the disease, but others in the wider community, who have not received the treatment, also benefit as there will be less carriers of the disease overall. The statistical likelihood of contracting measles is now reduced. In this case the social benefits of the programme exceed the private benefit to the individual.

Summary

Negative externalities are a direct consequence of economic activity. If private producers exclude the costs imposed on other people from their output calculations they will produce more of the good than is socially desirable. The direct result will be negative externalities, as outlined earlier, and a welfare loss to society. Some pollution, however, is socially acceptable because the enormous cost of reducing many types of pollution to zero may pose even more limits on society.

It has been suggested that it is in the economic interests of individuals and companies to accept the consequences of these externalities. This view, which encourages negative externalities, may be blinkered. Short-term benefits of having more and cheaper products to consume may not be in the wider long-term interests of the community and the environment. However, organisations in some parts of the world are often encouraged to take this short-term view by their shareholders as they strive for greater returns. Having considered the difference between the private and social optimum output, we now need to examine the role of the government.

MEASURES AVAILABLE TO LIMIT EXTERNALITIES

There is a disincentive for organisations to develop or install new, more environmentally friendly equipment, because the cost of so doing is likely to be a reduction in their competitiveness. The UK shoe industry, for example, has a dilemma regarding the harmful effects that can result from the extensive use of adhesives in the manufacture of shoes. The excessive cost of pollution control equipment will increase costs overall and, perhaps, result in an inability to compete with cheaper, less environmentally conscious, overseas competitors. However, taking no action may mean that stricter legislation is imposed on the industry.

Governments do not have to let all negative externalities persist. They can intervene in the market by a range of means, including adopting policies that use, or improve, the price mechanism, or by employing extra-market policies. Cost is a key consideration for government and the organisations when deciding upon the appropriate type and timing of intervention. In this section we discuss five ways of limiting externalities:

- promotion of bargaining;
- taxes and charges;
- marketable permits;
- grants or subsidies; and
- regulation and anti-monopoly legislation.

The principle is designed to encourage businesses to improve processes and is achieved by setting standards and controls which companies have to comply with in order to avoid incurring any extra costs through taxes or fines.

Organisations will usually try to pass on their increased costs to the consumer. Some consumers will refuse to pay the increased price and consumption of the good will fall. As was noted earlier in the chapter, this will reduce the level of externalities, for example pollution, and result in a more socially-efficient level of production.

Promotion of bargaining

If it is possible to identify the legal rights of the parties involved then bargaining may be viable. For example, a paper mill producing pulp may be willing to

compensate a sailing club that owns a stretch of water if the latter accepts a certain amount of pollution. In return the mill will save money on its waste treatment.

Four problems with the use of bargaining are evident:

- it is difficult to establish the legal rights involved;
- it would be impossible to list everyone who is affected by noxious emissions from a particular factory for the purpose of compensation;
- there might be no bargaining machinery in place;
- the costs to an organisation of administering such a system, even if agreements were reached, could be enormous.

Because of these problems bargaining is unlikely to be successful. As the market finds it very difficult to respond to the problem, many argue that there is a need for government intervention.

Taxes and charges

The tax mechanism can be used to impose extra costs on both producers and consumers. The increased use of financial instruments, such as regulatory charges, landfill levies and fines, are all manifestations of the 'polluter pays' principle (Welford and Gouldson, 1993).

The Swedish government has indicated that tax is 'one of the few efficient tools for reducing CO_2 emissions because when it comes to economy and industry, this task requires the market's own tools' (Boulton, 1995). A firm could be forced to pay an indirect tax, such as the carbon taxes imposed by the Danish and Swedish governments, on each unit of its polluting emissions. The effect of the tax is to increase the costs of production for manufacturers and reduce the output of pollutants (see Figure 6.9).

In 1995 about 70 per cent of UK waste went to landfill. In October 1996 the UK government introduced a new tax on waste going to landfill sites. The tax was levied at £2 per tonne for inactive waste and £7 per tonne for other wastes (Croner, 1996). The scheme is designed to encourage greater use of incineration, recycling or waste minimisation in the first place and to reduce this percentage to 50 per cent by the year 2015 (Lascelles, 1995). Amid questions of whether the tax was achieving its aim the standard rate on active waste rose to £10 per tonne from April 1999 and will rise by a further £1 per tonne each year until 2004.

In March 1998 the UK Chancellor, Gordon Brown, created a task force, led by Lord Marshall, to consider how targets set at Kyoto in 1997 (discussed in more detail below) for the reduction of greenhouse gases could be achieved. A report was published in November 1998 and in the 1999 budget the Chancellor announced an industrial energy tax to be introduced from April 2001, which will apply to all industrial and commercial energy users. It is estimated that carbon emissions should be reduced by 1.5 million tonnes a year.

If a tax reflects the full external environmental cost then the externality has been fully internalised. This is a very big 'if', since the issue is whether the tax can

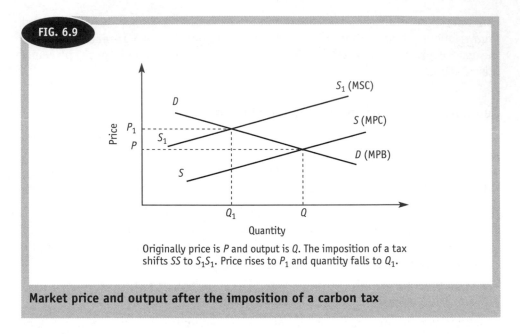

FIG. 6.9

Originally price is *P* and output is *Q*. The imposition of a tax shifts *SS* to S_1S_1. Price rises to P_1 and quantity falls to Q_1.

Market price and output after the imposition of a carbon tax

ever accurately reflect the external cost. The aim is to impose a tax that will result in the socially-efficient level of output. In such situations organisations have a choice: they can continue to pollute and pay for it or invest in anti-pollution measures which will, in the short term, reduce their tax liability and, possibly, save them money and/or offer competitive advantages in the long term.

Marketable permits

Under a marketable permit system, a government issues a fixed quantity of permits giving authorisation to discharge a certain level of waste. In America, for example, clean air legislation sets a cap on emissions of nitrous oxide and sulphur dioxide from power stations. Companies are given annual permits to emit a certain amount of the gases.

These permits are tradable, allowing those companies which find the cost of pollution control to be relatively low to sell their rights for a fee or allow those which have invested in long-term 'clean-up' measures to sell to their permits to those whose emissions exceed their permit.

Organisations will buy rights to discharge, as long as the cost of the permit is below the cost of the pollution control measures they would otherwise have to undertake. Having such a market means that resources are used more efficiently to control the overall level of pollution.

Grants or subsidies

Grants can be provided to polluters as an incentive to reduce the amount of discharge and encourage environmentally-friendly forms of behaviour. Farmers

can obtain subsidies under the Common Agricultural Policy (CAP) for land improvement schemes that enhance the environment. One key reservation is that the use of grants or subsidies flies in the face of the 'polluter pays' principle (discussed above).

Regulation and anti-monopoly legislation

A common method of intervening in the market to force organisations to address negative externalities is by regulation, usually by imposing a set of legal obligations upon organisations or individuals. Regulations are commonly used to impose external costs on producers. Regulations can take many forms which include (Lee, 1994):

- prohibiting the abstraction, use or disposal of particular substances, products and processes which are considered to be environmentally damaging (e.g. CFCs have been banned because of the damage they cause to the ozone layer);
- setting maximum limits for the abstraction of particular natural resources (e.g. water from rivers);
- setting maximum limits for discharges of pollutants to air, water or land (e.g. exhaust emission standards must be met by all cars taking an MOT test in the UK);
- prescribing the technology which may be used for particular processes of production or the materials which may be used in particular processes (e.g. catalytic converters must be used on cars to cut emissions);
- establishing ambient quality standards.

Regulations are used because they are easier than other types of intervention to administer. Taxation of, for example, CO_2 discharge into the atmosphere such as that discussed above requires sophisticated and costly monitoring. Regulations may not require this level of monitoring as spot checks may be enough. Through regulation, such as the placing of a legal maximum on the amount of pollution that a business organisation can produce, an organisation could be prohibited from producing more than the socially-efficient level of output.

Alternatively, regulations can be applied to change the way goods are produced in order to reduce the amount of pollution. In the United Kingdom, for example, the Environment Act 1995 makes producers responsible for ensuring that certain types of products are recyclable, for example, milk bottles and newsprint. Although the amount of materials which are recycled in the UK is increasing, other European countries are much better placed. Recycling rates in Germany and Denmark are around 80 per cent. In Germany, for example, household waste is sorted by householders into separate containers to facilitate recycling.

However, regulations do cause problems. Because the legislation is often uniformly applied it tends to be costly for the industries affected to keep up with the changes. This may mean that the government will 'tone down' legislation under pressure from powerful lobbyists or that there is no incentive to improve

performance beyond compliance with the regulation. It has even been suggested that trying to make industry cleaner, by applying tighter standards, may protect old, dirty technology already in place and discourage cleaner innovation.

Regulations, however, may also be able to promote business activity. Opportunities will flourish in the waste clean-up industry, giving export opportunities as other countries adopt similar regulations that tend to minimise waste. Porter (1990) argued that environmental regulations can create new jobs. It is possible that the imposition of strict regulations can actually improve the ability of a firm to compete. Stringent standards for product performance, product safety, and environmental impact can stimulate companies to improve quality, upgrade technology and provide features that respond to consumer and social demands. Easing standards, however tempting, is counterproductive (Porter, 1990). The environmental technologies industry could be losing as much as £2 billion in annual sales due to the weak regulation and enforcement of legislation requiring these safer processes on the rest of industry (Environmental Industries Commission, 1996).

Environmental standards can also act as a barrier to entry (see Chapter 2): those car manufacturers which had already fitted catalytic converters on cars for sale in the United States lobbied in favour for their adoption in the European market.

Organisations that are based in countries with substantial regulations, such as Sweden, may be in a position to gain competitive advantage over organisations operating under a more lax regime. As legislation changes and converges throughout Europe and the world, those organisations which have worked under the strictest regimes will have a distinct competitive advantage. Scania, the multinational truck manufacturer, has used the strict legal environment in Sweden to compete successfully in the truck industry (see Case Study 6 in Part II). Murray and Fahy (1994) suggest that the advantage to the early movers is most likely to arise from

- positive consumer perceptions and attitudes which become attached to companies and their brands;
- the accumulated experience of dealing with new materials, technologies and processes;
- the ownership of proprietary design, recovery and recycling technologies and processes.

It may be difficult for organisations that are left behind to catch up.

Anti-monopoly legislation may be necessary to prevent the abuse of monopoly power which could include infringement of environmental regulations. Firms may be taken into public ownership and their output controlled to take into account both public and private costs. How ineffective this may be can be judged by reference to the high levels of pollution in the former Soviet Union. One of the key foundations of environmental policies adopted by the Conservative government in the United Kingdom from 1979 was that effective regulation did not require legal ownership of industries.

A number of approaches can be used to reduce externalities. Exhibit 6.1 discusses the increasing problems posed by road congestion and a range of options open to governments.

Tackling road congestion head on

In the UK the Confederation of British Industry has estimated that traffic delays cost industry in excess of £15 billion a year. This excludes adverse health and environmental effects.

The UK government, using the price mechanism, is committed to increasing the private cost of motoring in an attempt to reduce the number of journeys and consequent pollution. Duty on petrol is being increased at a rate higher than inflation. In the 1998 budget, the price of petrol went up by more than three times the rate of inflation, and tax accounted for around 80 per cent or 50p of every 63p litre of petrol. Future budgets are likely to maintain this approach. In the 1999 budget unleaded petrol rose by 4.25p per litre.

The government reports that cars are becoming cleaner and polluting less, so that although traffic is growing, CO_2 emissions are falling. The government hopes to encourage smaller, cleaner cars by reducing road tax by £55 for owners of cars with engines of less than 1100 cc as from June 1999. Others measures that are part of the government's plan to reduce greenhouse gas emissions by 2010 include congestion management techniques – for example, trip reduction techniques and traffic management systems.

Trip reduction techniques are designed to entice motorists away from single-occupancy cars to public transport, car pools, cycling or walking. Telecommuting and staggered working hours have also been encouraged.

In the UK the Road Traffic Reduction Act 1997 imposed a duty on County, District and Unitary Authorities to draw up, within a year, a plan to curtail the growth of road traffic in its area. These plans could include schemes to encourage cycling and walking, calm traffic, create pedestrian-only zones etc. There is also a duty on the Secretary of State to draw up a national traffic reduction plan.

The UK government and the European Union have jointly funded a £2.5m project in Leicester to study the preparedness of private motorists to use alternative transport. Sixty motorists were given smart cards worth £120 to pay road charges and told they could keep any savings from using buses. Road charges were continuously adjusted to find the point at which cars would be left at home. Interim results show that 25 per cent of the sample used buses throughout the period and that 38 per cent decided to use buses when tolls reached £10 for one month. The system of bus lanes showed the buses to be quicker than using cars (Joint, 1998).

Northampton faces serious traffic jams due in part to a public transport system that is inadequate (Howe, 1998). In October 1998, the Northampton County and Borough Councils signed a charter agreement along with Rapid Transport

International giving priority status to the development of a 40 km network of 'guided bus' system together with a series of park-and-ride sites. The estimated cost of the proposed system was said to be £40 million. This type of initiative is likely to be important as bus use outside London has fallen since deregulation. The number of passenger journeys per year has fallen by 29 per cent from 4.5 billion to 3.2 billion in 1996.

In Europe the problem of traffic congestion is being tackled by pedestrianisation of city centres and the provision of more public transport. In Oslo many vehicles pay to enter the city electronically via a system of electronic tagging.

In Singapore car buying permits are necessary before anyone can purchase a car. Additionally, high import duties, which increase the purchase price of a car, high road tax and road pricing in the central business district all serve to reduce demand for cars. Allied to this is a very efficient public transport system.

In the USA, government programmes have been set up to assist people with finding suitable car-share arrangements; in Washington the Ride Finders Network has reduced the number of car journeys by over 2500 daily since 1993. Los Angeles has special lanes for cars carrying more than one person.

Alternatively, traffic management systems attempt to speed up traffic flow through techniques such as light synchronisation, widening intersections and designating one-way streets and protected turning lanes.

Although a number of initiatives are in progress, the second Dobris environment assessment (see p. 241) published by the European Environment Agency pessimistically notes that public transport is losing out to private transport across Europe. This raises the question of whether the political will exists to reach the Kyoto targets for the reduction in greenhouse gases (see below) and to encourage new patterns of settlement and production which reduce the need for transport.

QUESTIONS

1. Within your own region outline the responses of government at all levels to controlling congestion. Under which heading can the responses be categorised?

2. Environmental problems are, by their nature, transnational. Identify some recent international agreements. To which areas of economic and business activity do the agreements apply?

3. Governments may intervene in order to limit pollution. Identify and assess some recent measures that have been proposed.

GOVERNMENT REGULATION AT DIFFERENT GEO-POLITICAL SCALES

The marketplace is overseen by government at various geo-political scales, from international to local. Increasingly, much of the development of policy relating to environmental issues is taking place at global and regional scales. Nation states,

which will have participated in the formulation of policy, will then often have to give domestic effect to such things as international treaties or European directives via legislation and appropriate executive action. Various global and regional institutions monitor activities in different nation states.

Regulation at global/regional level

At the global level regulation is primarily concerned with nation states agreeing to environmental protection initiatives via international summit meetings such as that on climate change at Kyoto in December 1997. The Kyoto agreement will come into force when ratified by at least six developed countries representing at least 55 per cent of the total 1990 levels of greenhouse gases emitted. The agreement takes the form of a legally binding protocol to the Rio Convention on Climate Change in 1992. The total agreed level of emissions by developed countries has been estimated at about 5 per cent below 1990 levels.

At this global level the chief guiding concept is sustainable development assuring that, for the sake of generations to come, the amount and quality of what has been called 'natural capital' – for example, atmosphere, water, tropical rainforest and biodiversity – is not reduced by economic development. From the early 1980s onwards a range of key reports from institutions, such as the World Commission for Environment and Development and the World Bank, made pleas for integrating environmental considerations into policy making on economic development.

Often progress at this global scale is slow. At the Berlin Conference on climate change, in March 1995, it became evident that little progress had been made towards reaching the greenhouse gas targets agreed in 1992. At Berlin the tensions between rich and poor countries provided an interesting focus for the issue of trade-offs between environmental protection and economic growth. The traditional and underlying assumption is that environmental regulation impedes growth.

We turn now to the regional scale to discuss the role of the European Union in respect of environmental regulation. The signatories to the Treaty of Rome (1957), which created the EEC, were not particularly concerned with environmental issues. This oversight was rectified by the Single European Act (SEA) 1987 which adopted the specific environmental objectives in article 130R, namely,

- to preserve, protect and improve the quality of the environment;
- to contribute towards protecting human health;
- to ensure a prudent and rational utilisation of natural resources.

These objectives were extended by the Treaty of European Union (1992) (the so-called Maastricht Treaty) to include

- sustainable and non-inflationary growth respecting the environment;
- promotion of measures to help resolve global environmental problems.

The European Commission, through Directorate General DG XI, is responsible for the environment. DG XI takes the role of initiating and implementing European Union policies on the environment. EU policy intentions are set out in its Environmental Action Programme. To date there have been five such programmes, the first from 1973 to 1976 and the fifth from 1993 to 2000. EU policy has, over the years, changed in its scope. In the past, European environmental initiatives tended to be reactive and based on regulation; they are now becoming more market-driven and voluntary. The 'polluter pays' principle, discussed above, is now at the centre of much EU legislation.

It has also been recognised by the fifth programme that legislation is a toothless beast without compliance, so there is now increased emphasis on the enforcement of existing legislation. Towards the end of 1993 it was agreed that a long-planned European Environment Agency (EEA) should be set up in Copenhagen, Denmark. One of the major tasks of the EEA has been to set up a European Information and Observation Network to provide objective, reliable and comprehensive scientific and technical information at a European level. The aim is to provide data to enable the European Union to 'take the steps necessary to protect the environment as well as to assess the results of their actions' (CEC, 1994).

The EEA co-ordinates a system of national networks to enable it to achieve its objectives. Collaborative activity is important in order to avoid duplicating work being carried out by other bodies. It published its first report on the environment in 46 countries in 1995, the Dobris assessment, which uses a wide range of headings to analyse the extent of any progress, including

- climate change;
- stratospheric ozone depletion;
- acidification;
- tropospheric ozone;
- chemicals;
- waste;
- biodiversity;
- inland waters;
- marine and coastal environment;
- soil degradation;
- urban environment;
- technological and natural hazards.

A second version followed in 1998. Conferences of European environment ministers, such as those in Sofia in 1995 and Aarhus in 1998, aim to use these assessments to help to develop principles and policies designed to bring about environmental improvement and convergence upon a more sustainable pattern of development in Europe. A useful summary can be found at www.eea.dk/Document/3-yearly/Dobris2/summary/en/gencon.htm.

As we turn to consider regulation at a national level, it is important to note that the environmental laws of EU member states are increasingly determined by the Union, 'while the mechanisms through which these objectives are to be reached are determined nationally' (Welford and Gouldson, 1993). Furthermore, as industries are becoming increasingly globalised, organisations need to comply with varying environmental legislation and respond to action from cross-border pressure groups which may differ widely from those in their home market.

Regulation at national level

In the United Kingdom, the task of central government in regulating health and environmental issues or providing support for organisations is largely carried out through the Department of the Environment (DoE). The main legislation in this field is the Environmental Protection Act 1990 (EPA) and the Environment Act 1995 (EA). Chien (1991) suggests that legislation is based on the 'four Rs'. It includes reduction of the amount of waste produced, reuse of durable items, recycling of natural resources, and regeneration of discarded products for use as new materials or products. Support is also provided by other ministries, such as the Department of Trade and Industry, whose Business Link scheme provides advice on environmental issues for small firms in particular.

If a business organisation produces waste it has a duty of care in respect of that waste under the EPA 1990. Managers in such businesses need to be aware that breach of this duty of care can lead to fines and prison sentences in addition to civil liability for causing damage to environmental or human health by waste. (Legal issues are looked at in more detail in Chapter 7.) The EPA 1990 can grant authorisation to make emissions from any 'prescribed processes' but the process must satisfy a test known as BATNEEC ('best available technique not entailing excessive cost'). BATNEEC obliges organisations which are polluting to adopt cleaner technologies than those in place, providing they are not 'excessively' costly. However, the definition itself is ambiguous, and subject to a test of 'reasonableness'. Welford and Gouldson (1993) note that organisations which have developed self-regulation schemes such as BS EN ISO 14001 (discussed below) 'will be at a considerable advantage when gathering the information and applying the criteria of BATNEEC'.

Additionally, the EPA 1990 subjects the most polluting processes to an 'integrated' scheme of pollution control. Here, control is integrated in the sense that the impact of an organisation's emissions to air, water or land must be treated in a holistic way, in order to achieve what is known as the 'best practicable environmental option'.

Enforcement notices may be served if an organisation is in breach of the terms of its authorisation to emit. More serious risks which cannot be dealt with in this way will result in the issue of a prohibition notice, which can force the closure of a facility until an organisation complies with its authorisation.

The Environment Agency (EA) is a key body in respect of such enforcement issues in the UK. It came into existence in April 1996. The EA 1995 established this

body for England and Wales; it combines all the functions previously undertaken by H.M. Inspectorate of Pollution, the National Rivers Authority and the waste regulation authorities under one umbrella. The EA 1995 established the principal aim of the agency as to protect or enhance the environment as a whole and make a contribution towards attaining sustainable development. In an attempt to approach environmental issues from a holistic perspective the EA has identified nine key themes in environmental management:

- addressing climatic change;
- regulating major industries;
- improving air quality;
- managing waste;
- managing water resources;
- delivering integrated river basin management;
- conserving the land;
- managing fresh water fisheries;
- enhancing biodiversity.

Considerable similarity may be noted with the approach of the European Environmental Agency discussed above. We turn now to examine regulation at the local level.

Regulation at local level

In the UK, local authority environmental health departments have the responsibility for regulating food hygiene, health and safety (together with the Health and Safety Executive), pest control and air and noise pollution. Local authorities are also responsible for planning, licensing and trading standards.

The issue of planning controls is a crucial one in terms of more localised environmental issues. In England and Wales a series of Town and Country Planning regulations between 1990 and 1995 gave effect to a European directive on Environmental Impact Assessment which required member states 'to consider the environmental effects of new developments before planning consent is given' (Croner, 1998). The regulations require developers to produce an 'environmental impact statement' to help the planning authority make a decision.

The Environment Act 1995 set up an improved network of centres for monitoring air quality; by the end of 1996 there were expected to be 36 such locations in the UK. This local authority responsibility is the only area not incorporated into the work of the Environment Agency, discussed above. The European Union is also emphasising local regulation in its current Environmental Action Programme.

The city of Leicester was the first in the UK to receive the designation 'Environment City'. The City Council's experience of this project suggests that the greatest progress at this local scale results from local authorities developing links with community groups and both local charitable and business organisations. A

number of local businesses, including the brewers Everards, are reported to have made savings as a result of 'waste minimisation' reviews encouraged by the project (Gosling, 1996). At the end of 1998 UK legislation was in place that allows councils to charge motorists for journeys into towns and cities.

In summary, it is true to say that progress at the global level in taking ecological regulatory action is often slow. However, since most serious ecological concerns tend not to be confined within particular geographical boundaries, the ability to make progress at this global level is critical to the effective tackling of many of the earth's ecological problems. Action at regional, national or local levels often stems from these wider global initiatives.

QUESTIONS

1. Consult the Dobris website at www.eea.dk/Document/3-yearly/Dobris2/summary/en/ gencon.htm. Do you see signs of the global targets for pollution reduction being achieved within European countries?

2. Give examples of national regulations that have evolved from a global initiative. Trace the progress of the issues. What has been the impact on business organisations?

ORGANISATIONAL AGENDAS

Exxon faced a $2 billion (£1.3 billion) clean-up operation and fines of a similar amount, resulting from an oil spillage, when the tanker *Exxon Valdez* ran aground in March 1989. This caused oil contamination to about 4000 km of Alaskan coastline, killing substantial numbers of wild creatures including at least 32 000 birds and millions of fish. However, Cannon (1994) has estimated that loss of market share, disruptions to supplies, compliance with new regulations and the effect on share price cost the company a further substantial sum – between $8 billion and $15 billion (£5.2–9.7 billion). Rebuilding consumer confidence in such cases may prove very difficult.

All organisations cause environmental problems and disasters as a direct result of their activities. Taylor *et al.* (1994) identify three categories of company.

- High penetration companies have the greatest impact on the environment. They include agriculture, chemicals and plastics and metals and mining.

- Moderate penetration companies have some impact, and can save money by cutting wasteful practices. They include electronics, leisure and tourism, and packaging and paper.

- Low penetration companies feel that environmental matters do not concern them. These include advertising, education, and local government.

It is evident that organisations also have responsibilities. Hutchinson (1996) outlines four responsibilities of business, which are shown in Figure 6.10.

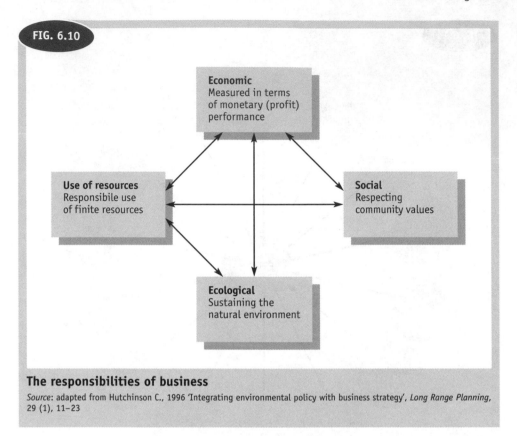

FIG. 6.10

The responsibilities of business

Source: adapted from Hutchinson C., 1996 'Integrating environmental policy with business strategy', *Long Range Planning*, 29 (1), 11–23

Given the nature of the business environment facing them, it is clear that organisations throughout the world realise that there is a wide range of responses available to meet the changing environmental agenda. More are discovering that they need to be seen to be responding to this changing context. Hamel and Prahalad (1994) suggest that radical change is necessary if lasting solutions are to be found, and government, business and individuals have a role to play. The future is about sustainability. Companies are competing for the future but can only do so if they are farsighted, regenerate their core strategies, innovate and use new ways of thinking to transform their organisations. Of importance to this agenda are changing stakeholder views, which we will explore in the next section.

The environment and stakeholders

Stakeholders are groups or individuals who have a stake in, or an expectation of, the organisation's performance (see Figure 6.11 and also Chapter 1). The environmental stance of an organisation is influenced by the perceptions of its stakeholders and the relative power which each possesses. In the United Kingdom we have grown accustomed to road-building and the export of live animals being accompanied by protests carried out by some stakeholders. However, an event in

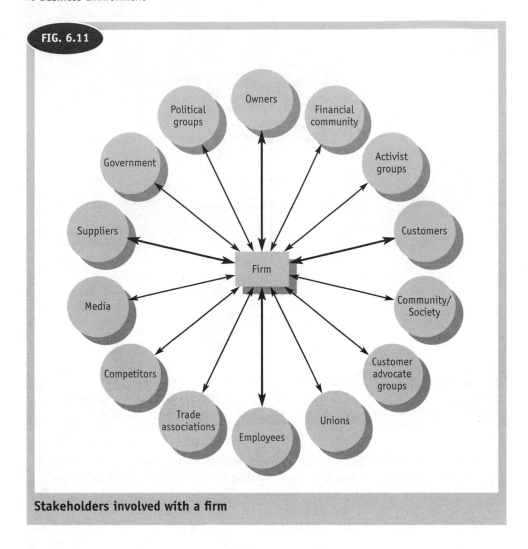

FIG. 6.11

Stakeholders involved with a firm

Nigeria shocked the world in November 1995. The military government of Nigeria executed Ken Saro-Wiwa and eight other environmental activists on what was believed by many international governments to be questionable evidence and after an unfair trial. Saro-Wiwa had encouraged his fellow Ogoni people to protest about the effects upon their lands of thirty years of oil exploitation by Shell Oil. This provoked further consumer backlashes against Shell, similar to those experienced during the Brent Spar incident discussed below. Body Shop founder, Anita Roddick, promised to pressurise Shell's shareholders to reform the company and banned the use of Shell products by her staff at work. The Body Shop, like the Co-op Bank (see Exhibit 6.4 on pp. 257–8), believe that 'good ethics' and consideration of wider stakeholder interests will pay in the long term (these two companies could be described as being good performers).

The influence of stakeholder power

Argenti (1980) identifies three categories of stakeholder:

- those internal to the enterprise, such as employees/management and shareholders;
- those immediately external to the enterprise, for example, suppliers and customers;
- other external stakeholders, such as the community and pressure groups.

The expectations and aspirations of stakeholder groups differ. The short-term profits desired by shareholders are often given priority over the interests of other stakeholders. Company managers have traditionally managed shareholder value, at the expense of other stakeholder requirements, by maximising shareholder returns through higher dividends or a better capital return from the sale of shares that have increased in value. This requirement frequently conflicts with the adoption of more socially and environmentally sound policies.

The expectations of the local community may substantially differ from that of a company, resulting in a conflict of interests. How do these wider social needs for more jobs, improvements in local amenities and minimum pollution correspond to the aims of a company? A major problem for the external stakeholders, such as the local community, is that they have insufficient power to influence company strategy because of their fragmented nature. Ansoff (1984) suggested that the dominant coalition, those in positions of power, such as the board of directors, can bias strategy toward their own preferred course of action. In this way senior management can initiate strategies to support shareholders' wishes which may be to the detriment of the environment and the local community. It would be unusual for external stakeholders to be part of the dominant coalition, so their influence is rarely felt.

Pressure in respect of environmental performance can be applied on the organisation by pressure groups, media and insurers (Welford and Gouldson, 1993). Thilo Bode, head of Greenpeace International, stated at the Rio summit in 1992, 'Big corporations today have a responsibility that goes beyond their aim to make a profit. The focus is on social, moral and ethical considerations.' A survey into managerial attitudes to ethics in the conduct of business, employee relations, social conscience and the environment was published in 1993 by the University of Westminster. It showed some ambivalence in respect of green issues. Although awareness of the issues was high, managers often lacked the motivation to take specific action. The survey also suggested that the closer executives were to responsibility for company profit, the more they seemed prepared to act against the best interests of the environment. However, the situation is not at all clear-cut. A later survey by Entec in 1996 suggested that green issues were moving up the corporate agenda (Caulkin, 1996). In November 1997 an Institute of Management survey of 423 companies found that 24 per cent were fully committed to environmental issues at board level, with a further 34 per cent taking a proactive stance towards environmental issues (Charlesworth, 1998). Clearly this leaves a

substantial minority which, at best, can be said to be reactive to environmental problems; these often did not have an environmental policy.

We must be careful not to suggest that all shareholders are short-term investment opportunists seeking a return at any cost. Differences of approach can be seen between companies and countries. In Germany and Japan, for example, shareholders are more likely to take a longer-term view than their American or UK counterparts.

In much of our coverage of factors in the business environment we have noted that the way in which organisations perceive changes is dependent upon their unique 'perceptual filters'. Divergent stakeholder interests add another level of complexity. It must be recognised that changing stakeholder views are beginning to have an impact on how organisations perceive the environment, and are likely to have effects on business and profit.

The importance of the organisation's environmental context

Organisations need to respond to the question of how the environment is viewed in the country or market in which they operate. It is important because the environmental context will have a direct impact on the way that the organisation operates.

Multinational companies are key players in the economic development in less developed countries (LDCs) as they are 'footloose' and can choose to locate anywhere in the world. The proliferation of legislation in Europe and the United States, as well as increasing costs, has caused the development of 'pollution havens' as some organisations have relocated to developing countries in order to escape tougher environmental legislation in their home markets (Croner, 1996). Mexico's *maquiladora* zone is home to blue-chip American companies such as DuPont, General Electric and General Motors. There is a clear trade-off between business growth and concern for the environment as these companies exploit the less stringent environmental controls of many LDCs. Is this an example of organisations trying to shirk their environmental responsibilities?

We will examine this activity with reference to the work of Azzone and Bertele (1994), who outline five environmental contexts which relate either to national context or to the situation prevailing in certain product/service markets:

1. *Stable context*. Here there may be either slow changes or no changes in environmental legislation. There may be a of lack of public perception of environmental issues or an almost complete lack of consumer power. Organisations in these circumstances will find it easy to ignore legislation and adopt a non-compliance stance. This could be the case in developing countries of South America, for example the *maquiladora* zone in Mexico or the former Eastern bloc nations.

2. *Reactive context*. Here environmental problems are known by small groups, consumer interest is limited and legislation evolves slowly. In this context, organisations may comply with legislation, responding only slowly when the

pressures build up. Many UK firms have opted for this approach to dealing with environmental problems.

3. *Anticipative context*. Here the public are more aware and have the ability to move issues onto the political agenda. It is more difficult for firms to influence the political process. Legislation and regulations become more demanding and organisations need to develop a compliance-plus strategy, anticipating changes and using technological developments to ensure that new standards can be met. The regulatory regime in the European Union and the United States is increasingly encouraging this approach (see Exhibit 6.3 on p. 254).

4. *Proactive context*. Within this context 'green' consumers are said to have a major impact. Organisations may need to demonstrate more concern for the environment if they are to prosper. Commercial and environmental excellence may provide a competitive advantage in the short term but may be indispensable if an organisation is to compete in this environment in the long term (see Case Study 6 in Part II).

5. *Creative context*. Here public opinion is extremely aware of environmental problems but there is a lack of accepted technological solutions to problems. A leading-edge company will be at the forefront of the technological push for the optimal solution. The cost of this could be substantial, but the rewards from developing and controlling a proprietary technological development can be enormous.

Clearly organisations need to be aware of the context in which they operate and need be able to respond to changes. Organisations that adopt a stance which is out of line with the context in which they operate may not survive in the long term. The next section examines some options based on Roome (1992) and gives some illustrations of how organisations, because of growing environmental concerns of a diverse range of stakeholders, might be following a path toward a more environmentally concerned way of operating.

Environmental options

Roome (1992) sets out a continuum of five possible environmental options for organisations:

- non-compliance
- compliance
- compliance plus
- commercial and environmental excellence
- leading edge.

The first three options may be taken by businesses whose primary reference point is legislation.

Non-compliance

An organisation that adopts a non-compliance position may, because of lack of resources or managerial inertia, be unable to satisfy legal requirements. Some may make a policy decision not to comply with the regulations in order to secure lower costs.

Compliance

The 'compliance' standpoint is clearly a minimal response and focuses efforts upon the action required to satisfy the minimum legal requirements.

These two stances are essentially reactive. By adopting a reactive stance it is possible that a company may fall behind competitors who are developing products and processes to meet the tougher environmental conditions. In fact because of European Union objectives it is becoming evident that organisations cannot take decisions without reference to environmental consequences. Policies will have to have an environmental dimension at the early stages of formation. This may cause a change in direction for many organisations as business decisions may take on a completely different perspective depending on the applicable environmental legislation.

Internal and external pressures are said to have prompted over 50 per cent of companies to go beyond compliance with existing legislation and 75 per cent have begun developing environmental management systems. The evidence shows that UK industry is lagging behind foreign competitors in appreciating the strategic benefits of operating at high environmental standards. Arguably, it is a case of recognising the opportunities rather than counting the cost of investment in environmental improvements. For example, the Environment Agency, in a joint project with Allied Colloids, identified savings of up to £4.5 million on one of the company's sites, based on an immediate investment of only £70 000. Prevention can be better than cure by being cheaper in the medium to long term (Caulkin, 1996).

Compliance plus

During the 1980s a shorthand reference to environmentally concerned organisations – and consumers – was use of the word 'green'. 'Green' organisations, such as the Body Shop, had a positive and proactive stance toward environmental issues. The 'compliance-plus' option demonstrates that a proactive stance towards legal standards can benefit the organisation. The reduced probability of fines associated with non-compliance is a demonstrable benefit of taking this option. Recognition, for example gaining the Queen's Award for Environmental Achievement, can also enhance image. Such an organisation might aim to integrate an environmental management system into its overall business strategy via a standard such as BS EN ISO 14001.

Commercial and environmental excellence and leading edge

Roome's two remaining options incorporate Kleiner's (1991) approach, which identified three key components of green companies:

- They will have developed a mechanism for placing a monetary value on the complete life cycle of their products, from raw materials through production to distribution, consumption and disposal. Such 'cradle-to-grave' or 'life-cycle cost' accounting will assist in the development of products and limit environmental impact.
- They will record and publish environmental data, possibly thereby averting environmental disasters and improving community relations.
- They will be committed to reducing waste at source, for example via some form of Total Quality Management programme.

A business focused on 'commercial and environmental excellence' would ensure that its core corporate and managerial values always take account of environmental management issues; 'leading-edge' businesses set the standard for a particular industry through the adoption of 'state-of-the-art' environmental management systems.

This more proactive stance can be illustrated by the systems adopted by Shanks and McEwan, a major UK waste management company. The company integrates the management of environmental issues throughout all areas of the organisation. Key elements of its approach are

- a corporate environment policy;
- the use of the quality management standard BS 5750 for quality assurance;
- the setting up of an 'independent' advisory board; and
- the use of regular audits and assessments.

A brief examination of a range of company Annual Reports, such as those of ICI, suggests that shareholder expectations in respect of a company's environmental record may be increasing. This may be partly due to pressure groups, which have sought to purchase shares in order to gain access to annual general meetings and be in a formal forum to put over their views. There is evidence, also, of the increasing popularity of 'green' investment funds.

It is thought that around 25 per cent of UK company Annual Reports make some sort of environmental disclosure (Maddox, 1995). Thorn EMI and Unilever are two multinationals which report extensively on environmental issues and progress.

A proactive stance may require substantial amounts of initial capital investment and put an organisation at a cost disadvantage in relation to more reactive competitors. However, there are a number of cases of organisations who justify investment in, for example, waste minimisation schemes, as making hard-headed, if long-term, business sense. The increasing cost of landfill dumping may cause

more organisations to make such decisions. One such organisation is 3M (see Exhibit 6.2).

EXHIBIT 6.2

3M

Some companies have put in place ecological strategies that seek to eliminate emissions, effluents and accidents through preventative action and continuous improvement at every step of the production process (Shrivastava, 1994). This preventative approach is more efficient than controlling discharges at 'end-of-pipe', which involves pollution control to purify air or water before they leave the plant. End-of-pipe control is often viewed by companies as cheaper than pollution prevention; however, there is an argument that an effective pollution prevention strategy is cheaper in the long run. One company that has taken the longer-term view is the multinational 3M (Minnesota Mining and Manufacturing Company).

3M has a diversified portfolio of businesses, based largely on its wide expertise. It has a strong reputation for product innovation, an example being 'Post-it' notes. 3M develops product lines around a series of small, discrete, free-standing products. The company forms new venture units comprising of small, semi-autonomous teams, led by a product champion to develop its new products.

One of the key tasks of this team is to minimise pollution from the first phase of product development. 3M's 'Pollution Prevention Pays' (3P) programme is designed to cut pollution at source. The programme is in four stages:

- product reformulation, where the issue is whether products can be made using fewer raw materials or less toxic materials;
- process modification, in order to cut down on waste;
- equipment redesign; and
- resource recovery. Can waste be salvaged, reused or sold?

Each project undertaken by the 3P programme must meet four criteria:

- eliminate or reduce pollution;
- save energy or material and resources;
- demonstrate technological innovation;
- save money.

As a direct result of the programme, waste per unit of output fell, though the reduction was not enough to satisfy the company. In 1989 3M introduced Pollution Prevention Plus (3P+), committing itself to stricter environmental controls and increased R&D expenditure. Their current goal is to reduce their rate of waste generation by 50 per cent from 1990 levels by 2000. Consistent with Kleiner's (1991) definition of a green company, 3M have a life-cycle management system

designed to improve the environmental, health and safety impacts of products throughout their life cycle. In 1995 3M also became the first company to sell an asthma inhaler which did not require CFCs.

Source: www.mmm.com/profile/envt/epr/products.htm

Organisations with some of the 'greenest' credentials tend to be engaged in self-regulation schemes of one type or another. Clearly, such companies are in the category of 'compliance plus', or beyond, in Roome's (1992) classifications.

Self-regulation

Global, European and national voluntary self-regulation schemes are having a considerable impact. These self-regulation schemes require organisations to 'sign up' to regimes which typically involve making information available to the public, principally via an environmental policy statement, together with clear targets and objectives needed to meet the policy. In such schemes, considerable stress is placed on plans to achieve continual improvements and of integrating environmental issues with those concerns of general management. Environmental audits and further statements on the progress made in respect of environmental objectives tend to be the final pieces of the jigsaw. The concept of environmental audit, in particular, requires organisations to monitor and collect detailed information in order to judge whether improvement has been achieved.

At the global scale there is an extensive range of such self-regulation schemes sponsored by the International Chamber of Commerce (ICC) and the International Standards Organisation (ISO), among others. The ICC's 'Business Charter for Sustainable Development', for example, outlines a range of actions to integrate the management of environmental issues with the general policies and activities of organisations. Perhaps the best known scheme is BS EN ISO 14001 – introduced in September 1996 as *the* international standard for environmental management. This superseded the old UK standard BS 7750.

An example of self-regulation at a European level, however, is the system sponsored by the European Petroleum Industry Association (EUROPIA) and the Eco-Management and Auditing Scheme (EMAS), requiring voluntary eco-audits. EMAS came into operation in April 1995 and applies principally to industrial sites, whereas BS EN ISO 14001 is applicable to all organisations. Although schemes are voluntary, in the future customers might place considerable pressure on supplier organisations to 'sign up'.

The Institute of Wastes Management (1998) believed that 50 sites were EMAS certified, whereas BS EN ISO 14001 certified sites were in excess of 430 in October 1998. Exhibit 6.3 illustrates how BS EN ISO 14001 can help the environment and the organisation (see also Case Study 6 in Part II).

Whatever the response to the environment that an organisation adopts, it is likely that an increased level of activity will be necessary as the environmental

---

EXHIBIT 6.3

Volvo

Volvo, the Swedish car manufacturer (part of Ford Motors since the beginning of 1999), achieved the environmental standard BS EN ISO 14001 in January 1998 at the distribution site of Volvo Car UK. In order to achieve the standard, the company had to

- draw up an environmental policy to show that its operations complied with European Union and UK legislation;
- show that proper procedures were in place to deal with an environmental crisis;
- demonstrate that it had an effective environmental communication programme.

Volvo concentrated its efforts on three areas of its business that were potentially damaging to the environment, namely,

- the amount of waste created by packaging;
- the effect of goods transport on the environment; and
- whether suppliers and contractors were environmentally sound.

Action plans were established, targets set and monitored. The environmental improvements have not only demonstrated the commitment of Volvo to the environment but have also brought business headway. Waste produced has fallen by 20 per cent and the percentage of waste being recycled has increased from less than 25 per cent to over 70 per cent.

Source: adapted from 'Environmental recognition for Volvo', *Daventry Calling*, no. 20, Summer 1998, p. 7

---

context moves from stable, at one end of the continuum, to creative, at the other. It is important to recognise the extra costs that will be incurred by an organisation as it moves from one stance to another (see Table 6.3).

To summarise, it is evident that there are many non-legally binding reasons why organisations need to be aware of their impact on the natural environment and, perhaps, to take action to improve the situation. The sort of environmental agenda which an organisation adopts will be influenced by both its environmental context and the extent of stakeholders' power and interest.

QUESTIONS

1. Conduct a search of recent press articles on environmental concerns. Can you find examples of organisations which fit each of Roome's (1992) categories?
2. What benefits are likely to accrue to an organisation and its stakeholders from compliance with BS EN ISO 14001?

TABLE 6.3   Organisational implications of environmental stances

	Stable	Reactive	Anticipatory	Proactive	Creative
			The context		
Environmental problems	None	Problems addressed when defined	Anticipates new legislation	Examines opportunities for products and company	Searches for new technology
Activities involved					
● R&D	No	No	Yes	Yes	Yes
● Production/logistics	Limited	Yes	Yes	Yes	Yes
● Marketing/sales	No	No	No	Yes	Yes
● External relations	No	Limited	Yes	Yes	Yes
● Legal	No	Limited	Yes	Yes	Yes
● Finance	No	No	No	No	Yes
● Environmental department	No	No	Usually	Usually	Usually
● Top management	No	No	Sometimes	Yes	Yes

Source: adapted from Azzone and Bertele (1994)

THE POSITION OF THE CONSUMER

Environmental issues are becoming increasingly important in consumers' buying decisions. Many consumers are ready to reward companies by buying the products of an organisation they believe to be ethical. They may be prepared to pay a higher price or actively seek out those companies which they believe to be ethical (Creyer and Ross, 1997).

It is, however, difficult to be precise in the use of the term 'green consumer'. The characteristics of 'green' consumers have been summarised by Elkington and Hailes (1988). These consumers will avoid products likely to

- endanger health;
- cause significant environmental damage or consume a disproportionate amount of energy during manufacture, use or disposal;
- cause unnecessary waste;
- use materials from threatened species or environments;
- involve unnecessary use of, or cruelty to, animals or adversely affect other countries – particularly those in the developing world.

Clearly consumers can only act in a 'green' way if they possess reliable information about the relative effects of a range of products on the environment. In the UK, toward the end of the 1980s, the ability of consumers to respond in an

environmentally sound manner was much enhanced by best-selling guides like *The Green Consumer Guide* by Elkington and Hailes (1988), although information was still patchy.

Azzone and Bertele (1994) suggest that as eco-labels with third-party certification are developed, such as the Blue Angel in Germany, 'green' qualities of products will become more obvious and 'green' consumers will become more important. It is easier for Germans to adopt 'green' purchasing habits because they have a comprehensive system of eco-labelling. This provides them with better quality information about products and the effects which their production, use or disposal might have on the environment.

The real test for 'green' consumerism is whether consumers will pay premium prices for environmentally-friendly products. A Mintel survey in December 1994 showed an 11 per cent decline in the numbers of British people expressing worries about environmental issues between 1990 and 1994. During recessionary times such as the early 1990s, it is to be expected that consumers will be less prepared to pay premium prices for such goods. This has been compounded by consumer scepticism about the quality of many products for which 'green' claims have been made.

There is a lack of published data comparing the 'greenness' of consumers between countries. One of the few examples is the 1992 Eurobarometer which suggests that 46 per cent of a sample of consumers from twelve member states were prepared to buy an environmentally-friendly product, even if it was more expensive. The pattern of response was not uniform throughout the European Union: for example, 75 per cent of former West German consumers were 'green' compared to 53 per cent of consumers in former East Germany.

It is interesting to examine the collective power which consumers can exert in respect of ecological issues. During the 1980s and early 1990s Greenpeace mounted many successful campaigns. These included the threat of a poster campaign to gain concessions from car companies regarding catalytic converters. They also lobbied shoe companies concerning the use of kangaroo hide in the manufacture of sports shoes. In 1995 Shell were forced to abandon plans to dispose of the Brent Spar oil storage buoy in deep water as a result of the Greenpeace campaign and boycotts of Shell petrol, particularly in Germany. Shell were thought to have lost about 70 per cent of trade at some petrol stations and hundreds of millions of pounds in revenue. Consumers are also reacting against the introduction of genetically modified foods. Significantly, Heinz, Kelloggs, Asda and Iceland foods have refused to use such food in their branded items.

Neither is government immune to the actions of committed and well organised groups. Road protesters at Newbury are credited with prompting the government to cancel over a hundred road-building schemes because of their effectiveness in stalling the Newbury bypass. The protest over the £700m Birmingham northern relief road is likely to be just as protracted and costly.

There is some suggestion that consumer power is starting to be influential in respect of products made using child labour. Adverse publicity has caused the Levi Strauss company to amend their sourcing arrangements and for retailers of rugs,

like IKEA, to seek assurances about the circumstances of manufacture. A shift to 'ethical consumption' and 'ethical investment' may be the next step from 'green consumption'.

To date around £1.93 billion has been invested in ethical funds by more than a quarter of a million people (Insley, 1998). Such funds include TSB Environmental, AXA Sun Life Ethical and Standard Life Ethical. Funds like these often screen out, for example, companies which produce pollutants, pesticides, or arms, and those which test on animals. However, some have recently relaxed the screening of companies involved in tobacco and alcohol production in an attempt to enable investment in more FTSE 100 companies. The Ethical Investment Research Service provides information on the following (Slavin, 1998):

- positive achievements of companies in respect of products with a positive environmental benefit;
- involvement in the community;
- disclosure of information;
- negative screening.

As can be seen from Exhibit 6.4, the Co-op Bank is an organisation which is very clearly stating its ethical principles.

EXHIBIT 6.4

Co-op Bank

The Co-op Bank was established more than 120 years ago and is currently the most profitable part of the Co-operative Wholesale Society. In 1997 pre-tax profits rose by 24 per cent to £45.5 million.

Part of this recent success can be attributed to its public stance on a range of ethical issues, although it is hard to quantify this. In 1992 the Co-op Bank published a 12-point ethical policy statement which included statements to the effect that it will not do business with any regime or organisation

- which oppresses the human spirit, takes away the rights of individuals or manufactures any instrument of torture;
- which involves the manufacture or sale of arms to countries with oppressive regimes;
- which speculates against the pound sterling;
- which enables drug trafficking or tax evasion to take place;
- which manufactures tobacco;
- which experiments on animals for cosmetics;
- which involves 'exploitative' factory farming or the production of animal fur; or
- which involves blood sports.

Exhibit 6.4 continued

The policy statement also states that the bank will actively seek out business compatible with this ethical position and that it will encourage its existing customers to take a proactive environmental stance. Terry Thomas, Managing Director of the bank, said, 'We say to all concerned people: If you're our kind of people, we're your kind of bank.'

The Co-op Bank conducted a detailed survey of customer attitudes which revealed that 84.2 per cent of those asked said it was a good idea for the bank to have a clear ethical policy. The types of activity identified in the policy statement had struck some significant chords with their customers.

It was the Bank's view, expressed in a press release of April 1995, that its advertising campaign, highlighting the strongly ethical stance which it had developed, had led to growth in both business and personal banking sectors. Since this time the bank has continued to expand quite rapidly.

Source: Press releases supplied by the Co-op Bank and *Ethical Attitudes: How Upright Is British Business?*, Co-op Bank

Of even greater significance is the growing number of organisations 'sleeping with the enemy'. Partnerships between organisations and environmental groups are aimed at promoting organisational goals by adopting 'market-based environmentalism' to reduce costs and create product differentiation. Hartman and Stafford (1997) identify a number of green alliances involving McDonalds, The Body Shop and Friends of the Earth.

To summarise, it is clear that individual consumers have limited influence either upon the environmental stance of organisations or upon government policy in this regard. However, there is increasing evidence to suggest that consumers can, when mobilised by environmental pressure groups, have considerable influence upon organisations, most particularly via the threat of a mass product boycott.

QUESTIONS

1. Using published materials outline the Shell Brent Spar case and its development since the case came to public attention in 1995. Comment on the role of the stakeholders involved.

2. Do you think that the Co-op Bank's ethical stance gives it a sustainable competitive advantage?

3. Identify other instances where consumer pressure has forced an organisation to re-think its actions. Comment on the impact on the organisation.

CONCLUSION

Since it is often difficult to confine ecological problems within individual countries it is becoming increasingly apparent that 'world solutions' need to be sought. There is also an increasing recognition that in order to address ecological problems it is no longer possible for environmental campaigners and businesses to snipe at each other from entrenched positions. Both sides are recognising the importance of agreeing trade-offs between economic development, which is important in terms of providing people with the means to live, and environmental protection, which seeks to ensure that the natural environment is used sensibly. The essence of this 'trade-off' is encapsulated in the principle of 'sustainable development' – the notion that we need to protect the natural environment for the sake of the generations of people which will follow us on the earth.

SUMMARY OF MAIN POINTS

In this chapter we have identified some of the issues that are important to the well-being of the planet and models that enable us to compare the different stances of organisations with respect to ecological issues. The main points are:

- The Earth is facing a number of serious environmental issues, including the greenhouse effect.

- The operation of the market is based upon the law of supply and demand.

- The concept of externalities describes the situation where an organisation has not fully internalised its costs. Most polluting emissions are, therefore, seen as negative externalities.

- Governments can use a range of actions to monitor and regulate the output of pollutants from economic activity, including taxes and charges; marketable permits; grants or subsidies; and regulation and anti-monopoly legislation.

- Progress at the global level in ecological regulation action is often slow since it operates via a series of International Summit meetings, such as that at Rio in 1992. However, since, most serious ecological concerns tend not to be confined within geo-political boundaries the ability to make progress at this global level is critical to the effective tackling of many ecological problems.

- The viewpoints which organisations can adopt in respect of ecological regulation range from non-compliance and compliance, through to some more proactive stances, and culminate in the use of state of the art processes by what have been called 'leading-edge' organisations.

- The ecological viewpoint adopted by an organisation is likely to be strongly influenced by the nature of its business environment and by its perceptions of the interest and power of stakeholders.

- The extent of individual consumer power in respect of ecological issues is clearly weak. However, there in an increase in single-issue action taken by environmental pressure groups which is capable of having a serious effect on how organisations view their stakeholders.

NET SEARCH

http://www.greenchannel.com/tec
From the Environment Council, an independent charity. Site includes:

- news, which is a little dated;
- information on seminars, briefings, events and courses;
- environmental services for business;
- environmental links page.

http://www.cedar.univie.ac.at/
Site of the International Society for Environmental Protection.

http://www.greenpeace.org
Home page of Greenpeace. Includes a whole host of environmental issues and links with other organisations.

http://www.foe.co.uk
Friends of the Earth website, frequently updated with current issues.

http://www.planetark.org
Home of the Reuters World Environment News. Access to Envirosearch, a search engine dedicated to environmental issues. News is current and software is available.

http://www.wri.org/
Home page of the World Resources Institute of New York. Provides access to sites covering a variety of environmental issues around the globe.

http://www.webdirectory.com/
This an environmental organisations web directory with search facility.

http://www-genie.mrrl.lut.ac.uk
Global environmental network for information exchange in the UK.

http://ceo.gelos.org
Gobal environmental information location service. The site provides access to a virtual library of environmental data and resources.

REFERENCES

Ansoff, I. (1984) *Implementing Strategic Management*, Englewood Cliffs: NJ, Prentice Hall.
Argenti, J. (1980) *Practical Corporate Planning*, London: Allen and Unwin.
Azzone, G. and Bertele, U. (1994) 'Exploiting green strategies for competitive advantage', *Long Range Planning*, 27 (6), 69–81.

Boulton, L. (1995) 'Higher carbon tax heats up debate', *Financial Times*, 14 June, p. 20.

Brown, P. (1995) 'Global warming summit at risk', *Guardian*, 25 March.

Cannon, T. (1994) *Corporate Responsibility: A Textbook on Business Ethics, Governance, Environment: Roles and Responsibilities*, London: Pitman.

Carter, F.W. and Turnock, D. (1993) *Environmental Problems in Eastern Europe*, London: Routledge.

Caulkin, S. (1996), 'Tarmac melts under pressure', *Observer*, 26 May.

Charlesworth, K. (1998) *A Green and Pleasant Land*, Institute of Management.

Chien, E. (1991) *Working Towards Environmental Quality in the 21st Century*, Environmental Protection Administration, January.

Commission of the European Communities (1994) *Background Report: The European Environment Agency*, ISEC/B6/94, 11 February, CEC, London.

Creyer, E. and Ross, W. (1997) 'The influence of firm behaviour on purchase intention: do consumers really care about business ethics?', *Journal of Consumer Marketing*, 14 (6), November/December.

Croner Guide (1996) *Environmental Management*, Croner Publications.

Croner Guide (1998) *Environmental Management*, Croner Publications.

Elkington, J. and Hailes, J. (1988) *The Green Consumer Guide*, London: Victor Gollancz.

Environmental Industries Commission (1996) *Croner's Environmental Briefing*, 19 March, no. 62.

Gosling, P. (1996) 'Cleaner investor in Leicester', *Financial Times*, 10 March.

Hamel, G. and Prahalad, C.K. (1994) *Competing for the Future*, Boston: Harvard Business School Press.

Hartman, C.L. and Stafford, E.R. (1997) 'Green alliances: building new business with environmental groups', *Long Range Planning*, 30 (2), 184–96.

Howe, S. (1998) 'Green light for business plan', *Northampton Herald and Post*, 29 October.

Hutchinson, C. (1996) 'Integrating environmental policy with business strategy', *Long Range Planning*, 29 (1), 11–23.

Insley, J. (1998) ' "Nutty" funds are no crackers after all', *Observer*, 15 November.

Institute of Wastes Management (1998) *Environmental Management Systems*, IWM Business Services.

Joint, J. (1998) 'Case for road pricing gathers speed', *Financial Times*, 12 June.

Kleiner, A. (1991) 'What does it mean to be green?', *Harvard Business Review*, July–August.

Lascelles, D. (1995) 'Time to take charge of waste', *Financial Times*, 17 May, p. 6.

Lee, N. (1994) 'Environmental policy', in Artis, M. and Lee, N. (eds) *The Economics of the European Union*, Oxford: Oxford University Press.

Lipsey, R.G. and Harbury, C. (1992) *First Principles of Economics*, London: Weidenfeld & Nicolson.

Maddox, B. (1995) 'Green light turns amber', *Financial Times*, 21 June.

Murray, J.A. and Fahy, J. (1994) 'The marketing environment', in Nugent, N. and O'Donnell, R. (eds) *The European Business Environment*, London: Macmillan.

Porter, M.E. (1990) 'The competitive advantage of nations', *Harvard Business Review*, March–April.

Radford, T. (1997) 'glowing, glowing . . . gone?', *Guardian*, 25 November.

Roome, N. (1992) 'Developing environmental management systems', *Business Strategy and the Environment*, Spring, part 1.

Shrivastava, P. (1994) *Strategic Management: Concepts and Practices*, Cincinnati: South-Western.

Shrivastava, P. (1995) 'Environmental technologies and competitive advantage', *Strategic Management Journal*, 16, 183–200.

Slavin, T. (1998) 'Green – or just cabbage looking', *Observer*, 15 November.

Taylor, B., Hutchinson, C., Pollack, S. and Tapper, R. (1994) *The Environmental Management Handbook*, London: Pitman.

Welford, R. and Gouldson, A. (1993) *Environmental Management and Business Strategy*, London: Pitman.

THE POLITICAL AND LEGAL ENVIRONMENT

Alistair Sutton
and Jamie Weatherston

LEARNING OBJECTIVES

On completion of this chapter you should be able to:

- identify political activity at global/regional, national and local levels;

- outline the roles of key EU institutions and the implications of EU developments for organisations;

- be aware of the role of EU legislation in supervising competition;

- understand the framework in which both UK and European decisions on regional aid issues are made;

- outline the workings of the UK constitution, including the role of Parliament, the Cabinet, the civil service and the judiciary;

- outline the main sources of law and the court system in the UK;

- correctly use legal terminology applying to different ways of classifying law in England and Wales and Scotland.

KEY CONCEPTS

- monetarism
- competitiveness and restriction of competitiveness
- regional policy
- Agenda 2000

- lobbying
- democratic government
- classification of laws
- sources of law

INTRODUCTION

The main aim of this chapter is to examine political institutions and developments at a range of geo-political levels: global/regional, national and local. We distinguish between each level to ensure that readers are aware of the bodies which exist and appreciate the fundamental role of each body within a specific context. However, the processes involved in making any decisions, particularly ones at global/regional levels, are very complex, and sometimes the rational institutional approach adopted as a framework for this chapter may not fully reflect the extent of 'horse-trading' involved in policy and decision making.

The regional level of decision making, in particular, has a significant impact on organisations. The European Union is important to business and competitive activity throughout the world. We will explore its background, its institutions, and the processes and mechanisms by which policies and decisions are made.

Although the title of the chapter includes the word 'legal', this element is not treated as extensively as the political area. The discussion of specific legal considerations relating to the legal system of England and Wales concentrates upon outlining the sources of law, the nature of the court system and the ways in which law may be classified. In addition, the section on the European Union contains detailed discussions of relevant treaties and of competition legislation. This will help the reader develop the vocabulary necessary to understand the areas of legal debate within the book and to appreciate the impact which legislation may have upon business organisations. It is not the intention of the chapter to provide a comprehensive coverage of all the law which may affect organisations. For details of laws which apply to business refer to Owens (1997), or to the original statutes or law reports. The law of Scotland is somewhat different to that which applies in England and Wales, particularly in respect of criminal law, the law of property and constitutional and administrative law. The Internet search section at the end of the chapter gives other useful sources.

It is appropriate to combine the legal and political elements in one chapter because they interlink in our discussion of issues connected with democratic

institutions. This discussion covers a range of areas such as bills of rights, the concept of separation of powers, the role of the judiciary, the issue of parliamentary lobbying, the standards of conduct expected of Members of Parliament (MPs), and the role of the House of Lords. These areas require a fusion of the legal and political elements to provide a rounded discussion.

THE IMPACT OF POLITICAL DECISIONS AT DIFFERENT GEO-POLITICAL SCALES

Decisions which affect business organisations are made at all geo-political levels. The oil shocks of the 1970s brought about by the supranational OPEC cartel and the entry of the UK into the European Community in 1973, for example, both had profound consequences for many organisations.

Competition policy in the United Kingdom (see also below and Chapter 2) is determined by the European Commission and national governments but is also monitored by local authorities through, for example, trading standards departments. Political decisions, such as those on economic policy, social policy, the control of pollution and support for technology, each of which is examined elsewhere in this book, all have an impact on business activities. The business environment is liable to change as a result of radical political shock, gradual shift, or a combination of the two. The Asian economic crisis in 1998 illustrates such a combination (see below).

Organisations will perceive political change differently; some may feel threatened, others may see the changes as offering business opportunities. It is evident that decisions and actions made at the higher geo-political scales can have an impact on organisations, both large and small. This is the context of our analysis of the political environment. The analysis will concentrate on three geo-political scales: global, national and local. This is followed by discussion of one of the most significant regional scales, the European Union.

Global scale

The changing international scene, with its powerful interests, has an enormous impact on the operating activities of many organisations. The international agenda is increasingly being set by international protocols and transnational bodies. For example, the World Trade Organisation (WTO) agreement on basic telecommunications services came into force on 5 February 1998. The agreement was signed by 69 countries, and covers 90 per cent of the world's $650 billion telecoms services market, with a possible turnover of $1 trillion in 2000. The European Union and Japan have agreed to open competition, though some EU countries were allowed to delay for one year from 1 January 1998.

The relationship between politics and business organisations is not a 'one-way street'. Business is not so weak that it always has to pander to politicians.

Governments are often keen to encourage multinational companies to invest, and offer financial incentives because of the jobs they may provide. Political parties too can benefit from closer alignments with business, especially media organisations. For example the *Sun* newspaper, owned by News Corporation, switched support to the Labour party in the run-up to the 1997 general election. After coming to power the Prime Minister, Tony Blair, was alleged to have canvassed the Italian Prime Minister, Romano Prodi, on behalf of News Corporation in a proposed takeover of Mediaset, an Italian television network.

Political changes are likely to create opportunities or present threats to organisations. In this section we consider a number of such changes in different parts of the world, and look, in general terms, at their impact upon business.

The Far East

In the recession of the early and mid 1980s, which largely affected the manu-facturing sector, a substantial number of job losses in the UK were a result of multinationals transferring capacity to cheaper NICs (see Case Study 3 in Part II). Around the world 'job-for-life' employment philosophies are gradually being replaced. More recently, in June 1998 Japan, for example, announced that it was in recession. With unemployment rising fast, the Prime Minister was replaced. The situation in Japan reflected the economic slump across Asia. Thailand went into recession in 1997. Malaysia's deputy prime minister was sacked and in September 1998 strict foreign exchange controls were introduced in an attempt to restore confidence in the economy. In Indonesia the recession caused full-scale riots; President Suharto was deposed as unemployment rose. South Korea was also in recession and even Hong Kong, a few months after its return to Chinese sovereignty, experienced a contraction in the first quarter of 1998.

Before these events the creation of new jobs in Europe, and particularly the UK, by Japanese, Taiwanese and Korean multinationals had led governments to provide significant grants in many cases and to reduce obstacles to such invest-ments by, for example, relaxing planning regulations. However, on 4 September 1998 Fujitsu announced the closure of its D-Ram microchip plant in Durham. This followed the closure of a similar Siemens plant on Tyneside and the abandonment of Hyundai's new plant in Scotland and that of LG in Wales. Job losses were substantial. Furthermore, Europe may see an influx of cheap imports from Asia as companies try to export their way out of trouble, hitting European companies further and precipitating additional job losses.

The impact on exporters to the region is equally problematic. Waterford Wedgwood opened a store in Tokyo's Ginza district in 1997, following two years of buoyant sales. By 1998 the fall in the value of the yen made its products much more expensive. As a result sales, in cash terms, dropped substantially (Hadfield and Smith, 1998).

As the business world is increasingly globalised, the extent of knock-on effects from regional crises becomes more acute.

The collapse of Communism and the peace dividend

The collapse of Communist systems in the former Soviet Union and throughout the world, the establishment of fledgling market economies and the opening of Communist China are bringing problems to some organisations and offering opportunities to others. The European Union itself seems to be undergoing an eastward shift as relations between Central and Eastern European countries have progressed significantly since the introduction of political and market reforms. The European Union is politically committed to enlargement, to embrace 25 members, or even more, early in the new millennium.

The former East Germany has presented enormous opportunities to business and has succeeded in attracting substantial funds as it continues to rebuild its crumbling infrastructure. In 1991, following the reunification of Germany in 1990, Volkswagen secured a 70 per cent share of Skoda of the Czech Republic for £480 million. In eight years Volkswagen have ploughed in excess of £5 billion into the company. They have succeeded in turning a brand that was often derided as cheap and poor quality into one that now occupies a favourable position in the market, with strong consumer backing and sales growth. German companies have provided a substantial proportion, around 50 per cent, of foreign direct investment into the Czech Republic in the 1990s.

Foreign companies are being allowed access to China, particularly in the special economic zones. The reduced labour costs enjoyed by the incomers, mostly multinational corporations (MNCs), have enabled them to become more competitive on a world scale. However, other competitors outside of China and the NICs have found themselves unable to compete with the cost advantages enjoyed by these 'transplants'. This has led to redundancies or even closure of factories. The British shoe industry, which is still relatively labour-dependent, has suffered because of cheaper Chinese competition.

Global location decisions

Organisations are increasingly operating in a diverse range of countries. A number of factors are relevant when making decisions about the countries in which to locate any business activity. Clearly, certain countries, particularly developing ones, may be attractive because they are potential sources of important natural resources and lower labour costs. It is, however, also important to assess the stability of the political, financial, social and cultural systems when evaluating a potential base in a given country. If companies export, or have production facilities outside their home bases, action by foreign governments may present both opportunities and threats. These include the following possibilities:

- governments may nationalise an organisation and freeze assets, as proposed by Russian Communists in 1998, or curtail overseas sales contracts;
- exchange controls may be imposed which can reduce the amount of money organisations can draw out of profit-making overseas subsidiaries, as in Malaysia in 1998 (see above);

- the privatisation of former nationalised industries may present opportunities for investment and trade. The willingness of some American utilities to buy out regional electricity companies in the UK must suggest a reasonable profit potential to the acquirer (see Chapter 2);

- import barriers may be raised or lowered, making an organisation's product or service more or less competitive in a foreign market. Restrictions on the import of Japanese cars into the EU are due to be lifted in 2000.

Import barriers may be:

- quotas which limit the number of goods entering a market;
- tariffs paid to the government; or
- technical requirements – for example, that a product must be of a particular standard or that it must not contain certain substances. (Vehicle exhaust emission standards in the United States are such a case. These standards have placed an added cost on manufacturers exporting to the American market.)

Organisations will place high priorities on peace and political stability (see Exhibit 7.1).

In other instances political decisions have forced companies to miss potential investment opportunities. American companies were left behind in the early rush to invest in Vietnam because of the trade embargo dating from the end of the Vietnam war in 1975. Companies from Singapore, Taiwan, Japan, France and Australia, in particular, took advantage. In the six years prior to American participation investment totalled in excess of £5 billion. It was only much later, in February 1994, that the embargo was lifted and American companies were given the green light to enter a potentially fast-growing market.

Even non-commercial organisations are increasingly having to operate against a background of changing political and economic issues. Oxfam, for example,

EXHIBIT 7.1

The Russian predicament

The economic and political unrest in Russia following the devaluation of the rouble and the collapse of the Russian stock market in 1998 resulted in a considerable undermining of confidence in the Russian economy. The outcome of this was a rise in the popularity of the Communist party. The party, under the leadership of Gennardy Zyuganov, was the largest in the Duma (the Russian parliament). The Communist party pointed to serious consequences following the collapse including hyper-inflation, mass unemployment and economic collapse. Possible solutions, under a Communist leadership, and proposed by Zyuganov, included nationalisation of private businesses. A policy of this nature is likely to have serious ramifications for both home-based and foreign-owned businesses.

has to be fully aware of these issues both at home and internationally and to be sensitive to the different motivations around the globe. Mary Cherry, Oxfam's chair in 1993/94, suggested that 'the constant challenge facing a charity was to change to meet the needs of the times and yet to retain our core values undiminished'.

At this global scale a large range of interactions takes place, involving such groupings as supranational bodies, governments, multinational companies and international pressure groups. The activities of these groups will often result in new law or policy being formulated, which will have implications for organisations. Some of the political pressures which manifest themselves at the national and local scale will have their origins at this global scale.

National scale

Some commentators, for example Ohmae (1995), claim that given the increasing globalisation of markets nation states are of diminishing importance. He argues that 'Nation states are no longer meaningful units in which to think about economic activity. In a borderless world they consign things to the wrong level of aggregation.' Ohmae lists a number of what he calls 'natural economic zones', which do not recognise geographical or political boundaries. These include northern Italy; Hong Kong and Southern China; and Singapore and its neighbouring Indonesian islands.

However, in most cases, despite the global pressures discussed above, nation states still possess considerable autonomy and the capacity to 'do things differently'. For example, the extent of government intervention in the economy varies enormously between countries (see Chapter 8). Even when a government is trying to maintain a 'hands-off' approach its actions can have an impact on an industrial sector. The political systems adopted by each country vary as a result of independent evolution over hundreds of years. It is important to recognise that the local political system will have an important impact on the operation of business in a given nation state.

Not all countries have democratic systems; a number of military governments exist, such as those in Iraq and Burma. However, there are still considerable differences between systems which share democratic governments. The proportional representation system in Italy has, for example, created a much more volatile environment for business than the system in use in the UK. Italy has had a succession of unstable coalition governments for most of the post-1945 period. In the UK, a 'first past the post' system is used to elect 651 members of parliament (MPs) to serve in the House of Commons. However, in October 1998 the Jenkins Commission recommended the adoption of a form of proportional representation, which will be tested by a referendum. It is thought that since the present voting system almost invariably brings to power a party with a majority in the House of Commons there may be some reluctance to change. Although the proportional representation model predominates in Europe, 'first past the post' systems apply to 49 per cent of the world's electors (*The Week*, 1998).

The impact of government: the UK case

In the UK the leader of the largest party is, normally, appointed as Prime Minister. The Cabinet makes policy which is debated in the House of Commons and the House of Lords. Changes in policy often require legislation and much of the work of both Houses is in reviewing and debating the contents of new Bills. Policy is implemented administratively by civil servants and quangos. Bills become Acts of Parliament or statutes when given the Royal Assent. Every year a large number of new Acts are added to the statute books.

Exhibit 7.2 shows how the actions and attitudes of government (at many scales) and society can impact on a particular sector. The influence of the government on the public sector is explored in Chapter 8.

EXHIBIT 7.2

Advertising and the law

Advertising is a business activity that has a wide impact and requires a framework in which to operate to ensure an acceptable standard of behaviour. This framework may be self-regulatory or provided by statute.

The law impacts on advertising in a number of ways. The first statute passed in the UK to protect consumers from unethical advertising was the Advertisement Act (1889). Now over a hundred statutes affect advertising. In June 1996, The Body Shop were cited by the Metropolitan Police for illegal flyposting under the Town and Country Planning Act 1990 and the London Local Authority Act of 1996 (Lee, 1996).

Legal and regulatory bodies have been established to monitor and control the activities of advertisers. In the UK these include the Advertising Standards Authority (ASA), the Independent Television Commission (ITC) and the Radio Authority (RA). In France it is the BVP, Commission for the Control of Advertising. Transnational bodies such as the European Advertising Standards Alliance (EASA) also have a role to play.

The ASA was established in 1963. Its role is to ensure that everyone who commissions, prepares and publishes advertisements in the non-broadcast media within the UK observes the British Codes of Advertising and Sales Promotion. The ASA codes state that advertisements should be 'legal, decent, honest and truthful, socially responsible and prepared in line with the principles of fair competition' (ASA, 1998a). In 1997 the ASA found that 98 per cent of poster advertisements, 96 per cent of press adverts and 85 per cent of direct mail advertisements complied with the code (ASA, 1998a).

If an advertisement breaks the rules, the ASA will ask the advertiser to withdraw the advertisement. Companies whose advertisements have provoked public complaints include Peugeot, Lee Apparel and Gossard (Boshoff, 1998). Benetton are (in)famous for their global advertising campaigns, which began in 1984. Their

1991 advertisement of a man, David Kirby, dying of AIDS was banned in the UK, and the BVP in France asked the media not to use it. As a result it was only published in the magazine Max. Virgin have also come under the regulatory spotlight. Virgin Interactive Entertainment (Europe) Ltd produced a poster for a Sony computer game 'Resident Evil', showing a bath full of blood. The ASA decided that the advertisement should only be allowed in adult magazines. In 1998 the ASA banned three advertisements produced for Virgin Cola Company Ltd (ASA, 1998b).

The Radio Authority came into being in January 1991 following the Broadcasting Act 1990. It is the responsibility of the authority to monitor the obligations of its licensees, all commercial radio stations, as required by the Broadcasting Acts of 1990 and 1996. One of these is to regulate programming and advertising. The ITC, established at the same time, undertakes the same task for commercial television.

There is also much reliance on self-regulation. The Committee of Advertising Practice (CAP), comprising twenty trade and professional associations representing all sectors of the advertising and media industries, give direction and guidance to advertisers through regularly updated codes of practice. The EASA was co-founded by the ASA in 1991 and achieved legal status in January 1994. It is an alliance of 23 European self-regulatory bodies and has three principal aims:

- to promote and support self-regulation in Europe;
- to co-ordinate and administer the cross-border complaints system;
- to provide information and research on the self-regulation of advertising in Europe.

Other legislation is also of key significance to organisations and consumers. The annual budget often has an impact on specific interest groups. In the 1999 UK Budget the price of a packet of cigarettes increased by a further 17.5p on a packet of 20 cigarettes, an increase of 7.5 per cent. The Tobacco Manufacturers Association and manufacturers had further grounds for concern. Specific legislation, such as the National Minimum Wage Act 1998, established a legislative framework for the national minimum wage. Regulations arising from the Act are likely to have a significant impact on many organisations.

The monetarist approach

The 1979 general election proved to be a significant political milestone. The new government turned away from traditional economic thinking, based on the Keynesian approach, to controlling the economy by adopting a 'monetarist' philosophy. The Keynesian approach rests on the assumption that the economy is inherently unstable and in need of active government intervention, largely through fiscal policy (see Chapter 3), to control demand in the economy. It is believed that the level of activity in the economy can be controlled, business cycles smoothed out, peaks and troughs eliminated and unemployment limited. However,

the orthodox Keynesian model was unable to deliver a strong economy. The 1960s and 1970s saw increasingly high levels of unemployment and inflation which could not be explained by Keynesian theory or solved using traditional demand management policies. Keynesian theory was open to criticism, especially by the monetarists. The monetarist approach, in contrast, regards the economy as inherently stable and suggests that fiscal policy has no role in regulating the economy. In fact monetarists argue that fiscal policy can actually exacerbate business downswings. Monetarists argue that firm control of the money supply will not affect the business cycle and that policy should be targeted at the supply side of the economy. Exhibit 7.3 takes a closer look at supply-side economic measures and how they may impact on organisations.

EXHIBIT 7.3

Supply-side measures

The goal of supply-side policy is to remove barriers which prevent or deter organisations and individuals from adapting quickly to changing demand and changes in production and, therefore, to increase efficiency and promote economic growth and employment. Conservative governments, from 1979, introduced a number of measures aimed at improving the supply side and giving organisations flexibility.

Taxation

Prime Minister Thatcher suggested that 'if people find too big a chunk of their pay taken away in tax they won't work so hard'. Measures have been introduced to ensure that people were better off in work: direct taxes such as income tax have been reduced, to be replaced by indirect taxes such as VAT; thresholds above which people start paying tax have been raised; and unemployment benefit is now taxed. Companies, particularly small and medium-sized enterprises, have also benefited from reductions in, for example, corporation tax.

The labour market

The government have introduced a number of training schemes designed to promote work skills, an example being the Youth Training Scheme. Whether these schemes have been successful is open to debate. Certainly the UK is still some way behind competitor nations such as Germany in the provision of quality training. Other measures have attempted to safeguard the interests of individuals in the workplace and to restrict trade unions (see Chapter 5). These measures aim to create a more flexible labour market and reduce unemployment.

Deregulation

Deregulation is the process of dismantling regulations governing the activities of business organisations. Deregulation has opened many other markets to greater

competition and aims to make consumers better off by increasing competition. For example, the telecommunications sector was opened up to competition so that Mercury communications could use BT's cable infrastructure to carry calls. Other sectors that were deregulated include road haulage, national buses and the capital market (see Chapter 8).

The capital market and financial sector

This is the market to which companies and the government turn when they need medium- and long-term funds. A whole range of controls have been abolished in the capital market. Foreign exchange controls were abolished in 1979; hire purchase controls in 1982; deregulation, the 'Big Bang', increased competition in the stock market in 1986, especially from foreign securities houses; the Financial Services Act 1986 and the Building Societies Act 1986 allowed non-banking financial institutions to provide services previously closed to them. These changes are seen as a way of encouraging competition and, therefore, improving the competitiveness of UK businesses.

Privatisation

Privatisation usually implies the transfer of assets from the public to the private sector. The aims of privatisation are: to introduce competition into previously monopoly-controlled public sectors and increase efficiency; to increase the extent of share ownership and to reduce government borrowing by raising revenue (see Chapter 8).

While we may support or oppose political decisions, depending on our political leaning, some important changes affecting managers and consumers have been made in the years since 1979. These will have a lasting effect on business. The change of emphasis and thinking in the 'corridors of power' has had some influence on the values and assumptions held by managers. In turn, this has affected the way managers consider customers, employees and other groups with an interest in their organisation (the stakeholders). In essence, the role of government intervention in the economy has been reduced and the importance of self-reliance emphasised. This important theme is further developed in Chapters 8 and 9.

Local scale

In the UK, as in many other countries, local authorities are run by elected councillors whose powers are laid down by parliament. They provide services and have regulatory responsibilities. Local government in the UK has traditionally been organised into a series of tiers such as County and District Councils. A Local Government Commission was set up in 1992 to investigate the structure of local government. Since then it has created a substantial number of new 'unitary' (single-level) authorities, for example by merging former County and Borough

Councils. Such changes may simplify the dealings of many organisations with local government, as there will only be one body with which to deal in a unitary authority. In the long term, efficiency gains may result in a lower business rate. The UK government also introduced a Local Government Bill in late 1998 which, if enacted, will allow cities to elect executive mayors. It aims to reform local government and encourage greater participation in it.

It is paradoxical that many organisations, for example grant-maintained schools, NHS Trusts and civil service agencies, are managed at the lowest local level but funded and controlled at the highest, that is by central government (in these cases by the Department of Education and Employment, the Department of Health and the Treasury). This is also the case for local authorities. The government controls what each local authority can spend; see Exhibit 7.4.

Local authorities can, however, raise further funds by borrowing for major capital investment schemes. Despite recent moves towards devolution of power, some disquiet has been raised regarding the trend towards centralisation by the UK government and the use of non-elected bodies to administer policy. It is argued that excessive centralisation has resulted in many local initiatives being stifled. Some feel that the fact that quangos now do much of the work previously carried out by local councils has raised a serious question about democratic accountability. Members of quangos do not need to seek election, or re-election, as local councillors do.

If we accept that the political system in the UK has become increasingly centralised then it should not surprise us that many consider the system has little to offer them. In Chapter 9 we examine the 'disconnectedness' of many young

---

EXHIBIT 7.4

Northamptonshire

In Northamptonshire spending in 1998/99 was increased by 4.5 per cent to £405.2 million. The funds are raised via:

1. Business Rates. These are charged on all non-domestic properties. An assessment is made by the government and a uniform charge applied to all businesses. The charge for 1998/99 was 47.4p in the £ (rateable value).

2. Revenue Support Grant. The amount received from this general grant is the amount that the government estimates that each authority needs to spend to provide a standard level of service. The amount is based on the Standard Spending Assessment (SSA). Together the business rate and the revenue support grant fund approximately 75 per cent of the budget.

3. Other smaller grants are received, but can only be used for specific purposes.

4. The Council Tax provides the balance of funding. This is levied on every household. The amount collected in Northamptonshire in 1998/99 was £104.4 million.

people in the UK from the established political system. In this section we have noted the impact of decision making on business at three different geo-political scales: the supranational level, by central government and by a more locally accountable means. In moving on to look at the European Union, we will examine a major area in this debate.

THE EUROPEAN UNION

The European Coal and Steel Community (ECSC) was established by the Treaty of Paris in 1951 between Belgium, the Federal Republic of Germany (West Germany), France, Italy, Luxembourg and the Netherlands. A treaty is a document which binds two or more countries to do something together. It is therefore a collection of commitments which are negotiated, ratified and implemented. The aim of the Treaty of Paris was to establish a unified market which could prosper from reduced barriers to trade. In 1957 the Treaty of Rome, signed by the six countries, created the European Economic Community (EEC) and the European Atomic Energy Community (Euratom). The Treaty extended economic ties by creating a customs union and common market. These three communities came together to establish the European Community (EC) in 1965. The first enlargement was in 1973 when Denmark, Ireland and the UK became members. Greece joined in 1981, followed in 1986 by Portugal and Spain.

The signing of the agreement on the European Economic Area in May 1992 created the world's biggest free trade area. Austria, Finland, Norway, Iceland and Sweden joined the European Community twelve and established an integrated economic entity with a 372 million population and enormous opportunities for trade and commerce. In 1995 Austria, Finland and Sweden became full members of the European Union. The Community has evolved largely through amendments to the original treaties, notably via the Single European Act (SEA) 1987 and the Treaty of European Union (TEU) 1992, more commonly known as the Maastricht Treaty. Most recently the Treaty of Amsterdam was signed on 2 October 1997.

The SEA 1987 changed decision-making procedures within the Community. Prior to its adoption, decisions had to be agreed by a unanimous vote; this condition was replaced by the ability to adopt decisions subject to qualified majority voting, clearing the way for speedier decision making within the community. The SEA 1987 also required that the Single European Market (SEM) should be in place

by the end of 1992. Its objectives were to improve the environment for business by providing for the free movement of labour, capital, goods and services within the Community and to facilitate closer co-operation between countries on a range of other matters. It was anticipated that the benefits would include increased growth, higher employment, lower prices and wider choice for consumers. The adoption of the SEM enhanced the ability of European business to compete in world markets by reducing non-tariff barriers that governments introduced partly to protect home industries. The most important non-tariff barriers are identified in Table 7.1.

The SEA 1987 represented an important supply-side initiative. Following the creation of the SEM it was envisaged that businesses would have unrestricted access to the European market and face lower costs and gain economies of scale. The UK industries that gained from the SEM include airlines, telecommunications and pharmaceuticals. However, a more open market also brings with it increased competition.

When the TEU 1992 came into force on 1 November 1993 the European Union came into being. The European Union comprises the European Community, a Common Foreign and Security Policy, and a common approach to Justice and Home Affairs: the so-called three-pillar structure (Thomson, 1995). The TEU 1992 was the focus for much internal disagreement in both the Conservative and Labour parties in the United Kingdom, and debate in Denmark and France where it was only ratified following referenda. Perhaps the most contentious issue in the TEU 1992, as far as the UK and Danish governments were concerned, was the Social Chapter, which included minimum requirements on

- health and safety;
- consultation between management and employees;
- working conditions and the working week;
- equality between men and women regarding job opportunities and treatment at work.

TABLE 7.1   The most important barriers to trade

Barriers	West Germany	France	Italy	UK	Euro 12
National standards and regulations	1	1	4	1	2
Government procurement	8	7/8	2	4	8
Administrative	2	2	1	2	1
Physical frontier delays and costs	4	4	3	3	3
Differences in VAT	5/6	3	7	8	6/7
Regulations on freight transport	5/6	5	8	5	6/7
Restrictions in capital market	7	7/8	5	7	5
Community law	3	6	6	6	4

Note: range of ranks 1 (most important) to 8 (least important)

Source: adapted from Paolo Cechini, The European Challenge, Wildwood House, 1988

The idea of applying regulations to the labour market was totally contrary to the supply-side approach that the government had adopted since 1979 (see above). The Conservative government felt that the costs to business would result in substantial job losses. By opting out of this part of the Treaty the government hoped that the low-cost environment it created within the EU would prove attractive to inward investment. The Social Chapter was only included as a protocol annexed to the Treaty, as a result of the opposition by the UK government. The Treaty was ratified by the UK Parliament in 1993, though the UK (and Denmark) secured an opt-out clause on significant parts of the treaty such as the section on Economic and Monetary Union.

An agreement was made to revise the TEU 1992 around the middle of the decade, hence Article N was included in the treaty, providing for a conference to be convened in 1996. The inter-governmental conference lasted more than a year (see later) and came to an end in Amsterdam with the political agreement on the new treaty. The Treaty of Amsterdam has four main objectives:

1. To place employment and citizens' rights at the heart of the Union;
2. To sweep away the last remaining obstacles to freedom of movement and to strengthen security;
3. To give Europe a stronger voice in world affairs;
4. To make the Union's institutional structure more efficient with a view to enlarging the Union.

The future development of the European Union will require further agreement so that more treaties are inevitable. The role of the European institutions is set by the treaties. We will now examine their roles.

The European institutions

The European Union has created a number of key supranational bodies. The four most important such bodies are

- the European Commission;
- the Council of Ministers (the Council of European Union);
- the European Court of Justice; and
- the European Parliament.

Other bodies may have a lower profile, but play an important role in economic life. These are examined in Table 7.2 and include

- the European Investment Bank
- the Economic and Social Committee
- the Committee of the Regions
- the European Environment Agency

TABLE 7.2   European Union institutions

The European Investment Bank (EIB)

Based in Luxembourg, the EIB is a non-profit-making, independent institution, established by the Treaty of Rome. It obtains finance from member states and raises funds on international money markets to provide long-term loans and guarantees for priority investment projects, particularly in the less developed regions.

The Economic and Social Committee (ECOSOC)

Made up of representatives of various interests, including trade unions, employers, and consumer associations. It is consulted on legislation and can draft opinions on matters of concern, though its influence is limited.

The Committee of the Regions

Created by the TEU, its role, to some extent, overlaps that of the ECOSOC. It is a consultative institution which represents local and regional authorities. It is consulted by the Council or Commission on issues affecting the regions.

The European Environment Agency

Established in 1990 to achieve the aims of environmental protection and improvement. The agency publishes a report on the state of the environment every three years. Certain areas of work are given priority, such as air quality, water quality, waste management, land use and natural resources (CEC, 1994b). The work of the Agency is discussed in more detail in Chapter 6.

The European Monetary Institute (EMI)

Established in 1994 following the TEU. Its role is to help establish the conditions necessary for EMU. The main objectives are the co-ordination of monetary policy, development of the Euro and preparation for the European System of Central Banks (CEC, 1994b). The EMI will eventually be replaced by the European Central Bank.

The Court of Auditors

Established in 1975. It was introduced to improve efficiency of resource-use and identify corruption. It monitors the EU budget, examines accounts and oversees budgets. It produces an annual report.

Source: Commission of the European Communities 1994 *The Institutions of the Community*, Background Report, ISEC/B7/94, London, CEC

- the European Monetary Institute
- the Court of Auditors.

Readers should be aware that many more such bodies, each with a specific role, do exist, for example the European Training Foundation and the Agency for Health and Safety at Work.

The European Commission

The Commission is headed by the Commission President and includes 20 members (commissioners), approved by the European Parliament and appointed by national governments to a specific portfolio for a period of five years (renewable). The Brussels-based Commission is the civil service of the European Union. The Commission's role as the 'guardian of the treaties' is:

- to mediate between governments to secure agreement on legislation;

- to manage the technical details and day-to-day policing of agreed policy, for example the Common Fisheries Policy, and ensuring compliance by governments, companies and individuals;
- to represent the European Union in negotiations, for instance within the World Trade Organisation (WTO), and to defend collective interests.

The Commission is divided into 26 Directorates General. DG I (external relations) has three subdivisions. It carries out preliminary research and makes proposals for directives and regulations in consultation with the Council of Ministers and the Parliament (see Figure 7.1 and Exhibit 7.5). Clearly the Commission is at the centre of decision making in the European Union. At the beginning of 1999 the Commission came under scrutiny because of allegations of corruption. New legislation must take account of three basic principles:

1. Subsidiarity: action at a European Union level must not be proposed if action can be more effectively carried out at the level of national governments.

2. Proposals have to be in the interests of the European Union as a whole.

3. The Commission has to consult widely before making a legislative proposal.

All member states have the opportunity to make their input before a legal measure is finally adopted by the Council and becomes law in the form of directives and regulations. National legislation must be enacted by member states,

EXHIBIT 7.5

Working time regulations

In the UK, working time regulations came into effect on 1 October 1998. The regulations implement an EC directive 93/104/EC: the Directive on Certain Aspects of Working Time. The directive sets out the rights and responsibilities of the parties involved in the workplace. In general a worker will be someone to whom an employer has a duty to provide work. The majority of agency workers and freelancers will be classed as workers. The regulations provide the following new rights for workers:

- 3 weeks' paid annual leave, rising to 4 weeks in 1999;
- 11 hours' rest a day;
- a day's rest a week;
- in-work rest breaks;
- a maximum limit of an average of 48 hours a week which a worker can be required to work;
- a maximum limit of an average of 8 hours' work in 24 hours for night workers and a requirement to offer these workers health assessments.

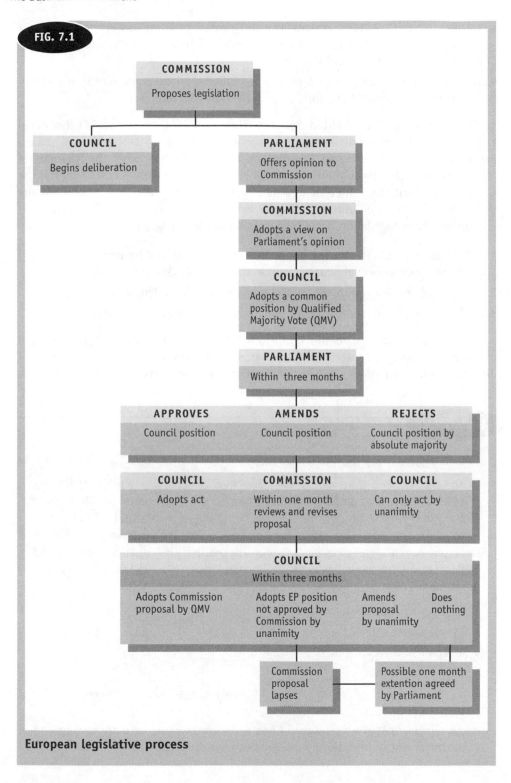

FIG. 7.1

European legislative process

Exhibit 7.5 continued

In the light of these new rights employers will need to consider whether their working practices need to be changed; clearly this could have substantial cost implications for a number of organisations. The regulations, however, do allow for some measures to be adopted through agreements between workers and employers so as to allow the flexibility to take account of the specific needs of local working arrangements.

Other organisations may see the new regulations in a different light. The DTI Minister of State Ian McCartney said that 'nobody profits from working too many hours'. There are a number of sectors (e.g. doctors) where the regulations do not apply, though the Commission has announced its intention to bring forward proposals to extend some rights to these workers.

A fascinating case study exploring the ways in which the previous Conservative government attempted to avoid the impact of the directive can be found in Le Sueur and Sunkin (1997).

according to traditional parliamentary practices, to turn these directives and regulations into national law.

The Council of Ministers

The Council of Ministers is the main decision-making body of the European Union. It makes the final decision on adopting proposals from the Commission. Each Council meeting is attended by the national minister responsible for that particular subject (e.g. economics and finance, transport, agriculture). Much of the work of the Council is undertaken by the Committee of Permanent Representatives (COREPER) which screens proposals before passing them on to the Council. The presidency of the council is held by each member country in turn and lasts for six months. It is the role of the president to chair the meeting of the Council. The Council takes some decisions by a unanimous vote. However, more decisions are now being taken by qualified majority voting (QMV) following the provisions laid down in the SEA 1987 and the TEU 1992. As well as significantly increasing the speed of decision making in the Council, QMV also means that, because member states have lost their right to veto, the risk of unfavourable policy outcomes for business is increased. This has forced organisations to develop proactive and individual European lobbying strategies. The decision to ban tobacco advertising in December 1997 was approved by 15 to 11 which is the narrowest margin acceptable under the QMV rules. The ban, under which cinema and hoarding advertising will be banned after three years, newspaper advertising after a further year and sponsorship a further year later, is likely to be appealed to the European Court of Justice by the Tobacco Manufacturers Association.

The Council of Ministers should not be confused with the European Council which meets twice a year. This is a forum for the heads of government of member

countries which is important in the strategic development of the European Union; its proposals are passed on to the Council of Ministers for transposition into law.

The inter-governmental conference (IGC) is another important EU forum. It is necessary for an IGC to prepare the ground for a new European treaty. The Turin European Council launched an IGC on 29 March 1996. This was continued at successive European Councils in Florence (21–22 June), Dublin (5 October), Dublin (13–14 December) and Noordwijk (23 May 1997). From the discussions a consensus emerged on the Amsterdam Treaty (see above).

The European Court of Justice

The European Court of Justice (ECJ), based in Luxembourg, is concerned with the application and interpretation of EU law. It follows directives and regulations and through its judgments ensures the compliance of member states. It interprets legislation and European treaties. The ECJ consists of 16 judges (one from each member state), one nominee and six advocates-general. Cases can be brought to the court by individuals, companies, and governments as well as by the Commission. Member states are bound by the Court's rulings. It is likely that organisations and individuals will increasingly feel the effects of the judgments of the Court. A subsidiary court, the Court of First Instance, was established by the SEA 1987 to deal with certain cases, particularly those brought by companies. Exhibit 7.6 shows how the Court can impact on multi-million pound businesses.

EXHIBIT 7.6

The Scotch Whisky Association *v* Compagnie Financienne de Prises de Participation (Cofepp) and Other

The Community Regulation on the definition, description and presentation of spirit drinks does not allow the use of the term 'whisky' in the name of a spirit drink containing whisky diluted with water, with an alcoholic strength of less than 40 per cent.

On discovering that Gold River, made by blending various Scotch, Canadian and American whiskies together with water and having a minimum alcoholic strength of 30 per cent, was being offered for sale, The Scotch Whisky Association, a Scottish company set up to protect and promote the interests of the Scotch whisky trade, brought proceedings against the companies involved before the Tribunal de Grande Instance in Paris, which asked the Court of Justice to give a ruling. The Court held that a drink such as Gold River was a spirit drink within the meaning of the Regulation, but not a whisky and, thus, could not be sold under that description.

Source: Press and Information Division, press release No. 47/98, CJ, 16 July 1998 Judgment of the Court of Justice in Case C-136/96. For the full text of the judgments, consult Internet page http://curia.eu.int.

The European Parliament

Since 1979, the European Parliament has been directly elected by member states on a five-year mandate. It is located in Strasbourg where it meets for twelve week-long sessions each year and Brussels where additional plenary sessions are held. Following the 1995 enlargement of the European Union the number of MEPs rose from 567 to 626, with 87 from the UK. The powers of the Parliament have gradually been extended, principally by the SEA 1987 and the TEU 1992, to amend and adopt legislation so that Parliament and the Council now share power of decision in a large number of areas. It retains control over the EU budget and must ratify proposals made by the Commission and the Council of Ministers. It has the power to amend or reject legislation and dismiss the Commission.

Legislative procedures

The procedure for drafting legislation was put in place by the SEA 1987. The new procedure represents a democratisation of the legislative procedure, as can be seen in Figure 7.1. Under the former system decisions were taken by the council with very little recourse to the European Parliament.

All the bodies of the European Union, particularly the four main ones outlined in this chapter, have the power to influence the day-to-day activities of all European business organisations. A closer examination of competition policy in the following section illustrates the influence that the European Union has on business activity.

QUESTIONS

1. Identify an issue and an interested lobby group (e.g. the Tobacco Manufacturers Association and the ban on tobacco advertising) and investigate how that group has used its influence with the Commission.

2. Give an assessment of the impact of the working time regulations on a business organisation or a sector.

THE EUROPEAN UNION AND COMPETITION POLICY

Competition policy in the UK is increasingly influenced by the European Union. When Swiss-owned Nestlé acquired Rowntree in 1988 the bid was not referred for consideration by the MMC, despite creating a new entity with over 25 per cent market share. The new enlarged company had less than 25 per cent of the European market. In this situation European considerations took precedence over UK competition policy.

Competition policy in the European Union is the remit of Directorate General (DG) IV. The specific objective of the Commission is to

prevent any agreement or practice that may distort competition. Accordingly, any restrictive practice that affects or is liable to affect trade between Community countries is prohibited, and any agreement between organisations having such characteristics is null and void. (CEC, 1993)

Competition is largely governed by Articles 37 and 85–94 of the TEU 1992. Articles 85 and 86 are arguably the most important. Each focuses on a particular aspect of competition:

- Article 85 on anti-competitive agreements between two or more organisations;
- Article 86 on exploitation of monopoly power or a dominant market position.

Over recent years competition policy has become more rigorous in its pursuit of the free market and the diminution of monopoly power.

Agreements that restrict competition

Article 85 controls oligopolies by regulating agreements. In general terms agreements are liable to be prohibited if:

- they have the object or effect of restricting competition; or
- they have an appreciable effect, either actual or potential, on trade between member states.

Agreements that prohibit competition can be placed into two categories. They can be either horizontal or vertical agreements. In this section we will investigate both types of agreement.

Horizontal agreements are between actual or potential competitors, that is, organisations at the same stage of production. The car industry may provide an illustration of this type of agreement (see Exhibit 2.6). Horizontal agreements are restricted if they lead to one or more of the following (CEC, 1993):

- joint fixing of prices by competitors;
- market sharing;
- setting of production quotas;
- tie-in sales clauses;
- discriminatory sales practices;
- joint purchasing by competitors;
- joint sales;
- sales promotion which restricts participation at commercial fairs or joint labels or trade marks, where this leads to an alignment of commercial strategy;
- exchange of information if this may lead to collusion.

Vertical agreements are between organisations operating at different levels in the distribution process. This may be an agreement between a manufacturer and a retailer (see Exhibit 2.6 and the Unilever example in Exhibit 7.7). As a general

principle, European policies presume that collectively imposed vertical restrictions are harmful, unless proved otherwise, even though economists can produce evidence that vertical agreements may, in some cases, actually promote inter-brand competition.

Vertical agreements are restricted if they lead to one or more of the following (CEC, 1993):

- a compartmentalisation of the market through an exclusive or selective distribution agreement or a franchise agreement (for example, export bans);
- restrictions in the choice of suppliers or customers;
- prices not being set freely;
- an exclusive purchasing obligation for an unlimited period and in respect of a broad range of products;
- discriminatory exclusion of certain types of retail outlets through an exclusive retail agreement.

The tough line has been epitomised by the action of European competition watchdogs. Recent cases that have come to the attention of competition authorities at both European and national level are shown in Exhibit 7.7, and mark the latest in a series of drives by Brussels to stamp out uncompetitive activities by EU-based companies. If found guilty of anti-competitive activities, companies can be fined up to 10 per cent of their worldwide annual turnover.

EXHIBIT 7.7

Regulation of competition by the European Commission

The Commission, under merger regulations in force since 1990, has been notified of 529 instances of potential conflict. The Commission deemed that in 33 the operation raised serious doubts as to its compatibility with the common market and undertook an in-depth (phase 2) investigation. By the end of 1996, 30 of these investigations were completed, and 7 mergers were forbidden, 16 were authorised, subject to resolving competition problems identified by the Commission, and 7 were cleared without conditions (European Commission, 1998a).

A recent proposal by Airtours, the UK's second-largest tour operator, to buy a stake in Germany's third-largest package holiday group, LTU, is being examined by the German cartel office. The cartel office is also looking at the German digital pay-TV joint venture proposed by Kirch Group and CLT-Ufa. Because of the closer co-operation which the agreement is likely to bring to free to air television, dominated by the two companies, the cartel office has recommended that Brussels block the deal (Studemann, 1998).

Under Articles 85 and 86 a separate decision was taken on 11 March 1998 to condemn the exclusivity condition imposed by Unilever as part of its terms for

> **Exhibit 7.7 continued**
>
> supplying freezer cabinets in the Irish ice-cream market. The condition was that freezers had to be used exclusively for the storage of Unilever products and this limited retailers to supplying Unilever products. As a result, Unilever had effectively closed the market to a substantial number of competitors, in breach of Article 85, and abused its dominant position in the market, in breach of Article 86 (European Commission, 1998b).

The European Commission has not been afraid to use its powers under Article 93 to investigate state aid to companies. In 1998 the Commission raised serious concerns as to the use of government aid (European Commission, 1998b).

Conversely, the European Commission is also able to approve aid to companies without raising high levels of opposition. An organisation needs to pass five key tests to allow the aid to be paid (Tucker and Riding, 1994). These are:

- the company must be restored to profitability within a 'reasonable' time;
- measures must be taken to offset any adverse effects on competitors;
- the aid must be kept to the strict minimum needed;
- the restructuring plan must be implemented in full;
- there must be detailed reports to monitor progress.

One of the main roles that a government has to play is through public spending on infrastructure, such as roads, railways and hospitals. Public expenditure supports a significant amount of economic activity. The European Union is seeking to secure equality of treatment and opportunity for organisations bidding for public works contracts. European Commission public works directives require that all public contracts of more than 200 000 ecus should be advertised in the Official Journal of the European Communities. The Commission is eager to ensure that companies from all member states have the same prospect of winning a contract as those from the home country. However, the vast majority of public procurement in the European Union is awarded to companies from the home country.

Cuts in government expenditure are likely to have a significant adverse impact on businesses that supply those sectors. Increased private sector investment in projects may partially offset the loss of public works. More recently, projects in the UK such as the Birmingham northern relief road and the new Severn road bridge have been financed by the private sector.

Not all companies have to be limited by national boundaries and, therefore, by individual government decisions. When one government makes a decision to cut expenditure it is important for companies to look elsewhere for business. Key projects such as the construction of the new airport in Hong Kong or infrastructure building in Europe provide opportunities for companies from many countries to

bid for business and gain valuable contracts. The international nature of the market has never been more evident, and nor has the need for effective monitoring of the wider environment.

SUPPORT FOR INDUSTRY AND THE REGIONS

Regional policy

One way in which government can support industry is through selective regional policy. Governments in many countries have intervened to correct regional imbalances and unemployment differentials by taking work to the workers, and have, as a direct result, gained electoral support.

The UK experience

Traditionally, industry support is made available through a number of diverse schemes. Gradually this support is being made available on a much more selective basis. Aid is now apportioned on more of a 'need' basis, rather than automatically as it tended to be in the past. The free-market enterprise culture fostered by successive administrations in the UK since 1979 has also been applied to regional aid. Furthermore, the thrust of the policy has moved away from manufacturing and towards the service sector.

The regional aid map, effective from August 1993, has a two-tier system of assisted areas in addition to Northern Ireland (see Figure 7.2):

- development areas;
- intermediate areas; and
- Northern Ireland.

Areas are defined as being in need of aid if economic conditions, particularly employment, are below a notional national average. The 1993 configuration saw a shift of aid away from the north in favour of the south of Britain. This was in response to the substantially higher levels of unemployment suffered by southern areas in the recession of the early 1990s. The two main types of grant available are Regional Selective Assistance and Regional Enterprise Grants.

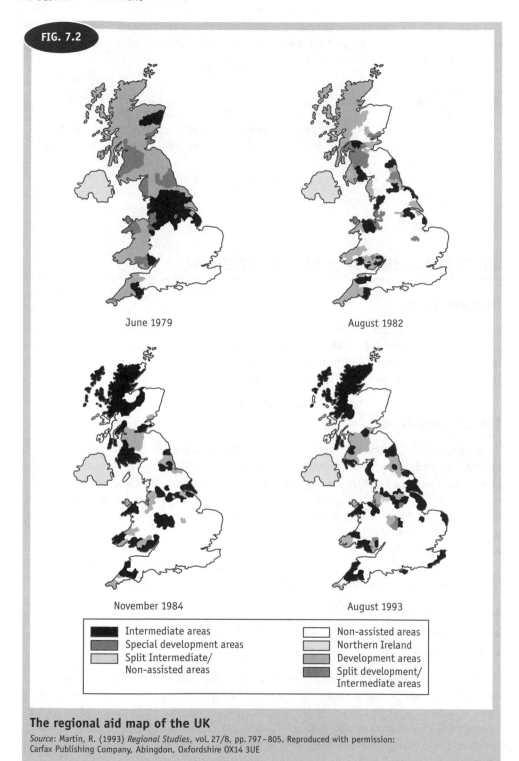

FIG. 7.2

June 1979

August 1982

November 1984

August 1993

■ Intermediate areas	□ Non-assisted areas
■ Special development areas	▨ Northern Ireland
▨ Split Intermediate/ Non-assisted areas	▨ Development areas
	▨ Split development/ Intermediate areas

The regional aid map of the UK

Source: Martin, R. (1993) *Regional Studies*, vol. 27/8, pp. 797–805. Reproduced with permission: Carfax Publishing Company, Abingdon, Oxfordshire OX14 3UE

Regional Selective Assistance (RSA), the main form of aid, is also discretionary and available to any organisation in an assisted area. It is granted to secure employment and increase regional competitiveness and prosperity, particularly in areas of deprivation (DTI, 1998a). Grants of up to 15 per cent of eligible project costs are made in order for a company to carry out an investment project. The grant awarded depends on the area, the needs of the project, the number of jobs safeguarded or created, and the impact on the local economy (DTI, 1998b). In the future RSA will focus support on high-quality, knowledge-based projects which provide skilled jobs (DTI, 1998c). From June to September 1998, 291 RSA offers, valued at over £44 million, were made.

Regional Enterprise Grants are discretionary and available, particularly, to help small and medium-sized enterprises (SMEs) in the start-up phase and to facilitate their growth. Two types of assistance are available under this scheme: regional investment grants and regional innovation grants.

While it is possible to outline some of the current systems and programmes it must be recognised that government intervention is ongoing and it is beyond the scope of the book to look in detail at all that is available to business. Two key developments that are important to organisations are reviewed below. It is clear that the impact of the European Union on this policy is of growing importance. New EU regional aid guidelines were adopted by the UK government in December 1997, and these will guide policy for the foreseeable future (see below).

Business Link

Business Link was launched in 1993. There are now 89 Business Link partnerships with about 240 outlets helping businesses, especially SMEs, to compete by providing a 'one-stop shop' offering a range of business support opportunities, services and information from personal and specialist business advisors, including guidance on

- developing business ideas;
- selling and marketing;
- developing people;
- doing business abroad;
- quality;
- new ideas and innovation;
- IT and computers;
- money and financial management;
- legislation and regulation;
- business start-up.

Business Links are run by private-sector-led partnerships of Training and Enterprise Councils (TECs), Chambers of Commerce, Enterprise Agencies, Local

Authorities and government. Further information on each of these bodies can be accessed at www.open.gov.uk/ or directly by their own web pages.

Regional Development Agencies

The government signalled further developments when it published a consultation paper in January 1998 proposing the establishment of Regional Development Agencies whose primary task is to drive forward a new co-ordinated regional policy and produce an economic strategy for a region through

- fostering economic development and regeneration;
- promoting business efficiency, investment and competitiveness;
- encouraging links between business and higher and further education;
- enhancing the development and application of skills;
- helping to maintain and safeguard employment;
- contributing to the achievement of sustainable development.

The White Paper published in December 1998, *Our Competitive Future: Building the Knowledge Driven Economy*, supports the provision of extra funds for RDAs to address regional competitiveness. The rationale for this latest development is 'strong regions, strong Britain'. The proposal assigns a role to all the agencies mentioned above and calls for closer collaboration with the European Union (see below). The framework is outlined in Figure 7.3.

The evolution of voluntary Regional Chambers may even be a stepping stone to push forward the government's devolution agenda and lead to directly elected Regional Assemblies.

The European dimension

Over the last ten years the European Union has become a key source of funding for regional regeneration. There is a growing desire in the European Union to develop an integrated regional policy, largely through the Committee of the Regions, to overcome disparities between the rich and poor regions of the European Union. An integrated policy is more important now because of the restructuring effects accompanying SEM and EMU. The TEU 1992 sets out its goal:

> *To promote its overall harmonious development, the Community shall develop and pursue its action leading to the strengthening of its economic and social cohesion. In particular the Community shall aim at reducing disparities between the various regions and backwardness of the least favoured regions, including rural areas*
>
> *(Council of Ministers, 1992)*

Structural funds have helped to underpin regional development strategies. There are at present four separate funds.

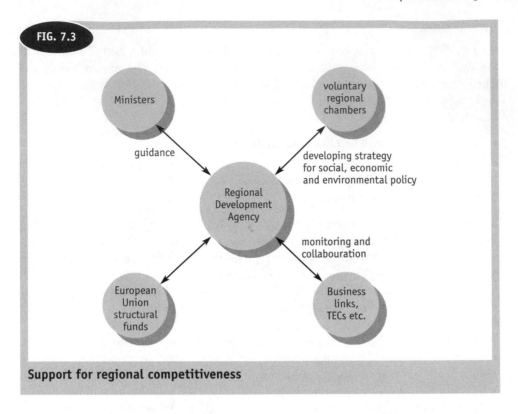

FIG. 7.3

Support for regional competitiveness

1. The European Social Fund (ESF) is targeted at training and reducing labour market discrimination, specifically;
    *   developing active labour market policies to combat unemployment,
    *   promoting social inclusion and equal opportunities for all in accessing the labour market,
    *   developing educational and training systems as part of a life-long learning policy,
    *   improving systems to promote a skilled, trained and adaptable workforce, and
    *   improving the participation of women in the labour market.

2. The European Regional Development Fund (ERDF) contributes to the financing of actions that will promote economic and social cohesion by correcting regional imbalances and participating in the development and conversion of regions.

3. The European Agricultural Guidance and Guarantee Fund (EAGGF) provides investment for farming and for stimulating the non-farm sector of the rural economy.

4. Financial Instrument for Fisheries Guidance (FIFG) covers the whole of the fisheries sector and is used for many activities in the sector.

Agenda 2000

In July 1997 the European Commission published Agenda 2000, a blueprint for the future proposals and budgeting implications for the expansion of the European Union, the reform of the Common Agricultural Policy and a review of regional policy. A new system will be in place from 1 January 2000. The review of regional policy aims

- to reduce the overall level of aid to industry;
- to reduce the proportion of the European Union's population covered by regional aid from 51 per cent to between 40 per cent and 35 per cent (it is currently 34 per cent in the UK).

The reform of the structural funds post-2000 aims at simplifying the number of Objectives, from seven to three, and Community Initiatives. The European Commission has made its proposals for new regulations which the European Parliament is considering and which the Council of Ministers is due to adopt early in 1999. Areas eligible for assistance have been established under a set of three objectives. These 'objective regions' represent an adjustment of the European Union map of regional aid. The criteria proposed will exclude many UK areas of need.

In broad terms Objective 1 covers assistance to the most disadvantaged areas. The new Objective 2 provides support for development in areas experiencing decline and structural change and comprises four strands – industrial, rural, urban and fishing. No more than 18 per cent of the EU population will be covered between 2000 and 2006. The new Objective 3 will cover activities funded under the old Objectives 3 and 4.

Around 70 per cent of structural funds will be allocated to Objective 1 regions; the dominant share will go to Italy, Spain, Greece and Portugal. In the UK, only Northern Ireland, Merseyside and the Highlands and Islands of Scotland come under the Objective 1 banner. However, a number of regions are classified as Objective 2 and, overall, the UK will be the fifth-largest recipient of funds in the European Union. Table 7.3 shows the priority objectives of the structural funds.

Further Community initiatives have been designed to support specific projects and industries. Information on current initiatives is available on www.open.gov.uk/ or www.Europa.Eu.Int.

Aid, as we have seen, is available to business on a discretionary basis, from both national and European sources. The availability of aid could be a decisive factor in a business organisation's location or expansion decisions. It is clearly a big incentive to an organisation if it is to receive substantial funds to facilitate a project.

Lobbying

The gradual transfer of regulatory functions from national to European Union institutions and the establishment of the single market have all contributed to the Europeanisation of business politics (Coen, 1997). In response to the power

TABLE 7.3 Assistance available and funds responsible

Priority objectives	Funds available
Objective 1: directed at regions lagging behind with a GDP per head of 75 per cent of the EU average based on the three most recent years	ERDF, ESF, EAGGF, FIFG
Objective 2: availability of aid relies heavily on unemployment measured over three years	ERDF, ESF, EAGGF, FIFG
Objective 3: will support the adaptation and modernisation of policies and systems relating to education, training and employment, outside Objective 1 and 2	ESF

Source: adapted from European Union Committee of the Regions UK delegation members' briefing pack on Structural Funds Working, published by the Local Government International Bureau, 1998

wielded by government at the European level, organisations have had to develop ways of influencing the decision-making process. One way that they achieve this is through lobbying. Successful lobbying means establishing an organisational capability to co-ordinate potential alliances and to develop and reinforce political channels (Coen, 1997). The principal aim of lobbying is to influence the European Commission, which openly encourages lobbying. As the European Parliament becomes more directly involved in the legislative process, it is likely that it too will become a target for the lobby groups. Not only do organisations and groups try to manoeuvre their interests to the top of the agenda and keep their own members informed, they also provide valuable information to the Commission.

The SEA 1987 has led to the introduction of over 3000 public and economic lobbies. The business lobby can be divided into five main groups (Coen, 1997):

1. individual companies – through the SEA 1987 over 200 businesses have been allowed to form direct links for lobbying;
2. industry forums, which pursue collective interests, e.g. the Maritime forum and the IT and Telecommunication superhighway groups;
3. high politics forums, which bring together leading European industrialists to formulate European policy e.g. the Bangemann group formulated the European telecommunications policy agenda (Martin Bangemann is the Commissioner with responsibility for industrial affairs, information and telecommunication technologies);
4. European federations, which represent the federations' position to the Commission, e.g. chemical, pharmaceutical and oil industries;
5. professional lobbyists, hired by organisations to provide a complementary service to the organisation.

Policy-making, therefore, relies on a huge network of contacts and upon the effectiveness of each lobby group in getting its case heard. It is still the case that national interests are promoted through these groups.

It is not only at the European level that lobbying has a role to play. Recently, professional lobbyists, who act on behalf of sectional interests, have been given a higher profile in the UK because of their ties with MPs. Exhibit 7.8 illustrates the effect that lobbying may have on government decisions.

Lobbying by business is a widespread activity. Much of the activity in Europe has its roots in system of lobbying that has grown up in the United States, where lobbying at both state and federal level is highly developed.

EXHIBIT 7.8

The grey car market

Cars can be bought in many parts of the world more cheaply than they can be in the United Kingdom. Dealers travel overseas, buy vehicles and import them into the United Kingdom. In some cases cars that are manufactured in the UK are re-imported into the country. This is the grey market. For example in 1998 an MGF sports car can be purchased in Japan for £6500 less than its UK selling price. The Toyota Starlet is available at 87 per cent cheaper and the UK manufactured Ford Mondeo at a 58 per cent discount. The major problem for the grey importers is the restriction on importing only 50 cars of each model.

However, the government were committed to opening up the car market (see Exhibit 2.6) and reducing barriers to competition. The government had planned to remove the limit and allow more freedom for the grey importers. In a written answer to Parliament, Gavin Strang, the Transport Minister, announced a 'U-turn', stating that the limit would remain so that safety and environmental standards could be maintained. Why the change in policy? Government inspectors had already announced that they were happy with the standard of the grey imports and were ready to accept more. Manufacturers such as Toyota had lobbied heavily to encourage the turnaround. In a letter, Toyota described the U-turn as a very positive step. It looks as though the government has been strongly influenced by the powerful sectional interests.

Source: adapted from *The Car Cartel Panorama*, BBC1, 6 June 1998

QUESTIONS

1. Present a report outlining the aid which may be available to a company which is thinking of locating to your area (or a specified area). Use a variety of sources.

2. Businesses can influence the decision-making process by lobbying. Choose a particular issue and analyse how lobbyists have influenced the outcome.

DEMOCRATIC SYSTEMS OF GOVERNMENT

Constitutions and the role of the legislative, judicial and administrative functions of government

This section considers the formal basis of democratic systems of government and looks at the legislative (law-making), judicial (law-applying) and executive or administrative functions which play crucial complementary roles within such systems of government.

British parliamentary democracy has been influential as a model of democratic government in, for example, Germany and Malaysia. However, it is ironic that until the passing of the Human Rights Act 1998 the UK was the only Western European country without either a bill of rights or domestic legislation which gives its citizens the ability to seek redress, in its own courts, for breaches of the European Convention on Human Rights. The Act passed into law in late 1998 and comes into force in 1999/2000. It will finally incorporate the European Convention into UK law (the full text of the Act can be found at http://www.hmso.gov.uk/acts1998/19980042.htm). The Convention includes such human rights as the right to life, freedom from torture and slavery, and freedoms of thought and expression.

The United States of America has a written constitution and a clear 'separation of powers' in that the legislative, judicial and administrative functions are kept distinct. It is often thought that such checks and balances are important for the effective operation of a democracy. One of the hallmarks of a totalitarian regime (an example being Nigeria) is thought to be the lack of a clear separation of the judicial function from the legislative and executive functions.

The UK, however, is not completely fussy in ensuring that there is a rigid separation of powers. The Lord Chancellor, for example, is a member of all three of the aforementioned groupings: being a member of the Cabinet (the executive), sitting in the House of Lords (the legislature) and being in charge of all the judges (the judiciary). In the UK, the province of each of the three groups is ever-changing. The role of the judiciary, for example, within the constitution has increasingly come to the fore in recent years. The number of cases of 'judicial review' of administrative actions increased to 3604 in 1995. Judicial review is the mechanism by which Ministers, government departments, local authorities or public bodies exercise discretion or carry out their duties. Nearly half of the cases involve decisions about homelessness taken by local authorities and immigration decisions by the Home Office. Authorities may be challenged for three broad reasons:

- for illegality in carrying out particular statutory and common law powers and duties;
- for unreasonableness in the reasoning on which decisions were made;
- for not following common law principles of fairness in the way a claim was dealt with.

A recent case decided that the government had unlawfully misused £234 million of foreign aid under the Overseas Development and Co-operation Act 1980 by tying it to a construction contract for the Pergau Dam in Malaysia in 1993. The pressure group, the World Development Movement, successfully challenged the then Home Secretary, Douglas Hurd, in the Pergau Dam case (see *R v Secretary of State for Foreign and Commonwealth Affairs, ex parte* World Development Movement [1995] 1 WCR 386). This case gives an indication of the increasing number of pressure groups who might be able to establish an interest in a government executive decision. It is evident that this kind of intervention may have a wide impact on specific organisations and business in general. Following the Pergau Dam affair the Malaysian Prime Minister, Dr Mahathir Mohammed, banned UK companies from bidding for work with the Malaysian Government, because of accusations, mainly in the UK press, of bribery of Malaysian officials by UK government and business. This was at a time of enormous spending on infrastructure projects, such as the new international airport outside Kuala Lumpur.

The increased willingness on the part of the judiciary to review administrative decisions, particularly those made by ministers, indicates that the interrelationships between the legislative, judicial and administrative functions in the UK is in a state of flux. Many would argue that the willingness of judges to develop the law of judicial review compensates for the lack of a written constitution in the UK. It has also been suggested that judges would not have shown such willingness to extend the boundaries of judicial review if Parliament had proved to be a more effective vehicle for keeping the activities of the administrative branch of government in check.

Judges are also seen to be suitable persons to conduct independent reviews such as those relating to standards in public life (the Nolan Committee) and the Dearing inquiry on student and university finance. By the end of 1998 the Labour government had established over a hundred inquiries, reviews and task forces. The role of judges in the UK will be much enhanced when the aforementioned Human Rights Act comes into effect. Indeed judges have already commenced training for this momentous change.

The increased centralisation of government in the UK, implied above, has made Parliament somewhat vulnerable to lobbying activity by individual pressure groups (discussed earlier). Such was the level of concern in 1994 that the Prime Minister set up a Commission chaired by Lord Nolan which reported on the activities of MPs in July 1995 (see Exhibit 7.9). The UK is not the only country where politicians have been brought into disrepute; the situation is not unknown in Europe. In Italy, for example, many politicians, including two former prime ministers, have come under scrutiny because of their close links with business and the Mafia. This type of relationship between politicians and businesspeople has been the subject of debate in many countries, not least in Japan, which has seen the resignation of a prime minister because of bribery allegations.

In summary, one of the key features of a democratic system of government is the ability of the judicial, legislative and administrative functions to operate in a

EXHIBIT 7.9

Standards in public life

The Nolan inquiry into standards in public life was set up in October 1994 following a wave of allegations about the behaviour of Members of Parliament. The inquiry comprised a permanent standing committee. In respect of the conduct of MPs the inquiry took evidence from a range of groups including ministers, public servants, experts, academics and pressure groups. The committee recommended that

- a Parliamentary Commissioner for Standards should be appointed to investigate complaints, complemented by a disciplinary panel of MPs whose hearings would be in public;
- MPs should not work for lobbying firms and must disclose details of any other parliamentary services performed;
- the long-established Register of Members' Interests should be made clearer and updated electronically;
- both MPs and Ministers should be given new Codes of Conduct. Ex-ministers should wait three months before taking a job outside Parliament and all appointments should be vetted by the committee which currently deals with such matters for civil servants. Where there appeared to be a conflict of interest a delay of up to two years could be advised;
- a new Public Appointments Commissioner should be appointed to oversee the fairness of appointments to quangos.

In November 1995 MPs voted to

- appoint a Parliamentary Commissioner for Standards;
- ban paid advocacy by all MPs, including the tabling of questions, motions and amendments to legislation, and restrict the right of MPs to speak in debates on behalf of outside paid interests;
- require MPs to disclose their earnings from consultancy work arising from their parliamentary role and to register details of all contracts with the parliamentary commissioner from March 1996;
- approve a code of conduct.

Other important topics that the committee reported on include public appointments, business jobs for ex-ministers, national and local quangos and local government.

In November 1997 Lord Nolan was replaced by Sir Patrick Neill. The Committee's report was published in October 1998 and featured 100 recommendations, including those on

- the disclosure of large political donations;
- the amounts which should be spent at elections;
- strict rules requiring government neutrality in referendum campaigns.

> **Exhibit 7.9 continued**
>
> An Election Commission would ensure that rules on the banning of foreign donations were not eroded and a committee of Privy Counsellors would ensure that there was no linkage between political contributions and the award of life peerages. These proposals were felt to be necessary to build public confidence in the system and reduce the feeling that political influence could be bought. The government expressed its intention to legislate in line with the broad thrust of the proposals – but it is unlikely that these proposals can be put into statute until 2000.

reasonably autonomous way so as to be able to provide a system of 'checks and balances'. In the UK we have noted the willingness of judges to develop the concept of judicial review, perhaps to compensate for the lack of a written constitution.

QUESTIONS

1. What do you understand by the doctrine of the 'separation of powers'? Discuss the doctrine in the context of a range of countries with which you are familiar.
2. What do you think will be the consequences of the enacting of the Human Rights Act in the UK?

CLASSIFYING LAWS

As we noted in the introduction to this chapter, the main purpose of this section is to develop a basic vocabulary which is necessary to understand the range of types of law. Laws may be classified in a large number of ways. Each main classification used below has a number of sub-classifications.

We start by examining international law. This can be subdivided into two sub-classifications: public and private international law. Public international law is the law regulating the relationships between nation states. It is also concerned with international bodies like the United Nations. The Rio Convention in 1992, discussed in Chapter 6, is an example of this type of international law.

Private international law, sometimes known as the 'conflict of laws', involves decisions about which courts have jurisdiction and which laws are applicable in cases where disputes arise between individuals or organisations based in different nation states. Clearly, the growth of multinational and transnational corporations and the increasingly global nature of economic activity mean that such questions may arise more frequently than in the past. However, such issues are normally resolved by the contracting parties, in advance of any dispute, via a standard contractual term.

All nation states will then have some public laws and some private laws. Public law is made up of a number of branches, and includes constitutional laws concerning the relationships of the different organs of government, criminal law setting out offences against the state, administrative laws which concern administrative actions taken by ministers and officials, EU law and laws involving the state itself, such as those on citizenship and immigration. There is then a huge range of private laws which are designed to regulate the behaviour of individuals and groups in areas which are not criminal. Private law offers ways of obtaining redress for individuals or organisations with grievances in areas such as the law of property, contract and consumer law, company and partnership law, the law of torts (for example, civil wrongs like negligence) and the laws of succession and trusts.

In October 1998 Sam Mansell, a boy of 11, was awarded £3.28 million in the largest medical negligence settlement in a British court. Sam has athetoid cerebral palsy as a result of oxygen starvation when he was being delivered by Caesarian section in a Haverfordwest hospital. The basis of the liability of the Dyfed Powys Health Authority is, as in all negligence cases, that it had broken the duty of care which it owed to the defendant. The settlement was approved by the High Court in Manchester.

For consumers who suffer product-related injuries a key question will be whether or not a contractual relationship exists. Contractual liability on retailers, for example, will often be 'strict', which means that the consumer does not need to prove fault on the part of the retailer. This situation is discussed in more detail below. However, if there is no such relationship then there may be a need to prove negligence (a very costly and time-consuming procedure) except in cases where a claim can be made under the Consumer Protection Act 1987. To succeed under this Act the injured party must be able to show that the injury (or property damage) was caused by a defective product and, on this basis, they may be able, subject to certain conditions, to obtain damages from the producer of the product.

It is important to understand that the different classifications of law, particularly the distinction between criminal and civil law, involve distinct sets of terminology and are largely dealt with in different courts. It is also important to note that words like 'prosecute' and 'guilt' are used only in respect of the criminal law and that the civil law equivalent terms are to 'sue' and to be found 'liable'. Since many business transactions involve the provision of goods or services in exchange for money then the notion of a contract underpins a lot of commercial activity. Increasing trends towards privatisation and the outsourcing of certain services mean that it is important for managers to have a grasp of basic contract law. One of the key questions relates to the point in time at which a contract comes into existence. This is a crucial matter since it is at this point that one party's failure to comply with its part of the bargain can result in the other party being able to sue for a remedy: either rescission of the contract, that is treating the contract as over, *and damages* for breaches of contractual 'conditions', or for *damages only* in cases of breaches of 'warranties' (less serious contractual terms).

If an organisation is involved in providing products or services to other organisations or to individuals it is important that the implications of a wide range of Acts of Parliament are understood. Relevant Acts in this context are:

- the Consumer Credit Act 1974;
- the Unfair Terms Contract Act 1977;
- the Sale of Goods Act 1979;
- the Supply of Goods and Services Act 1982;
- the Sale and Supply of Goods Act 1994.

Detailed consideration of this legislation is beyond the scope of this book. However, it is important to understand that such Acts include many instances where Parliament has deemed it necessary to intervene in freely negotiated contractual relationships between individual consumers and businesses by giving the former some 'extra' rights. The method of intervention most often used in the United Kingdom is the use of an 'implied term' such as the implied condition of 'satisfactory quality' in respect of goods sold 'in the course of a business', as implied by section 14 (2) of the Sale of Goods Act 1979 (as amended by the Sale and Supply of Goods Act 1994). Supermarkets, for example, must offer a consumer who has bought goods which are not of 'satisfactory quality' a remedy under section 14 of the Act. Such implied terms operate irrespective of what was agreed between the parties themselves at the time the contract was made. The economic rationale for such interventions is to redress particularly glaring inequalities of bargaining power.

As can be seen from the dates of the above-mentioned Acts, the high point of this legislative intervention in the UK was in the 1970s. The torch of consumer protection now seems to have passed to the European Union, as instanced by the directive on Unfair Terms in Consumer Contracts (93/13 EEC OJ 95, 21 April 1993). The directive was put into effect in the UK via the Unfair Terms in Consumer Contracts Regulations 1994. These regulations, which came into effect on 1 July 1995, apply a general concept of 'fairness' to terms in contracts for the supply of goods and services, excluding certain contracts such as contracts of employment, which have 'not been individually negotiated' (regulation 3(1)). The Regulations are, therefore, targeted at standard-form contracts where the consumer has had no opportunity to influence the terms of the contract. Regulation 4(1) states that an unfair term is one which,

contrary to the requirement of good faith causes a significant imbalance in the parties' rights and obligations arising under the contract, to the detriment of the consumer.

Here, again, we can note that inequality of bargaining power is the basis for intervention.

As far as organisations are concerned, the areas of relevant criminal law are areas of serious wrongdoing such as theft or fraud, and more minor breaches of 'regulatory' criminal offences, such as false descriptions or misleading prices in respect of goods or services. Although breaches of some criminal offences may be minor in terms of legal scale, organisations need to be aware that the publicity resulting from breaches of the criminal law tends to be rather wider than that arising from civil law liability.

To summarise, we have noted that it is important to understand how laws may be classified, in order that appropriate vocabulary may be used to frame any discussion of the impact of particular laws – for example civil or criminal – upon organisations. As noted in the introduction to this chapter, the aim is not to provide a comprehensive discussion of all the areas of law likely to affect organisations. Students requiring detailed coverage of particular areas of law are referred to the sources listed in the chapter introduction.

QUESTION

Identify, using newspapers and other sources, a number of legal cases which have a significant impact on business organisations. Identify and classify the particular laws referred to in the reports.

SOURCES OF LAW AND THE COURT SYSTEM IN ENGLAND AND WALES

The expression 'sources of law' is usually taken to mean the different sorts of law used to solve a legal problem. There are two principal sources of present-day law: statutes, and decisions taken by judges (case law).

Statutes

Statutes, or Acts of Parliament, are, constitutionally speaking, the supreme source of law in England and Wales. Thus, Parliament can, by an Act, make any law it sees fit without any legal limitation. Under the previously mentioned doctrine of separation of powers, judges cannot question the legality of any statute and their only latitude in interpreting an Act exists where there is ambiguity.

Parliament is supreme, but it can authorise others to pass 'delegated legislation', for example local authority by-laws. European law is logically an extension of this idea of delegated legislation as it is under the European Communities Act (ECA) 1972 that the English courts will take note of European law and, where a conflict exists, will enforce it in preference to any other. Thus, in theory, Parliament remains supreme because the ECA *could* be repealed. In practice, however, a considerable amount of legal sovereignty has been surrendered to the European Union.

Decisions taken by judges

Judicial decisions form case law. Nowadays, much case law involves interpretation of statutes passed by Parliament. However, many are based upon long-established 'common law' principles. It is often difficult to be clear about the law in a range of areas, particularly where competing rights are being asserted. A court decision represents a definitive judgment on the law as it applies to a given situation. By virtue of the doctrine of 'judicial precedent' judges are bound to follow rules of law established in previous court decisions. Detailed rules exist to establish under what circumstances a judge will be bound; they are too specialised for consideration in the present text.

The court system

The English court system strongly reflects the distinction between civil and criminal law (discussed above). Normally, small civil law claims are brought in the County Court; larger civil claims, like that involving Dyfed Powys Health Authority (see above), are processed in the High Court. The vast majority of criminal cases in the UK are dealt with by the magistrates' courts. Magistrates are only paid expenses, are not legally qualified people and operate, in respect of matters of law, under the guidance of a Clerk who must have considerable legal experience. More serious criminal cases will be heard in the Crown Court, before a judge and jury. There are then two levels of appeal court in the UK: the Court of Appeal and the House of Lords. Beyond this lies the European Court of Justice (discussed earlier in this chapter) for certain types of case.

In summary, we have noted that the two main sources of law are statutes and case law. Government policy is often translated into legislation. This tends to generate further case law in order to obtain definitive applications of complex statutory wording to particular situations. It is beyond the scope of this book to look in detail at case law and statutes. Finally, this section concluded with a very brief summary of the court system in the UK. Here we emphasised two features of the system: its hierarchical nature and the division into civil and criminal courts.

QUESTIONS

1. What have been the implications for the sovereignty of Parliament of the United Kingdom joining the European Community, as it then was, in 1972?

2. What is the relationship between statute law and case law?

CONCLUSION

It is important for managers in organisations to understand the level (global, regional, national or local) at which different political decisions are taken in order that lobbying can be carried out effectively. If an organisation is keen to influence a political decision then it may employ professional lobbyists who understand the detail, for example, of the UK or EU political processes. Many organisations are prepared to pay considerable sums of money to achieve such influence, perhaps in the hope of trying to persuade government, for example, to either relax or tighten the applicable regulatory regime depending upon their assessment of their position in the competitive marketplace. The activities of some UK MPs in this regard was instrumental in introducing a much tighter regulatory regime in respect of their behaviour.

Clearly, most organisations will want to ensure that appropriate staff have a good general idea of the law and of the legal system; it will generally be of considerable benefit to an organisation if its staff understand when their actions might have legal/regulatory implications. Nevertheless, most organisations will retain solicitors and barristers to give them advice on specific legal disputes.

SUMMARY OF MAIN POINTS

This chapter has examined a range of political issues and outlined a number of key areas of legal terminology important to the context of the book as a whole. The main points made are that:

- Political change can occur at all three levels which we have identified: global/ regional, national and local.

- At the global scale there is a huge diversity of interactions which will cascade downwards to the lower geo-political levels and affect the activities of a substantial number of organisations.

- There needs to be awareness by organisations which wish to compete across a range of countries that the interests of those countries may, on occasions, conflict with their own goals. As a result they must be prepared to respond flexibly when local political factors demand.

- Organisations can, and do, take action to influence political decisions at all political levels, for example by lobbying. In this way they can seek to neutralise political threats posed by political change or enhance their business opportunities.

- The roles of key European Union institutions need to be understood in order that organisations can understand the implications of developments at this level.

- The European Union has established a number of mechanisms by which business activity can be monitored and controlled.

- Organisations can obtain considerable benefit from domestic and European regional aid schemes.

- In the UK the relationship between the judicial, legislative and administrative functions is in a state of flux. Here it is important for citizens and organisations to be aware of the possibility of bringing a claim for judicial review of certain administrative decisions.

- It is important to recognise the different classifications of UK law in order that appropriate legal terminology may be used.

- One of the key areas of civil law for organisations is the range of statutes which regulate contractual activity.

- The rationale for legislative intervention in freely negotiated contacts between businesses and consumers is often to attempt to make up for a lack of bargaining power on the part of the consumer.

- In the UK, although Parliament is the supreme law-making body, case law is often required in order that judges can clarify the meaning and application of particular statutes.

- The distinction between the criminal and civil law is critical to understanding the legal system of England and Wales; the distinction is reflected, particularly, in the court structure.

NET SEARCH

http://www.pavilion.co.uk/legal/welcome.htm
The site is maintained by Delia Venables and provides access to many legal resources in the United Kingdom and Ireland, as well as links to other countries. Information is available via general subject areas including employment law, environmental law and business/commercial/financial/corporate resources.

http://libservb.ukc.ac.uk/library/netinfo/intnsubg/lawlinks.htm#spec
The site is maintained by the University of Kent. It is a miscellaneous collection of specialised sites and includes contract, business and finance, civil rights and many more. There is also a link to the Internet law library.

http://www.law.warwick.ac.uk/ncle/html/uk.html
This is law resources UK; the site is maintained by the University of Warwick. The site includes access to Acts of Parliament, journals, law reports. Good links to search engines and subject areas.

http://www.sol.co.uk/j/jmackenzie/scottish.htm
A number of links are gathered together which take you to both primary sources and information about the law of Scotland.

http://curia.eu.int/
For the full text of the judgments of the European Court of Justice and the Court of First Instance. Provides useful press releases and publications.

http://www.open.gov.uk/
This site is provided by the UK Central Computer and Telecommunications Agency (CCTA). It includes a number of useful features including an information locator with an organisational index which provides access to government departments, local authorities and quangos. A functional index with alphabetically arranged access to a range of areas, e.g., Acts of Parliament; link to UK Houses of Parliament www service; the Home Office; DTI; DE&E. There is also a search facility to locate UK national and local government information published on the World Wide Web.

Government – Online provides a useful gateway to some of the technological aspects of the business environment. The UK National Inventory project gives all UK counties and projects being undertaken within that county.

http://europa.eu.Int/
This is the European Union's server. Information on the EU includes

- historical development;
- institutions;
- policies;
- documents;
- political agenda;
- publications;
- news;
- governments on-line – which gives web addresses for member states;
- updates on issues relevant to the EU;
- search engine.

Access to the main UK political parties is available as follows:

Labour Party: **http://www.labour.org.uk**
Conservative Party: **http://www.conservative-party.org.uk/**
Liberal Democratic Party: **http://www.libdems.org.uk/**

REFERENCES

ASA (1998a) http:/www.asa.org.uk.

ASA (1998b) *ASA Monthly Report*, 14 (3), March.

Boshoff, A. (1998) 'Advert complaints show a shocking decline', *Daily Telegraph*, 31 March.

Coen, D. (1997) 'The European business lobby', *Business Strategy Review*, 8 (4), 17–25.

Commission of the European Communities (1993) *Small Business and Competition: A Practical Guide*, 10th edn, Brussels: CEC.

Commission of the European Communities (1994a) *Your Ministers Decide on Europe*, factsheet, London: CEC.

Commission of the European Communities (1994b) *The Institutions of the Community*, Background Report, ISEC/B7/94, London: CEC.

Council of Ministers (1992) *Treaty of European Union*, Brussels: Council of Ministers.

Department of Trade and Industry (1998a) *Review of Assisted Areas Map. A Consultation Paper*, URN98/809, July, DTI.

Department of Trade and Industry (1998b) *Regional Selective Assistance*, http://www.dti. gov.uk/support.rsa.htm.

Department of Trade and Industry (1998c) 'Mandelson announces new approach to industrial policy in the English regions', Press release P/98/1036, DTI, 16 December.

European Commission (1998a) *Bulletin of the European Union*, Office for Official Publications of the European Communities, Luxembourg.

European Commission (1998b) Supplement A: Economic Trends 11 – November 1997, *European Economy*, Office for Official Publications of the European Communities, Luxembourg.

Hadfield, P. and Smith, D. (1998) 'The vanishing yen', *Sunday Times*, 14 June.

Lee, J. (1996) 'Body Shop faces fine over illegal posters', *Marketing*, vol. 6, June.

Le Sueur, A. and Sunkin, M. (1997) *Public Law* (Longman Law Series), London: Addison Wesley Longman.

Ohmae, K. (1995) 'Putting global logic first', *Harvard Business Review*, January–February.

Owens, K. (1997) *Law for Business Studies Students*, London: Cavendish Publishing.

Studemann, F. (1998) 'German joint venture: digital pay TV', *Financial Times*, 17 March.

Thomson, I. (1995) Editorial, *European Information Association*, January, pp. 5–20.

Tucker, E. and Riding, J. (1994) 'Brussels approves £1.33 billion rescue for Bull', *Financial Times*, 13 October.

The Week (1998) 'Is Blair cool on electoral reform?', *The Week*, p. 9.

8

THE PUBLIC SECTOR ENVIRONMENT

Ian Brooks

LEARNING OBJECTIVES

On completion of this chapter you should be able to:

- discuss the rationale for the existence of public sector organisations;
- examine the changing political agendas and objectives which influence public sector activity;
- understand the wider business environmental forces acting upon public sector organisations;
- recognise the scale, scope and implications of privatisation, market testing and competitive tendering within public sector organisations;
- understand the structural and managerial changes that have occurred within the public sector;
- demonstrate an awareness of the unique characteristics of the public sector environment and differentiate these from those of commercial organisations' environment;
- understand the nature of the drivers and resistors of organisational change within the public sector.

KEY CONCEPTS

- public and private sectors
- public goods
- ideology
- privatisation and deregulation
- market testing and competitive tendering

- consumerism
- private/public sector collaboration (PFI)
- structural change and the new public management
- force-field analysis

DYNAMISM IN THE PUBLIC SECTOR

Given the global context in which all organisations now operate it is not surprising that the nature of the public sector and its business environment have fundamentally changed in recent decades. This has created a state of flux where many organisations have changed ownership from public to private sector and others have been so transformed as to be virtually unrecognisable. There is little doubt that the complex array of political, social and economic objectives of governments over the last two decades has created enormous pressures for change within publicly owned organisations, bringing a state of near-permanent tension between different interest groups. So radical are the changes that the term 'new public sector' is in common usage.

Both the scale of the public sector and the rate of change within its environment make it a valuable, but often neglected, field of study. This chapter takes a closer look at the economic, social, competitive, legal and technological forces which influence the public sector, although emphasis is placed on the political arena where most pressure for change originates. Public sector organisations conduct government business, are largely funded from the public purse and are usually accountable to government at some level. As the vast majority of funding and support for most public sector organisations is provided from taxation, it is the duty of government to ensure that proper care is taken when dispensing these resources. Hence, government at local, national and international levels has a pervasive and powerful influence over public sector bodies, particularly in their role as legislators and resource providers. Consequently, we pay particular attention to the role of government within this chapter.

A theme of environmental change or dynamism, together with ever-increasing complexity and uncertainty, prevails. The environmental changes are themselves part of a global transformation in the nature of public sector organisations. The chapter illustrates how the private sector environment is increasingly influencing public sector activity. It also aims to explain why publicly owned organisations exist. Attention will be focused on the political influences on the public sector, first, by analysing the changes that have taken place in political agendas in recent decades, and then by exploring the broader aspects of the public sector business environment, embracing competitive, technological, ecological and social concerns operating on a global scale. We then take a closer look at privatisation and the contracting-out of services. Finally we concentrate upon the structural and managerial changes which have evolved since the early 1980s.

In most countries the public sector is a major employer and service provider. It also accounts for a significant proportion of Gross Domestic Product. In the United Kingdom in 1999 government expenditure was about 41 per cent of GDP and around 5 million people were employed within the public sector, although this figure had fallen from almost 7.5 million in 1979. Nevertheless, the public sector far outweighs any branch of industry in scale and importance. Somewhat flippantly we can illustrate the changes that have occurred in the past two decades within the mixed economy by re-writing a quote from Brown and Jackson (1992) which aimed to demonstrate the importance of the public sector. The original reads:

> *most of us in the United Kingdom were born in public sector hospitals, are tended by public sector doctors, were educated in public sector schools, colleges and universities, play in public sector parks, are protected by the public sector, will end up in a public sector hospital when we are old and will be buried in public sector graveyards.*

This cradle-to-grave philosophy is fast waning, and the above statement could, in the not too distant future, read:

> *most of us in the United Kingdom were born in quasi-independent NHS Trusts where many of our mothers determined the method of delivery, rented a private room and were tended by GP fundholding doctors. We increasingly pay full market rate prescription charges, were educated in private, grant-maintained or locally managed schools and in private or quasi-independent universities as no-grant, fee-paying 'customers'. We play in poorly maintained public parks or lavish privately operated commercial adventure parks, are protected by private security firms and police forces supported by privately run support services, will end up not receiving state pensions, relying instead on private pension schemes, will be nursed in private nursing homes and will be cremated and buried on EU 'Set-Aside' farming land or other privatised graveyards by our dependants.*

The scope and pace of change in the public sector since 1980 has been both dramatic and rapid when compared to virtually any period in the United Kingdom's history.

The market system, public goods and change

It can be argued that the existence of the public sector is due to the failure of the free market system to provide all the services required by the general public and by government. However, both the scope and scale of the public sector in any country is in part the result of prevailing political ideologies, or those that prevailed in the past. A multitude of other factors also influence both the level of government involvement in the economy and the scale of public expenditure. However, there is no indisputable law of economics which argues that the public sector should, for example, operate the full range of services found in most developed countries. Neither is there, at any time, a 'correct' or indisputable level of government expenditure.

There are a certain, strictly limited, number of services which most politicians, academics and the general public agree should be conducted by the government or at least under its tight scrutiny. Relatively uncontroversial examples include the judiciary, the police and the armed services – although, as we will discover, some non-core 'support' roles for these services are subjected to market pressures and private operation. However, there are a large and growing number of activities which are the subject of considerable public debate in many countries regarding the most appropriate form of ownership and operation.

Many politicians and some academics believe that private markets are capable of providing some services that are more usually regarded as 'public goods'. These include health care (supported by private insurance) and education (backed with means-tested student loans and private schools). Others argue that this would lead to a multi-tiered system and a restriction of access to high-quality services for a significant section of the community. They further argue that the indirect benefits of a healthy and well-educated population are shared by all, so that the costs should also be shared. Additionally, objectors to the idea of a market economy argue that the conditions necessary for perfect competition rarely, if ever, exist, while critics suggest that competition in the provision of many public services, such as health care, is morally unacceptable and practically unworkable.

However, there is widespread recognition that in many circumstances the market is a sound and appropriate mechanism for the allocation of scarce resources (refer to arguments in Chapter 2). As such the marketplace, via the price system, allocates goods and services to individuals and organisations. It is increasingly being recognised in many countries since the collapse of Communism in Eastern Europe that the marketplace is the most efficient system of allocation of many, but not all, goods and services. Although the market economy is far from faultless, the alternatives are not necessarily guaranteed to be more efficient or effective in servicing the needs of society or individuals.

The trend towards a mixed economy, where economic activity is shared via both public and private ownership, proceeded apace in the developed industrialised world with the introduction and growth of government services throughout the nineteenth and twentieth centuries. The scope of government activity in most countries grew to include responsibility for education, health, law and order, defence and other services. Additionally, for example in the United Kingdom from 1945 to 1975, many industrial organisations were nationalised, so that they were not owned by private shareholders but by government on behalf of the nation; examples were the steel, gas, railway, electricity and water supply industries. As this chapter will reveal, there has been a major reversal of this trend since the early 1980s in the UK and in the 1990s across most of Europe, with the market economy once again becoming more dominant. Hence many outputs previously classified as 'public goods' are now provided by privately owned profit-making companies.

Political ideology and economic circumstances: the roots of change

It is without doubt the political environment which is of foremost importance to public sector organisations. Although we cannot easily disaggregate each environmental force, this brief section will focus upon the power of political ideology to shape public opinion and public organisations. The changes outlined within this chapter stand as testimony to the powerful influencing role of government. Of course economic, social and technological forces inform and otherwise influence government policy. However, government and political activity 'filter' these forces and impose constraints or afford opportunities on the public services. In short, governments draw up the agenda for change within the public sector.

Although it is often said that the arrival of the Thatcher government in 1979 signalled major political change in the UK, the origins of the transformation that was to occur stem from earlier developments. Following the World War II (1939–45) there existed a broad consensus in British politics which favoured the development of the role of the state in the economy. A mixed economy, with many industries in state control, was considered appropriate. This consensus ensured that annual government expenditure on the NHS, education and the civil service increased steadily, funded by economic growth made possible by full employment. However, the 1970s saw a period of recession, high inflation and increasing unemployment. Many academics and politicians began to realise that the growth of spending on the public sector, which included large publicly owned industries, would have to be reduced. In 1976 the Labour government was forced to seek a sizeable loan from the International Monetary Fund (IMF), a condition of which was to further control public expenditure. Unfortunately for them this coincided with a steady increase in the demand for public services. By the mid 1970s UK government expenditure amounted to about 45 per cent of GDP.

The 1970s also saw an acceleration in the decline of traditional industries, a sharp rise in the price of crude oil, strong overseas competition and the UK's entry into the European Community in 1973. These wider economic and political changes altered the 'ground rules' for the UK and many of its neighbours. No longer was low inflation, steady economic growth and near full employment assured. The economic and social changes in the 1970s coincided with the rise of the 'new Right' and a political ideology which, although not new, became increasingly appealing to middle- and working-class voters. This ideology emphasised individual choice and endeavour and advocated a reduction in the role of government in the economy and in the lives of individuals. Margaret Thatcher was a prime proponent of the new ideal. Although the Heath government of the early 1970s toyed with change and the Callaghan administration which followed started the process under the direction of the International Monetary Fund (IMF), it was the Thatcher government from 1979 that effectively broke the post-war consensus and brought about a fundamental change in the role of the state.

Thatcher exhibited a thinly disguised hostility towards the public sector, with which she associated bureaucracy, waste and inefficiency. She promoted the role of the free market and freedom of choice. No longer were 'lame duck' industries to be saved by government intervention, despite the social consequences which might ensue (even the British Labour government in 1998 ruled out any possibility of intervening to protect jobs in the motor industry; subsidies by the left-wing French government to a number of its companies remain but are being increasingly challenged as anti-competitive). Attention changed from a prime concern for levels of employment to the monetarist agenda and a preoccupation with inflation and control of the money supply. The New Right also pushed for reductions in taxation, especially corporation and income tax, so releasing funds for investment and giving the public greater choice over their spending. The 'enterprise culture' became paramount within the political economy of the 1980s. Growth in the number of small and medium-sized enterprises (SMEs), it was widely believed, would lead to national economic prosperity. Keat and Abercrombie (1991) summarise the prime characteristics of the time:

- continual process of privatisation;
- deregulation of industries;
- structural reorganisation of publicly funded bodies;
- diminution of the culture of dependence, including reduced reliance upon government agencies for support;
- competitive market organisation and commercial modes of operation becoming the dominant role model for all organisations (including those in the public sector).

Clearly, these 'environmental' changes have far-reaching consequences for public sector organisations and this new orientation, embracing market values and objectives, ensured that the public sector became something of a problem for the New Right. The Thatcher government believed that the public sector required both restructuring and cultural change if the ambitious attempt at national turnaround was to be successful. It was assumed that such a radical departure from perceived practice could only come about via government intervention. Major reforms were introduced within public sector organisations. Many of these changes, which aimed to achieve significant productivity gains and 'better value for money', are discussed in this chapter. The term 'value for money', probably more than any, symbolised government intention to reform the public sector. This term is defined as 'the provision of the right goods and services from the right source, of the right quality, at the right time, delivered to the right place and at the right price' (HMSO, 1993).

In broader evolutionary terms academics have argued that the last three decades of the twentieth century have witnessed a fundamental change in the way organisations operate. Since the success of Henry Ford in mass-producing motor vehicles at a fraction of the cost of many of his competitors, manufacturing and many service organisations broadly followed Ford's doctrines. Hence most tasks were tightly prescribed and mechanistic, management control and central-ised planning was crucial and customer choice limited. Post-Fordism (after or following from Henry Ford's mass production culture) has meant that organisa-tions, private and public, have sought new managerial and operational forms including flatter and leaner structures, greater decentralisation, flexibility, team-working and informality (Hoggett, 1987).

However, new pressures on the public purse have ensured that significant reductions in the scale of government spending have not been realised. Figure 8.1 shows recent levels of government expenditure benchmarked against average expenditure in the 1970s and 1980s in the UK. Short-term fluctuations are clearly related to the fortunes of the economy, that is, they are cyclical. In times of relative boom, such as in the mid to late 1980s, expenditure (as a percentage of GDP) declined as a result of reductions in unemployment and other social welfare claims. Additionally, tax revenues rise as the economy booms due to increasing tax receipts. In the longer term, structural cycles occur as a result of, for example, changing demand for old age pensions, child support and education. The UK is certainly not alone in experiencing continued pressure on the public purse as public spending in most OECD countries shows signs of considerable in-built growth. It is proving very difficult to achieve real decreases despite government efforts (see Figure 8.1). It is increasingly becoming apparent that further signific-ant falls in government expenditure (as a proportion of GDP) may not be achieved and a rate of around 40 per cent of GDP may represent an ambitious target.

Table 8.1 indicates the relative stability in government expenditure (as a proportion of total GDP) in the United Kingdom over the last three decades. There is, however, a significant difference in government expenditure between countries in the EU. This reflects both the historical context within each country and the

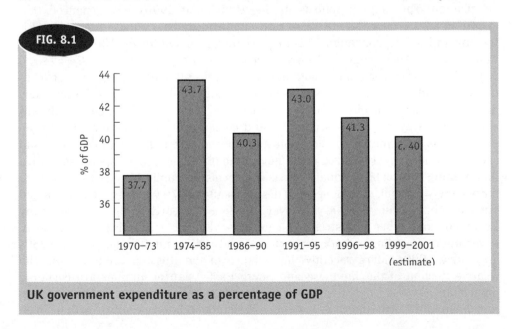

FIG. 8.1

UK government expenditure as a percentage of GDP

TABLE 8.1   General government total expenditure as a percentage of GDP, 1970–99

	1970–73	1974–85	1986–90	1991–95	1996–98	1996	1997	1998*	1999*
Belgium	43.2	56.5	56.8	55.4	53.0	54	53	52	50
Denmark	42.1	53.0	56.8	60.4	58.4	60	58	57	55
Germany	40.1	47.6	46.0	49.2	49.0	50	49	48	47
Spain	23.0	32.6	41.9	47.1	43.8	45	43	43	43
France	38.2	47.2	51.0	53.5	53.8	55	53	53	52
Ireland	35.5	46.7	44.7	39.6	35.3	36	35	34	33
Italy	34.8	43.2	51.4	54.1	51.3	53	51	50	48
Holland	43.4	55.1	57.0	55.0	50.0	51	50	49	48
Finland	31.5	40.5	45.5	59.6	56.8	59	56	55	51
Sweden	44.9	59.4	60.5	68.5	64.3	67	65	61	60
UK	37.7	43.7	40.3	43.0	41.3	42	41	40	40
EU average	36.7[1]	45.4[1]	47.8	50.8	49.5	51	49	48	48
USA	33.6	36.5	38.9	39.2	34.9	35	35	35	35
Japan	21.2	30.7	32.0	33.6	36.8	37	37	37	36

[1] EU without Greece   * estimate

Source: European Economy Supplement A, No. 12, December 1996, p. 21

broad political objectives of each government. Greater economic and political convergence, particularly through European Monetary Union (EMU), may lead to a convergence in levels of government spending between countries. It can be seen that whereas between 1970 and 1986 the UK was more in line with EU norms of government spending, its efforts in the 1980s and 1990s have ensured that spending as a proportion of GDP is now significantly below that of its major EU trading and political partners. This may create a problem for the United Kingdom in its efforts to seek economic 'convergence'.

Changing macroeconomic conditions directly influence successive governments' spending patterns. These economic conditions have become increasingly driven by external or global forces. For example, post-war affluence was threatened in 1973 by the Arab–Israeli war and consequent dramatic increases in oil prices. This contributed to recession and consequent high unemployment and rapid inflation. It also threatened government public sector spending plans. Maintaining a sizeable annual increase in levels of public expenditure became increasingly difficult, and indeed less desirable after 1979 when government acted out the Thatcherite agenda. However, Table 8.1 clearly indicates that many European and other industrialised countries allowed a significant increase in government spending in both proportional and real terms throughout the 1980s and early 1990s. More recently the collapse of the Russian economy and the relative decline of the Japanese and South-East Asian economies are certainly having an adverse impact in terms of economic growth and stability on every European and North American economy. A reduction in economic growth or even recession will lead to an increase in unemployment, lower tax revenues and increases in social payments. This in turn influences government's ability to control public spending and will necessitate either increased government borrowing in order to maintain spending plans or restraint in government spending. For example, as a result of the recessionary period of the early 1990s in the UK, schools, universities and the NHS suffered sometimes stifling budgetary constraint.

Although it is difficult to be specific, many public sector organisations experience a funding climate which is perceived to be related to the popularity of government and its need to court public support. Awarding a popular public service an additional tranche of funding, or denying public sector organisations funds in order to reduce taxation, are tactics often considered by government. This is particularly the case when a general election is approaching. Governments are frequently accused of manipulating public sector organisations in order to achieve party political objectives. Although many such accusations are undoubtedly unfounded, the Conservative government openly discussed in 1995 the need for spending and tax cuts in order to 'win back disenchanted voters', although, to be fair to that government, reductions in taxation were a long-term objective outlined in their manifesto. Nevertheless, such activity did not prevent their very heavy election defeat and the incoming Labour government, with a massive majority in parliament, found it easier to continue public spending constraint in the initial years of holding office.

In conclusion, it is true to say that attempts to reduce the role of government in the economy have led to a relatively small increase, but an increase nonetheless, in the 'incidence' of taxation and levels of public expenditure (in real terms) between 1979 and 1999. However, when compared with many of its EU and OECD neighbours, the UK government has resisted large-scale increases in public expenditure. During the first two years of office the Labour government (1997 to date) has largely maintained the previous government's spending plans, although it intends from 1999 onwards, to increase government expenditure in real terms and, depending on the state of the economy, this may also lead to an increase in government expenditure as a proportion of GDP.

The wider public sector 'business' environment

The political forces outlined above are themselves driven by powerful economic, social and technological changes within the global arena. Wider environmental changes inform political agendas and mould ideologies. However, the mechanism of influence between the wider environment and political activity is two-way, as government decisions profoundly influence those environmental forces. For example, whereas changing social needs create dynamism to which government and public organisations have to respond, those same social changes are, in part, the result of government policy and behaviour. For example, the income level of people in the poorest 10 per cent of UK society actually declined during the 1980s and 1990s. This has resulted from a lack of political will to address the problems faced by this sector of society through more progressive taxation or welfare policies, although the present Labour government have introduced employment and other welfare-related measures to tackle social and employment exclusion. The relative poverty of this group has contributed to many social problems such as urban deprivation, long-term unemployment, crime, drug abuse and social exclusion. As a result government and public sector organisations are faced with a social environment which is, in part, a consequence of their previous activity. Figure 8.2 illustrates some of the environmental influences on government and public sector organisations, together with the two-way nature of some of these relationships.

Prevailing and evolving competitive, economic and social conditions and information technologies are stimulating and facilitating moves towards further decentralisation and competition among current, or previously, publicly owned organisations. Emphasis on efficiency and effectiveness, customer orientation and performance management are partly a result of more fundamental and widespread global change.

Forces within the business environment impinge upon and otherwise influence public sector organisations every bit as much as they do commercial companies. Technological change, for example, is not discriminatory. It does not merely influence private companies. Information systems have transformed the work undertaken by many UK civil service agencies, while societal changes profoundly influence the objectives of public organisations. For example, demographic changes (see Chapter 5) have been a powerful influencing force upon many public sector organisations. The NHS, like health care organisations across Europe, is facing a steady increase in demand for its services due partly to the rapidly ageing nature of Britain's population. Older people tend to require more health care provision than their younger counterparts. This ageing population, combined with high levels of unemployment since the 1970s, have created an ever-increasing

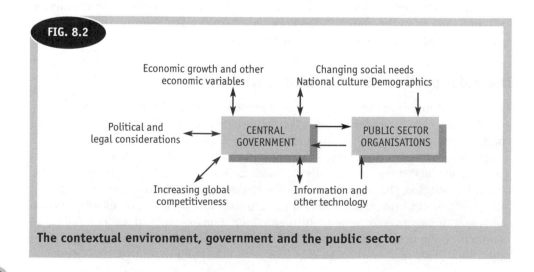

FIG. 8.2

The contextual environment, government and the public sector

burden on the state's social services. National culture is also changing with the development of a more sophisticated, assertive and less subservient population (Isaac-Henry *et al.*, 1993). Consumers today are demanding better quality service (e.g. convenient and responsive services) and proven value for money. These changes create added pressure on all service providers.

Information technology, telecommunications and automation have influenced both private and public organisations significantly in recent decades. The pace of change has become more rapid during the 1990s as information has increasingly become recognised as a vital tool for strategic planning, budgetary control and devolution of authority. For many public organisations the introduction of new technology has been problematic. Lack of expertise, individual resistance to change and poor technology management have often been cited as reasons for the failure or underachievement of information and other technologies in some organisations. Process technology which may enhance or replace traditional manual operations, and may lead to a reduced need for labour, is making inroads in many respects yet progress has been fraught with difficulties.

Many of the environmental forces discussed in previous chapters apply equally to public sector organisations so that there is no reason to repeat information here. However, you are urged to refer to the relevant chapters and sections.

Private and public sector environmental contrasts

There are important 'environmental' conditions within which the public sector operates which, by and large, are alien to the private sector. One important difference is the degree of public accountability government organisations are obliged to assume. Each civil service department, for example, is accountable to a government minister and to the general public who both vote for government and provide funds, via taxation, to run the public services.

The extent and significance of public, political and professional accountability within a typical NHS Trust hospital wields far greater influence over management practice than it does in a similarly sized commercial organisation. Table 8.2 illustrates this by comparing two organisations, one public, the other a private company, in Kettering, a town in Northamptonshire in England.

QUESTIONS

1. What are 'public goods'? Why is there considerable disagreement concerning the correct level of public sector activity in the economy?

2. Undertake research using primary sources, the media and other secondary sources of data into the effects of information technology on specific public sector organisations.

3. Having read Chapter 5 on the social and demographic environment, summarise the potential effects of the UK's changing demographics on the activities of the public sector.

4. Identify the fundamental drivers of public sector change.

TABLE 8.2   A comparison of the public, political and professional accountabilities of a private and a public organisation

External forces	Kettering General Hospital NHS Trust	Weetabix Plc (Burton Latimer, Kettering)
From the general public	• KGH NHS Trust serves the local community, providing accident and emergency and a wide range of services • funded from taxation • activities frequently reported in the local press; keen community interest in its future • employs 2400 people • incineration and disposal of toxic and other wastes • traffic flows in the vicinity of the hospital (now by-passed)	• emissions from the manufacturing plant have been the subject of some concern by local inhabitants • it employs local labour • access to a public footpath which runs through the grounds of the plant was restricted
From government or its agents	• accountable to and influenced by the Ministry of Health • Regional Health Authority • funding bodies (including Fund Holding GPs) • environmental health controls and planning legislation (local government)	• local planning legislation and control, e.g. planning permission for expansion turned down necessitating building in nearby Corby • environmental health controls (local government)
From professional bodies	• influence and control of standards and members' activities from numerous union and professional associations, including the BMA, Royal College of Nursing, and UNISON who aim to direct, monitor and influence practice within the hospital	• some relatively minor union influence. Some employees are members of professional associations

PRIVATISATION AND DEREGULATION

Perhaps the most radical and transparent indication of government intention to 'change the face of the public sector' is privatisation. The global phenomenon of privatisation has involved the transfer of ownership from public to private operation of literally millions of jobs and billions of pounds of assets across the world. The change of ownership has, in many cases, proven to be a major spur to change within the organisations effected. This is in part due to a range of new and evolving environmental opportunities and constraints facing the privatised companies. Many, although by no means all, have faced renewed competitive pressures which were largely alien to the old publicly owned entities. British

Airways now successfully competes on the world stage, while the UK regional water companies enjoy virtual monopolies in their core business.

The management agenda within the privatised companies has been transformed. Parker (1993) argues that privatisation 'implies a rematching of the organisation to its external environment to achieve "strategic fit"'. Under state control industries are protected from many environmental forces, notably competition, with the result that they are slow to change. Privatisation and deregulation often require management to utilise greater innovation and creativity and rely less on bureaucracy and the protection afforded by rules and procedures. Parker (1993) argues that the internal environment of privatised companies needs to change in order to cope with the challenges faced from the dynamic external business environment. These changes are often far-reaching and include:

- re-structuring, often involving 'downsizing' or 'rightsizing' (reducing the numbers employed) and delayering (reducing the number of levels in the organisational structure);
- alteration to human resource management policies and procedures including a reduction in the power and role of trade unions in pay negotiations;
- an emphasis on 'leadership' and extension of management accountability;
- changes in the product/markets and geographical emphasis, including attempts at globalisation;
- a transformation in business objectives.

Although privatisation was not invented in the UK, it was the Conservative governments of the 1980s and 1990s that led the way. This section focuses on the privatisation process in the UK as well as illustrating the unfolding events in the former Czechoslovakia (now the Czech and the Slovak republics). It also briefly reviews regulation and deregulation issues. There are many sound and in-depth analyses of the privatisation process in the UK and elsewhere, should the reader wish to go beyond this brief coverage.

Privatisation: aims, criticisms and the future

Privatisation has stimulated considerable debate concerning the wisdom and success of both the process and its outcome. It is a debate which will continue for many years throughout the world. The initial aims of the privatisation programme in the UK are a matter of some dispute. In broad terms, privatisation was a central policy tool to combat what successive governments through the 1980s and 90s saw as economic failure of state activity. More specifically government aims included a desire to

- reduce the scope and scale of the public sector;
- seek an increase in efficiency by introducing competition;
- reduce public sector financial commitment and associated borrowing requirement;

- provide proceeds from the sale of state-owned organisations to fund tax cuts;
- facilitate a reduction in the power of trade unions and professions;
- widen share ownership;
- encourage enterprise and customer choice, improve quality of provision, and reduce dependence on the state.

Criticism of the privatisation programme has been widespread and often fierce. Nevertheless, no mainstream political party in the UK has plans to re-nationalise large tracts of industry; on the contrary, the current Labour government plans to continue the process of privatisation.

Many of the problems created by privatisation continue to emerge as events unfold and knock-on effects take their toll. For example, the closure of many British coal mines and the subsequent decimation of the coal-mining industry have been linked with the privatisation of the electricity companies. Freed from the obligation to purchase British coal to fire thermal power stations, electricity generators increasingly switched to natural gas and imported coal as alternative raw materials in the 1990s, a trend which the current Labour government has, partially at least, sought to correct since 1997. Another longer-term implication of privatisation has been the political and social storm resulting from the sometimes massive salaries and bonuses many directors and chief executives have awarded themselves. Although not particularly significant in a competitive sense, or when compared to many of the more fundamental criticisms levelled at the process, it has contributed to a change of public opinion away from privatisation in the mid 1990s.

The prime criticisms of the privatisation programme are varied. Many of the previously nationalised corporations were effectively state monopolies. Privatisation of these does not in itself increase competition. Consequently, there are a number of privately owned and operated companies which now enjoy monopolistic market conditions and which are regulated by government or its appointed bodies. The regional water and electricity companies in particular, as well as British Gas and BT to some extent, operate in restricted markets and hence enjoy some of the benefits of restricted competition. The act of privatisation does not guarantee improvements in performance, and not all privatised companies have achieved productivity improvements (Parker and Martin, 1993).

Until the stock market crash in October 1987 the general public developed a distorted view of share ownership, seeing share subscription in the newly privatised companies as resulting in instant gain. For example, those subscribing to British Airways shares when they were first floated enjoyed an instant 36 per cent premium on their investment. This also indicated that government had underpriced many companies upon flotation, so 'selling the country's silver off cheap'. A more accurate estimate of the demand for shares would have led to substantial additional revenues earned by government which might have financed additional services or tax cuts. Again, it was British Airways which best illustrated this point as it was oversubscribed 36 times; BT was oversubscribed nine times and British Gas four times. Similarly the privatisation of Railtrack in 1996 was criticised as a politically inspired attempt to woo voters shortly before a general election and to raise money for government. Share prices in Railtrack rose significantly more rapidly than the Footsie 100 in the two years following privatisation, indicating that it might have been sold too cheap. Criticism was often levelled at governments in the 1980s and early 1990s for using the once-in-a-lifetime revenue from privatisation to fund spending or to reduce taxation rather than to invest in national infrastructure such as the rail and road network or housing stock.

Many privatised companies, such as BT, have shed thousands of employees so contributing to national unemployment and increasing the demands upon the welfare state. Additionally, with the loss of the old nationalised corporations, government is no longer in a position to use such organisations as tools of social, economic and regional policy. Finally, the cost of underwriting the multiple share issues in the 1980s was estimated at £325 million, while the advertising campaign to facilitate the sale of British Gas alone amounted to £21 million. The estimated total cost to date of selling the state-owned enterprises is in excess of £750 million.

Privatisation and other public sector structural changes led to over 750 000 jobs being transferred to private ownership between 1984 and 1999. The scope for further privatisation is now somewhat restricted as the most suitable candidates are already in private hands. Few straightforward businesses remain in the public sector. The Post Office/Royal Mail and the BBC, together with a number of local authority airports, the National Air Traffic Service (NATS) and transport companies could eventually be candidates for privatisation. So embedded now is the belief in privatisation that the Labour government is currently considering plans to partially privatise Royal Mail and National Air Traffic Service. It is hoped that

---

EXHIBIT 8.1

Privatisation in the Czech and Slovak Republics

As in Britain, the origins of privatisation in the Czech and Slovak Republics lie in political realignment following the perceived failure of state industry. But in the independent Czech and Slovak republics the change is of a different scale involving 'turnaround management' across the entire economy. In the mid 1980s around 97 per cent of Czechoslovakia's value added came from the state sector. In 1989, 61 per cent of its exports flowed through COMECON. However, by 1991 COMECON was disbanded and trade with the former communist states had collapsed.

Privatisation is taking place by many routes including:

- return of property to those dispossessed under Communism;
- direct sale through auctions and tenders to domestic citizens;

Exhibit 8.1 continued

- through a voucher scheme under which citizens purchase from the state, at nominal cost, vouchers to buy shares in privatised firms;

- sale to, or joint ventures with, foreign investors – a prominent example being the Volkswagen investment in Skoda.

By the end of 1992 over 31 000 small businesses, mainly shops and workshops, had been sold, largely by auction, under the October 1990 Small Privatisation Act. By mid 1992, 67 per cent of shares in over 1400 state companies had been sold through the voucher method and 171 firms had been completely privatised under the Large Privatisation Act of 1991.

Business has been privatised with the minimum of reconstruction. The speed of the desired privatisation, driven by the political need to dismantle state control quickly following the fall of the Communist government, has ruled out the low-risk strategies adopted in the UK. Consequently, failures amongst privatised businesses have occurred and have removed some of the economic distortions introduced by state planning. For overseas companies investment is high-risk. At the same time the republics need foreign investment, including involvement in joint ventures and strategic partnerships.

The privatisation programme has involved the management of transformational change. There are interest groups from within and outside the businesses which oppose change. The programme also requires management with a knowledge of how to succeed in competitive markets, something often lacking amongst incumbent administrators working according to central plans. Too many Czech and Slovak companies have suffered from low motivation at work and high absenteeism and have produced low-quality products which have sold in Western markets on price alone. Low prices alongside low productivity have led to inadequate surpluses for reinvestment.

In Romania privatisation has proven altogether more fraught. In 1997 only 825 privatisations were achieved against a target of 1600. The lack of political will and public support are reported to account for this.

Source: Parker, D. (1993)

the eventual sale of 51 per cent of NATS will raise around £250 million for the government.

Sizeable privatisation programmes are well under way in most European countries, although the election of centre or left-wing governments in Germany and France has delayed changes in this regard. In France the scale and scope of this programme is unlikely to match that of the UK in the past decade and a half, although a significant privatisation programme is under way. A global trend, which started before the collapse of Communism in Europe, has freed whole tranches of industry from direct government control. The long-term consequences of this transformation are as yet unknown.

Regulating privatised monopolies

The UK government has maintained some control over the more monopolistic privatised companies which might otherwise abuse their position. This has largely been achieved within a regulatory framework and through the appointment of official watchdog bodies. Table 8.3 lists some of the regulators.

However, the work of regulation is not without its critics. Many investors in the privatised utilities criticise the inconsistencies and uncertainties caused by the current regulatory system, while consumer groups and elements within the Labour and Liberal Democratic parties argue that regulation is not always sufficiently robust, nor conducted in the best interests of the public. It is a debate which is certain to continue as many public utilities are 'natural monopolies' which require some form of regulation or control if the interests of the general public, the nation and the consumer are to be upheld.

Deregulation

Governments through the ages have established a regulatory framework for many industries. Often the result of years of separate and well-meaning pieces of regulation, these frameworks sometimes restrict industries from growing and competing on the world stage. It has been a central tenet of government policy in the UK since 1979 to deregulate many industries to, as they see it, free them from unnecessary and unhelpful constraint. Hand in hand with deregulation, moves to ensure consumer protection, often in the form of new regulation, have taken place.

By way of example, in the 1980s the market for spectacles was largely deregulated. This resulted in greater competition and a reduction in prices to the consumer. It also led to the levying of a charge for eye tests, leading many to forego such 'treatment'. There has been an increase in the numbers diagnosed with eye diseases in the UK during the past decade. Bus services, outside London, have largely been deregulated leading to further competition and the growth of major transport operators. Public transport deregulation has led to the proliferation of bus services on some routes and total absence of regular services on others. As companies are largely responsive to market demand this has led to a reduction in service for those living in rural areas. The financial services industry has benefited from significant deregulation enabling a multitude of organisations to compete in

TABLE 8.3 Privatised companies and their regulators

Privatised company	Official regulator
BT	Office of Telecommunications (OFTEL)
Severn-Trent Water	Office of Water Regulation (OFWAT)
Northern Electric	Office of Electricity Regulation (OFFER)
British Gas	Office of Gas Regulation (OFGAS)

the growing pensions, insurance and other financial services markets. Government has also tightened or further regulated some sectors and industries as circumstances change. This is also true of the financial services industry where spurious new 'products' and means of marketing them have often led to renewed pressure to regulate. In 1999 the United Kingdom government introduced new tax-beneficial savings schemes (ISAs) and attempted to ensure that providers were encouraged to offer lower charges and greater flexibility to customers. Although the vast majority of the organisations which have benefited from deregulation fall within the private sector, their new-found freedoms stem from political and economic influence and the direct hand of government.

However, many politicians and consumers argue that insufficient regulation exists in certain fields (such as financial services and railways). The issue of regulation and deregulation is the subject of considerable political debate (refer to Chapter 7 for further details).

QUESTIONS

1. Conduct research into the privatisation process involving one company in the UK or elsewhere. Summarise the political, social, economic and other arguments given both in favour and against the privatisation. Which do you think are the more persuasive arguments?

2. What do you think are some of the potential long-term issues facing many previously privatised companies? What problems might governments and the general consuming public face following the privatisation of an industry?

3. To what extent do the regulators of privatised industries help compensate for the lack of competitiveness facing those industries? What are some of the inherent complexities facing the role of regulation?

4. Study the quality press and other secondary sources and write a short case study on the privatisation process in one country (e.g. Malaysia, France, Germany, Russia, Poland). Structure the case so that you comment on the scale and scope of privatisation, its pitfalls and problems, the likely benefits and the long-term aims and consequences of the programme. Focus on the 'new' business environment facing privatised companies.

CHANGING THE FACE OF PUBLIC SECTOR ORGANISATIONS

An equally powerful yet less controversial mechanism for changing the delivery of services is taking the place of the privatisation process. The NHS, the education services and large parts of the civil service and local government are being continually subjected to further market or competitive pressures. There have been three broad thrusts in government policy in this regard. First, compulsory competitive tendering and market testing of many local and national government services has taken place. Second, fundamental structural changes have been thrust upon the civil service and the NHS in particular and also the education service. Finally, the Private Finance Initiative (PFI) has sought to encourage collaboration between private and public sectors, particularly in developing new capital projects.

Exposing government services to competitive forces

As the scope for further wholesale privatisation has waned in the UK by the late 1990s, the scale of market testing and competitive tendering has grown to encompass areas hitherto considered 'safe' within both local and national government. At local government level political and media attention has focused upon a number of 'flagship' authorities which had embraced central government objectives with vigour in the 1980s and 1990s. Notable among these have been Wandsworth and Westminster, in London. Both councils reduced council tax to a fraction of that charged in some other London boroughs and claimed that lean and skilful management, including the contracting out of many roles and a reduction in 'non-essential' services, accounted for huge financial savings. Certainly, council taxes in these authorities were much lower in the early 1990s and remain low, yet the case has naturally raised a number of critical issues of relevance to local government across the country, not least accusations of favouritism. For example, the Conservative government in the early 1990s, an active and vociferous supporter of Wandsworth council, were accused of awarding the council sizeable tranches of grant monies and of showing 'favouritism' in other regards. Westminster Council was able to set one of the lowest council tax levels in England in 1994–95 (£245 for Band D properties) which represented a £50 reduction on the previous year. Critics argue that a combination of poor services and central government favouritism made this possible, although the council was at the forefront of extending competitive tendering into hitherto 'sacred' areas such as nursery education. Dame Shirley Porter, the figurehead of this flagship council, was no stranger to financial, political and legal controversy during her eight years as leader. She has faced various accusations including fraud and 'gerrymandering' and recently won an appeal against a successful prosecution.

It is clear that government departments and agencies, as well as local authorities, NHS Trusts and educational services, have been encouraged by their political masters to follow industrial trends and contract out non-core business. In 1985 the Ministry of Agriculture, Fisheries and Food (MAFF) broke new ground by market-testing the fisheries aerial surveillance service. However, compulsory and voluntary competitive tendering, a process where distinct services are identified and tenders or bids sought from service providers who wish to run the service, had been used extensively prior to this date as a mechanism for encouraging both competition and 'privatisation'. Many of the organisations successfully tendering to operate public services have been private profit-making companies. As a result of competitive tendering there has been a vast increase in contracted-out work, that is, services and goods supplied to public 'customers' by private or voluntary organisations. In such cases public authorities such as Northamptonshire County

Council still hold the responsibility, for example, for refuse collection, but their direct employees do not deliver the service (unless representatives of those direct employees were successful in tendering for the service). Contracting-out is very common in certain fields such as refuse collection and disposal, cleaning of local or national government buildings, and the provision of catering facilities for government employees.

Government have argued that market-testing holds many advantages; they believe that

- competition helps ensure value for money;
- a focus on performance outputs will produce clear standards;
- an improved quality of service will result;
- an explicit customer/supplier relationship will be apparent;
- it enables both external and in-house bidders to be more innovative in their field;
- the monitoring of contracts and service-level agreements focuses on outputs, objectives and targets in order to improve efficiency and effectiveness.

Naturally, these claims are the subject of considerable ongoing debate.

At the national level, market-testing and competitive tendering had increasingly broadened in scope throughout the 1990s, with few government departments exempt from their influence. Many 'support' functions which can be differentiated from the core business of a department have been identified for such 'privatisation'. For example, the armed forces' fleet of 95 000 support vehicles is targeted for private operation. A pilot scheme was established in 1995 which aimed to place non-combat Land Rovers, trucks, vans and cars under private management. The vehicles will be owned and maintained within the private sector and leased or rented back to the Ministry of Defence. The 'Competing for Quality' White Paper (HMSO, 1991) emphasised the role of public service managers in buying services on behalf of the citizen as opposed to automatically providing them internally. It aimed to move a minimum of £2300 million, or about 10 per cent of MOD expenditure, into the private sector by the year 2000. Other market-tested MOD services include:

- Royal Navy – operation of the tug and tanker fleet;
- Army – provision of logistics information to the quartermaster;
- RAF – engineering support for the Hawk jet trainers and the operation of training aircraft.

These, and many private business incursions into the civil service, will undoubtedly result in a reduction in staff requirements. Naturally, trade unions and employee associations have grave reservations concerning competitive tendering and market-testing. They fear not only job losses but also a reduction in the quality of services offered. Following proposals in late 1994 to allow private companies to compete with Inland Revenue staff in the collation of potentially sensitive financial information on individuals and companies, concern was expressed about potential lapses in confidentiality. The Inland Revenue Staff Federation fear that such information may be used for other, non-legitimate purposes by a less than scrupulous private operator. Similar concerns have been expressed over the privatisation of a dozen prisons which has taken place since 1995. The BBC is also engaged in the process of market-testing some of its services.

In many cases, however, there has not been a great deal of interest shown by suitable private companies who wish to operate government services. Additionally, the department's own tender is often financially the most attractive, so that the service remains in public hands. For example, catering facilities at Kettering General Hospital NHS Trust are run by the trust's own staff who have successfully bid against private operators. In many cases however, internal bids have been discouraged or even forbidden. Almost three-quarters of the first £1.1 billion of directly contracted-out civil service work was awarded to private sector operators while in-house bids were not allowed. Where in-house bids were acknowledged, over half of the market tests were won by the public servants. Similarly, estimates of the actual financial savings made by contracting out services vary significantly. Some not uncontroversial government data has indicated that the policy is proving to be a growing success in financial terms. The government claimed that a saving of 23 per cent was made on that first £1.1 billion of contracted-out services which involved a reduction of 14 500 civil service jobs with just over 12 000 transferring to the private sector.

EXHIBIT 8.2

Public sector reform in New Zealand

The concept of the 'New Public Management' was warmly embraced by the Labour government in New Zealand (1984–90). They brought in dramatic changes to both the organisation and management of the state sector. The aim was to improve efficiency and accountability. The government has

- commercialised many of the functions performed by public organisations;
- separated commercial and non-commercial operations;
- transferred trading activities to private operation;
- moved away from national pay bargaining to decentralised/enterprise based systems;
- introduced accountability systems for Chief Executives which include fixed-term contracts, performance-related pay and annual performance reviews.

There has been a great deal of contracting-out of public services and the sale of many public assets, although widespread privatisation has not occurred.

Consumerism: charters and league tables

Another mechanism governments have employed to encourage both public accountability and quality improvement is a variety of quality charters, publicly disclosed quality standards and measurements of performance. These charters set service standards which individuals might rightfully expect. They have, by and large, been imposed on public sector organisations. Hence, in the UK, we have the Citizens' Charter, the Patients' Charter, and School and Hospital league tables where individual units are 'benchmarked', enabling comparisons to be made between similar providers on the quality of outputs for example.

The Education Reform Act of 1988 gave parents the right to send their children to the school of their choice. Schools were obliged to provide information, including information on examination performance, to facilitate that choice. It is now possible to obtain a league table of schools within each local authority ranked according to the level of achievement of their pupils in internal and external examinations. What is more, each authority is ranked for its overall performance (see Table 8.4) and results are used to benchmark performance across schools and districts. Including base-line assessment for 4-year-olds, introduced in 1998, data now exists on pupil performance at ages 4, 7, 11, 14, 16 (GCSE) and 18 (GCE A-level/AS-level and GNVQ) in most non-private schools and for all education authorities.

Like so many of the public sector 'reforms' introduced since 1980 charters and league tables have been a source of bitter dispute between organisational managers, trade unions, government and other interest groups. League tables of performance, such as that shown in Table 8.4, invite the public to compare organisations or, in this case, local authorities. Those who have been responsible for the introduction and dissemination of such 'performance' measures argue that they serve to inform the general public, and to improve the quality of services.

TABLE 8.4   Extracts from school league tables by local authority (ranked 1 to 108)

LEA	GCSE A–C (%), 1998	Truancy	Social deprivation
Isles of Scilly	67	1st	1st
Kingston-upon-Thames	59	10th	38th
Sutton	58	3rd	42nd
West Sussex	52	4th	4th
England average	46		
Lambeth	29	100th	107th
Southwark	29	107th	102nd
Tower Hamlets	28	106th	106th
Islington	23	103rd	104th

Sources: Department of Education and Employment; Department of the Environment

Many public sector organisations, such as individual schools, feel that league tables disguise a whole host of relevant and critical information which parents should be aware of when making a decision about choice of school. They also argue that such figures can be thoroughly misleading, especially if taken at face value. For example, let us assume two schools, one located in the Isles of Scilly (refer to Table 8.4) and another in Southwark. School league tables will measure the GCSE and GCE A-level results and the truancy rates of both sets of students and probably indicate that the Scilly Isles school fared best. What the tables do not show is the 'value added' to students by their whole school experience, nor do they measure things such as artistic or creative development or the sporting excellence of students. They do not clearly show how some schools, despite enormous difficulties with social deprivation and related problems, are indeed 'successful', while others located in prosperous, relatively trouble-free areas may indeed be rather complacent and mediocre. In other words, school performance measures have not embraced the 'value added' concept, nor have they sought to benchmark schools operating in similar socio-economic circumstances. Value-added measures were introduced in 1998–99 but remain rather crude, relying at this early stage on various proxies for entry ability such as the proportion of children receiving free meals as a measure of social deprivation. Nevertheless, the relative wealth and sophistication of government data on key stage tests and GCSE and A-level results will now enable schools to benchmark themselves against comparator schools and so enable more accurate evaluation of performance and facilitate improvement.

Criticisms of the Patients' Charter, which sets out standards of care for the NHS and invites patients to insist upon such standards being met, has led to a vast increase in the number of complaints about the quality of service. Additionally, many government-funded organisations, such as NHS Trusts and Training and Enterprise Centres (TECs), have recently been required to seek user/customer feedback on the quality of services offered. For some time most university students have enjoyed the opportunity to express their views on quality standards as part of formal quality assurance procedures. Whereas charters, league tables and customer surveys may introduce a certain amount of competition, provide useful information and indirectly encourage some 'quality' improvement, public organisations often argue that they have insufficient resources to deal with the problems highlighted.

Structural changes in the public sector

The reader would be excused for assuming that there was very little of the public sector remaining after the privatisation and contracting-out processes outlined above. However, public sector expenditure still accounts for over 40 per cent of GDP. The NHS alone employs over a million of the total UK workforce of about 26 million and, as such, is the largest single employer in Europe. Although the public sector has changed it still accounts for a very significant element of Britain's economic activity.

A great number of the changes that have been introduced to the public sector are primarily structural in nature. That is, the organisational structures and reporting relationships have altered significantly. These transformations have, in turn, led to other 'softer' operational changes which have influenced prevailing management style and cultures. We will first focus on these structural changes before looking at management practices.

Structural changes have occurred within the public sector on a grand scale. The civil service, the NHS and the education service have been characterised by a degree of decentralisation. Distinct units within these services, such as a hospital or a school, have been encouraged to 'opt out' or accept further local management responsibility and become semi-autonomous. Some secondary and a few primary schools had taken themselves out of local government control prior to 1997 before the election of a government not sympathetic to 'opting-out', and are funded directly from the Department for Education and Employment (DfEE). They have been given additional budgetary responsibilities and freedoms and required 'to stand on their own feet'. Many have thrived under their newly granted powers released from the constraints and regulations that an additional tier of control may have imposed. However, there have been problems both within some 'opted-out' units and for those that remain as 'managed' units. Similarly the issue of dual or multiple standards has arisen.

Most of the civil service and most of the NHS are now managed within such opted-out units, referred to as 'Agencies' and 'Trusts' respectively. Schools have, by and large, been more reluctant to opt out, preferring instead to work within a local government framework. However, with Local Management of Schools (LMS) and the Education Reform Act of 1988 they have assumed greater responsibility for budgetary and staffing matters than was previously the case.

Public and private sector collaborative partnerships

Considerable political attention has been paid in recent years to the furtherance of private and public sector partnerships. The right wing of the Conservative party had argued for some time that the state ought to have an enabling rather than controlling role. That is, the state should facilitate and co-operate with private organisations in providing public services rather than assuming those services should be offered exclusively within a public framework. This basic ideology has been taken on board by the other major political parties. However, the Conservative governments through the 1980s and 1990s had only limited success in operationalising this belief. More left-wing proponents see such partnerships as an opportunity for local governments to concretise their influential role within the community. The growth and acceptance of such partnerships would begin to recast the prime role of the state as that of an 'enabler' as opposed to a 'provider'. Ironically, it has been a Labour government which appears to have made progress in this regard: the Millennium Dome is a case in point. The Private Finance Initiative (PFI), which was launched by Norman Lamont, then Chancellor of the Exchequer, in 1992 and attracted just £500 million of private money for public projects in the first two years of operation, aims to promote private/public sector partnerships. The relative failure of this initiative is in large measure due to uncertainty about rates of return to investors combined with cumbersome procedures. However, the scope for private/public partnership in both developing and operating 'public' projects suggests that this approach may achieve greater success in the future. A £150 million computer system to store National Insurance records is the first project of its kind to be funded through the 1992 initiative. The significance of the PFI scheme continues to increase and it has become an important feature of the Labour government's public sector capital expenditure plans. It embraces the concept of collaboration, an important theme in current public/private sector activity. The current government is planning to develop PFI-style arrangements allowing the private sector to exploit a variety of government assets including intellectual property. In October 1998 the government announced a further £4.25 billion in 30 new PFI projects. These included £730 million for hospital building, £480 million related to schools and schemes to develop IT case management at the Crown Prosecution Service and digitisation at the British Library. This comes after the announcement of the PFI scheme to build the Channel Tunnel Rail Link announced earlier in 1998.

QUESTIONS

1. What are the objectives of competitive tendering and market-testing for (a) the public sector organisation concerned, and (b) the government of the day? Assemble evidence to debate whether these objectives are being met.

2. What is the purpose of school league tables? Outline some of the key contentious issues concerning their use. How might such league tables improve, or otherwise change, managerial and professional activities within schools?

3. How might some of the structural changes discussed within this chapter influence managerial processes and the quality of services?

4. Utilising library and/or primary sources, explore the future possibilities for private/public sector partnership.

THE CONSEQUENCES OF ENVIRONMENTAL CHANGE: MANAGERIALISM

Private managerial practices and public objectives

During the 1980s and 1990s governments have been concerned to develop within the public sector a 'business-like' approach to management which draws upon private sector practice. Largely spurred on by the efforts of a number of policy advisors such as Griffiths (NHS, 1983) the view prevailed that core managerial roles and skills should be portable between private and public sectors. It became widely acknowledged that the public sector had a great deal to learn from private organisational practice (not, notably, the other way round).

Public sector organisations have imported a succession of management techniques strongly associated with notions of good practice in the private sector. These include devolved budgetary control, Total Quality Management (TQM), Business Process Re-engineering (BPR), target-setting and benchmarking. Many ideas are associated with notable management gurus, best-selling texts and local interpretations of 'the enterprise culture'. In general, attempts at adoption of such initiatives reveal a strong desire among key managers to mimic good practice elsewhere, yet often insufficient consideration is given to the suitability of the model to the specific public sector organisational context.

Many administrators, managers and, notably, 'professionals' within public service have resisted moves in this direction as they view them as inappropriate to their roles. Practices which are suitable for commercial profit-orientated companies are not, they argue, easily transferred to public service, nor is their adoption entirely desirable. The objectives of the public service differ sufficiently from those of private firms, it is argued, to ensure that transferability of styles, skills and practices is often inapplicable.

The public sector has long assumed distinctive goals from those of most private firms, such as the 'pursuit of equity, justice and fairness, accountability and the enhancement of citizenship' (Isaac-Henry et al., 1993). McKevitt and Lawson (1994) have identified both a private and public sector model which is abridged and simplified in Table 8.5.

The distinctive conditions within the public sector, such as the greater role of collective choice, citizenship and issues of need and justice, are not as apparent in the private sector. Fundamental differences exist with regard to the role of the marketplace. Even NHS quasi-markets remain heavily regulated and, far from wanting to stimulate demand, most public organisations are required to ration the service they offer.

Traditionally, public sector employees are seen as motivated by public service ideals and driven by a desire to serve the public and the country, as opposed to the business or oneself. However, 'public choice theory' suggests that public officials are motivated, amongst other things, by budget-maximising goals, that is, they

TABLE 8.5 Private and public sector management models

Private sector model	Public sector model
Individual choice	Collective choice
Demand and price	Need for resources
Closure (in private domain)	Openness (in public domain)
Market	Need
Search for market satisfaction	Search for justice
Competition	Collective action

Source: after McKevitt and Lawson, 1994

seek to increase their power and status by increasing their departmental budgets. Nevertheless, the public sector administrative culture embraces meritocracy and acts as a guarantor of probity. The rise of entrepreneurial and enterprise orientated management is seen as a threat to such values. In other words it can be, and often is, argued that the fundamental values of public sector managers and organisational objectives differ from those of the private sector. Differences in values encourage a divergence in managerial behaviour such that the 'private sector' model of management fails to 'fit' many public organisations.

Partly as a consequence of the differences between private and public sector objectives and roles, researchers and policy makers have sought new insight concerning the appropriate form for management in the new public sector. Much attention is now focused upon the difference between the two sectors as opposed to their similarities. The following section briefly investigates this issue further.

New public management

Increased attention has been focused on the concept of the 'New Public Management' both in the UK and internationally (Ferlie *et al.*, 1996). This has created pressures upon managers to change inherited roles and behaviours. These changes have had political implications as the power of managers in many public services, not least the NHS, has been in the ascendancy while that of 'professional' groups is, in relative terms, in decline. Many public sector arenas, previously dominated by professional groups, have been brought within political and 'managerial' control. For example, more exhaustive forms of auditing and inspection have been introduced within higher education in relation to the 'quality' of both teaching and research. The outcome of such audit and monitoring influences future funding arrangements. In the NHS even the powerful stakeholder group comprising doctors and consultants is seen to be losing ground to the new management. For example, Ferlie *et al.* (1996) suggest that many contracts in the new style quasi-market within the NHS are now signed-off by managers as opposed to consultants. Consequently, public sector managers, in relative terms at least, can be seen to have gained as a result of change while professionals have, by and large, become less powerful.

Ferlie *et al.* (1996) suggest four 'variants' or management models in evidence during the last two decades (Table 8.6). In reality many of the themes and indicators which portray each model are present in different public organisations at different times. It is not the case that one variant was universally dominant for a brief period before the next took precedence.

Private sector practices have made inroads within public organisations. Decentralisation and devolved budgetary control are now more common practices within the public sector. Progress was, however, slow at first partly due to a lack of clarity in the objectives of various change initiatives. In the early years of Margaret Thatcher's government the prime concern was with efficiency; a war on waste was declared. Rather than attempt to radically alter the culture of public service the Thatcher government established the Efficiency Unit, fronted by Derek Raynor, in

TABLE 8.6   Four 'new public sector' management models

	Themes and indicators
Variant 1	Value for money; efficiency improvement; market-like mechanisms; greater competition; strong general management spine; external audits
Variant 2	Organisational downsizing; search for flexibility; greater customer orientation; increased decentralisation of strategic and budgetary control; increased contracting-out
Variant 3	Emphasis on organisational development and organisation learning (bottom-up); organisational cultural change; vision; leadership (top-down)
Variant 4	Concern with quality; 'value-driven'; empowerment

Source: after Ferlie *et al.*

1980. Its primary aim was to secure efficiency savings and better value for money. The work of this Unit made little impact. Consequently it was followed by the development of a Management Information Systems for Ministers (MINIS) which provided government ministers with more financial and other information about their departments. It aimed, as did the Financial Management Initiative in 1982, to further decentralise budgetary and management responsibility within the civil service. These measures were attempts to devolve management responsibility and to encourage the development of managerial skills and awareness at lower levels than had hitherto been the case.

Change was initially slow to take root; however, the development of civil service agencies and structural changes within the NHS and the education services has hastened the speed of reform. 'Managerialism' has now infiltrated most public service organisations and indeed many professions (Brooks, 1998) although it is enjoying mixed fortunes in terms of both public and employee perceptions and when evaluated against measurable organisational outcomes. Although this is a subject of dispute, many academics, public sector managers and informed members of the public would argue that the changes have held many advantages, which include

- the reduction of bureaucracy which has enabled organisations to respond more rapidly to environmental changes;
- increased flexibility and the development of a customer orientation, which have improved the quality of service offered (at the same time, customers have become more vociferous in their complaints and more demanding generally of the public sector);
- improvements in efficiency and effectiveness as a result of clearer organisational and individual objectives and greater accountability and increased value for money.

The civil service

This section discusses the nature of structural and managerial changes within the civil service since the late 1980s. It illustrates the strong and pervasive influence upon the public sector of its political masters.

In 1987 the 'Next Steps' report commissioned by the government showed how little in the way of real financial and management responsibility was devolved down the line within the Civil Service (HMSO, 1987). This was despite the Financial Management Initiative of 1982. The report revealed that decentralised budgetary control had not been introduced in many departments and where it had, budget centre managers were invariably members of the senior management team. Decision making resided in the centre of departments or with senior management and problems that demanded resolution were all too often delegated upward. The Treasury remained meddlesome and the conservative and cautious culture continued to prevail. The report recommended a real devolution of power over budgets, manpower, pay, hiring and firing to executive agencies in areas of activity embracing the 95 per cent of the civil service involved in the delivery of services. The structural changes suggested have largely been achieved and civil service executive functions are conducted by over a hundred agencies employing over 350 000 civil servants. Agencies range in scale from the Social Security Benefits Agency, an organisation employing 65 000 civil servants, to the Wilton Park conference centre in Sussex with 30 employees.

The dawning of agency status in the civil service signalled what was probably the most radical departure from current practice the civil service had known in the twentieth century. Agency status, although some way short of privatisation, gives each executive unit opportunities to develop a structure, systems, style and culture which suits its environment. A Civil Service Agency represents a newly created identity for an organisation, or part of a previously larger unit, which manages a set of predetermined government functions, such as administering the Common Agricultural Policy of the European Union. Thus government functions are parcelled off into manageable units of similar operations. Each agency is responsible to its parent department or directly to a minister of the government. The Treasury closely monitors running costs. Agencies are required to set a framework, tailored to the job to be done, which specifies policies, objectives, the results required, the resources available and their indicators of performance. Clearly, government in the UK has attempted to encourage a degree of self-determination, especially among agencies with income-earning capabilities. Many agencies have 'trading fund status'. By enabling them to actively market and deliver their services widely this increases their capacity to supplement running costs by income generation. Some agency functions have been the subject of 'market-testing' to assess the feasibility of conducting these activities within the private sector.

Change within the civil service has involved major structural realignment and attempts at fundamental change to managerial practices. However, the ultimate aim is to transform the organisational culture of the civil service and to make it more responsive to customers, less bureaucratic and more effective, that is, to achieve better value for money. Many critics argue that levels of both efficiency and effectiveness within the current civil service are already high and that further change would adversely effect service quality. As if to symbolise continued government determination to slim down and change public service organisations,

---

EXHIBIT 8.3

The Intervention Board Executive Agency

The Intervention Board was established as a government department in 1972. It administers the market regulation and production support measures of the European Union Common Agricultural Policy (CAP) within the UK. This role involves the licensing of imports and exports, the payment of subsidies and the collection of levies together with the buying, storage and sale of agricultural products. It became a government agency on 1 April 1990.

The Agency employs just over 1000 staff and has a turnover in excess of £2.5 billion. On becoming an agency the Intervention Board established a corporate plan inclusive of a mission statement, strategic and financial objectives and performance targets. Additionally, the Chief Executive is responsible for developing a policy and resources document detailing the Agency's aims, responsibilities and delegated authorities, which was issued to all staff. The Agency aims to achieve 2 per cent efficiency savings annually, against a Treasury demand of 1.5 per cent. Its customers are the food and agricultural industries. It has been making efforts recently to improve both the service it gives its customers and its own corporate image. The Agency now has a customer care policy and publishes a booklet endorsing its services under the 'Citizen's Charter'.

There are nine levels of hierarchy within the Agency, that is, from Grade 3 (Chief Executive) to Administrative Assistants. The 'clerical factories', those parts of the Agency where claims are processed, are largely staffed by administrative officers and assistants and their first line supervisors, executive officers. In many ways, the change of identity and external structure have had little effect on internal structures and work organisation. The strong civil service organisational culture largely remains intact.

---

significant internal changes were announced in late 1994 to the Treasury, which lies at the very heart of the civil service.

Numerous other civil service agencies and departments are experiencing competitive tendering and market-testing which may involve the transfer of many services to private sector operators. This illustrates the depth of change that has occurred within the very bastion of British public service. However, whether a radical change in managerial and organisational behaviour has taken place within all agencies is a matter of some debate (Brooks and Bate, 1994). Undoubtedly some have enjoyed their new-found freedoms while others have proven less determined to 'go their own way'.

A more recent attempt at civil service reform comes in the shape of the 'Continuity and Change' (HMSO, 1994) proposals. The White Paper sets out the previous government's plans for building on the reforms aimed at improving efficiency, effectiveness and quality. The paper expresses the continuing need to separate policy making and service provision, embodied within the Next Steps initiative and the Citizen's Charter, and for further delegation of management responsibility by developing appropriate management structures and flexible pay systems and by further developing staff. Civil Service Agencies are encouraged to apply key management techniques such as priority-based cost management, benchmarking and process re-engineering. Further strategic contracting-out, privatisation and market-testing were encouraged in the White Paper (HMSO, 1994). However, it should be noted that a change of government may lead to changed priorities and practices.

Case Study 4 in Part II of this book explores in more detail the environmental characteristics and managerial issues facing the NHS. However, Exhibit 8.4 on Hong Kong illustrates the global nature of concern surrounding an all-important element of public provision, that is, health care. It looks at one province's attempt to come to terms with change. It explores the dynamic political and environmental influences which acted upon the health care system in Hong Kong shortly before its reunification with the Republic of China, and outlines the responses that the system has made to these external changes and pressures.

EXHIBIT 8.4

The Hospital Authority of Hong Kong

For many years prior to the commissioning of a consultant report on the public hospital system in Hong Kong the government had become concerned about the rising cost of providing medical services and the increasing community expectation of the service. Other concerns focused on the perceived lack of flexibility and management competence within the health care system. It was little surprise that the consultants recommended establishing a statutory hospital authority, structural changes within hospitals, measures to reduce overcrowding in hospitals, new staffing and management structures and further cost control and recovery measures.

A Provisional Health Authority was established and reported that the future hospital management structure should 'ensure staff serve the patients in a more efficient and effective manner'. In 1991 a new Hospital Authority took control of all public hospitals.

The Hospital Authority aimed to integrate government hospitals into a single system and to provide uniform terms and conditions of employment for its staff. It was also charged with encouraging further public participation in the operation of the public hospital system and thus inviting direct accountability to the public. In addition to the structural changes, the reforms hoped to achieve a 'cultural transformation' in public medical care, replacing a culture centred on the values of professionalism, specialisation and hierarchical management with a patient-centred approach emphasising empowerment of staff, teamwork, continuous improvement of service quality and overall organisational effectiveness. By 1994

▶

Exhibit 8.4 continued

the Hospital Authority had developed a mission statement, corporate plan, business plans and had articulated its corporate values.

The environment

The Authority is funded almost exclusively by government and had an operating budget of approximately £1.4 billion in 1995/96, which represented about 10 per cent of the government's recurrent expenditure.

Prior to the establishment of the Hospital Authority, decision making was centralised. It is argued that this led to the hospital system becoming out of step with its environment. This was particularly significant in areas of non-medical technology and hospital management practices. Critics suggest that clinical decisions were often made without consideration of the financial implications and service development was led by medical professionals. Services were criticised for not being customer-orientated. This was politically unacceptable.

The Hospital Authority is responsible for identifying the future medical needs of the population of Hong Kong. Estimates are based upon information such as population growth and distribution, including the recognition of a rapidly ageing population structure, and other health indices. It is estimated that as many as 50 per cent of Hong Kong residents aged over 65 years have some form of chronic disease and 20 per cent some form of disability. The identification of gaps in service provision, often created by changes within the external environment, is an important dimension of the authority's work. For example, currently there are few resources focused on the growing adolescent problems of drug abuse and suicide.

With increasing affluence in Hong Kong, better education and improvements in communication, there is greater awareness of the benefits health care can offer and increased customer expectations. A more informed public in a changing socio-political environment results in the emergence of demands to be involved in the decision-making process. This necessitates information-sharing and the invitation to active input from political and non-political groups.

The changing social structures in the province have had an effect on the care for the elderly who are becoming increasingly institutionalised due to a process of extended family breakdown. Although common in the West, this is a relatively new phenomena in South-East Asia.

Public sector change: drivers and resistors

Environmental and organisational change is a theme that has run throughout this chapter. The 'business' environment facing public sector organisations is in a state of flux largely, although not exclusively, due to changes in political ideologies and agendas. No public organisation is immune from change yet internal resistance is rife. There are within most organisations, not least publicly owned entities, both active and passive forces which encourage a state of stability and which serve to

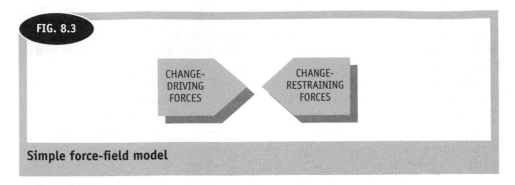

FIG. 8.3

CHANGE-
DRIVING
FORCES

CHANGE-
RESTRAINING
FORCES

Simple force-field model

reduce the potency of the forces for change. Hence a dynamic balance exists between the forces which promote change and those that favour stability. Both sets of pressures comprise a combination of external environmental and internal organisational forces.

Lewin (1951) encompassed such tensions within a force-field model. He argues that the two sets of forces 'push' against each other. If the forces for change, the 'drivers', are more pervasive and powerful than the 'resistors' then change will occur. Conversely, if resisting forces are more powerful they may well scupper the intentions of change agents. Hence an intense, continuous and highly political process of change and stability is unfolding within the public sector. Figure 8.3 shows the force-field model.

Table 8.7 identifies some of the forces for change and stability in the public sector. These are not ranked according to their potency. Nor is this an exhaustive

TABLE 8.7 Conflicting forces for change and stability within the public sector

Forces for change	Forces for stability
Margaret Thatcher, 17 years of Conservative government and the new right ideology	Organisational cultures: accepted practices and behaviours; taken-for-granted beliefs concerning how activities should be conducted; attitudes to colleagues, members of the public and politicians; fundamental public service values
Only moderate economic growth	
High levels of unemployment	
Increasing resource demands on welfare provision	Hierarchical organisational structures, formal reporting relationships and historically accrued bureaucracy
Ageing population	
Cultural change, e.g. increasing community expectation; power of the media; consumerism	Statutory and regulatory duties and procedures
Technological advance, e.g. in medicine and information technology	Employee organisations, e.g. trade unions (UNISON), BMA and other individual or group vested interests
Globalisation, e.g. restructuring of industry; deregulation; increased competitive forces	Lack of 'ownership' of change i.e. top-down imposed model is usually favoured
New blood, e.g. management trained/educated elites; managerialism; benchmarking	Resource constraint
Public accountability	Individual and group overt and covert resistance
New Labour	Public accountability

list. The forces encouraging change are largely, but not exclusively, external to public sector organisations. These have been outlined within this chapter. Factors encouraging stability and other resisting forces are largely internal to public organisations. Table 8.7 lists just some of the two sets of forces.

Although the causal relationships between many of the factors are not shown in the force-field model, it does indicate the complexity of the tensions that exist. It is also curious that some items, such as public accountability, can act as both a force encouraging change and reform and a pressure to guard against the flux and uncertainty which change often involves. This model could just as easily be applied to any single organisation or government department.

Just how much real change has occurred within the public sector over the past two decades is, like so many aspects of public policy, hotly disputed. There has been significant transfer of activity to private operators and major internal restructuring has altered patterns of responsibility and accountability. Whether organisational culture and workplace behaviour has altered radically within the public sector is far less certain.

CONCLUSION

The reinvention of government activity has proceeded apace during the last two decades of the twentieth century. This transformation has embraced a desire to focus on results rather than procedures. It is characterised by decentralisation (but firm control of costs and quality imposed by the centre), performance measurement, accountability and competition. The range of mechanisms government has employed since 1979 include privatisation; restructuring; contracting-out government and public sector services; quality charters, league tables and published performance targets; performance management and performance-related pay; more effective complaints procedures; tougher and more independent inspectorates; public/private sector collaboration; and better redress for the citizen when things go wrong.

The number of people employed within the public sector in the UK declined by about 2 million in the final two decades of the twentieth century. Much of this decline was due to the privatisation and contracting-out processes; general government staffing has shown only a slight decrease. In fact many services, such as the NHS and the police, have shown increases since 1979. Despite overall reductions, the UK public sector still employs about 22 per cent of the total workforce and 30 per cent of all professional workers.

SUMMARY OF MAIN POINTS

This chapter has focused on public organisations and their 'unique' business environment. The prime points made are:

- Prevailing political ideologies, priorities and practices are particularly important for public sector organisations, although dynamism and complexity are key characteristics of the public sector business environment.

- Although certain services are always likely to be in public hands, there is little agreement considering the extent of government involvement in the provision of goods and services.

- Economic and social circumstances and global environmental changes all influence public organisations, however, the government of the day often filters and interprets these external forces.

- Privatisation and deregulation processes are ongoing in many countries and seek to reduce the role of government in the economy and increase commercialisation and competition.

- Many government services in the UK and elsewhere have been exposed to competitive forces by privatisation, deregulation, competitive tendering and market-testing.

- Benchmarking and other mechanisms aimed at increasing competition and consumer involvement have been developed since the early 1980s.

- There have been major structural changes in the public sector.

- Public/private sector partnerships are increasing and continue to be given government support.

- Managerial practices within the public sector have been exposed to external change and influence.

- Managerial values and organisational culture, organisational objectives and environmental conditions often vary significantly between private and public sector organisations.

- A dynamic tension exists within the public sector between forces encouraging change and those seeking stability.

- The role government plays in the economy is subject to major ongoing debate.

REFERENCES

Brooks, I. (1998) 'Managerialist professionalism: the destruction of a non-comforming sub-culture', *British Journal of Management*, accepted for publication 1999.

Brooks, I. and Bate, S.P. (1994) 'The problems of effecting change within the British civil service: a cultural perspective', *British Journal of Management*, 5 (3).

Brown, C.V. and Jackson, P.M. (1992), *Public Sector Economics*, Blackwell.

Ferlie, E., Ashburner, L., Fitzgerald., L. and Pettigrew, A. (1996) *The New Public Management in Action*, Oxford: Oxford University Press.

HMSO (1987) *Improving Management in Government: The Next Steps*, Efficiency Unit, Cabinet Office, London: HMSO.

HMSO (1991) *Competing for Quality*, White Paper presented to Parliament by the Chancellor of The Exchequer (Norman Lamont), HM Treasury, London: HMSO.

HMSO (1993) *The Government's Guide to Market Testing: Efficiency Unit*, Office of Public Service and Science, London: HMSO.

HMSO (1994) *The Civil Service: Continuity and Change*, White Paper presented to Parliament by the Prime Minister, London: HMSO.

Hoggett, P. (1987) 'A farewell to mass production: decentralisation as an emergent private and public sector paradigm', in Hoggett, P. and Hamblett, R. (eds) *Decentralization and Democracy*, Occasional Paper No. 28, School for Advanced Urban Studies, Bristol University.

Isaac-Henry, K., Painter, C. and Barnes, C. (1993) *Management in the Public Sector: Challenge and Change*, Chapman and Hall.

Keat, R. and Abercrombie, N. (eds) (1991) *Enterprise Culture*, London: Routledge.

Lewin, K. (1951) *Field Theory in Social Science*, New York: Harper & Row.

McKevitt, D. and Lawson, A. (1994) *Public Sector Management: Theory, Critique and Practice*, London: Sage.

NHS (1983) *The Griffiths Report: NHS Management Inquiry*, London: DHSS.

Parker, D. (1993) 'Privatisation and the international business environment', *University of Birmingham WPC 93/15*.

Parker, D. and Martin, S. (1993) 'The impact of UK privatisation on labour and total factor productivity', *University of Birmingham Working Paper*.

9

CHALLENGES AND CHANGES

Ian Brooks
and Alistair Sutton

LEARNING OBJECTIVES

On completion of this chapter you should be able to:

- appreciate the main characteristics of the business environment and the prime themes identified within the text;

- understand the move towards greater dynamism, complexity and uncertainty (turbulence) in the business environment of most firms;

- outline the nature of chaotic and turbulent environments and the implications of these for long-term planning and flexible working;

- understand the characteristics of flexible firms and the advantages and drawbacks of flexible working;

- speculate about the future prospects for organisations, individuals, governments and groups in society as a result of environmental turbulence;

- discuss the influences that the changing business environment, and in particular the trend towards flexible working, have upon individuals and groups in the social community;

- debate the future role of government.

KEY CONCEPTS

- dynamism, complexity, uncertainty, turbulence and chaos
- long-term planning
- flexible firm

- flexible working
- social exclusion
- interventionist and laissez-faire government

INTRODUCTION

In this chapter we will outline the consequences for organisations, individuals, groups and governments of environmental and organisational turbulence. This will include analysis of the implications for long-range planning within organisations and of one major organisational response to environmental flux, that is, the growth of the flexible firm and of flexible working.

Throughout this text we have consistently suggested that the business environment is constantly changing, often in unpredictable ways. This implies considerable uncertainty for many organisations and can give rise to a near permanent state of internal flux as they attempt to respond to the changes in their environment. Broadly speaking, greater dynamism, complexity and uncertainty are synonymous with turbulence in the business environment. Such environments demand considerable flexibility on the part of organisations which wish to prosper. However, some evidence suggests that organisations operating in turbulent environments do not necessarily suffer a decline in profitability as the 'costs' of change are not always borne by the organisation initially influenced by such turbulence. Perrow (1986) argues that problems are often 'externalised' to dependent parts of the wider organisational system, such as employees (who may be made redundant), suppliers (who will lose orders) and other outworkers and persons responsible for non-core activities. This raises critical issues about how we define an organisation and where the boundaries lie between an organisation, its environment and its stakeholders. The organisation and its 'inner' or 'task' environment is itself undergoing major change and organisational boundaries are increasingly becoming flexible and dynamic.

We have identified, by way of a summary or stock-take, a number of dynamic environmental issues which have been raised in this book. These critical environmental trends include:

- globalisation in manufacturing, and increasingly in service provision, creating international competition and the development of new markets for goods and services;

- increasing emphasis on free market economics, competition and managerialism including the privatisation, contracting-out and 'marketisation' of public services;

- widely varying and volatile economic growth rates: for example, rapid growth around 8 to 10 per cent in the NICs in South-East Asia in the late 1980s and early 1990s turned to decline from 1997 while growth rates in Ireland reached over 7 per cent in 1998;

- the prevalence of long-term unemployment in Europe, and economic stagnation or decline in many African countries;

- the continuing integration of Europe, with the establishment of the Euro in 1999;

- technological advances in a wide range of fields, including information technology and communications, biotechnology and material sciences;

- growth in the power and influence of economic and political unions, such as the European Union, ASEAN and the World Trade Organization;

- the demographic transition typified by declining fertility rates and increasing life expectancy leading to an ageing population in most countries;

- dynamic national and international cultures;

- increasing availability of information and ease of communication;

- changing attitudes towards the family and health, and rising crime, including internationally organised felony;

- atmospheric, water, space, land and noise pollution, resource depletion and other ecological concerns;

- the spread of biological/chemical and atomic weapons capability, religious fundamentalism and the ever-present threat of international terrorism;

- ethnic divisions, such as those in Eastern Europe, the old Soviet Union and Iraq;

- increasing debate on the future role of government.

This list provides ample food for thought. Many of the issues raised have crucial implications for governments and organisations, groups and individuals. Collectively, these environmental forces are fundamentally influencing, and being influenced by, patterns of economic growth, employment and investment. They will ensure that organisations are required to be dynamic and that change will be an omnipresent feature of human existence. However, it is not the intention of this book to crystal-ball gaze or to explore, in detail, likely future events.

THE NATURE OF THE BUSINESS ENVIRONMENT

In Chapter 1 we identified dynamism and complexity as two key factors in the business environment of many organisations. These are the prime characteristics of a turbulent environment. The models discussed there help us to categorise environmental influences (using the LE PEST C model) and to devise lists of key organisational opportunities or threats (SWOT analysis). However, Johnson and Scholes (1999) argue that organisations need to understand the nature of their environments before they audit the individual environmental factors. Such an analysis might be expected to help an organisation decide upon the sorts of systems which are required to monitor and respond to environmental change.

If dynamism and complexity are key factors in analysing the nature of an organisation's business environment it seems reasonable to ask whether there are any academic models which may be of assistance in such a process. Miles (1980) devised a useful series of questions for evaluating the nature of an organisation's environment. The suggested process involves mapping an organisation's environment using a series of continuums, for example, from simple to complex and static to dynamic.

New technologies and increased globalisation of many markets encourage environmental turbulence, such that organisational planning cannot be seen as a continuous 'rolling out' of previous plans. If environmental factors are less predictable then planning needs to be seen as a more flexible, adaptive and responsive process. It is these two key areas, that is, the planning process and the need for organisational flexibility, which are given considerable attention in the next section. However, during this discussion we should be aware of the impact an organisation can have on its environment and the operation of the market by way of its strategic, tactical and operational actions.

Richardson and Richardson (1992) catalogue a range of increasingly 'commonplace' surprises which threaten today's organisations, such as major global accidents, terrorism, kidnappings, hostile takeovers, sabotage via product tampering, investigative journalism, equipment breakdowns, political upheaval and pressure group activity. Such events can be a trigger, creating problems or damage inside or outside the organisation; this might involve large-scale damage to human life and the business environment and significant economic and social costs.

There is a growing field of literature on crisis and shock event management, but consideration of this is outside the scope of a book essentially focused on the environment. Underlying analysis of such 'shock events' in the business sphere, however, is the developing body of knowledge about the concept of chaos. James Gleik's 1988 book *Chaos: Making a New Science* offers some fascinating insights into the discoveries about the behaviour of things in the natural world. These include the graphically-termed 'butterfly effect' in global weather forecasting: the notion that a butterfly stirring its wings today in one part of the world might transform weather systems next month in another far-off area. This effect underpins an equation written in 1963 by Edward Lorenz which seemed to predict cloud patterns. Gleik (1988) says that such discoveries have begun to 'change the way business executives make decisions about insurance, the way astronomers look at the solar system, the way political theorists talk about the stresses leading to armed conflict'.

In the 1980s a number of American fund management firms looked for such chaotic patterns in the movements of the stock market, in an attempt to predict its behaviour. However, this work has been criticised because

- any small errors made at the start of the process would be likely to result in huge forecasting errors over time;
- huge amounts of data are required to model chaotic systems and these were unavailable in most markets; and
- the ability to spot chaotic patterns is small given the large number of variables which influence the markets – particularly if we think that new factors are now affecting performance.

Writers such as Stacey (1996) have looked at the business impact of chaos theory. He notes the tendency in many business cycles towards the sort of 'non-linear feedback loops' observable in the natural world. Although the value of chaos theory may be questioned it is possible that the mathematical models designed to explore non-linearity will generate useful analytical tools for managers in the future.

QUESTIONS

1. What are the key global trends in the business environment?
2. Which academic models help us audit and classify the various environmental influences on organisations?
3. List some 'shock events' which have affected organisations recently.

IMPLICATIONS FOR ORGANISATIONS

Whatever their objectives and legal status, organisations have, almost without exception, changed over the last decade. Very many have restructured internally, realigned their business processes to improve customer service, made focused strategic changes to their management control systems, developed their staff, improved their technological positioning and adjusted their product market portfolio. Most of these changes reflect a conscious response to turbulence in the business environment and a deliberate effort to influence that environment. Many organisations have undergone fundamental change because the environment has itself transformed.

A number of researchers, among them some notable management 'gurus', have attempted to predict the ways in which organisations will change in the next decade and beyond. Such predictions are often based on current trends and collective expectations together with a pinch of 'educated' guesswork. To a large extent it is the changing nature of the business environment that will dictate the nature of these changes and, in turn, the way organisations respond to change will alter the nature of the environment for all. The next section will first look at the implications of the changing business environment for long-term planning and will then explore one particular organisational response to environmental turbulence, that is, the growth of the flexible firm and of flexible working.

Implications for long-term planning

Operational plans have always been distinguished from strategic plans on the basis of the time period they cover and the scope and detail they contain. Strategic plans have tended to imply a planning horizon of about five years and to cover the organisation as a whole. To be able to plan over this sort of period implies a reasonable level of certainty about the business environment in which the organisation operates. However, turbulence in the environment leads to an increasing lack of stability and predictability which, in turn, makes long-term strategic planning hazardous. This has led many writers on strategy to question whether organisations should adopt long-term, centralised approaches to planning. Authors such as Quinn (1978) and Mintzberg (1994) believe that incremental and emergent approaches to the process of strategy formulation should increasingly be considered by organisations. Increased environmental turbulence also suggests that systems of planning which devolve responsibility to individual business units are likely to make organisations more adaptable and responsive to environmental flux.

Stacey (1996) questions many of the underlying assumptions used by firms in the process of long-term planning. He points out that many of these assumptions are based upon a range of quantitatively-based analytical techniques. These techniques contribute to an underlying assumption, on the part of some theorists and many managers, that there is a 'best way' to plan. However, as noted above, long-term organisational planning is becoming less and less reliable or valid in today's turbulent environments.

Perhaps we should not over-react; after all, Mintzberg (1994) reminds us that each succeeding generation tends to perceive its present situation as more turbulent than its predecessors'. He suggests the key factor is whether organisations can learn to think strategically and avoid inappropriately formal processes of planning. He reminds us that

> changes that appear turbulent to organisations that rely heavily on planning may appear normal to, even welcomed by, those that prefer more of a visionary or learning approach. Put more boldly, if you have no vision but only formal plans then every unpredicted change in the environment makes you feel that the sky is falling.

He also suggests that the perceptual filters discussed in Chapter 1 may operate differently in different countries. He notes that what was seen as turbulence in the USA was perceived as opportunity in Japan. Turbulence demands an organisational response. One such 'reaction' has been for organisations to attempt to develop far greater flexibility; hence the growth of the concepts of the 'flexible firm' and of 'flexible working'.

Flexible working

Many organisations have responded to turbulent environmental conditions by attempting to become more flexible. This real or perceived need for flexibility is increasingly influencing employment conditions. Within organisations, people are both the most vital and the most costly resource. Traditionally, however, they have been prone to inflexibility and inertia. As a consequence many individual employees and organisations have sought to achieve greater flexibility in employment conditions in recent decades.

The old 'industrialised' scenario of reliable employment, which allowed families shared times for shopping, travel, and leisure, together with patterns of work and retirement within the nuclear family, is metamorphosing into what some have called a 'post-industrial' age. Alvin Toffler (1985), a well-known writer about the future shape of work and of organisations, has termed such a society a 'super-industrial' age or a 'third wave'. Toffler likens this 'wave' to the Agricultural Revolution (the first wave) and the Industrial Revolution (the second wave). Others have referred to it as post-Fordism – that is, after or following Henry Ford's mass-production era. Bridges (1995) argues that we are in an evolutionary phase where certain types of work are in decline as other types of work are emerging. He draws an analogy between the present period and a time in the UK between 1780 and 1830 when riots, arson and killings accompanied a shift from rural land-based jobs to industrial, factory work. Both are periods where two systems overlap and cause us to think again about our underlying assumptions about the nature of work.

Key characteristics of this new age are expectations on the part of employers that workers will be very flexible (examined in some detail below) and be able to adapt products and services, almost at will, to meet the particular needs of customers. The enhanced capabilities of many organisations to customise products and services has been strongly influenced by developments, for example, in microprocessor technology and management techniques. Computers enable us to process and communicate data and information extremely rapidly. Advances in telecommunications technology (telephones, faxes, multimedia computers, satellites and the Internet) have delivered significant improvements in the quality of data about life and work throughout the globe. These technologies have been harnessed by organisations which wish to operate in a range of countries. Quinn (1992) conceives of intelligent enterprises 'converting intellectual resources into a chain of service outputs and integrating these into a form most useful for certain customers'.

Bridges (1995) identified some 'new rules' which are still evolving and are becoming operative in some parts of the economy more quickly than in others. The rules are divided into three key points:

- everyone's employment is dependent on the organisation's performance and, as a result, workers need to continuously prove their worth to the organisation and to behave more like an external supplier than a traditional employee;
- workers should, therefore, plan for career-long self-development by taking primary responsibility for health insurance and retirement funds and by renegotiating their compensation arrangements with each organisation when, and if, organisational needs change;

- wise companies will need to work closely with these new-style workers to maximise the benefits for both parties and to bring a range of projects to satisfactory completion.

Having looked at some of the assumptions which underlie recent trends we can now examine the different forms of flexible working which may be found. First, we can identify various types of 'numerical' flexibility, which generally affect employees' hours of work. These include long-standing practices such as overtime, homeworking, shift and part-time work and other increasingly common practices, such as flexitime, teleworking, annual hours and zero hours contracts, the use of temporary staff, and job-sharing. A few of these require some further explanation. Zero hours contracts are similar to temporary work. For example, Burtons, the retail clothes chain, terminated the contracts of 2000 of its staff in the mid 1990s. Some of these people were re-employed on part-time contracts but many others were offered work as and when required by the employer. These 'zero-hours' contracts enable the organisation to adjust staff levels in line with customer shopping patterns. Needless to say most of the employees concerned were less than satisfied with this arrangement as it introduced considerable uncertainty into their working lives. Another market-driven change is apparent in the electricity generating business. One company encourages some employees to engage in 'winter/summer stagger', where they work longer hours in the winter to accommodate demand. Hence people are employed on an annual hours basis. Employees of the Rover group agreed in late 1998 to accept annualised hours contracts and in early 1999 production of Land Rovers in Solihull was scaled down and workers' hours temporarily reduced. Many new NHS nursing contracts are also of this type.

There has been an increasing number of people employed as temporary and agency labour over the last few years. Table 9.1 estimates the numbers of 'temps' in various European countries. Temporary workers are employed in most sectors and at all levels including interim managers, industrial workers, administrative staff and medical workers.

Homeworking is not new, although the scale of this activity is increasing. However, teleworking goes a step further by connecting home-based employees by

TABLE 9.1 Temporary workforce estimates

Country	Temporary workforce 1995	Penetration (%) 1995	Temporary workforce 2005 (estimate)	Penetration (%) 2005 (estimate)
UK	340 000	1.3	798 000	2.8
France	370 000	1.7	811 000	3.5
Netherlands	180 000	2.7	401 000	5.5
Germany	176 000	0.5	685 000	1.8
Spain	60 000	0.5	239 000	1.8
Belgium	41 000	1.1	105 000	2.5
Switzerland	26 000	0.7	62 000	1.5

the use of computer modems to the organisation and/or other teleworkers. The availability of communications technology has also led to the 'virtual office' where laptop computers, modems, portable faxes and mobile phones enable people to work in any location. Linked with this is the practice of 'hotdesking' where employees 'touch base' at the office and use whatever work space is available, picking up messages on e-mail. Stanworth and Stanworth (1992) found that the most popular working pattern amongst teleworkers is a combination of home and office working which helps to overcome the inherent isolation of working from home and increases the feeling of belonging to a team. 'Telecottaging', where a local venue acts as a central point for teleworkers, may be one way of solving the problem of isolation. From an ecological perspective an increase in teleworking, which is particularly commonplace amongst management consultants, computing and sales personnel, may help reduce rush hour traffic and air pollution.

A second form of flexibility, referred to as 'distancing', is where employees are replaced by sub-contractors and employment contracts are replaced by contracts for service. Again this has been commonplace in many industries, such as construction and manufacturing, for many decades. However, the process is increasingly popular in other types of activity, including service industries, and in the public sector.

A third form of flexible working is broadly termed 'functional flexibility'. Although in many organisations strict lines of demarcation exist between jobs, these are seen as offering little flexibility and often prove obstacles to effective teamwork and subsequent productivity gains. Hence multi-skilling, where individuals are trained to undertake a broader array of tasks, is becoming more commonplace. Exhibit 9.1 illustrates one such attempt at flexibility in an NHS hospital.

EXHIBIT 9.1

Kettering General Hospital NHS Trust: generic working

An objective expressed in the Trust's business plan is to 'produce a multi-skilled workforce'. The relevant objective is stated as 'to introduce teams of generic hotel service assistants at ward level so as to improve flexibility and responsiveness to patient needs by combining the role of porters, domestics and catering staff'.

At Kettering hospital all domestics, unqualified nurses and ward clerks are to be based at ward level, a relocation which is involving severing many existing formal and informal relationships. Most of the 260 personnel are being trained in patient care, cleaning and portering skills in order to develop multi-skilled competencies. Staff will then undertake a wider array of tasks and be required to embrace flexibility and teamwork. There may be reduced role certainty. They will need to manage the interface with clinical and other staff groups on the ward. All existing formal status and pay differentials between the hitherto separate groups will be

▶

Exhibit 9.1 continued

removed. Some staff will be required to change their shift pattern and the total hours they work within any one week.

It is argued that successful implementation will help to 'provide good value for money' and 'make cost savings'. It will ensure, for the time being at least, competitiveness with external commercial players. The single grade and pay spine will reduce status differentials and simplify the highly complex bonus schemes that had evolved. From an operational point of view it will bring benefits of flexibility and simplify work scheduling. It will serve to even out the workload for staff and improve efficiency by avoiding waiting-for-action time and duplication of effort. Managers believe it will improve worker motivation as people will feel part of a team. They will, it is believed, take a pride in their work at ward level.

In conclusion, the philosophy underpinning the care assistant concept is a familiar one. A multi-skilled, flexible workforce is thought to facilitate operational planning and enhance both the efficiency and effectiveness of service provision. The assumption is that employees benefit from the resultant job enrichment and co-operative teamwork, cost savings are there for the making, via enhanced efficiency, and patient care is improved.

A fourth form of flexibility, pay flexibility, is increasingly commonplace. This may involve the harmonisation of terms and conditions, including the removal of artificial barriers between white-collar and blue-collar workers, such as differences in pension, sick pay and holiday entitlements. This is an approach that the Rover Group, the motor vehicle manufacturer, have used to encourage the development of a teamwork culture. Many organisations have, however, taken a contrasting approach, offering personal non-standard contracts.

Many flexible working practices find their ultimate focus in the concept of a 'virtual corporation'. Virtual corporations have been defined by Davidow and Malone (1992) as

> *almost edgeless, with permeable and continuously changing interfaces between company, supplier and customers. From inside the firm, the view will be no less amorphous with traditional offices, departments and operating divisions constantly reforming according to need.*

Such an organisation 'structure' is a clear culmination of a teleworking, information-based, constantly evolving enterprise.

Finally, there is a number of related concepts including career breaks, paternity and maternity leave, secondments, domestic leave for carers, childcare assistance and school holiday leave. Many of these measures may be considered as 'family-friendly' and are intended to help motivate and retain staff. In 1999 the Labour government's new employment law sought to promote family-friendly policies and introduced statutory rights to, for example, paternity leave and short-term absence to manage family crises.

There is strong evidence to suggest that flexible work practices are on the increase, although less agreement concerning whether this is part of a strategically planned reaction to changing environmental circumstances, including employee needs/wants, or the result of short-term economic expedience. Recent studies into flexible working in Europe suggest that although there is an overall trend towards greater use of flexible working patterns there is considerable variation in practice between countries, sectors and sizes of organisation. About 16 per cent of the workforce in the European Union works part-time, growth in this respect being most notable in Holland, Germany and the UK. Non-permanent employment has increased significantly in all European Union countries, as has subcontracting. Trailing the trend is Greece, where only 5 per cent of workers are part-time, compared to 7 per cent in Italy and 8 per cent in Spain. The equivalent figures for Britain and Holland are 25 per cent and 20 per cent respectively. In a survey of British part-time workers, 84 per cent suggested that they preferred part-time work. As shown in Figure 9.1, many part-time workers are female. Around 50 per cent of women employees in the United Kingdom work part-time; the EU average is just 30 per cent. The trend in Europe follows earlier movements in this direction in the USA. It is not necessarily coincidental that in the UK and Holland, the two

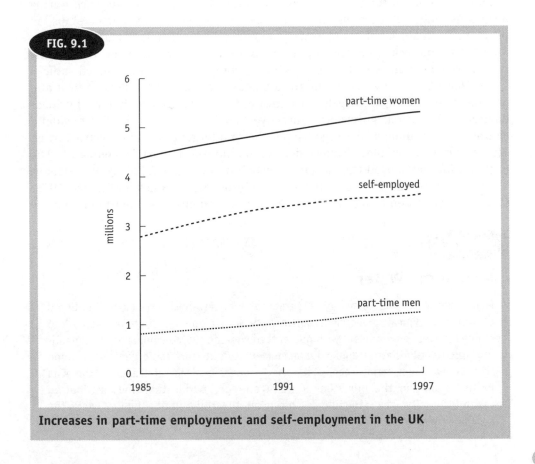

FIG. 9.1

Increases in part-time employment and self-employment in the UK countries with the most flexible labour market in this respect, unemployment is the lowest in the European Union.

The UK has the most flexible workforce in the EU with around 10 million people (almost 40 per cent of all employees) either part-time, temporary, self-employed, on a government training scheme or as unpaid family workers. This represented an increase of almost 2 million in a decade (1989–98). Over 80 per cent of all medium-sized and large organisations in the United Kingdom employ some temporary staff. The BBC, for example, now offers the majority of new recruits only short or fixed-term contracts, as do many universities.

In the UK there has also been an increase in the number of men working flexibly, from 18 per cent in 1986 to almost 30 per cent in 1998, while the proportion of women in this category remained stable and high at 50 per cent. Men in this category were largely self-employed; women were mainly part-time or on temporary contracts. Additionally, over 12 per cent, that is 2.6 million people, work flexitime, while 2 million, or 9 per cent of the workforce, have annualised hours contracts (most common in the professions). Over a million employees work school term-time only while about 200 000 people job-share. The Alliance & Leicester Building Society, for example, offer some employees, who are parents of school-age children (both mothers and fathers), the opportunity to work during term-time only, while Boots, the chemist, provide job-share 'partnerships' in positions from supervisor to pharmacy manager. These family-friendly measures attempt to motivate employees and help parents balance work and family demands. They also facilitate the retention of competent and well-trained staff.

Exhibit 9.2 illustrates some interesting characteristics of the flexible firm and organisational change. Largely as a response to changes within its business environment, such as government directives inspired by wider technological and competitive conditions, the organisation has undergone a major restructuring. The result is a smaller, leaner, delayered and more flexible company. The organisation has moved from a 'mechanistic' to an 'organic' (Burns and Stalker, 1961) structure and from a 'defender' to a 'prospector' (Miles and Snow, 1978) strategic orientation (refer to Chapter 1). It also demonstrates that the boundary

EXHIBIT 9.2

Melbourne Water

Melbourne Water was formed in 1993 from the long-established Metropolitan Board of Works, a typical government bureaucracy which operated in a protected and stable business environment with guaranteed superannuated employment. Impending privatisation has encouraged management to structure the organisation along competitive commercial lines as it aims to become a market leader in the Asia Pacific region in the provision of water storage, purification and distribution capabilities. The new structure is shown on the right in the figure, while the previous hierarchical structure is on the left.

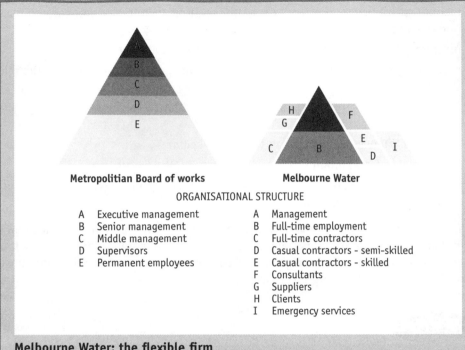

Metropolitian Board of works   **Melbourne Water**

ORGANISATIONAL STRUCTURE

A	Executive management	A	Management
B	Senior management	B	Full-time employment
C	Middle management	C	Full-time contractors
D	Supervisors	D	Casual contractors - semi-skilled
E	Permanent employees	E	Casual contractors - skilled
		F	Consultants
		G	Suppliers
		H	Clients
		I	Emergency services

Melbourne Water: the flexible firm

A layer of middle management has disappeared altogether. The executive and senior levels have been combined and supervisors have been reclassed as team leaders. The core workforce is now described as full-time and no one in the organisation is considered to have guaranteed life-long employment. All maintenance and construction activities are contracted out. Casual semi-skilled workers are employed as required on a daily basis and are recruited through specialist agencies. Much of the professional work is conducted by consultants. A number of major suppliers are now considered partners in the organisation as they are required to carry out some of the duties formerly conducted by employees.

between the organisation and its 'task' environment is not fixed but rather dynamic and flexible.

Changes in the external environment, which may have encouraged the moves towards flexible working, have been identified by Cole (1993), Curson (1986), Pollert (1991), Beardwell and Holden (1994) and others. These factors combined, they argue, ensure that the flexible firm and flexible working will become an increasing reality. Summarised here, they include:

- increased national competition;
- globalisation and consequent competitive pressures;
- uncertainty created by market volatility and, in part, a hang-over from recessionary periods;

- technological change, particularly in information technology and communications, which facilitates some forms of flexible working;

- investment in new plant requiring new and ever-changing skills;

- a move from Fordism to post-Fordism, from mass production to flexible specialisation;

- continued emphasis on costs and budgets and financial stringency in the public sector;

- political influence, particularly in the public sector;

- reductions in trade union power;

- increasing numbers of women and other employee groups 'demanding' alternative employment conditions.

In summary, it has been noted that as the business environment becomes more turbulent many organisations have sought ways of managing change. This has encouraged them to seek increased short-term operational flexibility and more adaptive approaches to long-term planning.

QUESTIONS

1. What are the implications of increased turbulence and chaos in the business environment for the ways in which organisations plan for the future?

2. What broad changes do you think are taking place in the nature of work? Illustrate your answer with examples from Exhibits 9.1 and 9.2.

IMPLICATIONS FOR THE INDIVIDUAL

When environmental change demands organisational change, as it almost continuously does, then we as individuals have to respond. It is becoming increasingly uncommon for people to work within a stable environment and undertake similar tasks and responsibilities for any length of time. Individuals are required to change at least as rapidly as the business environment if they are to remain effective. They need to continually develop their capabilities in order to function effectively within changing organisations. As Charles Handy (1989) reminds us, 'standing still is not an option'. We have to develop new skills and behaviours and, perhaps more importantly, new attitudes and ways of thinking, as the business environment demands flexibility and the capacity and willingness to seek personal development opportunities.

Moves towards greater flexible working and the growth of the flexible firm are of direct relevance to individuals in the workplace. It is individuals who are being made 'flexible' and it is they who will, or will not, cope with the changes in working patterns outlined above. Handy (1994) identifies the 'portfolio career' which many people experience these days. This is multifaceted and may include holding a number of 'loose' employment contracts, none of which are full-time or with just one employer. For example, a management consultant might work on a few short-term projects with a number of organisations, undertake to write a management textbook for a publishing company and work for a university business school as a part-time lecturer. Most individuals have been accustomed to regular '9 to 5', permanent, pensioned employment, so that new developments present personal challenges in balancing work and life patterns.

Increasing numbers of middle-aged and older people are having to adjust to changing employment patterns. The Organization for Economic Cooperation Development (OECD) calculated that only just over a third of the British aged over 55 years were in paid work in 1998. The equivalent figure for France was 27 per cent while for Italy it was just 11 per cent. Redundancy, early retirement opportunities and the lack of employment prospects for those over 50, together with youth unemployment and increasing numbers in higher education, ensure that the vast bulk of the workforce in Western Europe is between 25 and 55 years old. Many people's working life is restricted to just thirty years. In the 1960s the vast majority of young adults started work aged 15 and were expected to retire at 65 (male) or 60 (female) – a working life of up to fifty years. For some people changes in this regard have been unwelcome and have led to a reduction in their standard of living. Many have had to adjust their work-life expectations.

There is also a wider social implication for many millions who are not employed. They do not all do nothing! Handy (1994) suggests that there will come a time when no distinction will be drawn 'between full- and part-time work, when retirement will become a purely technical term ... and when "overtime" as a concept will seem as outmoded as "servant" does today'. At present, however, it is evident that many people have more time than they know what to do with, while others have far too little time to do what they want. Typical American and British citizens already work longer hours than they did in the 1980s. The average American works 164 hours a year longer than twenty years ago (equivalent to an extra month a year), concludes Juliet Schor (1992).

Successive Labour Force Surveys conducted in the UK by the Central Statistical Office have noted many significant changes including

- a medium/long-term decline in full-time male employment;
- a significant increase in part-time employment for both men and women (see data above and Figure 9.1);
- an increase in the numbers of self-employed (see Figure 9.1);
- an increase in the number of people with multiple jobs (approximately 1.4 million people in the UK have at least two jobs).

An increasingly 'flexible', self-employed and mobile workforce requires new forms of employment representation. Many trade unions are having to respond by providing different services and making different social responses. Increases in 'flexibility', which may often be forced upon employees, create personal uncertainty and anxiety about the future. Such uncertainties have complex implications. For example, uncertainty regarding the economy and consequent employment prospects was thought to be a contributory factor in the early 1990s to declining house prices and in the late 1990s to sluggish retail sales. Another response may be for people to actually save more. A perceived need for savings may be encouraged by a reduction in the value of state retirement pensions when compared with wages. Unfortunately many people are in no position to save a large proportion of their income as the poorest groups in the UK have, since the early 1980s, experienced little if any real growth in income. It appears that uncertainty, and all that it entails, is likely to be a permanent or long term reality, especially for low- and middle-income groups.

Of concern for the management of organisations which are undergoing seismic change is the potential for loss of worker motivation and commitment. Stevenson and Moldoveanu (1995) argue that anxious employees will ensure that their curricula vitae are kept up to date in case they fall prey to the latest round of re-engineering or restructuring. The authors contrast the mounting uncertainty for ordinary workers with improvements in certainty that senior managers gain from such things as golden parachutes, that is, the certainty of sizeable severance deals should their contracts be rescinded.

Previously predictable life-cycle patterns have, in the last two decades, changed considerably. Handy (1994) refers to the Sigmoid Curve (Figure 9.2) as an analytical model for depicting a person's working life-cycle. He argues that people start life falteringly, then make steady and consistent progress before peaking and enjoying a 'decline' during retirement. However, the time-frame for the Sigmoid Curve, rather like many product life cycles, is now being squeezed. This, he argues, means people need to develop new options for a second or even third career during their working lives. Evidence suggests that an increasing number of people switch careers at least once during their working life and undertake a seemingly different occupation (e.g. from executive to management lecturer or vice versa). Figure 9.2 shows this secondary curve superimposed on the Sigmoid Curve,

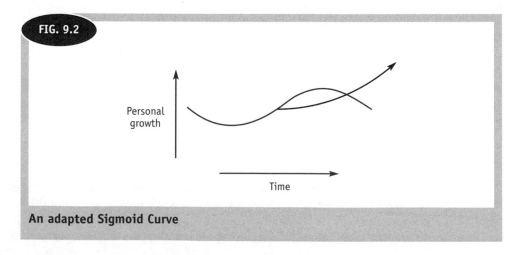

FIG. 9.2

Personal growth

Time

An adapted Sigmoid Curve

indicating that many people can sustain personal growth by developing a second career.

This discussion has highlighted a trend in society towards greater life and employment uncertainty. For many people flexible working improves choice and freedom while for others it constrains or sidelines them. Unfortunately, as individuals we are powerless to change societal trends or governmental policy. Globalisation and technological change conspire to transform our social and working worlds. What we can do is exercise some control over our own patterns of living. The paradox is that fragmentation and flexible working can offer new freedoms for those able to take advantage of them.

QUESTIONS

1. Assess the implications for individual workers of the increased use of flexible working practices by organisations.
2. Contrast your parents' work-life experiences with those of your grandparents. How do you expect your work-life experiences will differ from those of your parents?

IMPLICATIONS FOR GROUPS

In this section we look at the implications of environmental change on a number of groups – under-25-year-olds, the socially excluded, women and racial minorities – and at the increasing economic vulnerability suffered by many families as a result of the growth of flexible working.

A quarter of a century ago Pawley (1974) considered that Western society was withdrawing from 'the whole system of values and obligations that has historically been the basis of public, community and family life'. He was of the opinion that the sorts of technological developments discussed in this book, and which he termed 'socially atomising appliances', were fuelling a retreat into 'private lives of an unprecedented completeness'. During the 1980s the then Prime Minister Margaret Thatcher famously denied that there was such a thing as society, as distinct from groups of individuals. Pawley's assessment has, perhaps, proved to be particularly pertinent for young people in the UK.

Concern has been expressed about the degree to which young people feel 'disconnected' from the political and social system and about the generally acknowledged scale and growth of an underclass. In 1995, DEMOS, an independent think-tank, surveyed a number of people representative of the full spread of age groups. Their aim was to discover the percentage which believed they were not part of 'the system', and who would emigrate if they had the chance, who felt that they didn't belong to their neighbourhoods and would not agree that they would generally buy British. The results of the survey showed a marked contrast between the attitudes of young and old in society. Over 50 per cent of 18 to

24-year-olds were judged to be 'disconnected' from the British system whereas less than 10 per cent of 55 to 64-year-olds felt similarly. The survey showed a steady increase in the sense of belonging as age increased.

Moore (1995) draws attention to the fact that many young people have been attracted by single-issue campaigning on such matters as animal rights and environmental protection. She believes the attraction here is, as mentioned in Chapter 6, that the ethical basis of such campaigns contrasts sharply with the predominantly political atmosphere of parliamentary processes. She argues that,

> while the state has washed its hands of financial responsibility for the young, trapping them into economic dependence on their parents for longer and longer, it has intervened long enough to tell them that many of their leisure activities are illegal. The idea of voting once every five years is no compensation for the lack of say in the rest of their lives.

The use of the phrase 'underwolves' in the title of Moore's article reflects a feeling that increasing proportions of young people are not content to be 'underdogs' and are starting to fight back.

In the UK the Labour government launched the Social Exclusion Unit in 1997, bringing together the civil service, the police, business and voluntary sectors in an attempt to reduce homelessness and social exclusion, and address the problems of crime on many deprived housing estates. The emphasis is on trying to avoid one agency passing problems on to others and upon collaboration in order to try and prevent social exclusion from happening in the first place (Wintour, 1997). Crucial to the success of such policy initiatives will be the extent to which the 'new deal' initiative can encourage the long-term unemployed to find jobs. Similarly, attempts to improve educational standards and embed life-long learning are in part aimed at reducing the growth and scale of social, economic and political exclusion.

However, Hutton (1995) has argued that 'unemployment and low pay are no longer the sole measures of inequity and lack of social well-being'. He calls the UK a '30/30/40 society'. The bottom 30 per cent are the unemployed and economically inactive who are increasingly marginalised in society. The middle 30 per cent are a group he considers to be newly vulnerable to pressures beyond their control as a result of the 'the rise of new forms of casualised, temporary and contract forms of employment' discussed above. Hutton points out that much of the growth in part-time and insecure work has fallen to women, particularly to married women who are balancing work and family commitments. Such work is becoming essential to supplement family incomes. Nevertheless, 'When the capacity to avoid house repossession', for example, 'depends on earnings from an employer who can sack you at will, family stability hangs on a thread.' Further pressures to family life are caused by the fact that two-thirds of British workers now work more than 40 hours a week and a quarter work more than 50 hours. The available time to engage in social pursuits and community activities is consequently diminished. Even the European Union directive on maximum working hours (that is, 48 hours per week except by agreement) will do little to change this as many workers need the overtime payment.

The remaining 40 per cent, in Hutton's '30/30/40 society', are tenured workers. These, Hutton suggests, have reasonably certain prospects. An increasing number of workers in this group have been termed an 'overclass'. People in this group are competitive and ambitious and earn substantial salaries. Parallels have been drawn between this class and the underclass. It has been noted that both groups share an existence outside ordinary society, with the overclass being able to insulate themselves from many of society's services, for example, by 'buying into' private education and health care.

We have noted the impact of the growth of temporary and contract forms of work on female employment. According to a 1995 report entitled *Social Focus on Women*, published by the Central Statistical Office, the proportion of working women increased from 44 per cent in 1971 to 53 per cent in 1994 and is set to increase to 57 per cent by the year 2006. Just over a quarter of all women work full-time.

It can be argued that female job prospects have improved in the UK as a result of changes in the nature of work, the introduction of some more family-friendly policies and the increased availability of affordable childcare. Evans (1998) notes that only 9.8 per cent of mothers with children under 5 were unemployed in 1996, compared with 27.2 per cent in 1984. He argues that the availability of more part-time work, job-shares and the ability to work from home, ease women's return to work after childbirth.

In the UK more women are advancing into higher managerial and professional work, passing through what has been termed the 'glass ceiling'. The female proportion of this group rose from 9 per cent in 1984 to 22 per cent in 1998. However, about 11 per cent of the female workforce is engaged in highly routine low-skilled occupations; the comparable figure for men is just 5 per cent (Brindle, 1998).

Many countries have legislation designed to combat race discrimination in the world of work. Jaques (1997) feels that although blacks are hardly represented in the way the UK is governed there has been considerable progress towards a more inclusive and diverse mix within society. In particular, he identifies the extent to which young Asians are making an impact in the media, film and the professions and Afro-Caribbeans are making a crucial contribution to the development of the music and fashion scene. He compares the tendency of America to segregate white and black communities and notes that the 1991 census shows that the UK has many more inter-racial marriages: 40 per cent of Afro-Caribbean men and 21 per cent of Afro-Caribbean women between 16 and 34 had white partners.

QUESTION

Do you consider the social, political and economic situation for the under-25s, working women, families and racial minorities has improved or worsened since the early 1980s? Discuss the reasons for your answer.

IMPLICATIONS FOR GOVERNMENT

This section explores some of the implications for government of environmental change before discussing on the ongoing debate concerning the role of government. Government at local, national, continental and global levels is a powerful environmental force which influences the business environment of all organisations. However, there is a range of environmental phenomena which are themselves of major concern to governments at various levels. Many of these are listed in the introductory section of this chapter. We will look at just four of these changes and briefly assess the consequences for governments. These areas are:

- globalisation and consequent intense international competition;
- technological advances creating issues which many argue require a co-ordinated political and 'strategic' approach;
- the growth of the flexible firm and flexible working;
- conflicting pressures for both a reduced and an extended role for government.

Globalisation

Progress towards the globalisation of production and trade has been rapid in recent decades. It has been hastened by the successes of the General Agreement on Tariffs and Trade (GATT), now known as the World Trade Organization, by market and political union, and by many genuine attempts on the part of world leaders to reduce 'distance' between nations and communities.

Despite the volatility in economic growth, notably in Asia, the last two decades of the twentieth century witnessed large increases in global income and in levels of international trade in both goods and services. Many protective barriers have been removed or reduced, such that competition between nations and companies is, by and large, more fierce than in previous decades. It is now important for companies and governments to consider the level of national and regional competitiveness. Undoubtedly, some countries enjoy political, social, technological and economic advantages which encourage multinational, transnational or truly global companies to invest in them. A number of organisations and researchers have attempted to calculate national competitiveness and produce 'league tables'. They consider such things as average wage rates, workforce skills and capabilities, income and corporation tax rates and the degree of political stability (see the Case Study 3 in Part II).

Many individuals, groups and organisations in most countries argue that government should play a major part in attempting to maintain or improve their national competitiveness. By so doing they may facilitate the achievement of comfortable economic growth rates, better and secure employment opportunities and improvements in standards of living. Although most governments actively pursue policies which they believe will enhance the competitiveness of their country and its organisations, there is considerable disagreement on how best to achieve this aim. Some argue for a heavily 'interventionist' policy in which government plays a major role, for example, by directly investing in industry, providing training, building state-of-the-art infrastructure and facilitating international trade. Conversely, other arguments favour a more laissez-faire approach, such as was traditionally the case in the USA or Hong Kong and, since the 1980s, in the UK. Broadly, government's role in this scenario is to 'free' private enterprise from many 'constraints', such as high social costs and taxes, and to allow it to compete in free markets. Government does not significantly intervene, for example, to develop national industry or transport policies or to invest directly in industry.

Both broad schools of thought can claim successes. The USA and Hong Kong, for example, flourished by adopting a predominantly laissez-faire approach, while Singapore and Japan have experienced very rapid economic growth in the past thirty years, despite short-term setbacks, in part, it is argued, by active government interventionist policies. Whatever one's views, it is clear that national and/or regional competitiveness is increasingly becoming an important determinant of the material well-being of a population. Consequently, government has an obligation to its citizens to ensure they share in global successes.

Technological change

Technological change has a significant influence over economic growth. Government, therefore, has a role to play in the development of conditions suitable for technological advances to be made and transformed into economic wealth-creating opportunities. The approach governments adopt will largely depend on their ideological stance, as indicated above. One government may, for example, invest a significant element of revenue collected from taxation into research which might lead to economic wealth-creating opportunities largely for private industry. Another may prefer to allow market mechanisms to dictate research and development spending levels within industry. Clearly, the role of government, although crucial, varies considerably across the world.

It is reported, for example, that in Hong Kong multinational organisations have for decades been invited to invest, irrespective of the technological benefits they might bring to the province. However, the Singaporean government have been somewhat more vigilant and active in encouraging companies which bring transferable technological advances to their country.

In addition to creating the 'right' conditions for technological development and diffusion, government also has a regulatory role to perform. This role may involve prohibiting, or otherwise regulating, potentially unethical research and technological development. Many countries are currently debating issues concerning the advances in genetic engineering which have been made in recent years. There are important and far-reaching ethical consequences of many technological advances. Although self-regulation, by researchers and professional bodies for example, is important, many people expect governments to adopt an ideological and regulatory stance in this regard.

Flexible working and the role of government

The role of government in broad employment issues is multi-faceted. Beardwell and Holden (1994) argue that government policy needs to reflect the dynamism shown in employment changes. However, there are a number of highly contentious issues associated with flexible working. For example, centre-right government policy in the UK may favour a reduction in the legal restrictions on the hiring and dismissal of workers, which would most certainly increase flexibility. However, this would have significant, often harmful, consequences for many groups and individuals. Beardwell and Holden also suggest that government might remove all state intervention in pay setting and further extend the law to curb trade union influence over pay and employment. These measures were promoted by Conservative governments in the 1980s and 1990s. However, these policies often conflict with European Union legislation, which favours a statutory minimum wage and protection for workers, and takes a more interventionist, less free-market, approach. Additionally, the Labour government in the UK have introduced a minimum wage, albeit at a low level, and are 'mixed' in their support for the more focused pursuit of 'flexibility'. The introduction of new employment rights in 1999 suggested some attempt is being made to achieve a compromise between family-friendly policies and the perceived needs of industry. Nevertheless, for two decades in the UK, government departments have largely promoted greater labour market flexibility, both in White Papers such as *The Challenge for the Nation* (1985) and *People, Jobs and Opportunity* (1992), and in various policy initiatives.

Changes in employment and career patterns have important and far-reaching consequences for pension provision and some welfare payments. The government in the UK has responded to long-term change by increasing the age of retirement for women to 65 years, to match that for men, by strongly encouraging employees to take out additional private personal pension provision and by introducing new compulsory pension savings schemes. With an ageing population and increasing long-term unemployment, government fears the rising burden of pension and welfare demands upon the public purse.

Role of government

There has been a tendency in many countries in the 1980s and 1990s for governments to move away from direct provision of goods and services and towards a focus on regulating more and producing less. The range of mechanisms which government in the UK employed in the 1980s and 19890s included

- privatisation;
- deregulation;
- contracting-out public sector services;
- quality charters, league tables and published performance targets;
- performance management and performance-related pay;

- more effective complaints procedures;
- tougher and more independent inspectorates;
- better redress for the citizen when things go wrong; and
- private/public sector financial partnerships.

The Conservative government in the mid 1990s, and the Labour Party both in opposition and in government since 1997, conducted 'fundamental' reviews of current and likely future government expenditure. They have addressed some highly sensitive issues, such as welfare spending, and have identified areas where spending cuts may be made. The Labour government are addressing some controversial issues and the eventual outcomes for the nation will depend on the 'complexion' of the government(s) in power in the next decade and beyond and their resolve in dealing with these issues.

A reduction in the role of government will involve significant cuts in public expenditure. However, reining back growth in government expenditure is fraught with difficulties. There is considerable inertia from a series of built-in mechanisms which ensure future government commitment. For example, the rapid growth in higher education, seen as essential if the UK is to compete in the global economy, has meant that government has had to increase expenditure in this area. The expectation will be for even greater numbers to experience higher education. Additionally, the criminal justice system saw increases in the prison population during the 1990s, with consequent increases in government expenditure in part as a result of rising crime rates, but also due to 'get-tough' government policies. Governments, especially in the old Western industrialised world, are increasingly concerned about the long-term social and financial costs of unemployment. An ageing population continues to put increased demands upon the NHS and welfare system, necessitating increased government expenditure.

It is estimated that improvements in life expectancy and medical care, combined with changing demographic factors, will mean that long-term care for the aged in the year 2005 may account for up to 11 per cent of the GDP of the UK compared to a figure of just 7 per cent of GDP for the whole of the NHS in 1995 (source: evidence presented to Royal Commission on care for the aged, 1998). The government of the UK spends about £90 billion on social security and a further £36 billion on health. Together this amounts to over 38 per cent of government expenditure. Figure 9.3 illustrates government expenditure in the late 1990s.

Despite the 'radical' changes that have occurred within the public sector, such as privatisation and compulsory competitive tendering, the fact remains that the burden of taxation and the scale of the public sector have not declined. In large part this is because of the rise in welfare demands, including unemployment and housing benefits, social security payments, pensions and increases in health care costs.

The problem of potentially spiralling demands upon the public purse is certainly not unique to the UK. Many European Union countries experienced alarmingly rapid increases in government expenditure during the 1980s and 1990s and were

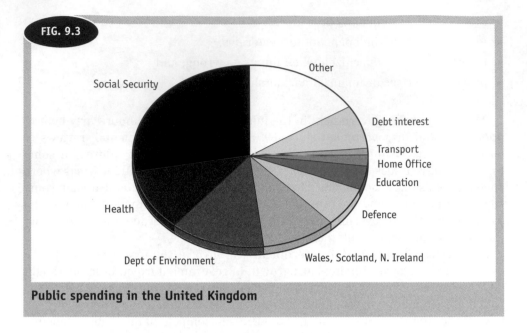

FIG. 9.3

Social Security · Other · Debt interest · Transport · Home Office · Education · Defence · Wales, Scotland, N. Ireland · Dept of Environment · Health

Public spending in the United Kingdom

obliged to reduce expenditure in order to qualify for first-wave Euro membership in 1999. Business leaders, employee representative bodies, right-wing think-tanks and politicians frequently call for major reform.

Many, especially those on the right of mainstream politics, argue for a fundamental rethink of the role of the state. Duncan and Hobson (1995) suggest that

> *after a decade and a half of cuts public expenditure is higher than at any time since the war. The burden of taxation is heavier than it was in 1979. One in every five workers is still employed by the state. There are more officials and regulators and policemen, enforcing more laws and more regulations, than in any previous era.*

They outline a controversial thesis concerning the role of government. This may involve substantial and truly radical changes to government social welfare policies and the scaling-down of the role of the state. Measures might include the privatisation of the national health and education services, deregulation in all walks of life, rejection of EU controls, and an end to many state old age pensions, sickness, housing and unemployment benefits. However, because of the enormous hardship, and subsequent outcry, such changes would create, and the potentially catastrophic consequences for society that might ensue, change of this nature is unlikely to occur, especially as public opinion is divided already concerning the success or otherwise of previous public sector reforms.

There are alternative ideologies. For example, a recent emphasis on one-nation politics by the Labour and Liberal Democratic parties advocates greater emphasis on financial, political and social equality. Such ideologies may reflect in policies which seek to maintain state welfare, education and health care provision at 'satisfactory' levels. Services may be increasingly paid by steady increases in taxation which might, in particular, be levied on high-income groups.

However, change is omnipresent and environmental flux within the broader public sector is a reality which faces all employees, politicians and members of the public. Environmental change will ensure that public organisations will be called upon to change, sometimes radically, and the role of government in the economy will remain a contemporary issue for the foreseeable future.

QUESTIONS

1. Discuss the opposing ideological positions concerning the role of government in encouraging national competitiveness and technological development.

2. Identify the 'winners' and 'losers' if the UK government were to radically reduce expenditure and taxation.

3. What are the arguments for and against (a) reducing, and (b) increasing, welfare expenditure in real terms?

CONCLUSION

In this chapter we have focused on many of the environmental factors outlined in this text and on the increasing dynamism and uncertainty in the environment. We then explored the implications of this for organisations, groups, individuals and governments.

We have tried to resist the temptation to predict the future and have concentrated on examining currently developing trends which we expect to continue to have a significant impact. In so doing we hope to have created a book which does not date too quickly, at least in its main thrust. The tendency with much factual data, however, is for it to become obsolete very quickly. This will, undoubtedly, mean that when you read this book there will be some points which no longer hold true. For this reason we trust that the most lasting impact of the book will be on the processes which you use to examine the business environment.

In respect of these processes we have placed strong emphasis on ways of evaluating the business environment. For example, we have stressed the importance of examining problems at a range of geo-political scales, that is, from international, through regional and national to local perspectives. It seems to us that a business environment textbook cannot confine itself to examining environmental factors at any one of these levels. We have also indicated that the methods which organisations adopt to monitor their environments will, to a large extent, influence both what is seen and whether changes are perceived as opportunities or threats. We have used the phrase 'perceptual filters' to describe this process. This, intentionally, placed the emphasis upon the human side of organisational activity.

SUMMARY OF MAIN POINTS

This chapter has focused upon the nature of change in the business environment and organisational, individual, group and government responses to environmental dynamism. The main points made are:

- The business environment is increasingly complex, dynamic, uncertain (turbulent) and even chaotic for many organisations, individuals, groups and governments.

- Major economic, political, technological and social changes have transformed the business environment in the last two decades, necessitating organisational change and increased flexibility.

- There may be a trend towards high profile 'shock events' and non-linear chaotic patterns in many areas of the natural world (to some extent such patterns are also observable in the business world) which suggests that organisations might do well to make contingency plans.

- The nature of the business environment calls into question the validity of organisational approaches to long-term planning and suggests the need for processes which build in flexibility and adaptability.

- There has been a rapid increase in previously considered 'non-standard' temporal and contractual patterns of work such as part-time work, teleworking, contracting-out, self-employment and temporary work.

- The position of many young people in the UK shows alarmingly large proportions are 'disconnected' from both the political system and from their local communities.

- Turbulent environments demand government attention.

- The future role of government is likely to remain a fiercely debated issue for some time.

REFERENCES

Beardwell, I. and Holden, L. (1994) *Human Resource Management: A Contemporary Perspective*, Pitman.

Bridges, W. (1995) 'The death of the job', *Independent on Sunday*, 5 February.

Brindle, D. (1998) 'Teachers get more class in social shake-up', *Guardian*, 1 December.

Burns, T. and Stalker, G.M. (1961) *The Management of Innovation*, London: Tavistock.

Cole, G.A. (1993) *Personnel Management*, 3rd edn, DPP.

Curson, C. (ed.) (1986) *Flexible Patterns of Work*, IPM.

Davidow, W.H. and Malone, M.S. (1992) *The Virtual Corporation: Structuring and Revitalizing the Corporation for the 21st Century*, Harper Business.

Dickson, T. (1995) 'The fight against "Exclusion" – European corporate initiatives to help the long-term unemployed', *Financial Times*, 8 May.

Duncan, A. and Hobson, D. (1995) *Saturn's Children*, Sinclair-Stevenson.

Evans P. (1998) 'Why has the female unemployment rate in Britain fallen?', *Bank of England Quarterly Bulletin*, 38(3), August.

Flexible Working Patterns in Europe (1993), Issues in People Management No. 6, IPM.

Gleick, J. (1988) *Chaos: Making a New Science*, Cardinal.

Handy, C. (1989) *The Age of Unreason*, Arrow.

Handy, C. (1994) *The Empty Raincoat*, Hutchinson.

Hutton, W. (1995) 'High risk strategy', *Guardian*, 30 October.

Jaques, M. (1997) 'The melting pot that is born-again Britannia', *Observer*, 28 December.

Johnson, G. and Scholes, K. (1999) *Exploring Corporate Strategy*, Prentice Hall.

Miles, R.E. (1980) *Macro Organisational Behaviour*, Sutt Foresman & Co.

Miles, R.E. and Snow, C.C. (1978) *Organisational Strategy, Structure and Process*, New York: McGraw-Hill.

Mintzberg, H. (1994) *The Rise and Fall of Strategic Planning*, New York: Prentice Hall.

Moore, S. (1995) 'Beware of dances with underwolves', *Guardian 2*, 28 September.

Pawley, M. (1974) *The Private Future*, Pan.

Perrow, C. (1986) *Complex Organisations: A Critical Essay*, 3rd edn, New York: Random House.

Pollert, A. (1991) *Farewell to Flexibility?*, Blackwell.

Quinn, J.B. (1978) 'Strategic change: logical incrementalism', *Sloan Management Review*, Fall.

Quinn, J.B. (1992) *Intelligent Enterprise*, The Free Press.

Richardson, B. and Richardson, R. (1992) *Business Planning: An Approach to Strategic Management*, Pitman.

Schor, J.B. (1992) *The Overworked American*, New York: Basic Books.

Stacey, R.D. (1996) *Strategic Management and Organisational Dynamics*, Pitman.

Stanworth, J. and Stanworth, C. (1992) *Telework: The Human Resource Implications*, IPM.

Stevenson, H.H. and Moldoveanu, M.C. (1995) 'The power of predictability', *Harvard Business Review*, July–August.

Toffler, A. (1985) *The Adaptive Corporation*, Pan.

Wintour, P. (1997) 'Ghetto busters to tackle poverty in can-do mood', *Observer*, 7 December.

CASE STUDIES

INTRODUCTION

The nine cases which form Part II of this book illustrate aspects of the business environment. They have been carefully selected to include an array of organisational types and operating environments. They comprise three commercial companies, a government service organisation, a higher education institution, three industries or sectors and an international region. Three of the cases are ostensibly concerned with international organisations and/or issues.

The table below indicates the relationship between each chapter in Part I and the case studies in Part II and uses the following guidelines:

* = minor relevance   ** = significant relevance   *** = prime focus.

Each case study includes a number of questions. It may prove beneficial to refer to the relevant chapter(s) when answering them.

Indication of Case Studies' relationship with chapters

Case Studies	Chapters in Part I						
	2	3	4	5	6	7	8
Case Study 1: Growth and dynamism in higher education: the case of University College Northampton		*		**		***	***
Case Study 2: Unilever	*	*		*	***	*	
Case Study 3: South-East Asia: boom to bust	*	***	*	**		*	
Case Study 4: Europe's largest employer: the National Health Service	*	*	*	**		**	***
Case Study 5: HP Bulmer Holdings PLC: living with new realities	***			**			
Case Study 6: Environment and competition: the case of Scania	**	*	**	*	***	**	
Case Study 7: Book retailing: the storm after the calm	**	*	**	*		*	
Case Study 8: Responses to change in the business environment: the case of Rugby League football	***		*	**		*	
Case Study 9: The hotel industry: an Anglo-French perspective	**	**	*	**		*	

GROWTH AND DYNAMISM IN HIGHER EDUCATION

THE CASE OF UNIVERSITY COLLEGE NORTHAMPTON

Diane Hayes

This case study uses one higher education institution in the UK to illustrate the impact of government policy. As well as the political and legal environment, the case highlights social and economic factors behind the growth in higher education from the late 1980s to the late 1990s thus demonstrating the dynamism of the business environment.

A decade of change

The environment within which higher education institutions operate has been subject to radical change over the period 1988 to 1998. This is amply illustrated by the development of Nene College in Northampton over that period.

In 1988 Nene College offered both further and higher education courses in a range of subject areas from the purely academic to the vocational crafts. Students ranged from age 16, through all levels to mature postgraduates. At the time there were approximately 4000 full-time equivalent students. Higher education (HE) is defined as post-A-level courses for the 18+ population and further education (FE) is defined as academic and vocational courses for the post-16 population.

In early 1999 the same institution received confirmation, from the Privy Council, of change of legal title to University College Northampton (UCN). It now concentrates almost exclusively on higher education courses and has approximately 9000 full-time equivalent students. The buildings and resource provision, and the staff numbers and job roles, have undergone major change. This transformation was brought about by a number of key developments nationally. There have been changes in legislation; in government policy towards higher education; in economic and workforce factors; and a doubling of the numbers of 18-year-olds entering higher education.

The impact of legislation

Until 1989 the colleges and polytechnics of the UK had been under the control of local education authorities (LEAs). Nene College (as it then was) was the responsibility of Northamptonshire County Council and its LEA. The LEA was responsible for the 'general character of the College' and it delegated its direct running to a Board of Governors, on which the LEA were well represented, and to the Director of the College. These powers were enshrined in the Education (No 2) Act 1968.

The Education Reform Act of 1988 determined that the colleges of higher education and the polytechnics would come out of local authority control and would become higher education corporations with newly constituted Boards of Governors, and Directors as chief executives, becoming more responsible for their own running and accountable directly to a new national funding body and the Secretary of State responsible for education.

Another piece of legislation, the Further and Higher Education Act passed in 1992, transformed the polytechnics into universities by giving the Privy Council powers to specify that an institution is competent to award degrees. Previously the polytechnics had awarded degrees of the Council for National Academic Awards (CNAA). From this point they were given powers to award their own degrees. Nene College had not sought institutional validation from CNAA but instead had a long-standing validation association with the University of Leicester. Nene students on most degree and postgraduate programmes were registered for University of Leicester awards.

In 1992, therefore, the category of polytechnic disappeared from the higher education scene in England and a new national funding council came into being – the Higher Education Funding Council England (HEFCE) – set up to manage the funding distribution to 135 higher education institutions and to 72 further education colleges that provide higher education courses (number of institutions as at 1998/99). At the same time as the polytechnics were given university title, criteria were established for colleges to apply for taught degree awarding powers and for research degree awarding powers and thereafter for university status. In 1993 Nene College applied for taught degree awarding powers. In November 1993, following an assessment process conducted by the Higher Education Quality Council, the Privy Council granted Nene College the power to award its own taught Bachelors and Masters degrees (BA, BSc, MA, MSc). The college continued to register some students for Leicester University research degrees (PhD, MPhil). It was expected that, when the college met the criteria laid down for research degree awarding powers, application would be made and thereafter progression on to full university status.

In the period since the 1992 Act, only one college has achieved university status. The University of Luton achieved the status change in 1993. Since then no further new universities have been created. The title issue received attention from the Government's National Committee of Inquiry into Higher Education, chaired by Sir Ron Dearing, which reported in 1997. Amongst 93 recommendations was one which referred to confusion of title and name, and recommended government action to end the scope for confusion. Behind this was the move by a number of colleges which offer higher education courses to use the designation 'University College'. Some of these colleges were mainly further education colleges offering a limited number of higher education courses, hence the potential for confusion. Government subsequently took up this recommendation and in the 1998 Teaching and Higher Education Act defined the title 'University College' as one which could legally be used by institutions that had degree awarding powers, or institutions that were fully part of a university. This legislation therefore created a legally defined category of university college.

The confusion up to this point had been around the meaning of the term college and of the description 'University College' or UCN. UCN is in competition with universities for students. The descriptor 'College' is most likely to be associated with further education providers. Some colleges which offered higher education courses, some of them with few 'university-like' characteristics, had used the designation University College for marketing purposes, presumably in the hope of attracting more students than would be the case by merely using the 'College' designation. Nene College deliberately chose not to take up an unauthorised title, recognising that not doing so might have some negative short-term effect on student recruitment.

Courses and students at Nene in 1988

Nene College was, at the time of the passing of the 1988 Education Reform Act, one of the larger colleges of higher education which had a mixed economy providing both higher and further education courses. The criteria for becoming incorporated, and hence obtaining significant freedom over future direction and management of finances, were related to size of HE student population, spread of activity, and the proportion of the HE students amongst the whole student population in the college. Those colleges meeting the criteria (of which Nene College was one) were funded from 1989 by a new national body, the Polytechnics and Colleges Funding Council (PCFC), the precursor of the HEFCE. The spread of activities at Nene College in 1988 are shown in Table C1.1. In 1988 the College had a 3:5 ratio of FE to HE and a 1:1 ratio of part-time students to full-time students.

At the time of incorporation the College had two main campuses, 2.3 miles apart. The older campus, Avenue Campus, opened in 1932, accommodated most of the further education work, particularly in art and design and in technology, including construction. The buildings on that campus are typical of the era – large, solidly built, with high ceilings and long corridors, expensive to heat and harder to maintain. The other campus, Park Campus, dates from 1972. It is on the outskirts of the town and had in 1988 mainly smaller, single-storey, flat-roofed buildings, of attractive but basic construction, not well maintained, set in a green campus with a lot of open space.

TABLE C1.1   Nene College: spread of activities by main subject area in 1988

| | Full-time equivalent student numbers | | | |
| | FE | | HE | |
	Part-time	Full-time	Part-time	Full-time
Art and design	84	169	0	103
Education and social science	64	0	210	693
Humanities	61	0	0	225
Management and business	284	31	297	373
Science	106	11	55	240
Technology	567	123	280	51
	1166	334	842	1685
				Total = 4027

In 1989 Nene College had a turnover of approximately £14 million, of which

- £6 million came as a grant from PCFC to fund the HE courses;
- £3.6 million from the contract with the LEA to deliver FE;
- £1.8 million from fees paid by students;
- the remainder being generated from other activities such as short courses, residential operations and catering.

Approximately 37 per cent of the student population were studying on further education courses, with nearly half of those on courses related to technology and construction. The 1685 full-time higher education students were recruited from across the UK with 21.6 per cent coming from Northamptonshire. By contrast it would be expected that the part-time HE and all FE students would be recruited from a largely local market. At that time Nene College had 200 residential places in halls of residence on Park Campus.

It is interesting to compare this data with that of ten years later.

Courses and students at Nene in 1998

Over the period 1988 to 1998 Nene College has grown substantially. By the latter year, turnover was of the order of £36 million:

- £17 million came from HE funding council grants (including teacher training);
- £1 million from the FE funding council;
- £12 million from fees paid by students;
- the remainder from other income-generating activities.

The course portfolio has developed to meet changing demand. The number of students on higher education courses has grown from 2527 full-time equivalents in 1988 to 8607 in 1998. There are now only 390 full-time equivalent students on further education courses compared with 1500 in 1988. This reduction was the result of a strategic decision to focus on higher education and to develop partnership arrangements with local FE colleges.

Of the full-time HE students, 77.2 per cent were recruited from outside Northamptonshire in 1997–98. The proportion of national recruitment is much the same as it was in 1988 but the absolute numbers have changed significantly. In 1988 just over 1300 students were non-local and on full-time courses, in 1998 the number is approximately 5800. Many of these will be renting accommodation on or off campus.

The 1988 Education Reform Act, coupled with the expansionist policy towards higher education of successive Conservative governments, signalled a period of transformation for Nene College. The physical infrastructure has been developed and upgraded. New buildings have been constructed on both campuses but mainly at Park Campus because of the availability of building space on that site. Teaching accommodation, shops, offices, a much expanded library, an IT centre, a restaurant, and a Senate building provide facilities for the working lives of UCN staff and students whilst there are now 1565 places in halls of residence to cater for the needs of students, mainly first-year students, who want to live on campus.

The change in student numbers and in the areas of curriculum is demonstrated in Table C1.2. We can see that the significant areas of development have been in

- management and business, including computing;
- humanities, including performance arts;
- art and design;

TABLE C1.2   Nene College: spread of activities by main subject area in 1998

| | Full-time equivalent student numbers | | | |
| | FE | | HE | |
	Part-time	Full-time	Part-time	Full-time
Art and design	0	131	9	551
Education	0	0	177	786
Social science including sport studies	0	0	28	1002
Humanities including performance arts	24	0	48	1050
Management and business	28	0	478	1694
Science including environmental science	0	0	7	361
Applied technology and applied design	163	12	157	373
Maths and computing	0	0	72	609
Health	32	0	171	1034
	247	143	1147	7460
				Total = 8997

- social science; and
- health, i.e. the professions allied to medicine, including nursing (particularly as a result of mergers with schools of nursing and other professions).

Numbers in technology and construction have declined in line with national trends, whereas student numbers for education courses have been more or less static.

Government policy

In the 1970s there were approximately 450 000 students studying HE courses in the UK (not counting students from overseas). During the 1980s these numbers grew fairly slowly to about 550 000, but from the beginning of the 1990s government policy triggered a period of great expansion. The aim of the policy was to increase participation in higher education so that by the end of the 1990s approximately a third of the cohort of 18-year-olds in any one year would enter higher education. Previously participation was around the 15 per cent level. Expansion was encouraged by the greater financial freedom given to the HE colleges and polytechnics by the 1988 Act. Planning controls on the development of new courses were taken away, and institutions had freedom to develop their individual mission statements and to produce expansionist strategic plans. HE institutions were funded on a per student basis, with a portion of the funding being in the form of a 'fee' paid by the student or by his/her LEA. Whilst the total unit of funding per student did not increase in the early 1990s, the 'fee' element increased as a proportion of whole unit of funding. Also, institutions were able to bid for extra student numbers on a competitive price basis. The greater importance of fees made recruitment over and above the contract numbers financially worthwhile. Whilst the increases in student numbers were funded by HEFCE, there was at the same time a gradual reduction in the unit funding per student as the government sought efficiency gains. In real terms, there has been a 40 per cent unit cost reduction in the grant to HE institutions from HEFCE over the twenty years to 1999.

The universities, polytechnics and colleges were very successful in recruiting more students to make government policy a reality. The expansion was so successful, in fact, that the objective set by the government in the early 1990s, of a one-third participation rate by the year 2000, had already been reached by the mid 1990s. By 1995, more than 1 million UK students were studying on higher education courses. There were other factors which aided expansion. Up to the 1990s, nurses had been trained in hospitals, where they achieved registered professional status whilst working as employees of the NHS and doing much of their training 'on-the-job'. Now all courses for first registration are operated by universities and higher education colleges via a contract with health authorities. Students on these courses are no longer employees of the NHS. They study for an academic award at the same time as gaining professional registration; and spend more time in the classroom than they did previously. UCN now has a large Centre for Healthcare Education which runs courses for nurses as well as other professions supplementary to medicine.

The economic factors

Another factor which fuelled expansion in the early 1990s was the economic recession in the UK, coupled with changes in the demand for different skills and qualifications. The workforce was becoming more skilled and more likely to be employed in the service sector rather than in manufacturing. The information technology revolution also meant that many of the jobs which school-leavers might have done ten, fifteen or twenty years ago were disappearing.

UCN is situated in an area that has been economically buoyant for thirty years. The County of Northamptonshire has had a growing population during that period and has developed many new employment opportunities. Unemployment is low. In July 1997 the unemployment rate for Northamptonshire was 3.6 per cent compared with 5.6 per cent for the UK as a whole. There is still a relative bias towards the manufacturing sector, by comparison with the UK as a whole. Nearly a third of output and a quarter of residents in employment are associated with manufacturing industries.

Northamptonshire currently has

- a rapid economic growth rate, annual growth in GDP 4.5 per cent from 1981 to 1991 compared with 2.4 per cent average UK rate; and predicted to be 3.2 per cent from 1995 to 2000 compared with a national average of 2.6 per cent;
- significant inward investment from the London area;
- significant net in-migration of population;
- relatively low unemployment levels.

Apart from manufacturing, the largest categories of employment are in distribution, hotels and catering, and public administration, education and health. Substantial numbers are employed in banking, finance and insurance. In comparison with the national picture Northamptonshire has relatively more people employed in manufacturing, distribution, hotels and restaurants. On a regional basis there are more people employed in banking, finance and insurance, and transport and communications.

In the county of Northamptonshire, UCN is the only major provider of higher education. The nearest major competitors are Coventry University, Leicester University, Leicester De Montfort University and Anglia Polytechnic University at Cambridge, all of which are more than 25 miles from Northampton.

A decision was made in 1992 to transfer most of the further education courses to local FE colleges. At a time of significant expansion of HE provision, this transfer was done to free resources for the additional degree students and to enable Nene College to concentrate on its major area of activity in the belief that a university is primarily about higher education. The reduction of income from FE contracts was compensated for by an increase in HE income. The small number of FE courses that are retained are in specialist areas. The emphasis on higher education has helped Nene College to offer more postgraduate courses and to develop research activity and income.

Assessment of performance

Prior to 1989 colleges and polytechnics were subject to inspection by Her Majesty's Inspectors (HMI). This system, run by the government's Department for Education, was similar to that operating in schools. Colleges and polytechnics which were validated by CNAA were subject to quite heavy scrutiny by that body. This covered all validated courses and institutional issues. Colleges like Nene, which was validated by the University of Leicester, were subject to monitoring by their validating university.

In the 1990s, with the creation of many more universities by the 1992 Further and Higher Education Act, and the demise of CNAA, a quality assurance 'industry' has grown up in higher education. Successive governments have been wary of accusations of falling standards and of dumbing-down of degrees. These accusations are frequently made by those people who are not fully persuaded by the case for the policy of expansion of participation in HE.

Universities and colleges of higher education have developed internal systems of quality assurance:

- validation of new courses;
- annual review of courses;
- student course evaluation;
- involvement of employers in evaluation and review;
- monitoring of performance.

There are many parties interested in the performance of universities:

- students themselves want to have a worthwhile experience and achieve as good a degree as possible;
- the government wants value for money for its expenditure;
- employers want a supply of suitably educated new recruits, and want to be able to send employees back to university for continuous development and updating;
- parents may be paying for their offspring's time in HE.

The internal quality assurance system of a university is backed up by external peer review. Individual fellow academics are used to quality assure new developments and, in the process of review, external examiners are used in all courses to assess the standard of students' assessed work and to ensure that standards are linked nationally across universities. The system that has developed demands that on a cycle of approximately five years, each subject area is subject to significant external scrutiny by a team of assessors; on a similar five-yearly cycle, institutional systems and procedures are tested by an audit team.

These quality processes put a heavy demand on staff, both academic and administrative. Staff employed in quality assurance units have grown in numbers.

This is only one of the areas of growth. In 1988 Nene College had only a small number of professionally qualified support staff and higher grade administrators. Up to then many of the necessary professional functions were carried out by the LEA. Over the ten years since then another change that has been seen has been in the development of professional support functions: marketing, personnel, finance, as well as academic registry and quality assurance, are all areas that needed to be developed. One of the benefits of growth, and of the level of turnover as it currently stands, is the ability to fund an infrastructure appropriate to a university. That infrastructure includes necessary support functions as well as the buildings to house the growing operations.

UCN – 1998 onwards

A new era for higher education began in 1998 with the introduction of fees for full-time undergraduate courses. Prior to this most people gaining places on full-time higher education courses, at diploma or first degree level, had fees paid on their behalf by their LEA, regardless of their individual circumstances. The new Labour government, coming into office in 1997, decided that individuals should directly contribute towards the costs of higher education if their income, or their parents' income, was above a certain level. In 1998 a fee of £1000 per year was set and LEAs given the job of assessing individual applicants as to whether they should pay all of or part of that fee. It was generally expected that LEAs would pay the whole fee for about a third of applicants; part of the fee for about another third; and to decide that the final third were responsible for their own full fee.

There were many predictions of the impact this fee introduction would have on higher education in general and on individual institutions in particular. It may encourage more students to study nearer to home to reduce their living costs whilst studying. It appears to be having an impact on the number of mature students applying for degree courses. It may mean that more students choose to study part-time and work while they study. It is very likely to make students more conscious of 'value for money', and more discriminating between institutions.

Higher education is a competitive business. Institutions spend money on marketing and promotion, aiming to be one of the six choices on the intending undergraduate's UCAS form. Marketing must be backed by real assets valued by applicants. These assets would include

- the courses that they want to study;
- good facilities for study;
- living accommodation, social facilities, and 'student life';
- a marketable qualification.

University College Northampton in 1999 is a very different institution to Nene College in 1988.

QUESTIONS

1. Using library and other information sources, compare the participation rate of UK school-leavers in higher education with those from the United States, France, Germany and Japan. What links are made between participation rate and indicators of economic success?

2. Identify four environmental variables that may effect UCN in the next ten years. Choose two competitor universities and conduct an impact analysis for those and UCN.

3. Who are currently the stakeholders of UCN? What is their relative power? Repeat the analysis for Nene College in 1988 and compare the two.

2

UNILEVER

Jamie Weatherston

Unilever operates in more than 90 countries and employs nearly 270 000 people. In 1997 worldwide sales were over £29 billion. It invests approximately £550 million in research and development and spends £3.6 billion a year marketing more than 1000 brands. One of the company's key organisational objectives is to become world class; this includes the way it manages the environmental impact of operations and products. Unilever was one of the first companies to commit to a wide range of environmental practices and published its ecological charter in 1990. It is committed to report publicly every two years on environmental performance. The reporting procedures are verified at different levels by independent experts.

An executive committee is responsible for the group's overall strategic leadership. The company is organised into twelve business groups, which develop regional strategies. Each group has its own chief executive. Unilever's products fall into three main categories:

- food products (five categories);
- home cleaning and personal care products (eight categories);
- professional cleaning under DiverseyLever.

Well known names in its portfolio include Wall's, Bird's Eye, Brooke Bond, Timotei, Calvin Klein cosmetics and Persil. Turnover by region and by product is shown in Figure C2.1.

Pressure from many quarters is mounting on industry to act to reduce its environmental impact. John Sharpe, in the *Lever and the Environment Review* of 1995/96, said, 'The environment is a top priority for Lever today. It is essential for

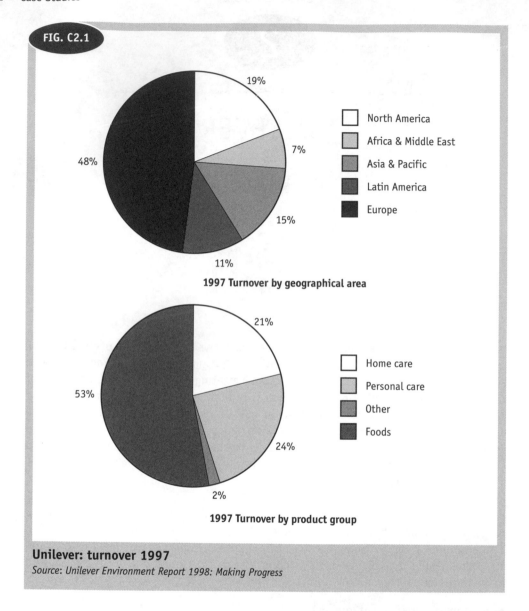

FIG. C2.1

19%

7%

48%

15%

11%

North America

Africa & Middle East

Asia & Pacific

Latin America

Europe

1997 Turnover by geographical area

21%

53%

24%

2%

Home care

Personal care

Other

Foods

1997 Turnover by product group

Unilever: turnover 1997
Source: Unilever Environment Report 1998: Making Progress

our success in the future that we deliver environmental progress as well as business progress.' Unilever recognises that if it is to maintain its growth and safeguard shareholders' interests it needs to find new, more sustainable ways of meeting customer needs. The company has achieved some measure of success. In 1996 Unilever was ranked eighth in terms of eco-performance in the Hamburger Umweltinstitut e.V. review. During the first quarter of 1996 each product category developed and agreed an environmental plan detailing their overall environmental objectives and highlighting priority areas to be tackled. Figure C2.2 shows the progress that Lever Europe has made in waste disposal and recycling.

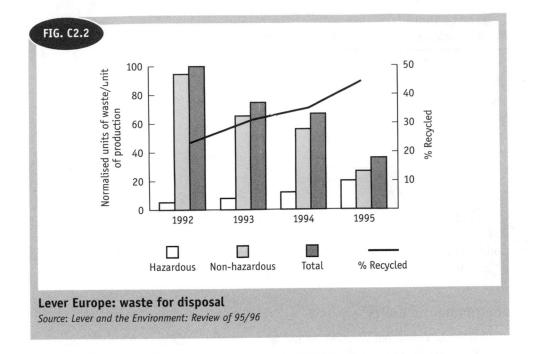

Lever Europe: waste for disposal
Source: Lever and the Environment: Review of 95/96

Although the number of initiatives is substantial, it is evident that a number of negative externalities result from business activity. Unilever does, for example, contribute to photochemical smog which results from the reaction of certain gases, in the presence of sunlight, to form ground-level ozone, which is a component of smog. Some of these gases are used in personal care products, e.g. aerosols, although they form a very small part of overall world emissions. Nutrification, the release of nutrients, such as phosphorous, nitrogen and organic carbon compounds, to surface waters, which can lead to over-fertilisation, is also a problem. Nutrification arises from the use of phosphates in laundry products and fertilisers. The Norfolk Broads have been severely affected by nutrient enrichment from sewage and agriculture. Environmental performance is being continuously monitored and measured. Unit loads for the year 1995/96 were:

- Chemical Oxygen Demand (COD) in waste-water – down;
- hazardous waste – up;
- non-hazardous waste – down;
- water use – down;
- energy use – steady, after rising;
- sulphur emissions – down;
- compliance – penalties down.

Table C2.1 summarises the penalties incurred for infringement of environmental regulations during 1993–96. The number of penalties incurred has fallen.

TABLE C2.1   Unilever:
Manufacturing environmental performance: compliance

Year	Number of sites	Number of fines	Total fines (£)
1993	407	25	53 534
1994	408	24	94 072
1995	444	16	203 641
1996	506	9	74 005

Source: Unilever Environment Report 1998: Making Progress

To build on its successes Unilever aims to bring the environment to the core of business activities. Unilever is a signatory of the International Chamber of Commerce Charter on Sustainable Development. The Charter has helped to guide its global environment policy and strategy.

Environmental policy

Unilever is committed to meeting the needs of customers and consumers in an environmentally sound and sustainable manner, through continuous improvement in environmental performance in all our activities.

Accordingly, Unilever's aims are:

- to ensure the safety of its products and operations for the environment;
- the same concern for the environment wherever it operates;
- innovative products and processes which reduce levels of environmental impact; developing methods of packaging which combine effective presentation with the conservation of raw materials and convenient, environmentally appropriate disposal;
- to reduce waste, conserve energy and explore opportunities for reuse and recycling.

Life cycle assessment

Life cycle assessment helps to identify and quantify areas of highest potential impact and so enable targeting of areas where action can be taken most effectively to make the most significant improvements. Unilever has identified three sections on which to concentrate.

1. Supply chain. Understanding their impact on the environment from raw material production to final product disposal.
2. Manufacturing. Implementing environmental management systems standards through training, auditing and target setting.

3. Consumption. Working with others to find new ways to meet consumers' needs sustainably.

The food business has adapted this approach to assess its own potential environmental effects. Three broad areas within the complete product life cycle are considered:

- production of raw materials (mainly farming and fishing);
- manufacture and distribution of goods;
- consumption of products.

Unilever recognises that it has direct control during the manufacturing stage, where water consumption and organic matter in waste-waters are key areas to manage, and is committed to reduce their overall impact. However, studies have shown that the use and consumption of their products have far more potential to affect the environment. Unilever is particularly concerned about excess amounts of nutrients which are introduced into the environment when fertilisers are used inefficiently in farming.

In the home cleaning and personal care division, energy used in both the manufacture and use of laundry detergents is a key factor to be considered because it contributes to global warming and the formation of acid rain. The division considers the reduction of energy consumption as especially important in those parts of the world where washing machines are used. Over the past twenty years the use of enzymes and low-temperature bleaches has cut the average wash temperatures by 20 degrees Celsius in Europe. Because new detergents wash at lower temperatures, the latest washing machines use only half the energy per wash cycle of those of a decade ago.

Sustainability: Unilever's approach

In order to achieve its aims Unilever believes that it needs to minimise the environmental impact of its activities by using a three-level approach.

Level: 1 Eco-efficiency

This involves producing safe products from clean processes as efficiently as possible.

Specialised environmental management systems are one of the ways to improve performance and to promote continuous improvement. These have been established in factories throughout the world. Unilever's systems are compatible with the ISO 14001, and 13 plants achieved certification by the end of 1997. A further 45 intend to be certified by 2001. Unilever has made progress in training and environmental awareness. Training courses have been established and 169 environmental managers/auditors have been trained. All sites will be audited by the end of 2000. Improvement targets have been set by most sites to cover factory emissions, waste, energy and water consumption.

For example, in packaging efforts have been made to minimise its use by:

- promoting refill packs to reduce packaging materials;
- concentration, for example of detergents, which allows the use of much smaller packs;
- lightweighting – between 1994 and 1997 Unilever reduced the weight of bottles in the Timotei range by over 60 per cent;
- increasing the use of recycled packaging.

Part of the rationale behind the minimisation is environmental concern, but it is also driven by legislation and the urge to reduce costs. Since May 1993 the Swedish government have held industry responsible for setting up their own systems to deal with packaging waste and to reach certain recovery targets. The Packaging Waste Directive from the European Union provides a further incentive.

At the Sacavem site in Portugal, Lever aimed to minimise industrial effluent in order to reduce the waste-water bill paid to the municipality. In 1995 the Liquids factory in Port Sunlight reduced effluent by 56 per cent with a cash saving of £529 000.

Total Productive Maintenance (TPM), the Japanese-inspired programme designed to increase manufacturing efficiency, is accepted at many Unilever factories worldwide, including those at P.T. Unilever Indonesia where the concept was first introduced in 1991. At the Home and Personal Care factory at Surabaya strict maintenance of machinery with the TPM guidelines has helped to increase skill levels and overall efficiencies, eliminate losses caused by stoppages, and lessen waste of materials. By strict attention to the smallest detail the factory has made savings of some US$200 000 a year in energy, water and waste minimisation.

Level 2: Sustainable consumption

This involves thinking about the sustainable use of natural resources used in the business and examining the overall impact of all activities on the environment.

Unilever aims to understand the total environmental impact of its business. This includes the whole life cycle of products, back up through the supply chain and down to ultimate disposal (see above). The tool it uses to evaluate the impact is the Unilever Imprint. Unilever calculates the impact that it has on the environment and compares that with its contribution to global GDP. The assessment shows that in most areas Unilever's environmental impact is roughly in line with its economic value added.

Developing sustainable agriculture practices is an essential element in the long-term health and prosperity of Unilever's business. Unilever further acknowledges that sustainability needs to be understood from different perspectives to find appropriate global, regional and local solutions.

Sustainable agriculture

More than two-thirds of the raw materials used in Unilever come from agricultural crops and livestock, fisheries and other renewable sources. With rising consumption placing growing demands on the productivity of the soil and the associated increase in the use of machinery and inputs such as fertilisers, pesticides and fossil fuels, a heavy burden is being placed on the environment. Unilever is working with farmers to encourage them to adopt standards aimed at reducing environmental impact and seeking ways to provide better consumer information about the ingredients in their products.

Level 3: Global solutions

Entails engaging in partnerships to look for radical changes in the way people's needs are met to address longer-term issues. The World Business Council for Sustainable Development, for example, provides a forum where companies can work together.

Conserving fisheries

Evidence is mounting that global fish populations are under serious threat from human activity. The decline in some fish stocks and the depletion of others, such as the Canadian Grand Banks Fishery, has put supplies to Unilever's fish business at risk and highlighted the possibility of extinction for certain species. Unilever formed a conservation partnership with the World Wide Fund for Nature in 1996 with the aim of using market forces and the power of consumer choice to encourage sustainable fishing. The Marine Stewardship Council, an independent, self-financing body, was set up in 1997 to promote sustainable fishing practices. Unilever has committed to source all its fish from fisheries certified to Marine Stewardship Council standards by 2005.

A brief look at oil palm plantations should show how Unilever's approach is having some practical effects.

Malaysia – healthy oil palm plantations

Unilever produces just over 1 per cent of the commercial world production of palm oil, yet in terms of innovation, productivity and environmental good practice, its plantations are widely recognised to stand comparison with the best anywhere.

In Malaysia, Pamol processes about 250 000 tonnes of fresh fruit bunches a year and manages 20 000 ha of oil palm, including 12 000 ha in the Labuk Valley, Sabah. This remote and beautiful plantation – accessible by dirt road and river – sets the highest standards. The combination of strong sun, high rainfall – one and a half times that of Western Malaysia – and rich alluvial soil gives exceptional yields. Yet fierce annual floods and soil erosion can cause problems if the land is not sensitively managed.

Ho Sui Ting is general manager at one of Pamol's young oil palm plantations in Sabah. 'Unilever's charter precludes the clearing of primary forest, or destroying habitats of specific scientific or cultural interest. We have learned in our business constantly to modify our practices to benefit the environment, which we realise is vital to our long-term success.'

Senior estate manager Muhiddin Aminuddin explains, 'We now leave a strip of natural forest alongside river banks, and encourage different species of trees and wildflowers to grow there. With this practice we minimise the disturbance of the river banks and keep the water clear.'

New planting is staggered to minimise soil erosion. 'And we no longer plant on steep slopes to allow the natural vegetation to protect the soil – good for wildlife, good for the palms below as well,' adds Muhiddin Aminuddin.

Effective use of terracing where appropriate and the planting of leguminous cover crops further decreases soil erosion and fixes nitrogen into the soil.

'We can harvest a palm tree within three years, but by 25 years it is too tall to harvest safely, and it's time to replant.'

Traditional practice was to burn or shred old trees, but people have learnt that this releases the nutrients too quickly so that they wash away before new palms can take advantage of them. General manager Ho Sui Ting explains: 'Now we simply stack the old palms in the interline and leave them to rot – in this climate it only takes a couple of years. Similarly, empty fruit bunches used to be burnt which caused bad pollution. Now we use them as organic mulch around accessible palms – it's better for the soil and cuts down on inorganic fertilisers. We also return excess liquid from processing operations to the fields.'

In general oil palm is relatively free of pests and therefore pesticides are hardly used on the plantation, but senior estate adviser Lau Kok Chin regularly checks for trouble. 'We use herbicides only round the base of the palms for the purpose of collecting fruits. Soft or broadleaf weeds growing between the rows are an advantage as besides decreasing soil erosion they provide a habitat for predators of pests that would otherwise attack the palms.'

Heavy machinery might seem a good idea in so large an area, but it damages the sodden soil. In the wettest parts harvesters work with their buffalo alongside, pulling a cart to collect the fresh fruit bunches which may weigh anything from 5 kg to 25 kg. Buffalo are cheap to run, don't break down, can cope with uneven terrain and – importantly – don't compact the soil.

The first principle behind all these endeavours is sound environmental practice. 'Good environmental practice is good agriculture,' says Ho Sui Ting.

Source: adapted from *Sustainability: Unilever's approach*, produced by Unilever Corporate Relations Department. *Lever and the Environment: Review of 95/96*.
Unilever Environment Report 1998: Making Progress, produced by Unilever Corporate Relations Department.
Introducing Unilever, produced by Unilever Corporate Relations Department.
Thanks to Huner Gulay at Unilever in Turkey for his assistance.

QUESTIONS

1. How does Unilever's environmental strategy suggest that the company has:
   (a) adverse and
   (b) beneficial impacts on the environment?

2. What are the benefits to Unilever of applying more stringent criteria to the environmental impact of their activities than is required by the law?

3. What do you understand by the principles of sustainable development and economic value added?

4. The case identifies some negative externalities produced by Unilever. What actions can Unilever take to reduce these externalities?

5. Identify new environmental legislation that Unilever has to consider. What action will Unilever have to take to meet the new legislation?

6. Unilever minimises its environmental impact by using a three-level approach. Identify and analyse this approach using the information given on 'healthy oil palm plantations' in Malaysia.

3

SOUTH-EAST ASIA

BOOM TO BUST

Ian Brooks

This case study examines the enormous success of South-East Asian economies up to the mid 1990s and explores the area's more recent troubles. The case study will demonstrate that the fate of each economy and of almost all commercial companies across South-East Asia, as elsewhere, is closely related to national and international economic and political circumstances and that economic growth and prosperity remain decidedly tenuous. Some South-East Asian economies (e.g. Hong Kong, Singapore) achieved, in the mid 1990s, per capita incomes comparable with those of the West, while others were expected to achieve that level within the first two decades of the twenty-first century. In the light of the recent (1997 to date) crisis, that increasingly looks to be a highly optimistic expectation.

In the first edition of this book, written in 1995–96 and published in early 1997, a case study entitled 'The industrialized countries of South-East Asia' examined the enormous growth and success of the South-East Asian countries. It explored the reasons for such rapid economic growth which brought prosperity, increasing employment and rich opportunities to most South-East Asian countries. As a measure of the volatility or turbulence of the business environment, in the short time since that case was written the economies of most South-East Asian countries have undergone decline, negative 'growth' has been experienced across Asia, investment in manufacturing and construction has plummeted, unemployment has risen considerably and the future looks decidedly less rosy than it did just a few years ago. South-East Asia is a testament to the consequences of the chaotic nature of the business environment, with the vast majority of the thousands of hitherto successful Asian organisations now in the midst of strife the scale of which was quite unpredictable in 1996.

The scale of economic growth in the NICs

There is little agreement concerning which countries in this region can legitimately be referred to Newly Industrialised. In order to avoid this largely technical and historical debate, for the purposes of this case study we will refer to the newly industrialised economies of Taiwan, South Korea, Singapore and Hong Kong, 'the four tigers', and Malaysia and Thailand, referred to as the ASEAN-2 (Association of Southeast Asian Nations). These six countries, known by the acronym DAE (Dynamic Asian Economies), together with Indonesia, the Philippines and Japan, are often referred to as the eight high-performing Asian economies (HPAEs). Table C3.1 clarifies these categories and includes others whose economies prospered until the mid-late 1990s.

Japan is generally considered to be an 'old' industrialised country and hence not classified as a NIC. Joining the ranks of the HPAEs in the recent years are two other economic dragons, the gigantic China and an enterprising Vietnam. In the period 1965–90, the eight HPAEs averaged a per capita rise in GNP of 5.6 per cent per year compared with just 2.3 per cent growth for all OECD economies (World Bank figures). The rate of growth in 'the four tigers' was closer to 8 per cent and remained at that level (e.g. Singapore 8 per cent in 1994–95) until the mid 1990s.

Economic prospects for the industrial countries of South-East Asia were promising. For example, if the growth rates of the 1980s and early 1990s had been maintained, the Asia-Pacific region (including Japan) would have been larger in GDP terms than the European Union by the year 2000. In the year 2025, it would have been twice the size of both North America and the EU. These might have been quite reasonable predictions to have made up to 1996, but they now appear quite fanciful. However, per capita incomes in Hong Kong and Singapore, for example, do exceed those of a number of European Union countries. In 1994

TABLE C3.1 HPAEs, NIEs, ASEAN-2: clusters of countries

High-performing East Asian economies (HPAEs)	Newly industrialised economies (NIEs): 'the four tigers'	ASEAN-2	Latest additions to high economic growth countries
Japan[1]			
Hong Kong	Hong Kong		
Singapore	Singapore		
Taiwan	Taiwan		
South Korea	South Korea		
Malaysia		Malaysia	
Thailand		Thailand	
Indonesia			
			China
			Vietnam
			Philippines

Note: [1] Data from Japan is not included in figures which refer to South-East Asia, the NIEs or ASEAN per capita incomes in Hong Kong and Singapore were US $18 634 and US $17 414 respectively.

Growth in China and Vietnam, the two most recent 'entrants' justifying the 'newly industrialised' label, was impressive in the early 1990s. China began its process of reform and opening itself to the outside world, a process referred to as *'gai ge kai feng'*, with historic policy shifts in December 1978 under the leadership of Deng Xiao Ping. Subsequently, the annual average growth in GNP of 9 per cent has captured the attention of economists and politicians worldwide. In 1993, for example, China approved a record 83 265 foreign investment projects amounting to over £70 billion (actual investment totalled £36 billion). These figures were equivalent to the accumulated total of all foreign investments attracted to China in the preceding fourteen years. Given the difficulties of accurate measurement and inter-country comparisons, some considerable debate exists concerning the current size of the Chinese economy. However, China's economy is now considered to be in excess of 45 per cent of the size of the United States of America. In 1993 the International Monetary Fund ranked China as the third largest economy in the world, behind only the USA and Japan.

Since the introduction of the 'Doi Moi' (renovation) policy in 1987, Vietnam has attracted considerable international investment. It achieved its first recorded trade surplus in 1992 and an economic growth rate of 9 per cent in 1994, but has recently experienced recession due to the South-East Asian crisis.

The export-driven manufacturing sector was particularly dynamic in the newly industrialised countries of South-East Asia. The four tigers together with Malaysia and Thailand accounted for 12 per cent of world exports in 1996, an increase from just 4 per cent in 1975 (OECD figures). Additionally, by 1989 Hong Kong, Taiwan, Singapore and South Korea had joined Japan and China in the world's top twenty exporters.

This rapid growth had contributed to a dramatic upgrading of human welfare measures. Just three decades ago all South-East Asian countries would have been considered to be impoverished Third World nations. Life expectancy in the HPAEs has increased from 56 years in 1960 to 72 years in 1996. Life expectancy in Hong Kong, Taiwan and Singapore, for example, is comparable to that found in Western Europe. The proportion of people living in absolute poverty, lacking such basic necessities as clean water, food and shelter, dropped substantively prior to the recent crisis – in the case of Indonesia from 58 per cent in 1960 to 15 per cent in 1996, and in Malaysia from 37 per cent to less than 5 per cent in the same period (World Bank). Such poverty was virtually non-existent within 'the four tigers'. Birth rates have declined significantly throughout South-East Asia. South Korea, Taiwan, Hong Kong and Singapore, the core NICs, had a birth rate of about 15 per 1000 in the 1990s, again very similar to that found in Western Europe. These countries are now experiencing a rapidly ageing population. The decline in fertility rates is partly due to birth control, which typically accompanies economic growth, but also due to measures to further encourage women into the workplace. Female representation in the labour force within 'the four tigers' and the ASEAN-2 countries averages over 40 per cent, just a little below that of the European Union.

By as early as the mid 1970s Hong Kong, Singapore, Taiwan and South Korea had passed the so-called 'Lewis turning point', going from unlimited to limited labour supply.

Competitiveness

The Swiss-based World Economic Forum analyses national competitiveness on an annual basis. It utilises a wide range of data in order to 'score' and rank 53 countries. Thus data ranging from GDP to gold reserves is combined with feedback from 3000 business managers responding to 130-item questionnaires. Although competitiveness is a notoriously contentious concept, the results of the WEF report are generally held in high regard. They showed in 1995, for example, that Singapore and Hong Kong were second and third, respectively, in the world (behind the USA) and Taiwan was eleventh. The UK was in eighteenth position. Each of the industrialised countries of South-East Asia had either entered the rankings for the first time in 1995 or been promoted to a higher position. In 1996 Singapore and Hong Kong were rated first and second and remained in that position to 1998 despite the crisis in South-East Asia. In 1998 Indonesia fell by sixteen places (to 31st place) and Malaysia by eight places (to seventeenth place). The WEF report of 1998 also noted that whereas in 1996 there was a net inflow of foreign capital to South-East Asia of $96 billion, in 1997 this had turned into a net outflow of $12 billion.

Decline: the uncompromising business environment

As early as mid 1996 many experts were predicting that the sustainability of outstanding economic growth in South-East Asia was in doubt: that said, they had been doing that for some time. This time they were right. Through 1996 and especially 1997 stock markets in all Asian countries plummeted, reflecting in part the poor prospects for continued growth (e.g. in Thailand the stock market fell by 55 per cent in the year to May 1997). Nevertheless, most economic forecasts in 1996 suggested that economic growth was set to continue at a rapid rate. For example, the International Monetary Fund gave Hong Kong an optimistic assessment in December 1996 predicting growth of over 5 per cent compared to a growth rate of just 4 per cent in 1996. In some of the newer 'tiger' economies growth rates were predicted in double figures. Yet also in December 1996 the Republic of China warned of the dangers of a 'meltdown' in stock markets and the damaging effect this might have on investor and consumer confidence (shares on the Beijing stock market fell by 10 per cent following this warning). Nevertheless, growth in exports from South-East Asia fell considerably in 1996 to 5.6 per cent from 22 per cent growth in 1995.

When the crisis led to massive stock market falls in 1997 many banks began to call in their debts, others went out of business, currencies were put under pressure and devaluation of many followed (e.g. Thailand in July 1997). Previous large-scale borrowing, for example to fund construction projects in Thailand and Korea, led to debts too high to be adequately serviced by rapidly declining economies. Added to this in September 1997 widespread drought and forest fires in many countries (e.g. Indonesia, Philippines, Malaysia) created lingering smog which severely damaged the tourist trade. Investors fled and many Asian manufacturing companies suspended their investments overseas and at home. The days of near or actual double figure economic growth appear, temporarily at least, to be over.

Social consequences of recession

The social consequences of recession in South-East Asia are generally more severe than when relative hardship hits Western countries. This is due in part to the fragility, or scarcity, of welfare systems in many newly industrialised countries and in part to the sheer depth of the current crisis. It is an unfortunate consequence of the crisis in Asia that millions of people have been pushed back into poverty, particularly, but not exclusively, those who had struggled to achieve a reasonable standard of living prior to the recession. Unemployment is at its highest level for two decades in many of the NICs and real wages have fallen while inflation, particularly the price of essential commodities, has risen. Social services in many countries, relying as they do on government finances, have been under pressure to cope. Further consequences include an increase in violence and other illegal and/ or undesirable social decline (World Bank report, 1998). In Indonesia, Thailand, Malaysia and the Philippines combined, a fall of 10 per cent in economic activity (GDP) will, the World Bank suggest, create a further 45 million officially categorised as in poverty. The safety net often provided by sophisticated welfare provision is simply not there in much of South-East Asia.

Consequences elsewhere

The crises in Asia and in Russia have affected economic growth potential around the world. Forecasts made in 1997 and 1998 of growth in Europe and North America for 1999, 2000 and beyond have been revised downward. Growth in the West has slowed (1998–99) and investment from South-East Asian countries has fallen considerably. Some foreign-owned manufacturing plants in the UK, for example, have closed while other proposed developments have been delayed or shelved altogether. As the economies in South-East Asia decline so does their need and capacity to import goods and services from Europe and North America. Hence trade between the West and South-East Asia has declined since 1997.

Whereas recessions in one country or trading area have for many decades stimulated problems elsewhere, this crisis has raised awareness of the global nature of the world economy. The G7 nations (USA, Japan, Canada, UK, Germany, France, Italy) agreed (1998) to attempt to take measures to help deal with the Asian crisis, and the American and many European governments have reduced interest rates in part as an attempt to ensure continued world economic growth. There is little doubt that the crisis in Asia is directly (e.g. by leading to a reduction in inward investment and in export potential) and indirectly (e.g. by damaging consumer optimism) influencing growth potential in all economies across the globe.

QUESTIONS

1. Undertake research using newspapers CD-ROMs, the Internet and other sources to explain why the recession in South-East Asia occurred with such scale and rapidity.

2. How has the business environment for South-East Asian manufacturers, such as Malaysia's Proton or Korea's Samsung, changed since the mid 1990s?

3. Explain the impact of large-scale unemployment on the economy of the country from the perspective of (a) government and (b) business.

4

EUROPE'S LARGEST EMPLOYER
THE NATIONAL HEALTH SERVICE

Ian Brooks

This case study discusses the highly complex and dynamic business environment facing the National Health Service (NHS) in the UK. It focuses, where relevant, on one particular Trust hospital, Kettering General Hospital NHS Trust (KGH).

KGH provides a full range of acute and midwifery services to a population of about 265 000, mostly in Northamptonshire. The hospital, which gained Trust status in April 1994, had an income of over £50 million in 1998/99. It employed over 2500 personnel (1500 full-time equivalents) in 1996.

This case study adopts a structured format by focusing on political, social, competitive and technological issues while briefly exploring ecological, legal and economic concerns.

Political environment

There is probably no area of public or private business that inspires such emotion as health care. The NHS lies close to the heart of the British public. Perhaps inevitably, the National Health Service is the subject of political contention and considerable academic debate. There is little which remains uncontroversial, excepting perhaps recognition that the technological, social, economic and political environments, all of which fundamentally influence the NHS, have undergone major change in the past two decades.

Most publicly funded health care systems, such as the NHS, operate in an environment in which demand exceeds supply. When a 'desirable' service, such as health care, is free at the point of use, this is always likely to be the case. However, government as the main provider of funds for the NHS has a responsibility to the taxpayer and the health consumer to achieve value for money and to enhance the overall effectiveness of the service. During the 1980s and 1990s UK governments attempted to control health care expenditure in the light of both their ideological stance and the increasing demands upon the public purse. Escalating health care costs have become a major issue elsewhere as most developed countries spend between 6 and 10 per cent of their GDP on health care. The United States is exceptional in spending about 14 per cent of its GDP in this area, much of which is accounted for by private health care. In many countries increases in health care expenditure have been facilitated by economic growth and consequent increases in receipts from taxation.

In the UK, NHS Trusts have been established in which managers experience greater decentralised authority in return for further accountability. A strong general management spine was introduced within the NHS and its Trust hospitals during the 1980s and early 1990s, so reducing the influence of powerful professional groups such as medical consultants. Salaries for these 'new' managers are generally higher than those given to previous 'administrators'. Many senior managers, such as NHS Trust Chief Executive Officers (CEOs), are largely employed on 'rolling contracts' and so have little job security. Many, therefore, face strong personal incentives to manage organisational change. Additionally, a non-elected Board of Directors, including a number of non-executive members, is responsible for the appointment of senior staff and for meeting the objectives of the Trust. Their role resembles that of a Board of Directors of a private company.

Central government change initiatives in the last decade include:

- the establishment of an internal market within the NHS involving the separation of purchasers and providers (also the imminent disbandment of that internal market);
- encouragement for hospitals and other discrete NHS services to seek Trust, or quasi-independent, status in response to the National Health Service and Community Care Act 1990;
- the Patients' Charter which has established waiting times and other patient 'rights' – replaced in 1998 by a new quality standards initiative;
- the new deal for doctors which is attempting to reduce their hours of work and alter other conditions, especially for junior doctors;
- Community Care (Caring for People);
- the Carmen Report on the training and career structure of medical staff;
- the private finance initiative which has sought to encourage greater involvement of private organisations in capital projects and increasingly in operational initiatives;
- a requirement to market-test and encouragement to contract out non-core services, such as catering;
- the establishment of an efficiency index by the Department of Health which attempts to assess value for money;

- the *Health of the Nation* (1995) report which provides a strategic approach to improving the overall health of the population, setting targets for improving health in five key areas and emphasising disease prevention and health promotion;

- attempts to signal a shift in resources towards primary care;

- government pressure and some funds to reduce waiting lists;

- league tables (suspended by the Labour government after 1998).

Implementing these initiatives, and dealing with the consequent operational and strategic changes, has many social and structural implications and involves considerable management effort. Collectively, these and other initiatives act as major forces for change within the NHS. On the ground each initiative has differential effects across the NHS as regional authorities 'interpret' central requirements and directives often independently of one another.

Intervention measures are largely consistent with priorities, and other changes within the public sector, instigated by the Conservative governments of the 1980s and 1990s. They directly influence the strategy, structure and operations of all aspects of NHS activity and, paradoxically, these interventionist policies tend to contrast with the Conservative party's espoused laissez-faire values. The Labour government (1997 to date) plan to reverse some of the competitive market initiatives (including GP fundholding).

Political influence in health care is largely considered to be one-way, that is, there is a deterministic relationship between government and NHS practice, with the former significantly influencing the latter. However, as health care is very much in the public domain, governments (not least a Labour government whose predecessors established the NHS in 1948) are concerned with public perception of the quality of service and value for money. Recent promised short-term injections of funds into the NHS aimed at reducing waiting lists are testimony to government concerns over public opinion.

Social and demographic environment

Flexible working at KGH

Sixty-two per cent of employees of KGH work part-time while over 80 per cent of all personnel are female. Forty-three per cent of staff have over five years' tenure. The staff turnover rate is rather low compared to many urban hospitals and is declining. Absenteeism for sickness currently stands at 3.6 per cent which compares favourably with many hospitals and other public and private sector organisations. Absenteeism among ancillary staff is about double the hospital average. About 80 per cent of the hospital budget is accounted for by wages and salaries.

Increasing emphasis is being placed on flexibility and multi-skilling within the hospital. Moves towards greater flexibility include attempts to combine the roles of porters, cleaning staff and catering assistants to form a single role of ward assistant. Such moves are driven by the need to demonstrate efficiency improvements and to compete with commercial organisations who may, following market-testing, manage the service currently run by in-house staff. Moves towards multi-skilling and flexible working are proceeding afoot within the private and public sector.

Consumerism

The general public were, prior to the 1980s, often reluctant to complain about the quality of service experienced within the NHS. However, a culture of dignified acceptance has slowly given way to one increasingly influenced by consumerist values. As a consequence of this, together with the provision of simpler mechanisms of complaint, there has been an increase in the number of complaints from the general public to almost every hospital and NHS service in the past decade.

The role of the media in this respect is not inconsiderable. Examples of poor practice are frequently exposed within national and local newspapers and television news programmes. Partly as a consequence most hospital trusts, and KGH is certainly no exception, are concerned how they are portrayed in the local press. In fact KGH actively manage their public relations. Interestingly, KGH Trust also 'uses' the media, and subsequent public support, to help ensure that the scale of services offered locally, as opposed to in Northampton, is at least maintained.

Expectations of the quality of life experienced by individuals within society have increased. Fostered by the changes in national culture, by consumerism and by the Patients' Charter, people are less accepting of levels of disablement than they once were. This manifests itself in high levels of demand for many specific health care services, such as hip and other joint replacements and cataract operations, which improve mobility. Additionally, people demand such items as hearing aids that are cosmetically acceptable. Consumerism, in part encouraged by government in the 1980s and 1990s, acts as a pressure to improve the quality of the service and leads to an increase in the demand for the service. The latter characteristic ensures that greater rationing is essential and/or additional spending on health care is required.

Demography

Changes in the age and gender structure of local and national populations have far-reaching effects on the providers of NHS services. Accurate demographic data is fundamental to the planning process. For any hospital trust, such as KGH, it is important to understand what is happening to the population in its catchment area. For example, if a large new housing estate is built which contains mainly starter and family homes, then it is likely that the number of women requiring maternity services will increase accordingly. Alternatively, if new sheltered housing for the aged is under construction, the hospital may well experience an increase in the demand for services more frequently demanded by this age group.

The emphasis given to particular specialisms within a hospital, such as maternity care or rheumatology, is related to demographic conditions. For example, rheumatology services cater more for old age groups, as does chiropody. Also of significance in this regard is the political influence of different groups in society. Elderly people tend to be less mobile and appreciate local accessibility to NHS services. As the proportion of elderly patients increases in society then their influence over policy decisions may also increase.

The United Kingdom has an ageing population. Generally speaking as people grow older they require greater medical care. There is little doubt that a significant element of the increase in the demand for NHS service experienced in recent decades is due to demographic ageing. This is a global phenomenon and one which has, in part, been created by improvements in health care which have progressively increased life expectancy and contributed to reductions in fertility rates. Increasing sophistication in drug regimes, surgery and other technologies and in medical knowledge has contributed to increases in life expectancy.

Racial mix within the local community served by a hospital is also an important characteristic which influences the nature and priority of services on offer. There are a number of ethno-specific illnesses. For example, mouth cancer is far more common in areas with large numbers of Asians who chew a plant root containing cancer-forming agents. In contrast, alcohol-related illnesses, for example, are far less common amongst Muslim populations. Additionally, many illnesses are related to social class and to occupational group. Hence the range of services offered by any hospital trust is influenced by a series of demographic and social variables.

Competitive environment

Funding for KGH and other Trusts come from a variety of sources. About two-thirds of General Practitioners (GPs) are 'fundholders' who currently can 'purchase' services for their patients from any suitable 'provider' such as KGH. Trusts can also compete for the income derived from treating private patients. Additionally, individual patients can, in specific circumstances, choose the provider of certain health care services. For example, maternity care is one of the most competitive services offered by KGH. Many expectant women are 'free' to choose which hospital they would like to attend, or whose services they require, to provide pre-natal, birth and post-natal care. In Northamptonshire, for example, both Kettering and Northampton hospitals run maternity units and hence 'compete' for patients.

Price is usually not the prime 'order-winning criterion' or reason for purchasing a service. Of greater importance in most cases is local accessibility and availability. In other words, people living in or around Kettering generally prefer to use KGH rather than travel to Northampton (about 15 miles) or Leicester (about 25 miles). Individual patients often view the services provided by hospitals as largely homogeneous and, of course, free at the point of delivery, suggesting that other criteria, such as accessibility, are of prime importance. Offering direct access, for example providing facilities for fitting hearing aids without prior referral from a specialist consultant, can give a hospital a competitive advantage. Especially in serious or more debilitating cases, timely availability of care is a crucial determinant in the choice of provider.

Rather than permitting purely competitive pressures to dictate the nature of services offered by any one provider, local health authorities often act as the arbiter in such cases. For example, in Northamptonshire, where there were three providers of vascular services in the early 1990s, the local health authority decided, largely on cost grounds, that two providers were sufficient. They felt that the duplication of these services did not represent value for money. The decision enabled some centralisation of expertise, equipment and other facilities and economies of scale to be realised. However, it has reduced accessibility for some patients.

Generally, there is little evidence to suggest that individual patients influence purchasing decisions. The Community Health Councils represent the needs of patients but many practitioners and academics have questioned their effectiveness in altering purchasing decisions or patterns of delivery.

Finally, there are new sources of direct competition for many of the services offered by a typical NHS Trust hospital. First, the growth of private health care and insurance (e.g. BUPA) proceeds apace. Curiously, the NHS itself provides facilities and other resources for private users. Additionally, GPs do some minor surgery, and nursing homes have removed many old people from hospitals. These changes are seen as largely complementary and in the best interests of patients. Rather, the major 'threat' of competition currently comes from other major NHS providers. Hence, in Northamptonshire, both KGH and Northampton General Hospital provide many services in common and consequently directly compete for continued funding from GPs and their mutual political masters, the local health authority. The local community in and around Kettering fear the reduction of services locally and the switch of resources to Northampton (the larger town). Although there may be some cost advantages for the providers, local accessibility to services would be denied if facilities are switched to the county town. The local political consequences of such an action are not inconsiderable.

Technological environment

Scientific breakthroughs and technological advances have made available new diagnostic methods and treatments for innumerable conditions which were not amenable to medical intervention in the past. Genetic science has developed, and continues to explore, a virtually endless array of possible treatments. Partly as a consequence of technological advance, and also the contribution made by changing demographics and increased customer awareness and expectations, health care specific inflation exceeds both retail price inflation and economic growth in the UK. Many more drugs have become available, some of which are very expensive, such as Beta Interferon for treating multiple sclerosis. In this case the existence of the new drug has raised the expectations of MS sufferers and necessitated it being rationed by health authorities.

Paradoxically, other technological changes have led to a reduction in the need for some treatments as new drugs, for example, can remove the need for more resource-intense care or hospitalisation. The increasing sophistication of many haematological treatments via a drug regime, which reduces the need for hospitalisation, is a case in point. Other improvements in medical and surgical techniques have significantly reduced the time patients spend in hospital. For example, minimal access surgery reduces recovery periods. Consequently, such improvements, which obviously improve patient care and reduce rehabilitation time and discomfort, also reduce the demand for many hospital services, such as the provision of hospital beds. Preventative medicine would also reduce demand for hospital services, other things being equal. However, the NHS invests sparingly in preventative medicine, partly because of the political issues involved in, for example, persuading people not to smoke. The Health of the Nation (1995), a preventative health campaign, is unlikely to achieve all of its rather modest targets.

Legal environment

Trust status has significantly altered the level at which legal responsibility lies. As a self-governed organisation, each NHS Trust now carries liability for all its activities. Hospitals use the services of legal advisers on a very frequent basis for advice on actions against the hospital, statements to the press about hospital activity, and the assessment of risk in such matters as access to property. Additionally, Trusts have many contractual and service agreements with providers of contracted-out services. Although NHS contracts between purchaser and provider have no basis in law, as they are merely service agreements, disagreements often go to arbitration or appeal via an array of established mechanisms.

Ecological environment

KGH is a very large user of energy and produces considerable waste, for example radioactive materials from radio physics and X-rays, and clinical waste including body fluids. It interacts with its ecological environment in very many respects.

CONCLUSION

Change in the NHS has been omnipresent since its establishment in 1948. However, few would disagree with the assumption that the pace of change has escalated in the last decade and taken the NHS in new directions. This has created many demands on management and staff.

At the local level, the internal market and the growing sophistication of financial and information systems have provided far more data on how resources are being used. Each Trust hospital is now 'closer' to the environment, and accountability for the consequences of its decisions is greater than in the past. This 'closeness' is demonstrated in the business planning process. For example, the NHS Executive, Anglia and Oxford region, require Trusts, such as KGH, to consider all possible environmental influences on their activity when undertaking their planning processes. The Executive suggested that these influences may include:

- advances in medical and surgical practice (technological environment);
- public awareness and expectations (social environment);
- demographic changes (social and demographic environment);
- the economic outlook (economic and political environment);
- the local health care market and other related markets (competitive environment);
- national priorities including Health of the Nation, Caring for People, Patients' Charter and Value for Money (political environment);
- local health commissions' and GP fundholders' priorities and future purchasing power/ capacity (competitive and political environment).

Despite this guidance (or some might argue, because of it) uncertainty within the NHS is rife. Meanwhile, the notorious short-termism in the NHS still prevails. Short-termism goes hand in hand with a growing recognition of political realities. Uncertainty about whether there will be a growth in private health care or the 'privatisation' of parts of the NHS prevails. Additionally, there is constant media attention, and individual Trusts are continually subjected to public scrutiny. In the 1997 general election the NHS was used as a 'political football'; despite attempts to make NHS activity apolitical, there seems little chance that this will occur.

QUESTIONS

1. Conduct a stakeholder analysis of Kettering General Hospital NHS Trust. Map the relative power and interest of the stakeholders. Based upon this analysis, assess which stakeholders are most likely to influence the direction of change in the NHS and attempt to assess in which directions you think the NHS may move in the next decade.

2. Conduct a PEST analysis of KGH.

3. What are the necessary conditions for perfect competition to thrive? Analyse the NHS internal market and assess the likelihood of perfect competition becoming established within the health care industry.

4. What are the consequences of demographic changes for the NHS?

5. Establish a small number of feasible scenarios for how the health care industry in the UK might develop within the next two decades.

HP BULMER HOLDINGS PLC

LIVING WITH NEW REALITIES

Graham Spickett-Jones, Jon Reast
and Crispin McKelvey

This case explores the competitive business environment influencing Bulmers, the Hereford-based cider maker.

The fruit of success

After trading for 112 years Bulmers like to describe themselves as the world's leading cider maker: 'Our mission is to remain the world's most successful cider company' (Annual Report, 1996–97). Much of the last decade has viewed the future of cider with rosy prospects. As a category, the cider market grew in size substantially through the early 1990s. This was partly driven by the introduction of new products, including premium packaged and white cider targeted at 18-to-24-year-olds. In 1996, the UK cider market was estimated to be worth £1065 million (Mintel), up 23 per cent in real terms from 1992.

In the UK, Bulmers claim a dominant market share and leadership in key parts of the cider market. This includes the dry, medium sweet and traditional sectors with their three 'pillar' brands, Strongbow, Woodpecker and Scrumpy Jack respectively. In the mid 1990s, the Strongbow brand alone accounted for a third of the UK's 112 million gallon cider market. Matthew Clark (MC), previously better known for products like Stone's Ginger Wine, became arch rivals when they bought Showerings in 1994 (with the Gaymers, Copperhead and K brands) and then acquired Taunton Cider in 1995 (with its Dry Blackthorn, Red Rock and Diamond White brands). At the time this gave MC a 41 per cent share of the UK cider market.

By 1996 Bulmers and MC held a virtual duopoly covering approximately 70 per cent of the branded cider market and a major share of the remaining market, largely retailer 'own label'. Other producer companies in the UK cider market have a modest presence. The largest, Merrydown, grew to hold a 3 per cent market share by volume in the middle of the 1990s, before seeing this share decline. They are followed by a small group of traditional firms, including H. Weston and Thatchers, with small regional markets. Most of the remaining 400 or so manufacturers operate on a farmhouse production scale.

Within the EU the UK is the dominant cider producer nation, accounting for approximately two-thirds of the European production. Apple juice is a major import but very little finished cider is brought into the UK market. Bulmers see themselves as having a commanding lead in the development of the international cider market. They claim to be the only major cider company with the resources and skills to capture markets around the globe and have recently been spending over £2 million a year developing export markets from the UK.

Bulmers' investment strategy through the 1990s

Much of the growth in the cider market in the early 1990s has been attributed to the sector's brand investment. From 1988 through to the early 1990s a substantial advertising spend was credited as having helped Bulmers develop the cider market and market leadership for the Strongbow brand. New product development and new packaging formats introduced through the early 1990s helped ride a fashion trend for white and premium packaged ciders. From 1993 brands like Diamond White and Red Rock from Taunton and Bulmers' own MAX helped to make cider shares glamorous as these products attracted new consumers. These brands helped equalise the seasonal trend for what is traditionally a summer drink, and spread cider into geographical markets outside the normal strongholds of the West Country and the counties bordering Wales. These new products effectively introduced cider into the brand repertoire of alcoholic beverages that younger drinkers would draw on, depending on the location or occasion for consumption. The long hot summer of 1995 then added extra sales volume from a more traditional area of the market. Cider shares boomed as a result.

Recently Bulmers' investment has included spending on new production capacity, a PET bottle blowing plant (to cope with greater take-home volume of large PET bottles), new warehousing, re-launching of Strongbow in a new packaging design, and the development of cider brands, including the Bulmers Heritage range. Bulmers have also invested in new markets and they now own companies in Australia, New Zealand and Belgium. They have supply arrangements that give the Bulmers products a presence in 40 countries and their share of the UK export market for cider is in excess of 80 per cent.

In 1993, in the face of increasingly competitive international market conditions, Bulmers sold off their interests in pectin, a jelling agent for the food industry. In 1994 it announced a further major step in repositioning its strategic focus when it changed its UK distribution business by withdrawing from major soft drinks, wines and spirit agency contracts to concentrate on its cider and beer activities.

In recent years Bulmers have been first to market with innovations like ice cider and smooth flow cider. The company owns the Symonds name and in May 1996 spent £23.3 million to acquire Inch's, a Devon-based cider maker, which came with a strong white cider brand, White Lightning, as well as a range of traditional brands and an established regional identity in the West Country. This has given Bulmers a broad portfolio of brands that supply both the on trade and take-home trade.

Along with their presence in the cider market Bulmers have developed a beer distribution business in the UK where they market strong brands, like San Miguel and Steinlager, which has helped the firm rise to be the fourth largest supplier in this sector of the UK take-home market.

Bulmers tend to take a long-term view on investment. In recent years they have established major new cider apple orchards in the UK and are experimenting with orchards in Poland and Australia. None of these will produce commercially usable fruit in the immediate future. Bulmers obtain nearly two-thirds of their apple juice from their own orchards and from UK contracts. This helps to make Bulmers far less dependent on imported juice and concentrates than its competitors.

Product sectors

Cider covers a broad set of products and formats. This ranges from low-alcohol to super-strong ciders, and from draught to various bottled and canned formats (including PET and premium packaged products). New packaging formats and the development of white ciders and fruit-flavoured ciders has opened up new category definitions. The cider product range now broadly fits into economy, mainstream and premium segments, and across each of these a tradition versus fashion axis has emerged.

Economy products are mainly amber ciders with an alcohol by volume (ABV) of up to 6 per cent but a new and growing white cider market is emerging, especially for strong cider with an ABV of up to 8.4 per cent.

Mainstream ciders tend to be amber, and medium sweet or dry, with an ABV of 3.5 to 6 per cent. This category includes Strongbow and Woodpecker and some of the newer white ciders, such as White Lightning (with an ABV of 7.4 per cent).

In the premium sector products tend to split into either strength, style or heritage brands. The stronger ciders, like Strongbow Super, typically have ABVs above 8 per cent and include White Lightning Super at an ABV of 8.4 per cent. Style ciders include premium packaged fashion-conscious products that have usually been formatted to fall into the lower of the two recently established duty excise bands (which tax ciders differently depending on whether they have an ABV above or below 7.5 per cent), e.g. Woodpecker Red (which has been lowered to a new ABV of 7.4 per cent since the introduction of the higher excise band). The heritage brands include products like the traditional Scrumpy Jack and the newly promoted Harvest Scrumpy and Bulmers Number 7 Fine Dry Cider.

A range of characteristics can divide the types of products:

- palate – sweet to dry, still or carbonated
- presentation – draught to large packaged to small premium bottles

- positioning – from premium (including strength, style and heritage) to mainstream and economy
- colour – from amber to white
- outlet – on trade and off trade
- excise duty band – above or below 7.5 per cent ABV (adapted from Mintel).

Bulmers have interests in all sectors of the market and spend approximately 2 per cent of sales on research and development. Over recent years this has helped the firm develop fruit-based cider and ice cider products along with a smooth flow delivery system.

Trading areas

Bulmers export to 50 countries from the UK, using a range of distribution agreements. They have seen export volumes rise by 12 per cent in 1997–98, with particularly strong growth in North America, Scandinavia and southern Europe. They also have established interests in continental Europe largely through their ownership of Cidrerie Stassen, the leading Belgian cider maker. Although the Belgian market is in decline, Stassen have forged new links with markets in Holland, Germany and France and are producing good growth in the sale of Bulmers UK ciders on the continent (where distribution of English ciders grew 81 per cent in 1997). Bulmers dominate the Australian cider market with Bulmer Australia and they have recently acquired the Harvest Wine Company, New Zealand's leading cider maker, which is being integrated with the Australian business.

The UK is far and away Bulmers' most important market (see Table C5.1). Data on consumers in the UK, from the mid 1990s, shows that consumer penetration of cider is in the order of 29 per cent (Keynotes) and that it has a strong appeal for both sexes. More than a third of adults claim to have drunk a pint of cider or more in the last month and 28 per cent will have drunk a pint or more over the last week. There is, however, a strong youth profile in the market with two-fifths of 18–24 year olds drinking cider. Heaviest consumption is by the social group D from this young age group in Wales and the north, who tend to drink the economy brands bought in large take-home containers.

The demographic trends in the UK population reveal that there will be a fall in consumer numbers between the 15–24 and 25–34 age groups in the early part of

TABLE C5.1 Bulmers UK operational analysis

	1998 £m	1997 £m	1996 £m	1995 £m	1994 £m	1993 £m
Turnover	264	276	228	218	223	218
Operating profit	21.6	30	26	23	22	20
Operating profit as % of turnover	8.9	10.9	11.3	10.6	9.6	9

Source: Bulmers Annual Reports and Accounts 1996–98

TABLE C5.2   Bulmers Australasia operational analysis

	1998 £m	1997 £m	1996 £m	1995 £m	1994 £m	1993 £m
Turnover	20.8*	20.5	18	19	17	14
Operating profit	3.9	3.5	3.2	3.6	3	2.3
Operating profit as % of turnover	19.5	17.1	17.8	19.4	18.1	16.4

Note: * The figure now includes New Zealand.

Source: Bulmers Annual Reports and Accounts 1996–98

the next century and this seems likely to influence sales levels for cider if new markets are not developed.

Australasia

After a downturn in volumes in 1996, Bulmers Australasia have reinvigorated the market and increased sales with new packaging, new advertising and a relaunch of Strongbow Ice (see Table C5.2). In 1997–98 local operating profits (as a percentage of net trading assets) rose 33 per cent. The integration with the recently acquired Harvest Wine Company in New Zealand promises to consolidate the position in this area of the world, which now includes the local production of Strongbow and the recent introduction of Scrumpy Jack.

A comparison of the level of operating profits to the assets employed in each region shows that Australia has a return in excess of 55 per cent (see Table C5.3).

Belgium

Operating in a depressed and shrinking market, Stassen have been able to supply a bridgehead into continental Europe and a test market area for future expansion (see Table C5.4). A major challenge has been to sidestep the cultural issue of cider being seen as a substitute for sparkling wine on much of the continent. Bulmers have tried to deal with this by presenting cider as an alternative to beer instead.

TABLE C5.3   Return on assets by region

	UK £m	Australasia £m	Belgium £m
Operating profits	21.6	3.9	0.9
Net assets employed	143.6	6.8	5.8
Return as % of turnover	15.0	55.8	15.5

Source: Bulmers Annual Reports and Accounts 1996–98

TABLE C5.4   Cidrerie Stassen operational analysis

	1998 £m	1997 £m	1996 £m	1995 £m	1994 £m	1993 £m
Turnover	13.8	14	13	11	9	7
Operating profit	0.9	0.9	0.9	0.8	1.3	0.8
Operating profit as % of turnover	6.9	6.6	7.2	7.6	14.7	11.5

Source: Bulmers Annual Reports and Accounts 1996–98

Rotten apples

In 1995 a major distraction in the sector was the growth of the alcopops market. This badly dented some of the cider industry's new style-conscious brands, like Diamond White and MAX. As well as establishing a new fashion trend amongst UK youth, alcopops gave young drinkers a new entry path into the alcoholic beverage market that had previously often involved cider. The unfavourable publicity attracted by alcopops, mainly from the claim that they appealed to under-age drinkers, was also credited as having tarnished the image of the white cider market.

The market for premium strength ciders, with an ABV above 7.5 per cent, was also badly dented by a 50 per cent increase in excise duty brought in by the UK government on 1 October 1996. Advance indication of this deadline created market distortions and swings in demand as extensive forward purchasing was seen in the trade, followed by a rapid decline in consumer demand as prices increased. However, as less than 10 per cent of Bulmers' volume was in top-strength ciders the damage to the firm's sales levels was relatively modest.

In March 1998 the Bulmers share value had fallen by almost 40 per cent from its high the previous year of 626 pence. This was in line with the other mainstream quoted cider makers, MC and Merrydown, who had seen shares roughly halve in value over twelve months. Confidence in the industry was damaged by disastrous trading results from Merrydown and profit warnings from MC. Merrydown had been hit by a collapse in sales of 34 per cent, mainly because of the rapid decline of its Two Dogs alcopops brand and by poor cider sales generally. In May 1998 Merrydown were forced to announce a £7m rescue deal that included a change of management and laying off 40 per cent of the 125 staff. Two profit warnings from MC in 1997 were spurred by a collapse in margins that MC's Chief Executive, Peter Aikens, partly blamed on what he called 'bare-knuckle fighting' with Bulmers over prices in the take-home markets. During the summer of 1997 MC had been force to cut the price of their two-litre Gaymers Olde English cider from £2.99 to £1.99. They also admitted to a four-point drop in market share in a declining market. In the face of a sharp decline in turnover, profits and share value, MC were being forced to consider demerging the group to separate its difficult cider business from its other more successful drinks activities, and they had to shelve plans to dramatically increase the advertising budget for their cider brands.

Many of the company's UK problems have been attributed to the growth of imported continental lagers. This includes the relatively high volumes being imported by individuals since the relaxation of controls on the personal importing of beers and ciders from other parts of the EU. The company also list the weakness of white cider brands and their price sensitivity as having resulted in trading problems.

UK distribution

Historically the pattern of cider consumption has been roughly equally split between take-home and on trade. In keeping with much of the rest of the alcohol industry, this has shifted dramatically in favour of the take-home trade through the 1990s. For cider, take-home trade had risen to approximately 60 per cent by 1997. The bulk of this now goes through the supermarkets, whose share of the take-home trade has grown rapidly. By 1997 the grocery multiples accounted for approximately 48 per cent of the total UK cider sales volumes.

The on trade has changed dramatically through the 1990s. The 1989 Monopolies and Mergers Commission Report *The Supply of Beer* resulted in legislation that helped lead to a restructure of the ownership of much of the on trade and sparked major shifts in its supply arrangements. This restructuring is still an ongoing feature of the on trade. One of the recent encouraging developments has been the emergence of theme-type cider pubs. Bulmers do not run their own retail estate, however, but mainly choose to supply brewers directly, or else distribute to trade wholesalers.

The on trade has seen a rapid drop in draught cider volumes and this is also the part of the market that has seen the most impact from new drinks, beers and alcopops. This decline was nearly 8 per cent during 1996–97. The problems of the on trade have been compounded by the control of distribution channels into the pub and club markets, which are largely in the hands of the brewing companies who are also effectively the main competitors for cider brands. While in the past many pub customers would have remained loyal to the same type of drink, Bulmers have had to accept that modern customers enjoy drinking across a wide range of different product types, which may be selected for reasons of mood or because of the event or location. In addition cider has had to compete with an increasing range of product options, making it increasingly difficult to retain its share of this shrinking on trade market.

In the face of these pressures Bulmers have been successful in limiting the damage to their core brand, Strongbow. This has declined at half the trend rate of the rest of the cider on trade, and at the end of 1997 Strongbow built a market share of 63.6 per cent in this sector.

Responding to the competitive environment

There was a sharp decline in the overall cider market of 7.1 per cent in the year to September 1997. Bulmers see themselves as being in the long alcoholic drinks market, which includes beers and ciders. In the year to March 1998 the total market consumption for this sector fell by 2 per cent and the decline in cider slowed to match this rate. Industry cider volumes have been less dented in the take-home trade than in the on trade. However, profit margins have been hit by the strength of the bargaining position of the grocery multiples and the rise in their share of the take-home market. This has been compounded by a price war through the mid 1990s between the major suppliers to win the business of the grocery multiples, particularly for volume sales at the bottom end of the market. Despite the low price points on offer the own-label and economy ciders have not performed well since their initial strong growth in 1995–96. The multiples have also been willing to use their bargaining power to buy branded products which they then offer at discounted prices, to build store traffic. This has been done without regard to the impact this can have on brand perceptions. The lack of experience of the cider industry in these markets and the pressures of these trading conditions have encouraged a switch in emphasis in the promotional effort of the cider manufacturers, through the 1990s, toward sales promotion and discounting at the expense of a decline in levels of brand-building support such as advertising.

By 1996 the weakness in the position of cider was visible in its decline in the share of voice (sov) in advertising support for brands in relation to other alcoholic products: 1996 saw only 39 per cent of the advertising spend of 1992. This is something Bulmers attempted to address in 1997 when the company agreed to increase its investment in media spend from £4.7 million to £8 million for the year to April 1998, and they allocated an extra £1.5m media support for Strongbow in the run-up to Christmas 1997. This level of media support helped the Strongbow brand rise to twelfth position in the UK at the end of 1997, from its previous fifteenth position. Between 1997 and 1998 Strongbow volume increased by 10 per cent overall (combining on and off trades) taking the brand from fourteenth to eleventh in the UK's long drinks league table.

Big brand investment has paid off for Bulmers in the past. From 1988 and over the following few years Bulmers made a relatively high level of advertising investment and by the early 1990s the company's profit margins and share price are thought to have directly benefited from this. In the year to April 1997, Managing Director and Chief Executive, John Rudgard, was frank about the intended increase in brand investment being likely to absorb any planned profit growth for the coming year. At the time Bulmers took the view that the investment they planned would help return the market to growth. Bulmers were aware that, at the start of 1997, a substantial lift in advertising budget had also been promised by MC, from £1.7 million to £10 million. In 1997 the HP Bulmer Board saw an increased advertising investment as a price they should be willing to pay to reinvigorate the market, even if this was at the expense of short-term growth. In a pain today but jam tomorrow approach, they believed that, in combination with a greater media spend by MC, this would produce long-term benefits for the popularity of cider. The company resolved to use its superior market position to maintain a higher sov (share of advertising voice) than rivals MC would be able to offer their brands, to maintain their market share.

A claimed success by Bulmers has been its progress in foreign markets but the benefit of this has been influenced by the relatively high value of sterling against many other currencies. This has made exports relatively expensive and distorted the return in operating profits from the foreign subsidiaries, when translated to sterling. The decline in profits coupled with a maintained investment programme has meant that the company's gearing has increased to 61.4 per cent. A gearing level above 50 per cent is considered as a warning signal on a company's financial stability.

By the industry's own figures, the twelve months to September 1997 saw a sharp decline in the UK cider market. Speculation and rumour have accompanied this decline and its accompanying loss in turnover and profit levels. Bulmers have been reported as exploring consolidation in the industry by looking at Matthew Clark as a possible takeover target. The giant French drinks group Pernod-Ricard have been reported to be exploring the new affordability of Bulmers, since their drop in share price, having dismissed MC as a possible takeover target. However, any takeover bid for Bulmers would have to satisfy the Bulmers family who, with a 23 per cent stake in the firm, represent a sizeable ownership block.

Taking stock at the start of 1998, 1997 had been a difficult year for Bulmers. The acquisition of Inch's, in 1996, had proved to be poorly judged. The closure of the plant was announced early in 1998, along with an exceptional cost of £2.5 million to cover expenses associated with the closure. An attempt to raise prices for white cider had failed in an embarrassing U-turn when rivals dropped their prices as a response. The Christmas promotional effort had proved a trading disaster (with a possible cost of £4.5 million). This was largely because supermarkets had sold 12-can packs of Strongbow at £4.99, instead of the normal £8.99, producing volumes that resulted in a substantial over-run in the company's volume-linked promotional costs, and which exposed weakness in internal management controls at Bulmers. A flood of cheap imported beers also damaged the Christmas cider trade, as the strength of the pound and lower foreign duty rates had encouraged the supermarkets to source vast quantities of beer on the continent. These were sold in opposition to cider, seducing customers away with much cheaper prices. John Rudgard, Bulmers' Chief Executive, told the *Independent*, 'It is the first time I can ever remember that beer was cheaper than cider at Christmas. A litre of beer was selling for 70p while a bottle of Strongbow was selling for £1.30.'

A warning in February 1998 that profits would fall by about a quarter proved to be optimistic when the results for the year ending 24 April showed that pre-tax profits were down 35 per cent (from £29.3 million to £18.9 million) on sales down 4 per cent to £298.2 million.

These figures mask the rapid deterioration in profits in the second half of the company's financial year (see Table C5.5). The seasonal bias to higher summer sales activity is reflected in the first six months' figures, to 24 October for each year. However, pre-tax profits for the second half (six months to 24 April) in 1998 fell by over 45 per cent from the first-half level. This compared to a 23 per cent fall for the corresponding period in 1997.

TABLE C5.5 Sales and profit performance, 1996–98

Period ended:	1997–98			1996–97		
	6 months 24 Oct 97 £m	6 months 24 Apr 98 £m	Year total 24 Apr 98 £m	6 months 24 Oct 96 £m	6 months 24 Apr 97 £m	Year total 24 Apr 97 £m
Sales	154.2	144	298.2	162.6	147.9	310.5
Operating profit	16.5	10	26.5	19.5	14.9	34.4
Pre-tax profit	14.3	7.8	18.9	16.6	12.7	29.3
Number of employees			1133			1095

In April 1998, John Rudgard took retirement two years early to make way for Mike Hughes. As new Chief Executive, Hughes was quick to reveal to the *Financial Times* some of the brighter sides to the Bulmers performance. The advertising investment in Strongbow had seen volumes rise by 10 per cent in a shrinking market and a new supply agreement with Bass promised to take Strongbow into another 1000 pubs. The international division was doing well and the net effect of the strength of sterling was positive to the tune of £500 000, because of the cheaper purchase of apple juice concentrates. The group had also finally managed to raise its prices for its white cider, White Lightning, in anticipation of investing in a brand-building strategy for the product.

QUESTIONS

1. Analyse the competitive environment facing Bulmers by applying appropriate tools, frameworks and concepts.
2. Consider what the impact of demographic changes may be on Bulmers in the future.
3. Consider how the Bulmers portfolio has been changed over the last ten years in response to competitive pressures within the environment.
4. Explore the extent to which the picture portrayed within the cider and beer market approximates to a situation of 'perfect competition'.
5. Discuss what market Bulmers are in, who their key competitors are and how this has changed during the recent past.

6

ENVIRONMENT AND COMPETITION

THE CASE OF SCANIA

Ian Brooks

This case study focuses on the ecological or 'green' issues facing Scania, a truck manufacturer. Because of the integrated nature of environmental forces, other areas, including technology, legal and political issues, are also addressed. It discusses some of the issues central to the heated debate concerning the growing use of road transport in the UK and in Europe generally.

Scania is a Swedish manufacturer and distributor of trucks, buses, coaches and marine engines. Their lorries, or trucks as they are referred to in the industry, are manufactured and assembled in Sodertalue in Sweden, Zwolle in Holland, Angers in France and a number of sites in Latin America. Scania trucks have been referred to as the Rolls-Royce of the truck industry. Trucks of this nature cost in excess of £50 000 excluding a trailer.

Trucks are primarily marketed through franchised dealers many of whom are separately owned companies. Each commands a territory and directly serves the customer. Their prime business comprises the sale of new and used trucks, servicing and repair. It is the lucrative aftersales market which yields the lion's share of their business profits. This marketplace is rapidly changing with the development of different forms of competition and a changing customer base. There has been a decrease in the importance of small haulage operators and a rise in fleet sales to large organisations. Contract hire and truck leasing are also rapidly expanding.

Environmental concerns

Until the mid 1960s there were few environmental issues at stake for commercial vehicle manufacturers. Legislation was limited, there was no significant body of opinion voicing concern and few facts were available to demonstrate that a problem existed. In those circumstances manufacturers' prime concern was to build trucks that would prove competitive in their marketplaces. In the late 1960s West Coast (USA) laws were established which began to regulate pollution from commercial vehicles. The United States of America still has some of the most stringent environmental legislation.

Progress was slow in Europe during the 1970s and the 1980s; it was hampered by the lack of clear-cut evidence and adequate methods of measurement. This has now changed, and while we are still a long way from the harmonised legislation sought by Scania and some other manufacturers, many standards for the present and future have been established. Environmental legislation in Sweden, the home of Scania (and of its major rival Volvo), is amongst the strictest in the world. For example, from 1998 all Swedish companies were obliged to provide information in their annual reports about environmental issues and activities, and car producers become liable for recycling costs.

To a large extent these standards drive change, although some 'environment-ally friendly' activity also improves competitiveness. Leif Ostling, the President and CEO, argues that technological improvements linked to emissions will have competitive pay-offs. Methods are being developed to improve the efficiency of engines; non-engine-related improvements can also reduce emissions and fuel consumption by increasing aerodynamic qualities. Improvements in aerodynamics and rolling resistance and reductions in weight have reduced energy consumption by up to 50 per cent in a little over two decades, Ostling argues.

Scania regards the integration of environmental work into all of its processes as a key competitive factor. Nearly half of Scania's product development work occurs in fields related to the environment. These include materials selection, exhaust emissions, noise, fuel consumption, alternative fuels and recycling of components and materials.

Nevertheless, the truck industry is an obvious target for environmentalists who brand it as a polluter of urban areas and the countryside. Yet road transport is, in most circumstances, the most economic form of transport for goods. It has also adapted well to changing economic and competitive conditions and to a variety of legal constraints imposed at both national and international levels.

Total road freight has increased rapidly in recent decades in most European countries. This rise is particularly significant when compared with the dwindling importance of rail in some countries. Yet in many ways rail transport, especially for bulk freight, is more acceptable to the environmentalist lobby. Switching freight from road to rail would reduce both road congestion and atmospheric pollution. Table C6.1 shows the relative growth and decline of road and rail freight transport in the UK and other European countries. The UK and France 'head' the table, a position of some regret to environmentalist groups and rail authorities. This decline is made more dramatic when one considers that total freight move-ment has increased vastly during the same time period. The increasing importance of road transport for industrial and consumer goods is particularly marked in those countries which have enjoyed sizeable growth in their economies.

TABLE C6.1   Change in total road and rail freight (tonne-kilometre), 1977–98

	Road % change 1977–98	Rail % change 1977–98
UK	+48	– 25
France	+51	−25
Spain	+85	−20
Sweden	+52	+19
Germany (West)	+95	+25
Italy	+160	+25
Portugal	+5 (est.)	+105

In 1998 around 1800 million tonnes of goods were transported on roads within the UK while a little under 110 million tonnes went by rail. Coastal and inland waterways account for a further 135 million tonnes of freight in and around the UK. Thus, excluding materials carried within pipelines, road transport in 1998 accounted for almost 90 per cent (by weight) of total freight movement within the United Kingdom.

Throughout Europe there is concern about road congestion. The EU forecasts that Europe's roads will carry 16.5 billion tonnes of freight by the year 2010. This would represent a doubling in a little over twenty years. In England, the M6 motorway north-west of Birmingham was built for a capacity of 80 to 90 thousand vehicles per day. It now carries in excess of 115 000 vehicles a day, and has done so for some time, although the majority of these are private motor vehicles. Meanwhile truck manufacturers, such as Scania, are pushing for an increase in the legally permissible size of lorries to 48 tonnes, arguing that this would reduce the number of journeys required. In Britain hauliers are restricted to 38 tonnes maximum weight until 1999 and just 40 tonnes thereafter. The Freight Transport Association argue that increasing the permissible weight limit to just 44 tonnes would remove some 9000 trucks from Britain's roads and save 300 million litres of diesel fuel annually. Such a move, however, may require some road bridges to be rebuilt and speed restrictions and other safety measures to be reviewed. Additionally, public perception of the effects of an increase in the size of lorries is far from favourable.

Considerable pressure is placed on governments across Europe to reduce their reliance on road transport and to improve public and rail freight services. The UK government provided grants between 1995 and 1997 for companies to establish private rail freight terminals. They have also shown some commitment to raising the price of fuel to further encourage movement off the roads (fuel tax is set to increase at twice the level of annual inflation). Critics argue these measures do not go far enough. Government, for their part, have been reluctant to impose extra costs on industry for fear of damaging its competitiveness overseas. For this reason the Conservative government in the mid 1990s rejected EU proposals for a carbon tax. However, at the world environmental summit in 1998 in Kyoto, Japan, governments agreed to reduce carbon dioxide emissions.

The Royal Commission on the Environment report published in 1994 (*Transport and the Environment*, Command Number 2674, HMSO, 1994) made a significant contribution to the sometimes heated debate concerning the increasing reliance on the use of roads in the UK for both passenger and goods transport. It contributed to a reduction in the road-building ambitions of the government of the day. The report argued that 'pollutants from vehicles are the prime cause of poor air quality that damages human health, plants and the fabric of buildings.' It continues, 'noise from vehicles and aircraft is a major source of stress. The transport system must already be regarded as unsustainable.' The Commission made a series of firm recommendations to government to ensure that World Health Organization guidelines for the year 2005 were met. These included the encouragement of the use of natural gas and electric-powered vehicles, stronger emissions controls and encouragement to use rail for freight transport. The commission argued for a target for rail's share of total freight movement within the United Kingdom to rise from 6.5 per cent in 1994 to 20 per cent by 2010. One proposed mechanism to achieve this is the encouragement of attempts to further extend the use of 'piggybacking' where truck trailer loads are lifted on to rail carriages and transported by rail. This may encourage some long-distance and continental loads off the roads.

Scania's environmental policy

A growing number of national and international organisations have developed an environmental policy which sets out their ecological position. Scania have long recognised that industrial production and ecological concerns often conflict. When an industry is primarily concerned with the manufacture of vehicles which burn fossil fuels and contribute to traffic flows, the environmentalist lobby is particularly watchful and active. However, partly perhaps due to their liberal and sensitive Swedish cultural origin, Scania are renowned within the truck industry for the attention they pay to ecological concerns. Scania's environmental (meaning, here, ecological) policy is enshrined in its mission statement and explicitly stated thus:

Scania's Environmental Policy

- *Scania shall achieve and maintain leadership within its field of competence in order to provide a better environment.*

- *Scania shall by foresighted research and development continuously reduce the environmental impact coming from its production, products and services.*

- *Scania shall actively promote internationally harmonised and effective environmental legislation – for Scania current legislation is the minimum standard.*

- *Scania shall increase the confidence in its environmental work through openness and regular environmental reporting.*

Scania also publishes an annual Environmental Report which sets out its annual environmental goals and evaluates progress against previous goals. Scania claims to match or improve upon all statutory environmental standards despite the inevitable cost of following such a policy. However, of equal certainty are the competitive benefits that ensue from the application of technology to forge a bridge between ecological concerns and competitive pressures. For example, Scania's designers have achieved a steady reduction in fuel requirements from the application of aerodynamic technologies. The 'Scania Streamline' has achieved reductions of up to 15 per cent in the coefficient of drag (Cd) compared with

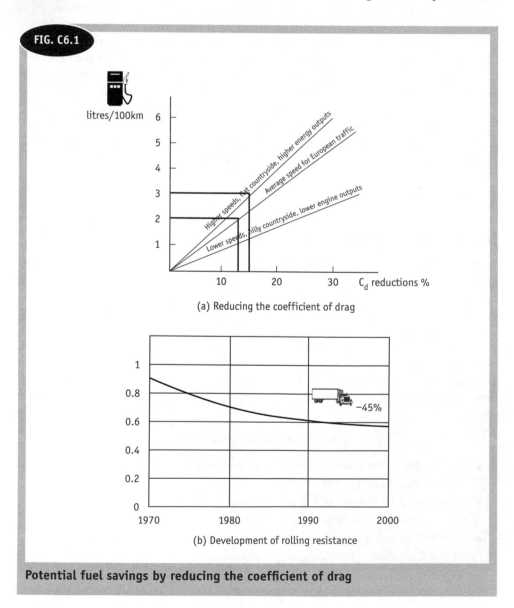

FIG. C6.1

(a) Reducing the coefficient of drag

(b) Development of rolling resistance

Potential fuel savings by reducing the coefficient of drag

standard models. The resultant Cd is around 0.5 compared to over 0.8 in the mid 1970s. This has led to a reduction in fuel requirements, as shown in Figure C6.1.

Additionally, engine designs have sought to reduce fuel consumption and exhaust emissions. Measured under laboratory conditions and expressed in grammes per kilowatt hour (g/kWh), specific fuel consumption (sfc) is the number of grammes of fuel an engine consumes for a power output of 1 kW over a period of one hour. Compared with family motor vehicles or light commercial vehicles, lorries are energy-efficient. For example, an average car (weighing a tonne) will require about 8 litres of fuel to travel 100 km, while a 40-tonne truck will only need about 0.8 litres for each tonne of its weight over the same distance. That is, the heavy truck is about ten times as efficient as the family car.

As Figure C6.2 shows, sfc has fallen by over 16 per cent since 1970. Another dramatic downward shift is seen in truck exhaust emissions. Figure C6.3 indicates the outputs of carbon monoxide (CO), nitrogen oxides (NO_x), hydrocarbons (HC) and particulates (PM) from modern (1997 figures) Scania engines compared to Euro 2 standards.

Of course the question still remains, given the clear improvements in exhaust emissions, fuel consumption and noise levels, have the truck industry gone far enough? Across the globe, although more pertinently in Europe, social protest against heavy lorries and road transport in general has increased in recent years. The wondrous Taj Mahal in Agra, India is being dangerously affected by pollutants created as a result of increasing industrialisation and use of road transport. This has necessitated urgent repair work. Similarly, the Parthenon in Athens is showing signs of rapid deterioration due in large measure to road vehicle emissions. High levels of exhaust emissions have been linked to all manner of human illness, not

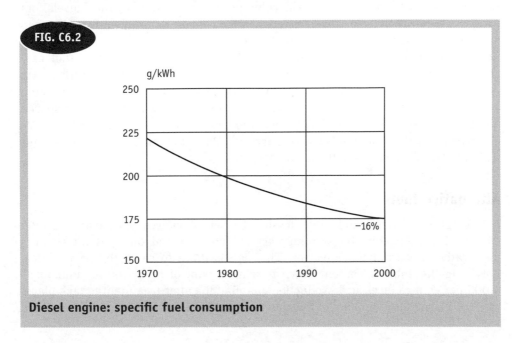

FIG. C6.2

Diesel engine: specific fuel consumption

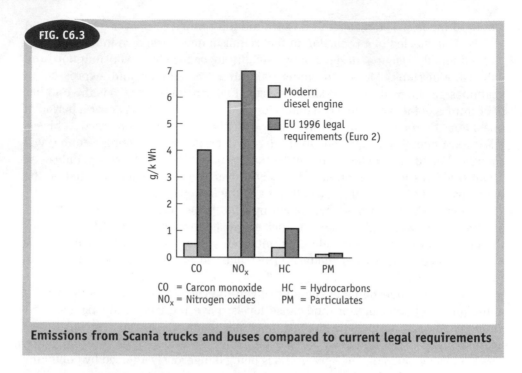

FIG. C6.3

Modern diesel engine

EU 1996 legal requirements (Euro 2)

g/kWh

CO NOₓ HC PM

CO = Carcon monoxide   HC = Hydrocarbons
NO$_x$ = Nitrogen oxides   PM = Particulates

Emissions from Scania trucks and buses compared to current legal requirements

least asthma and lung disease, and significant increases in these and other medical conditions have been recorded in many urban areas in the UK.

Noise pollution ranks high among concerns of those living and working close to busy roads. Scania has made considerable progress in reducing noise levels, but progress in future may be slowed as much of the remaining problem lies with road surfaces and the inevitable noise created by contact with that surface. However, new Scania trucks are fitted with air brake silencers to avoid the often ear-shattering hiss of air brakes. These limit sound emitted to 72 decibels (dB(A)). On engine sound levels it now takes eight engines to produce the same as one from ten years ago. *Coach and Bus Week* magazine reported that 'a Scania coach whispered along at 70 mph with 61 dB(A) measured throughout the top deck', while comparatively a typical family car registers 70 dB(A) at 50 mph whilst a passenger train at 70 mph registers at 98 dB(A).

Alternative fuels

It is sulphur in diesel and other fossil fuels which causes particular pollution worries. During burning the sulphuric acid which is created damages and renders inoperative any catalytic converter. The 'cat' is there to catch the particulates. Lowering the sulphur content down to a maximum of 50 parts per million or 0.005 per cent reduces acid production enabling the after treatment to take place. The OK Petroleum Company in Sweden now market low-sulphur diesel and Shell have joined them by opening the world's first ultra low sulphur diesel refinery which produces fuel with a sulphur content of just 0.001 per cent.

Alternative fuels come in all shapes and sizes. Ethanol and compressed natural gas (CNG) are already widely used. Scania engage in considerable research in examining alternative future fuels. They conclude that diesel will continue to provide the optimum business solution for the long term. Next on their favoured list is ethanol (alcohol), with CNG taking third place. In Sweden the wood pulping industry produces ethanol as a by-product of its operations, a factor that led SL, the Stockholm equivalent to London Transport, to start trials with 30 ethanol-powered Scania buses. By the year 2000 SL Bus will have 150 ethanol-powered buses in its fleet. This fuel reduces a number of harmful emissions when compared with diesel, including nitrogen oxides and sulphuric acid. However, currently ethanol is not as efficient a fuel as diesel. In a related development, Scania is now supplying 250 CNG-powered buses to Sydney, Australia, and British Gas have shown an interest in further developing and marketing CNG as a fuel source for domestic and commercial vehicle users. CNG is an effective suppresser of noise and will dramatically reduce NO_x emissions; however, it is still a fossil fuel product with all the inherent difficulties this involves.

Scania is in the process of introducing an environmental management system that fulfils ISO 14001 international standard. All operations in Brazil, the Argentine and Mexico were third party certified in 1997 such that all Latin American operations now have ISO 14001. This was achieved within Europe in 1998/99. The aim is now to examine environmental management at Scania's distributors.

Legislative emission control: the European Union

The European Union has established numerous environmental control standards, many of which directly apply to the truck industry. Whereas individual countries have targets for such things as carbon dioxide emissions, more specifically truck engine manufacturers must satisfy increasingly stringent, legally enforceable, standards.

The 'Euro 1' emissions standards were introduced by the European Union in October 1993, while 'Euro 2' were initiated in October 1996. Euro 2 represented a tightening of limits compared to Euro 1. 'Euro 3' standards are now driving developments. These standards require reductions in emissions of nitrogen oxides (which contribute to acid rain), carbon monoxide and particulates, principally diesel soot. These come into operation for all newly registered vehicles in 2001. Achieving these standards relies upon co-operation from the petroleum industry which needs to reduce the sulphur content of diesel fuel. Standards for measuring emissions are currently being prepared for the turn of the century. These will require trucks to undergo a new driving cycle which reflects 'real-life' road conditions in Europe rather than the current, rather artificial, test conditions. Preparatory work is already under way to establish even more stringent 'Euro 4' rules which will take effect from the year 2005.

Scania, together with its rival Volvo, are influential players in the European truck market. Their Swedish origin has assisted both companies in coming to terms with European environmental legislation. For many years successive Swedish governments have been at the forefront, within Europe, of legislative controls concerning all manner of environmental issues. Hence Scania have 'grown up' in an ecology-conscious environment. Scania engines met the Euro 2 standards some two and half years prior to the 1996 deadline. However, their competitors had also responded effectively. Cummins, Volvo, Daf, MAN and Mercedes all produce engines which match up to environmental regulations.

Recycling

In a recent report entitled 'The Greening of the Automotive Industry' consultants Coopers & Lybrand stated that vehicles are already surprisingly recyclable. Approximately 87 per cent of the materials in a Scania truck can be reused in some way or another. The report expressed concern, however, that a residue of glass, plastics, rubber, fibres and various fluids cannot be profitably recovered and is, therefore, buried in landfill sites. In Europe this mountain of 'auto crusher residue' represents close to five million cubic metres a year; this is the equivalent of burying a waste tip the size of Wembley stadium every twelve months.

One potential solution to the problem is to establish automotive disassembly plants which would provide a recycling structure to match current production and assembly systems. However, if not driven by legislation the viability of this idea

FIG. C6.4

THE SCANIA RECIPE	Kg
Steels (e.g. forgings, crankshaft, springs)	2400
Cast iron (engine block, brake drum)	1300
Sheet steel (cab shell, chassis frame members)	1200
Rubber (tyres)	600
Aluminium (flywheel housing)	1300
Plastic (wings, interior fittings)	30
Lead (batteries)	50
Copper (electric cables)	30
Zinc	4
Typical ex-factory truck comprises 8000 parts weighing 5.75 tonnes of which 87 per cent is recoverable. From the metal components forgings, iron castings, steel, aluminium, lead and copper are all recyclable. All rubber and plastic components are now marked in accordance with German VDA 260 standard enabling them to be sorted easily after scrapping.	

The Scania recipe – the make-up of a truck

will be governed by cost-effectiveness. In the United States, which actually produces less auto waste than the European Union, the big three manufacturers – GM, Ford and Chrysler – have formed a vehicle recycling partnership. In Switzerland a recycling levy of £30 is now placed on vehicles to cover the cost of incineration plants to render harmless parts that cannot be reused. One thought to ponder is that eventually manufacturers may have to guarantee that there are disassembly plants to dismantle every vehicle they construct. Figure C6.4 shows the material make-up of a Scania truck.

The debate concerning the increasing use of road freight transport is set to continue. If the industrialised nations are sincere in their espoused intent to reduce or even maintain current levels of traffic on roads and reduce carbon dioxide and other emissions, nothing short of drastic government action will be required at national, EU and international levels. The role played by the major truck manufacturers and car producers will be important in influencing future decision making in this regard. The future profitability and growth of manufacturers, such as Scania, and their hundreds of distributors across the globe is in balance.

QUESTIONS

1. Is road transport of manufactured goods the most ecologically sound form of transport? Discuss your answer with reference to alternative transportation methods and alternatives to mass transport of goods and people.

2. Why is it important for Scania to publish and otherwise promote the ecologically relevant improvements they have made to their truck designs?

3. How can a concern for the environment act as a source of competitive advantage to Scania? How might that concern, if taken to greater extremes, prove to be a liability?

4. What might be the consequences for Scania of 'going it alone' and developing new engine designs which utilise alternative fuel sources?

5. Why do you think companies like Scania are concerned to achieve a harmonisation of environmental legislation across the globe?

6. To what extent is collaboration between governments and industry needed to tackle environmental concerns? How can collaboration between companies in the same sector (e.g. manufacturers of trucks) and manufacturers in different sectors (e.g. Scania and Shell) make progress in environmental protection?

7. Discuss the potential consequences in terms of global competitiveness of the UK government enforcing controls to ensure far greater use of rail transport for freight.

7

BOOK RETAILING

THE STORM AFTER THE CALM

Ian Brooks

This case study analyses the competitive changes in book retailing in the three years following the collapse of the Net Book Agreement (NBA). It also demonstrates the influence of international competition, of lifestyle changes and technology, and of the breakdown of a long-standing industry agreement on an increasingly competitive retail business.

In the early 1990s and for countless decades before, booksellers had stuck to a negotiated agreement which fixed the price for each competitively sold book. The Net Book Agreement (NBA) provided a degree of stability to the book retailing (and publishing) industry while customers were assured that there was little value in 'shopping around'; if they knew what book they required, as it would be identically priced in all bookshops. Competition was most certainly not based on price. Under such conditions many bookshops, including over 2000 small book retailers, survived in a less than fiercely competitive environment. The shops tended to be small (although there have always been a small number of large bookshops in a few major cities), none-too-attractive, 'hushed' places. They tended to specialise in books, preferring to allow other stores to provide for stationery and music sales. W.H. Smith is a notable exception to this: they have been a major high street presence competing in the books, stationery, periodicals and music business for over a century.

Things have changed in the last few years. Most major retailers now discount certain, particularly best-selling, books. The supermarkets have entered the fray, together with a large American retailer, and there are increasing Internet sales. Add to this the mail order business, some 1700 independents and major players like Waterstone's, Books etc. and the ever-present W.H. Smith, and competition is particularly rife in what is a mature, slow-growth business.

In addition to the demise of the NBA, territorial copyright is also being challenged by an increasingly globalised book market, particularly by WWW sales and trans-Atlantic expansion. Currently, identical books retail often for significantly different prices in different market territories. With the increase in WWW sales and the expansion of Borders (an American company) and others this looks set to follow the NBA.

The market for books

In the UK the retail value of bookselling is around £3 billion, according to the Publishers' Association. Verdict, the retail consultant, estimate that book sales increased by just 3 per cent in 1997, although predicted sales growth for 1998 and beyond is a little higher. Nevertheless this is a mature market and one which experienced stable or even declining sales in the mid 1990s. A little over two-thirds of the market is in consumer bookselling, while academic, professional and school books account for less than 30 per cent of the market. Despite the rise in higher education students in the 1990s, sales to universities and to schools have remained fairly static in the past decade. UK schools spend just 2 per cent of their budgets on books, around £15 for each primary pupil and £30 for each secondary student each year. It seems unlikely that bookselling to schools or university students will provide a boost to this industry.

An increase in the value of books in audio (market size about £45 million in 1995) or multimedia form has been noted in recent years but growth, particularly of multimedia works has been disappointing.

To date the ending of the NBA has had little effect either on the price of the vast majority of books or on the size of the market. Research published by Books Marketing Ltd suggests that the market is dominated by a relatively small number of high-volume purchasers and those buying Christmas presents. It is believed that demand for books is relatively inelastic.

The main players

Table C7.1 shows the market share of the main players in book retailing. Borders opened its first (an American first also) shop, a superstore, on Oxford Street in London in mid 1998 and has four others planned (in London, Leeds, Glasgow and Brighton). Another American giant, Barnes & Noble, are considering development in the UK. It is predicted (by Verdict, the retail consultants) that this development will lead to a price war and attempts by retailers to differentiate their offerings. It may precipitate a shake-out of weaker independents and small chains.

Borders purchased Books etc. for £40 million in 1997 while Waterstone's has, since the failure of the NBA, become independent of W.H. Smith and has merged with Dillons. Waterstone's opened its first superstore in Glasgow in November

TABLE C7.1   Market share estimates in bookselling in the UK, 1997

Waterstone's (inc. Dillons)	20%
W.H. Smith (inc. Menzies)	18%
Book clubs (mail order)	10%
Ottakar's	2%
Other specialist chains	2%
Books etc.	2%
Supermarkets	7%
Department stores	1%
Confectioners, newsagents, tobacconists	6%
Independents (small bookshops)	30%
Others (inc. Internet)	2%

1997. They are the market leaders with a steadily increasing market share. They also have their own, small, Internet sales operation. In 1999 Waterstone's took out a lease on London's famous Simpson's Piccadilly store in an attempt to make this its flagship premises. This historic site contains almost 70 000 square feet over seven storeys and represents Waterstone's largest outlet and an attempt to fend off competition from Borders.

W.H. Smith is considering developing a mega-store format in order to compete. Of the prime players in the market, W.H. Smith is the most diversified. Nevertheless they have recently purchased the Internet Bookshop, a bookseller with over a million titles, operating on the Net.

Tesco, Asda and Sainsbury now sell mainly best-sellers and children's books. They frequently discount by around 30 per cent as do Borders and increasingly the other UK major booksellers. It is unlikely that supermarkets will venture beyond the best-seller or fast-moving stock section of the market, although their convenience to very many shoppers, added to the fact that possibly 50 per cent of all book purchases are made on impulse, suggest that they are assured of a significant, if not dominant, position in the market. Their 'best-seller' range offers less of a threat to the major booksellers, such as Waterstone's, than it does to generalist chains like Woolworths and W.H. Smith. Ottakar's, a relative newcomer, targets small towns and cities and is also enjoying growing market share such that it is the second largest specialist high street bookseller. Its market share is expanding as it seeks new sites which do not place it in direct competition with Waterstone's and the American giants.

Amazon.com, a US-based Internet bookseller, has enjoyed an enormous market growth (but from a zero base, of course). Internet sales are likely to be just £150 million worldwide in 1998 but growth is far higher than in the book market overall. They can offer choice (they do not need the physical space to retail books) and discounted prices (shops and other distribution facilities are expensive to maintain while Internet providers can eliminate considerable elements of cost encountered by traditional retailers). Verdict, however, suggest that Internet sales may only capture about 10 per cent of the market by the year 2010 despite this sector lending itself to electronic shopping.

Despite the fact that the independent book market has not been decimated by the demise of the NBA, market share of the specialist multiples has increased from 28 per cent to 34 per cent in the five years to 1998. The independent bookshops will find their traditional markets increasingly under pressure and will need to differentiate their offering.

In broader terms, in addition to competitive rivalry within the book market, booksellers also compete with other leisure activities for revenue. Hence, to an extent book sales compete with film, music and computer and other games.

The Bookseller magazine (3 May 1996) reported that the already sizeable disparity between the discounts offered by publishers to large and to small booksellers has increased recently. W.H. Smith has taken a tough stance with publishers, demanding large discounts in order to improve its own profitability. More recently, however, the publishers have met to discuss approaches to offset the power of larger booksellers. There has been a spate of mergers and takeovers in the book publishing industry in 1997/98.

The style

There appears to be a growing emphasis on 'lifestyle retailing' in bookselling. Borders' new shop in London has a fashionable coffee shop, is modern in its internal decoration and has an enormous array of periodicals (some 2000) with ample seating for customers who wish to browse. They also have an impressive CD section with 150 'listening posts', computer terminals (for Internet access), less of a 'hushed tone' and a more vibrant atmosphere. With opening hours from 8 a.m. to 11 p.m. on all but Sunday, they have signalled new competitive conditions for the industry. Book superstores appear to be the way forward and each major player is actively planning new stores. Originally, small book retailers managed stores of around 4000 square feet, while the superstores recently opened are of the order of 25 000 square feet. The planned new mega-stores are to have around 40 000 square feet of shop space.

The popularity of public libraries appears to be waning. Underinvestment and lack of marketing drive have not enticed large sections of the public into libraries. This bodes well for bookshops, although if children are not imbued with a liking for books from libraries the marketing of books as a desirable product becomes a more difficult task.

The Internet may change the face of book retailing. The pace at which the public become 'web-friendly' and the extent of acceptance of Internet purchasing will influence the degree of dynamism in this and many other retail businesses. Ironically, increased use of the Internet and other communications and informa-tion technology may lead to a reduction in the long-term demand for 'hard copy' books as people increasingly are able to access information in other forms and from multiple sources. Additionally, competition is set to become increasingly rife in direct, via the Internet, book sales.

QUESTIONS

1. To what extent has the abandonment of the Net Book Agreement led to change in book retailing?

2. Calculate an appropriate concentration ratio for the industry. What does this tell us about the nature of competition in the industry?

3. What are the prime forces for change in the bookselling industry?

4. Construct between two and four scenarios for the shape of book retailing in the year 2010.

8

RESPONSES TO CHANGE IN THE BUSINESS ENVIRONMENT
THE CASE OF RUGBY LEAGUE FOOTBALL

Graham Wilkinson

This case examines the pressures in the business environment that led to the professional clubs of the UK's Rugby Football League changing from playing fixtures in the winter months to playing in the summer. In particular, it looks at the competitive, technological and social changes that brought about the change and examines the role of various stakeholders in the process.

The sport of rugby league

The sport of rugby league came into existence in the summer of 1895 when 22 clubs from Yorkshire and Lancashire left the Rugby Football Union to set up their own competition. Although they still considered themselves as amateurs, players at these clubs wanted to be compensated for losing wages when taking time off work to play the game on Saturday afternoons. This idea was rejected by the rugby union authorities, who believed that it was a form of professionalism and, therefore, contrary to their amateur status.

For the next hundred years – until 1995 – the game in the UK remained largely confined to the two northern counties where it had originated, plus Cumbria. Some attempts at expansion had occurred, principally in South Wales and London, but the number of clubs in the 'professional' league never exceeded 36. The sport had been adopted enthusiastically in both Australia and New Zealand and, less successfully, in France. Players at the 'professional' clubs remained part-time, earning the majority of their income from jobs outside the sport.

The rules of the game have been subject to frequent change over the years of the sport's existence, in an attempt to make the game more attractive to spectators, the higher gate receipts being needed to pay the players' wages. The number of league and cup competitions also varied. Apart from two brief experiments with two divisions (1902 to 1905 and 1962 to 1964) the league fixtures were based largely on a geographic, county, basis with all results counting for position in one league table. As not all the teams played each other, the championship was decided via an end-of-season play-off. In an attempt to raise playing standards and increase spectator interest, a system of two divisions with promotion and relegation was adopted in 1973. Expansion of the game was again attempted, with clubs being formed in London (Fulham), Cardiff, Carlisle, Maidstone, Sheffield and Mansfield; of these clubs, only London and Sheffield are still members of the league.

FIG. C8.1

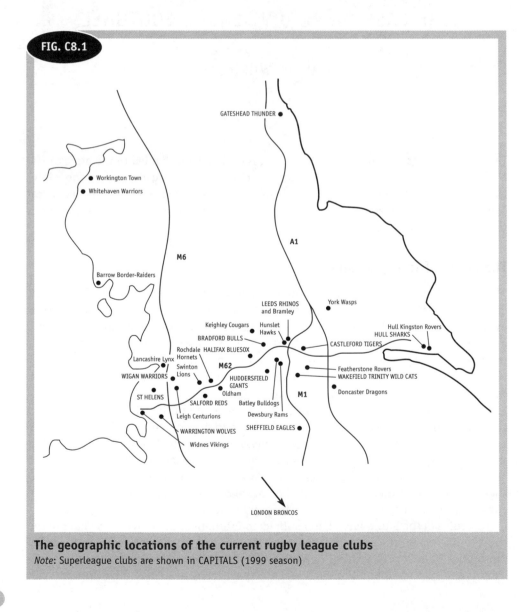

The geographic locations of the current rugby league clubs
Note: Superleague clubs are shown in CAPITALS (1999 season)

Recent changes

By the start of the 1990s, it was apparent that the game faced major challenges if it was to survive and prosper in the face of changing social habits and competition from other leisure activities. In this it was not alone. Other spectator sports – soccer, cricket and rugby union – were facing similar pressures. In rugby league it was also apparent that the quality gap between the top clubs (for example, Leeds, Bradford, St Helens and, especially, Wigan) and the rest was widening and that spectator interest, as measured by attendances, was declining. There were comments made that the game was dying and would be unable to survive in the changed environment. Optimists pointed out that major showpiece games, such as the Challenge Cup Final at Wembley Stadium, still attracted huge, often capacity, crowds and pointed to the strong community links which most clubs still had with local people in their area. Others worried that, despite these community links, the regular league games were being played in front of fewer and fewer people. Attendances at Division One games are shown in Table C8.1. The table shows considerable variations. From an average of around 4500 in the late 1970s/early

TABLE C8.1 Attendances at Division One games

Season	Average attendance
1976/77	3825
1977/78	4402
1978/79	4128
1979/80	4875
1980/81	5110
1981/82	5268
1982/83	4641
1983/84	4752
1984/85	4738
1985/86	4585
1986/87	4844
1987/88	5826
1988/89	7292
1989/90	6450
1990/91	6420
1991/92	6511
1992/93	6170
1993/94	5683
1994/95	5543
1995/96	5515

1980s, there was a sudden rise to over 7000 in 1988/89. But this was followed by a gradual decline to around 5500 by the mid 1990s. What, if anything, could or should be done to reverse the decline?

Stakeholders

Traditionalists have long viewed the clubs, the players and their fans – the paying spectators – as the only people with an interest in the game. However, it is increasingly apparent that this represents a limited view and that there are many other groups and individuals who have a stake in the game's prosperity. Even traditionalists would concede that the game's governing body – the Rugby Football League – is an important stakeholder. Important too are the fortunes of the national side in games against Australia, New Zealand and France.

What was becoming apparent was that other groups were also playing an increasingly important role. First, it was clear that spectators at the ground were not the only source of income for the clubs. Sponsorship, both of clubs and of various competitions, was playing a major part in generating revenue, as was the money received from various television companies to cover the game. In turn, it can be argued that the 'armchair' fan, someone who doesn't actually go to the ground but watches on television, is as important – or more important – than the fans who turn up. After all, they are likely to outnumber the five or ten thousand fans at the game many times over. For a sport committed to attracting more fans to the existing clubs, as well as expanding to other geographical areas, attracting new spectators is important. Exposure to the product via television is seen as playing a vital role in this process; the hope is that fans who have seen the game on television will be attracted by the skills, excitement and atmosphere and wish to experience it live for themselves.

Change in the social and competitive environments

The environment surrounding the sport of rugby league has changed rapidly in recent years. A wider variety of leisure activities is now available to the public, who are, arguably, less likely to simply persist in maintaining long-established habits. This has placed increasing pressure on more traditional activities, such as viewing rugby league, which in many ways have remained largely unchanged since the early years of this century.

The rugby league authorities, as seen above, had responded to earlier pressures, for example via rule changes to make the game more attractive. Changes in the structure of the league were also designed to have the same effect. But, apart from these and the switch to playing on Sundays to avoid competition from soccer – a change which took place as long ago as the late 1960s – the game, its stadiums and its outlook had remained largely traditional. As the figures for attendances show, however, by the mid 1990s it was apparent to many that the game was fighting a losing battle. Expansion was viewed as a pipe-dream by many, more concerned simply with the game's survival.

Other professional sports faced similar challenges. Soccer, for example, had also seen a decline in attendances, partly for similar environmental reasons and partly because of the perception of violence by fans at games. (The latter has never been a problem for rugby league, where segregation of fans and perimeter fencing have never been known or needed.) Soccer had reinvented itself in the early 1990s with the introduction of the FA Premier League, the change to all-seater stadia and the image of 'a whole new ball-game'. Should rugby league do something similar?

Technological change

Alongside these changes in the social and competitive environments, there is the role of technology, specifically the role of satellite television. Just as Sky had played a pivotal role in the rebranding of top-class soccer, they were to influence – some would say determine – rugby league's future. Rugby league had long been shown on the terrestrial television channels, live league and cup matches being for many years a mainstay of the BBC's Saturday afternoon *Grandstand* programme. In addition to this, the BBC had invented and sponsored their own trophy (the BBC2 Floodlit Cup) played on Tuesday evenings to boost audiences for their second channel. ITV had also shown games, though coverage was limited, with matches usually being shown only in the Yorkshire and/or Granada regions. In 1990, satellite TV was in its infancy – and, from January of that year, showing live rugby league to its few viewers. By 1992, Sky had increased its interest in the game and the Rugby Football League negotiated contracts with them for coverage of league games and overseas internationals for a further four years. The deal cost the broadcaster around £3 million. Alongside this a deal was negotiated with the BBC for a similar amount to cover the cup competitions and domestic internationals. However, as we have seen, attendances at games continued to decline. Nigel Wood, chief executive of Halifax, was one of many pessimists; the professional game was, he declared, 'insolvent'.

The game changes...

The sport of rugby league entered its centenary year of 1995 in a state of uncertainty, its future widely debated by optimists and pessimists, by those who favoured a 'business as usual' approach and those who believed that radical change was necessary for the game's survival. Most believed that the standard of play on the field, the product, was better than ever. This improvement had certainly been shown by Wigan – whose players had become full-time professionals some years earlier – and who were rewarded with eight cup wins in a row, the last six of these being accompanied by the league title. The only club that came anywhere near to challenging this dominance was Leeds, who had also gone full-time, albeit some years after Wigan. Many believed that if the standard of the competition was to be maintained, the only way was for the other clubs in the top division to follow suit. But, the question remained, how could this be afforded? Would the game change? And, if so, how?

The answer to these questions was provided towards the end of the 1994/95 season. After a meeting of the league clubs in April it was announced that the Rugby Football League had agreed a new, five-year deal with Rupert Murdoch's BSkyB. The extent of the changes stunned most observers. There was to be a new 'Superleague' of twelve elite clubs, the remaining clubs were split into two further divisions, Sky would have exclusive rights to all league games (both live and highlights programmes), there would be mergers of clubs to provide 'super-clubs' in selected areas and the season would be changed so that all the professional clubs' games were played in the summer rather than the winter. All this was to start the following year, with a truncated 1995/96 winter season being played, finishing in February to allow the superleague to start the following April.

The arguments started immediately. The followers of clubs that were to be merged (and many other fans) were, predictably perhaps, outraged that a century of tradition and community links were to be ditched for, as they saw it, purely commercial reasons. Others believed that for the game to survive the changes were perhaps regrettable, but necessary. Maurice Lindsay, the chief executive of the RFL, said that the change to summer was something that the clubs had discussed previously and would lead to an improvement in playing standards – firm, grass-covered pitches allowing for faster play and better handling than cold, muddy fields. An additional benefit was that this meant the British and Australian seasons coincided, allowing for the possibility of end-of-season play-offs between the top clubs in each country, which were to be covered by BSkyB.

The superleague concept was opposed most vehemently by the supporters of Keighley Cougars, who, as well being the first club to introduce innovative marketing ideas (including adding the Cougars suffix), had finished top of the second division but were not to be promoted. Indeed, of the sixteen clubs in Division One in 1994/95, only the top ten would be in the new elite, where they would be joined by London (who had finished 1994/95 some way below Keighley in Division Two) and the newly invented Paris club. Although the furore continued for some months (and the idea of mergers was abandoned, at least for the moment) the new structure of the game went ahead.

Given the scale of the opposition to the changes, it is worthwhile investigating why the clubs (even Keighley) agreed to them. The answer, it appears, is quite simple – money. The BSkyB deal was worth £87 million for five years, around £17.5 million a year, compared to the £0.75 million per year of the previous deal. With a similar deal eventually being concluded in Australia, after a season where Murdoch's superleague and the Australian Rugby League each ran their own competition, it seems that the worldwide competition and coverage that the broadcaster craves is now a possibility.

Success?

Have the changes to the game proved successful? After three years of summer rugby, the answer is far from clear; indeed, the answer may well depend on who is asked the question and which stakeholders are involved.

Spectator attendance at the top division games has increased to an average of 7087 (second only to the record of 7292 in 1988/89), but this masks big differences in the fortunes of individual clubs. For the 1998 season, six of the clubs recorded increases in gates, while six saw declines. It is arguable that the clubs that have most enthusiastically embraced the concept of superleague and improved their marketing efforts the most are the ones that have benefited from increases. The introduction of suffixes to team names (Bradford Bulls, Leeds Rhinos, Warrington Wolves, etc.) has been much derided by traditionalists. The clubs are, however, convinced that the new brand images have raised public awareness. There is certainly no doubt that the associated mascots (Bull Man, Ronnie the Rhino, Wolfie, etc.) are very popular with younger spectators and have helped to raise the profile of their clubs in the local media – Ronnie the Rhino even gaining several hundred votes in the last general election.

Of the original twelve members of the superleague, Workington were relegated at the end of the first season, and Oldham at the end of the second; Paris also saw their membership 'suspended' at the end of 1997, to be replaced by Huddersfield. With the promotion of Salford for 1997 and Hull for 1998, this means that, with the exception of the London Broncos, the superleague for 1998 was composed of teams entirely located in the traditional Yorkshire/Lancashire (M62 corridor) area. Hopes for expansion are, however, still alive, with Gateshead being admitted to the league for the 1999 season; applications for franchises from clubs in Cardiff and Swansea were both rejected, however, because of doubts about the viability of their business plans. The first division champions, Wakefield, have also been promoted, however, giving a fourteen-team superleague for 1999. A further change is that the remaining eighteen teams have been combined in a single division for 1999, rather than playing in two divisions as had been the case since the start of summer rugby.

BSkyB continue to say they are very satisfied with their involvement with the game, with viewing figures for club games being second only to their soccer coverage. Many, however, have expressed doubts about whether the deal will be renewed after the end of the current five-year period – or, if it is renewed, about how much money will be offered. The fact that terrestrial television coverage is now limited to the BBC showing Challenge Cup games, including the final, during March, April and May is another worry for many. They argue that a wider audience is needed for the whole season, if the game is to truly develop its appeal and expand.

As for the future, opinions vary widely. Optimists point to the increasing numbers of spectators overall, pessimists to the decline in attendances recorded by half the superleague teams and the increasingly large gap in revenues between the top superleague teams and the rest. Traditionalists say that the failure of Paris and the refusal to admit Cardiff and/or Swansea because of doubts about the viability of their business plans indicate that the game is returning to where it belongs, its roots in the culture and people of northern England. Radicals, on the other hand, argue that the existence of nationwide amateur competitions, the admittance of Gateshead to the superleague, the success of London Broncos (who attract bigger crowds to their home ground at The Stoop in Twickenham than do their landlords, the Harlequins rugby union team), the introduction of international teams representing Scotland and Ireland (as well as Wales and England), the high standard on the field of play and the support of high-profile companies such as Virgin, Compaq, Norweb, JJB Sports and British Gas as sponsors all indicate that the game is building well, though perhaps more slowly than they had hoped.

As the game and its environment continue to change, we must wait and see which views are proved to be correct.

QUESTIONS

1. Identify the various organisations/individuals who may be regarded as stakeholders in the sport of rugby league. How has their relative power changed in recent years?

2. What have been the main changes in the competitive environment facing the sport? Is pressure from these likely to increase or decrease in the future?

3. Can the sport accurately forecast changes in its environment? Outline various possible scenarios for its future development in a complex and dynamic environment.

4. How important is technological change to the future of rugby league and other spectator sports in the UK?

References

Butcher, T. (ed.) (1998) *Rugby League '98–99*, Brighouse: League Publications.

Clayton, I. and Steele, M. (1993) *When Push Comes to Shove – Rugby League, The People's Game*, Castleford: Yorkshire Art Circus.

Curtis, I. (1996) 'Murdoch tackles a new sports challenge', *Marketing*, Haymarket Publishing, 14 March.

Fletcher, R. and Howes, D. (1998) *Rothmans – Rugby League Yearbook 1998*, London: Rothmans/Headline.

Kelner, S. (1996) *To Jerusalem and Back: A Personal History of Rugby League*, London: Macmillan.

Moorhouse, G. (1995) *A People's Game: The Official History of Rugby League 1895–1995*, London: Hodder and Stoughton.

9

THE HOTEL INDUSTRY

AN ANGLO-FRENCH PERSPECTIVE

Jon Stephens

This case looks at some of the major factors affecting the business environment of hotels in both the UK and France and the extent to which the factors are common to both countries. From this the comparative nature of the industries will be assessed.

The hotel industry is significantly affected by changes in the national and international business environment and as a result tends to operate in a dynamic, rapidly-changing situation which demands proactive responses from hotel owners if they are to maintain competitive advantage in the market.

The market for hotels in Europe is a significant one, given the fact that Europe remains the number one holiday destination in the world and also that the impetus of the Single Market has led to increased business travel in Europe. The UK and France are two of the major markets, with the UK having 870 000 rooms compared to 1.2 million in France.

Whilst the hotel industry is usually linked with the leisure industry, it must not be forgotten that essentially it serves two main groups of customers, namely business and leisure users, and thus there are two distinct markets that should be examined to assess the critical factors that will affect the hotel industry in the two countries.

The tourism and leisure markets

The hotel industry is often classified as part of the leisure industry and is particularly linked to tourism, especially in certain times of the year. Tourism already accounts for 6 per cent of GDP in the UK and is even more significant in France. This is reflected in the profile of hotel users in the two countries.

In the UK, for example, business users in 1993 accounted for 45 per cent of market share and conferences for 11 per cent of the market leaving about 44 per cent of the market accounted for by leisure travellers. By contrast, in France there is a much greater reliance in the hotel industry upon the leisure traveller: in 1993, 76 per cent of demand was for leisure travellers, and 59 per cent of these were overseas residents. This suggests a higher reliance on the tourist trade from overseas in the French hotel market. This is accentuated when one considers that the average stay of a client in a French hotel is about six to seven days whereas in the UK it is only two days, which indicates the potential of leisure travellers for longer stays, although the business traveller is likely to pay the higher premium.

Tourists can be very sensitive to instability in a particular area and demand can drop quite dramatically when there is a risk of danger or unrest in a region. For example, the outbreak of the Gulf War saw hotel occupancy levels drop to 60 per cent of normal in London and Paris, primarily as a result of American tourists staying away because of concerns about travelling to Europe. More dramatic examples can be seen in Dubrovnik in Croatia which used to be a prime tourist resort before the outbreak of the Balkan conflicts and in Egypt where terrorist activity has severely damaged the tourist trade, although it is now beginning to recover. In the 1990s bombing campaigns by the IRA in London and Algerian fundamentalists in Paris have caused short-term fluctuations in demand.

On the other hand increased political stability can have the reverse effect by encouraging tourism and hence increasing the demand for hotel accommodation. This has recently been the case in parts of Eastern Europe, such as Prague and Budapest, which have seen significant increases in tourist inflows, and on a smaller level this has been identified in Northern Ireland as part of the 'peace dividend'.

The demand for travel and tourism and hence for hotel spaces will also be significantly affected by the economic conditions in both the host country and the countries visitors come from. Some of the key economic indicators of France and the UK can be seen in Table C9.1.

TABLE C9.1   Key economic variables in France and the UK

		1994–98	1999 (est.)	2000 (est.)
Economic growth (%)	UK	3.1	0.0	1.2
	France	2.4	2.0	2.0
Inflation (%)	UK	2.8	2.3	1.8
	France	1.5	0.7	1.0
Interest rates (%)	UK	6.0 (1996)	7.3 (1998)	
	France	3.7 (1996)	3.4 (1998)	
Current account (£bn)	UK	−2.0 (1998)	−8.0	−3.0
	France	38.0 (1998)	32.0	26.0

The relative levels of wealth and rates of economic growth will either encourage or discourage increased travel and tourism and use of hotels. In a recession people will have less disposable income for holidays or may be forced to substitute alternative and cheaper forms of accommodation when travelling, such as camping, gites and villas, rather than using the more expensive hotel accommodation. Alternatively they may look for greater discounts or cheaper hotels when they travel. This has led to the formation of cheaper hotel chains in both the UK and France, such as the 'Formule 1' range, where facilities are clean but minimalist and thus offered at a cheaper price. Conversely, with higher income levels, there would tend to be a higher demand for tourism and travel and perhaps a move away from, say, camping to a hotel-based vacation or to higher-quality hotels.

One area which can have a very significant impact upon the demand for hotel space from the leisure traveller will be the rate of exchange between countries. This will be particularly significant for hotel industries that have to rely for a substantial amount of their business on the overseas traveller. A substantial appreciation of an exchange rate will force up the cost of hotel stays and could even offset the impact of income gains discussed previously with negative consequences for the industry.

The period from 1993 has seen particular emphasis laid by the French government on its 'franc fort' policy which has deliberately kept the value of the French franc high for a range of economic and political reasons. The consequence has been a substantial reduction in British holidaymakers visiting France. The UK, with its relatively weak currency on the European stage, has fared better and is becoming an increasingly attractive holiday destination with increased demand for hotel spaces. However, the tables were turned in 1997 and 1998 when the pound sterling strengthened considerably against the franc, thus increasing the appeal of stays in France, boosted even further by the running of football's World Cup in 1998. It remains to be seen what impact the UK remaining outside the Euro will have on the industry.

One factor common to both countries is the trend for the leisure customer to demand better amenities and value for money. The general increase in health awareness is leading to an increased demand for additional facilities such as fitness centres and swimming pools, together with special facilities for younger children. Many of the leading hotel chains, such as Accor and Granada, have responded to this demand; however, it does have cost implications for the smaller independent hotel.

Both the UK and France have populations that are significantly ageing and this, coupled with the move towards earlier retirement, has resulted in a significant number of people of 'the third age' who are not only much more healthy and interested in travelling, but also have a much greater spending power than ever before which will enable them to undertake more travel. If one adds to this the anticipated increase in the numbers of people aged 45 to 59 in each country, caused partly by the post-war baby-boomers, then it can be seen that this group will be a significant market in the future for the hotel industry and where the competition from areas like camping will be less. Already some groups are responding, an example being the new chain in France, called 'Hotelier', which caters specifically for this group.

The business market

It has already been identified that the business sector is a significant group served by hotels and hotel chains. Hotels are used by businessmen and women who are travelling from one destination to another; they are also often used as a place to conduct business meetings and in many cases as a location for presentations, development workshops and full conferences.

With the advent of the Single Market there has been an increase in the cross-border utilisation of hotels as more companies seek closer European contacts or alliances in order to develop a European presence. The issues of costs, value for money and quality of accommodation are just as significant for this sector as for the leisure traveller, although the corporate customer is increasingly demanding more business facilities such as seminar rooms and conference facilities. Some hotels, especially in the well established hotel chains, are developing facilities such as teleconferencing, video conferencing and even satellite conference facilities in a bid to attract this market.

The Atria group of hotels in France are specifically aimed at the business sector and Granada in the United Kingdom have developed business television networks with British Telecom which use satellite transmissions to allow global conferencing.

Industry structure in France and the UK

The structure of the hotel industry in France and the UK, and indeed most of the rest of Europe, can be split into two groups; the independent hotels, often family-run and based in a specific or a limited range of locations, and the hotel chains run by well-known companies, having a wide portfolio of different types of hotels to suit different needs and frequently having a wide national and often international distribution of hotels. Examples of these hotel chains would be the Accor Group in France and the Granada Group in the UK, which are both market leaders in their respective countries but also compete globally. Table C9.2 indicates the range of hotel types available in these chains.

Independent hotels

The independent hotels still make up about four-fifths of the market in France and are still in the majority in the UK. These traditional hotels, often aiming at the leisure traveller in specific locations, are numerous for many reasons. One key factor is that there are limited entry barriers to setting up a hotel. There will be the original land and construction or conversion costs and limited marketing costs. Labour costs tend to be low as many of these hotels will be family-run businesses

TABLE C9.2 Positioning of selected hotel chains in the UK and France

	France	UK
Economy and budget	Formule 1 Etap Ibis	Travelodge Campanile
Mid-market	Best Western Mercure Novotel	Post House Swallow Garden Court
Upper market	Sofitel Holiday Inn Relais et Chateaux	Crest Holiday Inn Hilton

and additional labour costs tend to be very low in this sector given the part-time and seasonal nature of much of the employment.

In France the deregulation of the financial markets has led to easier access to finance and has encouraged investment in hotels at this level, although the Voisin Law does control the number of constructions at local level.

One advantage the small independent French hotels have over their UK counterparts is in the VAT rates they have to pay: France has a much reduced rate for hotels, while in the UK they are charged at the standard rate.

However, the UK independent hotel sector benefits to some extent from the fact that the UK had an opt-out clause in the European Social Chapter. In an industry which is labour-intensive by nature and which employs a considerable number of part-time workers, the UK has been less affected by legislation concerning part-time workers' rights and hours of employment and by national minimum wage levels than has France.

It has already been seen that demand can be volatile in the sector and this may frequently have a regional dimension, that is, national demand may rise but regional demand could fall because of factors specific to the local or regional business environment.

One economic factor that may be significant for the independent hotel operator is the rate of interest as not only will this have a bearing on consumer demand but it will directly affect hotels where they have had to borrow money, for example for expansion, or to comply with tighter health and safety regulations. These highly-geared hotels are at risk from any increases in interest rates. They particularly suffer in recessions when there is intensive competition to attract customers and there is a general increase in buyer power in terms of demands for bigger discounts and more value for money. In addition they are considerably at risk from consumers using alternative sources of accommodation such as camping, holiday centres or bed-and-breakfast establishments, and in a market with elements of overcapacity their profit margins get squeezed and many struggle to survive.

The hotel chains

The rest of the hotel industry consists of the hotel chains, which have been significantly increasing their share of the French and British markets. In France the top five hotels control 17.5 per cent of the market with the Accor Group alone controlling 12 per cent. In the UK the top five hotel chains control one-third of the market, making it one of the most concentrated hotel markets in Europe.

One of the main reasons for the growth of the hotel chains is the advantages that accrue to them through economies of scale. These are seen especially in the areas of purchasing, marketing and financing. For example, with purchasing, the major chains are able to own or control their chief suppliers, thus achieving the advantages of vertical integration. The Granada Group owns most of its suppliers and, like Accor, has a computerised purchasing database. In marketing the larger chains are able to advertise extensively and support the wide range of brands of hotels they own, thus enhancing brand loyalty amongst targeted segments of current and potential hotel customers. They use database-driven marketing, often linked up to a computer reservation system, such as the Resinter system at Accor, which makes the whole process of booking into a hotel considerably easier for the client.

In addition they can offer consistent quality in a range of locations and at different classes of hotel. This has undoubtedly attracted custom from the business traveller and conference markets and may have also benefited from such legislation as the EU Package Tour Directive which makes organisers of package holidays legally liable to the customer for all aspects of the package offer; as this includes hotels, they may benefit from the guaranteed quality they can provide.

On the whole the prospects for the industry in France and the UK look good with the continuing move towards leisure-based activities, but the market remains very competitive and is prone to overcapacity. The challenge for both the independents and the hotel chains will be to retain competitiveness in such a rapidly changing business environment.

QUESTIONS

1. Compare the business environment for hotels specialising in the business market with those in the leisure market. Which of these is the more volatile and why?

2. Assess the extent to which the business environment for the hotel industry varies between the UK and France. Is this a market where national tendencies dominate or is there evidence of a European market?

3. Compare an independent hotel in your home location and one in an overseas location that you may have visited and evaluate the key differences in their business environment.

4. To what extent do you feel that the hotel industry is becoming more concentrated in the UK and France and what are the likely consequences of this? What do you feel are the main competitive forces affecting the industry?

INDEX

447